Essential Law for Social Work Practice in Canada

Second Edition

Cheryl Regehr

Karima Kanani

OXFORD

UNIVERSITY PRESS

OXFORD
UNIVERSITY PRESS

8 Sampson Mews, Suite 204, Don Mills, Ontario M3C 0H5
www.oupcanada.com

Oxford University Press is a department of the University of Oxford.
It furthers the University's objective of excellence in research, scholarship,
and education by publishing worldwide in

Oxford   New York

Auckland   Cape Town   Dar es Salaam   Hong Kong   Karachi
Kuala Lumpur   Madrid   Melbourne   Mexico City   Nairobi
New Delhi   Shanghai   Taipei   Toronto

With offices in

Argentina   Austria   Brazil   Chile   Czech Republic   France   Greece
Guatemala   Hungary   Italy   Japan   Poland   Portugal   Singapore
South Korea   Switzerland   Thailand   Turkey   Ukraine   Vietnam

Oxford is a trade mark of Oxford University Press
in the UK and in certain other countries

Published in Canada
by Oxford University Press

Library and Archives Canada Cataloguing in Publication
Regehr, Cheryl
Essential law for social work practice in Canada / Cheryl
Regehr, Karima Kanani.—2nd ed.

Includes bibliographical references and index.
ISBN 978-0-19-543077-6

1. Social workers—Legal status, laws, etc.—Canada. 2. Public welfare—
Law and legislation—Canada. I. Kanani, Karima II. Title.

KE450.S6R43 2010   344.7103'2   C2009-906127-9
KF390.S6R43 2010

Cover image: Stockbyte Illustration/Veer

Printed and bound in the United States of America.

8 9 – 16 15

Contents

Preface

- Simon and Michael have been living in a committed relationship for five years. Last year, following changes to Canada's laws regarding same-sex marriage, they were married. In the past two years, Simon and Michael have spent a great deal of time talking about their wish to have a child to share their family and lives. Is adoption an option available to them?
- Isabel has received threats from her husband who is currently in a state of psychosis because of an exacerbation of bipolar affective disorder. Can she arrange to have him admitted and detained in a psychiatric hospital against his will?
- Twenty-year-old Joseph has been on life support in an intensive care unit for two weeks. He has just been declared clinically dead. Who decides to withdraw life support?
- Nela came to Canada and married a man she met over the Internet. Shortly after her arrival, he began to physically abuse her. If Nela leaves her husband, will she be sent back to her home country?
- Nancy has been told by a prospective landlord that she cannot rent in his building because he does not rent to single mothers. Is this discrimination? If so, what can Nancy do?

Individuals presenting for social work services frequently have problems that are complex and multi-faceted. A person with schizophrenia is facing criminal charges for assault. The parent of a child receiving services from a child welfare agency requires emergency psychiatric hospitalization but refuses to leave home. The family of a palliative patient is facing deportation. In each of these situations, social workers must not only be familiar with the legislation and legal procedures regarding their area of expertise, but they must also provide information to the client and the multidisciplinary team and broker community services regarding legal issues with which they are less familiar. Social workers are frequently asked questions of a legal nature. Can I and should I sue the person who sexually abused me as a child? What do I need to do to stay in Canada? Can I sign papers that will force my adult son to obtain psychiatric treatment? How do I get custody of my child and limit the access of the other parent? Social workers are not expected or authorized to give legal advice, but they must frequently advocate for the rights of clients, advise clients to exercise their own rights and freedoms, direct clients to seek legal assistance, or make decisions in their own practice that have legal consequences. In performing these professional functions, social workers have an obligation to be informed. However, although social workers may be more or less aware of laws in their own specific areas of practice, the clients they encounter generally present with multiple challenges in life. As a result, social workers need a quick way to access legal information in a broad range of practice areas in order to best serve their clients and to provide ethical and competent service.

In providing assistance to others whose problems interface with the law, social workers may themselves become drawn into the legal process. Records may be sought for legal purposes, reports may be requested for court, social workers may be called to testify as experts or fact witnesses. In addition, as members of a legislated profession, social workers have specific duties to uphold regarding their own competence, clients' rights to confidentiality and informed consent, and the safety of clients and other vulnerable members of society.

This second edition of *Essential Law for Social Work Practice in Canada* is for students in courses in the law for social work as well as a general legal guide for Canadian social work practitioners. Each updated chapter reviews case law and legislation pertaining to a particular area of law, including family law, adoption law, mental health law, child welfare law, health law, criminal law, immigration law, and human rights law. In each of these domains the processes that clients will encounter and the duties of social workers are carefully reviewed. As well, the elements of competent practice for social workers when their practice interfaces with the law are discussed, as are means for minimizing liability. Clinical case examples are used to demonstrate the application of law to social work practice and clients' lives. Most chapters open with one or two discussion-sparking case examples that a social worker might encounter and all provide questions related to the law that need to be answered. The chapters close by revisiting the case-example scenarios and discussing possible answers to the questions raised. Instructive figures outline legal processes and informative tables summarize similarities and differences in legislation across Canadian provinces and territories.

The intersection of law and social work practice is undeniable. It is imperative that social workers be able to appropriately direct their clients on the legal rights and resources available to them as well as be aware of their own legal responsibilities in their social work practices. Social workers must also aim to provide competent service that best meets the needs of their clients. To date, there have been few consolidated resources available for social workers as reference tools on the general laws and legal processes that may be applicable when client needs and issues involve the law. We hope this book will fill this information gap and be useful to social workers as a quick reference guide in their daily practices.

Consultants, Reviewers, and Advisors

In this book we have attempted to cover a vast range of practice areas and law. We would not have been able to do so without the generous sharing of time and knowledge from a wide variety of experts in the field. We are most grateful to the following professionals who acted as consultants, reviewers, and advisors in this process:

Beverley J. Antle, Academic and Clinical Specialist, Director of PKU Program, Division of Clinical and Metabolic Genetics, The Hospital for Sick Children, Toronto, Ontario

Marvin M. Bernstein, Children's Advocate, Province of Saskatchewan

Michael Birley, Lawyer, Miller Thomson LLP

Paul Brace, Lawyer, Miller Thomson LLP

Bryan Buttigieg, Lawyer, Miller Thomson LLP

Sharlene Craig, Professional Practice Leader in Social Work, University of Alberta Stollery Children's Hospitals, Edmonton, Alberta

Peter Dudding, Executive Director, Child Welfare League of Canada

Kathryn Frelick, Lawyer, Health Industry Group, Miller Thomson LLP

Graham Glancy, Forensic Psychiatrist, Assistant Professor Faculty of Medicine, Adjunct Professor, Faculty of Law, University of Toronto

Anne Huot, Director of Client Programs and Information, Ottawa Children's Treatment Centre, Ottawa

Joshua Liswood, Lawyer, Chair of the National Health Industry Group, Miller Thomson LLP

Steve Lurie, Executive Director, Canadian Mental Health Association, Toronto Branch

Suzanne McKenna, Executive Director and Registrar, New Brunswick Association of Social Workers

Susan Adam Metzler, Lawyer, Miller Thomson LLP

Roy O'Shaughnessey, Head of the Division of Forensic Psychiatry, University of British Columbia, Clinical Director Youth Forensic Psychiatric Services of British Columbia (1981–2005)

Jane Paterson, Director of Professional Services, Centre for Addiction and Mental Health, Toronto

Robin Pike, Manager of Divisional Operations and Support and Director of Migrant Services, Provincial Services Division, Ministry of Children and Family, Victoria, British Columbia

Bruce Rivers, Executive Director, Children's Aid Society of Toronto, and Executive Director, Child Welfare Secretariat, Ontario Ministry of Children and Youth Services

Valerie Wise, Lawyer, Health Industry Group, Miller Thomson LLP

Research Assistants

In the process of writing this book the following individuals identified, gathered, and synthesized vast amounts of information:

Students in the Faculties of Social Work and Law at the University of Toronto

Holly Andrade, Sandra Bertok, Aileen Cheon, Sharon George, Clara Matheson, Sarvenaz Kermanshahi, with a special thanks to Tiffany Lau for her work compiling the key terms in the second edition of the book.

Students and Clerks at Miller Thomson LLP

Tarsem Basraon, Heather Campbell, Soma Choudhury, Jody Clark, Christian Fortin, Chere-Lee Hollett, Matthew Husson, Alia Karsan, Andre Kuyntjes, Matthew Ledger, Adria Leung, Stephen McCotter, David Pooler, Andrea Sanche, Shaya Silber, Kelly Sinclair, Maanit Zemel, with special thanks to Katherine Salsman.

Funding Assistance

The research contained in this book was generously supported by:
The Sandra Rotman Chair in Social Work Practice
The Canadian Institute of Health Research Fellowship Program
Miller Thomson LLP

Author Profiles

Cheryl Regehr is the Vice-Provost of Academic Programs for the University of Toronto. She is a Professor in the Factor-Inwentash Faculty of Social Work and the Faculty of Law at the University of Toronto. Previously she was Dean of the Factor-Inwentash Faculty of Social Work, the Director of the Centre for Applied Social Research, and the Research Institute for Evidence-Based Social Work. In addition, she has been a member of several editorial boards for international scholarly journals and of committees adjudicating grants for national granting councils. Her practice background includes 20 years of direct service in forensic social work and emergency mental health and in the administration of mental health programs. As a forensic social worker, she specialized in workplace trauma interventions and civil litigation and criminal court assessments of trauma victims and violent offenders. Her current research focuses on the impact of workplace trauma exposure on performance and decision-making of emergency service and child welfare professionals. Professor Regehr's other books with Oxford University Press are *In the Line of Fire: Trauma in the Emergency Services* and *Mental Health Social Work Practice in Canada*.

Karima Kanani is a lawyer and Partner in the Health Industry Group of Miller Thomson LLP. She routinely provides legal advice to health care and social service organizations and professionals. She is a member of the Bar in Ontario, Canada, and in Massachusetts, United States. She holds a Juris Doctor and Master of Social Work from the University of Toronto and a Bachelor of Arts in Psychology and Women's Studies from McGill University. Her past experience in social work includes the Intensive Care of the Toronto Western Hospital, the Mediation Unit of the Ontario Human Rights Commission, and the Health Services Appeal and Review Board of the Ontario Health Boards Secretariat. In addition, Karima is presently a member of the Research Ethics Board at the Centre for Addiction and Mental Health (Toronto). Her research efforts to date have focused primarily on examining the intersections between law and social work and she has published in this area both nationally and internationally. In 2003, she was recognized for the quality of her research and writing, receiving first place in a national competition sponsored by Canadian Lawyers for Social Responsibility.

My contributions to this book are dedicated to my friend, colleague, and partner, Graham, whose knowledge, experience, and wisdom regarding forensic mental health have been invaluable in the preparation of this book and in my work centred at the interface of law and social work practice.

— *Cheryl Regehr*

My contributions to this book are dedicated to my loving husband who inspires me to chase my dreams.

— *Karima Kanani*

CHAPTER ONE

Introduction to Law for Social Work Practice

OBJECTIVES

- To describe the role of law in social work practice
- To review the structure of the Canadian legal system
- To outline how laws are enacted and how social workers may influence the law-making process

Individuals who need social work services have problems that are complex and multifaceted: a person with schizophrenia faces criminal charges for assault; the parent of a child receiving services from a child welfare agency requires emergency psychiatric hospitalization but refuses to leave home; the family of a palliative patient faces deportation. In each of these situations, social workers must not only be familiar with the legislation and legal procedures in their own area of expertise, but they must also provide information to the client and the multidisciplinary team involved, as well as broker community services regarding legal issues that are not familiar to them.

Social workers are also frequently asked questions of a legal nature. Can I and should I sue the person who sexually abused me as a child? What do I need to do to stay in Canada? Can I sign papers that will force my adult son to obtain psychiatric treatment? How do I get custody of my child and limit the access of the other parent? Although social workers do not provide legal advice, if they understand the law regarding these issues, they can assist clients through the various processes and direct them to appropriate resources.

Further, social workers themselves are required to comply with the law in their daily practice and are often faced with legal dilemmas. They may ask: Do I need to report a client's illegal behaviour to the police? I know that I must report child abuse, but what do I do if I know an elderly person is being abused? What do I do when I receive a subpoena for my clinical notes? What will they ask me if I testify as a witness? As an expert?

Therefore, in order to address issues facing their clients, to govern the manner and method with which they deliver social work services, and to participate directly within the legal system, social workers must understand Canadian law. In particular, there are two general but critical questions that they must consider: 1) What is the structure of the Canadian legal system? 2) What are the laws relevant to social work practice in Canada?

The Canadian Legal System

The legal framework within which Canadian social workers practise is multilayered: the Canadian Constitution defines the powers of government; the Canadian Charter of Rights and Freedoms protects the fundamental rights of Canadians; the legislatures make, alter, and repeal laws; and the judiciary and administrative bodies interpret and apply the law (Department of Justice, 2003; 2005).

Constitution

In 1982, the Constitution Act, part of the Canada Act of 1982, declared the Constitution of Canada to be the supreme law of Canada.

The Constitution sets out the basic principles of democratic government and defines the three branches of government as: 1) the executive, which includes the prime minister and other ministers, that is responsible for administering and enforcing laws, and that answers to the legislature; 2) the legislature that has the power to make, alter, and repeal laws; and 3) the judiciary that interprets and applies the law (Department of Justice, 2003).

The Constitution affirms Canada's 'dual' or 'federal' legal system that divides legislative and judicial powers between the federal government and the provinces/territories. Under the Constitution the federal government has jurisdiction to make laws concerning Canada as a whole, including but not limited to trade, entry of persons into Canada, national defence, and criminal. In contrast, the provinces and territories have power in areas such as education, property, civil rights, and hospitals. Local and municipal governments are created under provincial laws and they regulate such matters as smoking, pesticide use, parking, and construction (Department of Justice, 2005).

The Constitution also addresses Aboriginal rights. Under the Constitution the federal government has jurisdiction over Indians and lands reserved for Indians. The federal Indian Act generally applies to all registered Indians and Indian band governments and addresses some issues in relation to their rights and lands, known as 'reserves' (Kyle, 2009). Which persons are considered 'Indians' for the purpose of the Constitution is of particular interest to the federal and provincial governments because it is an important factor in determining which level of government is fiscally responsible for the provision of services (Isaac, 2004). Notwithstanding the jurisdiction of the federal government, provincial laws of general application apply to Indians so long as they do not interfere or conflict with federal jurisdiction and federal law. However, section 35 of the Constitution recognizes and affirms existing Aboriginal and treaty rights. No federal or provincial legislation may infringe on existing Aboriginal or treaty rights, unless such infringement can be justified. Justification includes a duty on the part of the government to consult with the Aboriginal group where their rights may be adversely impacted. 'Aboriginal peoples' include Indian, Inuit, and Metis. 'Aboriginal rights' relate to an element of practice, custom, or tradition integral to the distinctive culture of the Aboriginal group claiming the right. 'Treaty rights' are contained in treaties entered into by the federal Crown and Aboriginal people (Isaac, 2004). There is debate over whether the Constitution has recognized and affirmed an inherent right to Aboriginal self-governance and what 'self-government' means. Self-government takes many forms including band councils under the Indian Act. In 1995 the government released a policy document committing to recognize the inherent right to Aboriginal self-government under section 35 of the Constitution (Minister of Public Works and Government Services Canada, 1995). The policy emphasizes negotiation among the federal, provincial, and territorial governments with Aboriginal peoples on self-government and jurisdiction matters. The impact of relations between federal law, provincial law, and Aboriginal self-governance as it relates to social work practice is discussed in more detail in Chapter 3 on Family Law, Chapter 4 on Child Protection, and Chapter 5 on Adoption Law.

Charter of Rights and Freedoms

When the Constitution came into force in 1982, a fundamental part of it was the Canadian Charter of Rights and Freedoms, which enshrined protection of the fundamental human rights of Canadians in the Constitution. Since the Charter is entrenched in the Constitution, it applies to and takes precedence over all federal and provincial legislation. In general, Canadian laws, the Canadian government, and bodies created, supported, or connected to the Canadian government, may not violate the guaranteed rights of Canadians under the Charter. A law may only infringe Charter rights if the limits placed on these rights can be shown to be reasonable, prescribed by law, and justified in a free and democratic society. The idea is that the interests of society must be balanced against individual interests to see if limiting individual rights would be justified. However, in the circumstances where the reasonable and justified standard for limitation of rights cannot be met, the federal and provincial governments have retained some right to violate the Charter outright through a declaration under what is called the 'notwithstanding clause'. The notwithstanding clause is not used often and any declaration that is made under it must be reenacted (i.e., renewed) to ensure that the government remains accountable to the public. Rights under the Charter include fundamental freedoms (freedom of religion), democratic rights, mobility rights, legal rights, equality rights, language rights, minority language education rights, and Aboriginal rights. It is important to note that the Charter sets out the minimum level of rights only; the federal or provincial legislatures are always free to add to these rights (Department of Justice, 2005).

Legislatures

The Canadian 'legislature' or 'Parliament' has the power to make and change laws. As discussed earlier in this chapter, there are both federal and provincial legislatures. Laws enacted at either level are called 'statutes', 'legislation', or 'acts'. Laws originate as 'bills' in the legislatures. There are two types of bills – public bills that address matters of public policy and private bills that address special powers and exemptions from the general law by conferring a right on some person or group or relieving them

of responsibility (Government of Canada, 2007). All bills must pass through three 'readings' (either at the House of Commons for federal law or the Legislative Assembly for provincial/territorial law) and receive royal assent before they become law (Parliament of Canada, 2006). The first reading is where the bill is introduced, the second reading is when the scope of the bill is debated, and the third reading is where it is decided whether the bill should be adopted and ultimately become law. The legislative process can be long, challenging, and frustrating for advocates who are trying to get social issues addressed by the government in a meaningful way. Even private bills must be introduced by members of the Parliament or Legislative Assembly; so to bring a new law into consideration advocates must actively campaign for political support, often through organized movement of coalitions of persons or groups united for a common cause. Once a bill is introduced into the legislative process, a committee may be established to examine the bill and propose amendments to its scope. To this end, public hearings may be held where interested individuals and groups are invited to make submissions. Social advocacy can influence the law-making process. For example, EGALE (Equality for Gays and Lesbians Everywhere), a national organization committed to advancing equality and justice for lesbian, gay, and bisexual individuals, is funded almost exclusively by member contributions, and has appeared before numerous parliamentary committees, lobbied for amendments to a variety of federal laws, acted as an intervener before the Supreme Court of Canada, and is regularly involved in extensive public education campaigns (EGALE, 2005). EGALE played an important role in the birth of the Modernization of Benefits and Obligations Act, which received assent in 2000. This Act makes amendments to 68 federal laws, extending the rights and responsibilities of opposite-sex married couples to same-sex couples. EGALE was involved at nearly every stage of the legislative process, attending the first session of the House of Commons to identify the need for such a bill, testifying before the Senate Committee to express concerns regarding particular provisions, and more generally, engaging in media activities, developing action alerts, and meeting with MPs from all political parties (EGALE, 2000).

Both federal and provincial governments have constitutional authority to pass legislation governing areas in which social workers are engaged. Where the legislation is federal, practice across Canada will be more or less consistent. For example, the Criminal Code is federal, as is the Youth Criminal Justice Act, and therefore practices related to charging an alleged offender, trying his or her case, and sentencing him or her if found guilty, are (theoretically) the same across the provinces. Thus, if a person assaults another person and this comes to the attention of the police and justice system, the federal Criminal Code is followed by all police, prosecutors, and judges. However, where the legislation is provincial there may be stark differences across the provinces. For example, a social worker's responsibility for intervening in violence cases varies depending on jurisdiction. If an elderly person is abused by his or her adult children, social workers have a duty to report and intervene in the Atlantic Provinces even if the elderly individual does not want them to do so. However, if the person lives anywhere else in Canada there is no such duty to intervene and the social worker is bound by confidentiality not to disclose the information if the elderly client so deems. Similarly, child welfare legislation is also provincial. Thus, while the duty to report suspected child abuse is consistent across the country, whether the behaviour of a parent constitutes child abuse in a specific case varies somewhat, as do the penalties a social worker may face if he or she does not report.

A variety of legislation also directly regulates social work practice, for instance, the privacy of health records and the duty to report child abuse.

Judiciary

Law is more than statutes or legislation. The judiciary (judges in the various courts) is charged with the task of applying and interpreting the statutes for the facts in specific situations. This is known as the 'common law'. Common law, initiated in England in 1066 following the Norman Conquest, is a process by which each decision of the court rests upon previous decisions (called precedents). The principle of relying on decided cases is referred to in legal circles as the principle of *stare decisis* (Waddams, 2004). To ensure that like cases are decided alike, judges are called upon to determine whether the case before the court contains the same circumstances as previous cases. If this is so, the decision rendered must follow the precedents. However, if the circumstances are somewhat unique, a new decision can be rendered that then sets the precedent for the future. In Canada there are four levels of court as follows (Department of Justice, 2003):

1. *Provincial courts* handle most federal and provincial cases that come through the legal system, including but not limited to criminal offences, family law matters (except divorce), and young offenders. Some provinces and territories have established provincial courts dedicated to particular offences or offenders, such as Small Claims Courts, Drug Treatment Courts, Youth Courts, and Domestic Violence Courts.
    a) *Provincial/territorial superior courts* can hear a case unless it is specifically limited to a lower court. Typically, they deal with the most serious criminal and civil cases. Most superior courts have special family law divisions to deal with divorce and *property* claims.
    b) *Federal court* hears matters regarding intellectual property, maritime law, and federal–provincial disputes. The federal specialized courts include the Tax Court of Canada and the Military Justice System.
2. *Provincial and federal courts of appeal* hear appeals from the lower courts as well as constitutional questions.
3. *Supreme Court of Canada* is the final court of appeal from all other courts. Generally, the court must grant permission, or 'leave',

before it will hear a case, but in some circumstances the right to appeal is automatic. This court also decides questions on the Constitution and other controversial questions.

The levels of court are shown in Figure 1.1. Generally, a decision made in a lower court can be appealed to the next level of court until the case reaches the Supreme Court of Canada. Lower courts must follow precedents set by higher courts and thus decisions made by the Supreme Court of Canada direct decisions at all other levels. When new legislation is passed, however, the courts must include these directives in the decision-making process. Furthermore, as we stated earlier, the Canadian Charter of Rights and Freedoms must ultimately govern judiciary decisions in that the courts must ensure that legislation does not violate individual rights and freedoms.

Controversial cases before the courts often incite the interest of individuals and groups with strong opinions on the issues in question. There are two ways that social advocates can participate in the judicial process: as an intervening party or as an amicus curiae. Any person who is interested in a proceeding before a court can make an application under the rules of that court to intervene as a party. Under the Rules of the Supreme Court of Canada, the motion for intervention as a party must be made within a prescribed period of time and identify the person interested, describe the interest, the intended submissions, their usefulness to the court and prejudice that would be suffered if the motion is not granted.

Figure 1.1 Outline of Canada's Court System

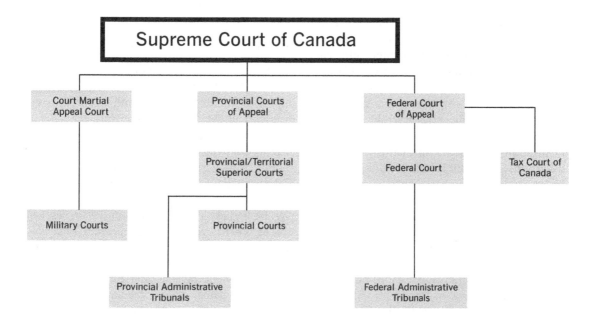

Source: 'Outline of Canada's Court System', from Department of Justice, *Canada's System of Justice* (Ottawa: Her Majesty the Queen in Right of Canada, 2005), p. 16. Reproduced with the permission of the Minister of Public Works and Government Services Canada.

Similar requirements apply in lower courts. In *Reference re Workers' Compensation Act, 1983 (Newfoundland)*, the Supreme Court of Canada discussed two factors they examine when considering a motion for intervention: whether the person has an interest (any interest is sufficient, subject to the court's discretion) and whether the person will be making submissions to the court that will be useful and different from the other parties (i.e., a fresh perspective on an important constitutional or public issue). The standard to intervene applied in lower courts can be higher than the Supreme Court because interveners in lower courts can introduce evidence and argument, which has the potential to prolong a trial (*Halpern v. Toronto (City)*, 2000). If permission to intervene is granted, the judge may impose terms and conditions on the intervener, such as the form of the submissions, the evidence that may be introduced or the amount of argument made in court. Generally, at the Supreme Court the intervener is first given an opportunity to make written submissions and once those submissions are reviewed then consideration is given to whether permission will be granted to give oral submissions. One example of the role of intervening parties is the 2006 Supreme Court of Canada case that considered the constitutionality of a school board's refusal to allow a boy to wear a kirpan at school (a religious object that resembles a dagger and is made of metal). In this case the World Sikh Organization of Canada, Canadian Civil Liberties Association, Canadian Human Rights Commission, and Ontario Human Rights Commission all participated as interveners (*Multani v. Commission scolaire Marguerite-Bourgeoys*, 2006).

The second way for an interested person or group to have their views considered by the court is as an amicus curiae. The amicus curiae is a friend of the court that makes written submissions but, unlike an intervener, is not a legal party to the case. A friend of the court is intended to be an impartial aid to the judge. The court or a judge may appoint an amicus curiae where they believe the person or organization will provide a valuable expertise or perspective (*Piexeiro v. Haberman*, 1994).

Although Canadians are not bound by statutory enactments or the decisions of the courts in other countries, the development of the law in the US and the Commonwealth countries informs Canadian law. This is evident, for example, in the issue of a therapist's duty to protect third parties from harm. In this instance, until a Canadian precedent was set, Canadian therapists assumed that, should such an issue arise in Canada, it would be dealt with in a manner similar to that in the US. Although Canadian law is independent, it does rely on the experience of other similar legal jurisdictions when entering new territory.

The exception to this common law model is the law in Quebec, which evolved from the Roman model and is based on a written civil code. The current Civil Code of Québec was enacted in 1994 and contains a comprehensive statement of rules to deal with any dispute that may arise (Canadiana, 2005). Unlike the common law model, under the civil code model, courts look first to the code and only after that consider precedent cases for consistency (Department of Justice, 2005).

Administrative Bodies

Due to the dearth of the laws that are enacted and the complexity of these laws, it would be nearly impossible for the legislatures and the judiciary to deal with all details of all laws. Thus, the federal and provincial legislatures often pass general laws creating and delegating regulatory authority to various administrative boards and tribunals, such as the Immigration and Refugee Board, the Human Rights tribunals, and the various professional regulatory bodies. These administrative bodies (as well as other government organizations) may be charged with the power to make subordinate legislation known as 'regulations', without having to proceed through the legislative process described earlier (Waddams, 2004). Regulations carry out the purposes of or expand upon the general laws. In addition, the administrative bodies may also serve an adjudicative function, hearing cases and interpreting and applying the law, including the regulations. The procedures before these administrative bodies are less formal than in the courts; however, to ensure that they only exercise the authority they have been given and that they do so with fair procedure, the courts retain the ability to review their decisions and proceedings (Department of Justice, 2005).

Social workers throughout Canada practise under regulatory legislation. Each province has enacted regulatory legislation and has established regulatory bodies to oversee regulation of social workers and to govern practice (see Chapter 12). The territories to date have not enacted such legislation. The primary purpose of regulatory legislation is the protection of the public through ensuring that professionals have a certain level of competence and that they adhere to certain standards of practice. Each regulatory body has established minimum requirements for licensing or registration based on educational requirements, years of supervised practice (in Alberta and Nova Scotia), and/or completion of a licensing examination (in Nova Scotia and Prince Edward Island). These bodies also determine standards for practice and a process for receiving, investigating, and dealing with complaints against social workers (CASW, 2003). In addition to complying with the standards of practice of the provincial regulatory body, social workers must follow the *Code of Ethics* of the Canadian Association of Social Workers (CASW, 2005) or risk facing disciplinary action by their regulatory bodies.

Types of Law

Laws can generally be divided into two categories: public law and private law. Public laws are the laws that govern the relationship between individuals and society and include criminal law, constitutional law, and administrative law. For example, criminal cases involve prosecution by the Crown. Similarly, violations of professional regulations involve prosecution by the professional regulatory body. In contrast, private law, which is also known as and generally referred to in this text as 'civil law', governs relationships between individuals and includes family law, contract law, and tort law (Department of Justice, 2005). An individual may be subject to both public and private law simultaneously. That is, a person may be subject to action by the state and other individuals at the same time, in respect of the same act. For example, an individual who commits an assault may face criminal prosecution by the state as well as a civil action in tort by the injured party who will be seeking monetary compensation for his or her injuries (Waddams, 2004). Although criminal and civil cases may proceed simultaneously in relation to the same act, it is important to be aware that the proceedings will be entirely independent of each other (see Chapter 9).

Clearly, therefore, answering any legal question related to social work practice is complex and requires a consideration of multiple factors including federal and provincial statutory legislation, judiciary procedures, common law precedents, decisions of administrative bodies, and professional regulatory and ethical requirements.

Law for Social Work Practice in Canada

It is essential for social workers to have a solid working knowledge of the legal system and laws of our country in order to be able to assist and empower clients, to comply with the law in the manner and method through which they deliver such assistance, and to participate in the Canadian legal system themselves. To aid social workers in this endeavour, this book surveys the legal landscape for social workers and demonstrates its application to social work practice. What follows is a brief synopsis of the areas of law relevant to social work practice in Canada that are examined in this text.

Human Rights

Human rights laws protect people from discrimination in employment, goods, services, and accommodation. Social workers need a working knowledge of human rights laws not only to be able to respond to the breadth of client inquiries they may receive but also to conduct their social work practice in a manner that respects the equality and freedom from discrimination that is demanded by the law. Chapter 2 provides an overview of federal and provincial human rights legislation and case law pertaining to the protected classes including race, religion, sex, age, disability, social status, sexual orientation, and criminal convictions. The role of the federal and provincial human rights commissions and the mechanics of the commission complaint process are discussed. The chapter also highlights Canada's role in protecting international human rights.

Family Law

Divorce and child custody disputes are extremely difficult and emotionally taxing experiences that affect every aspect of an individual's life—finances, residence, work, health, and relationships with family and friends. The far-reaching impacts of divorce and custody disputes call for all social workers to be aware of the parameters of family law rules and procedures. Chapter 3 surveys federal and provincial family laws and provides an overview of the choice of process available in family law disputes. Topics discussed include who can get married, the grounds and procedures for obtaining a divorce, the factors considered in child custody determinations, and the legal requirements for spousal and child support. The chapter also provides a discussion of family law issues as they impact contemporary family structures such as common-law relationships and same-sex marriages.

Child Protection

Most professionals are well aware of the obligation that they hold to report suspected child abuse to child protection services. However, even though the duty to report child abuse may seem obvious, in actual cases issues may not be clear. For instance, between birth and the age of 16, all provinces and territories have similar legislation and practices regarding the duty to report;

beyond that age, however, who constitutes a child and whether services will be delivered to young people over the age of 16 varies. How issues such as physical discipline, emotional abuse, and exposure to intraparental violence are addressed is not consistent throughout the country, nor are the consequences of not reporting. Once the report is made to child welfare services regarding suspected abuse, those outside the child protection system are frequently perplexed as to the process and annoyed that a child has or has not been apprehended, contrary to their expectations. Thus, Chapter 4 covers child welfare legislation across Canada and legally mandated processes for assessment and intervention. It discusses the rights of clients encountering the child welfare system, the process they are likely to encounter, and the responsibilities of social workers both within and outside of child welfare.

Adoption

Adoption is a time of great joy for parents who wish to have a child enter their family. It is also a time fraught with great frustration over procedural and legal requirements. These requirements are intended to balance the best interest of the child, the rights of birth parents, and the adoptive parents' rights, and at times the rights of disadvantaged groups whose children are adopted by those outside the culture. Adoptive parents wishing to adopt within Canada generally have two options: 1) public adoption (generally from a child welfare organization); and 2) private adoption (usually aided by private adoption agencies). In addition, approximately 2,000 children from other countries are adopted by Canadians every year. The social welfare laws that govern adoptions depend on the province or territory in which the adoptive parents reside and international law.

Consent and Capacity

Although social work may not be the primary discipline responsible for provision of health care, social workers are central members of the health care team. Frequently it is the social worker who discusses complex issues regarding consent to treatment, substitute decision-making, and advance directives for end-of-life care with ill individuals and their families. Issues frequently arise around access to health care records and information; social workers, as mediators between other health care team members and family, educate clients and their families regarding these issues and guide them through the process. Other serious concerns over disposition of property and donation of organs are frequently raised as someone becomes incapacitated because of medical conditions and, finally, as they reach the end of their lives.

Mental Illness

Mental health law deals with highly complex issues related to treatment of individuals who may not have the ability to make decisions about their own care or who may be a danger to themselves or others. Legislation in this area covers such issues as decisions regarding consent to treatment, substitute decision-making, and involuntary admission. Social workers are called upon to: instruct patients regarding their rights; instruct families regarding their ability to ensure that treatment is or is not provided to an ill loved one; and provide assessments regarding the capacity to consent. Each role requires an understanding of the laws pertaining to consent and treatment, essential elements of consent and capacity, and the process of review through provincially appointed boards. Additionally, at times, those with serious mental illnesses come into contact with the law through being charged with criminal offences. Social workers are frequently involved in various aspects of this process including participation in court diversion, providing assessments to the courts, and providing monitoring and follow-up after court disposition. Finally, when those with serious mental illnesses present a risk to others, social workers may have to make decisions and take actions regarding the duty to warn and protect others.

Youth Criminal Justice

In their work with multichallenged families and their children, social workers often have youth who come into conflict with the law among their caseloads. Over the history of youth law in Canada, policies regarding the legal treatment of young people have swung between punitive measures that have treated them like 'little adults' to social justice models that have viewed them as troubled kids who got in with the wrong crowd. The Youth Criminal Justice Act (YCJA) attempts to balance previous models, including the legalistic framework of the Young Offenders Act with the social justice approach of the Juvenile Delinquents Act. The YCJA clearly specifies a range of extrajudicial measures at each stage of the criminal justice process. Social workers have key roles not only in assisting youth and families that are navigating the justice system, but also in providing services that offer options to the courts and divert youth from the courts and jails. Chapter 8 describes the YCJA, the implications that it has for youth and their families, the processes that may occur when a young person comes into contact with the police, and the various options for extrajudicial measures.

Victims of Violence

Social workers regularly provide services for both victims and perpetrators of crime. When developing safety plans for victims of abuse, social workers must be aware of the legal remedies, including the processes of restraining orders and criminal charges. In working with victims of violence, social workers are frequently called upon to guide the client through the process of reporting assault to the police and subsequently to support those encountering the criminal justice system or pursuing civil litigation. Social workers provide reports to the court regarding the impact of a particular crime on the victim or on factors that aid in understanding a particular offender and his or her actions that may mitigate conviction or sentencing decisions. Chapter 9 reviews the process of both civil and criminal courts from the perspective of the victim.

Immigrants and Refugees

Canada's ever-increasing multicultural society guarantees that social workers will come across individuals from all corners of the globe. A social worker may face a battered woman whose immigration sponsorship is from her husband, an applicant for permanent residence who is under medical surveillance, or an infertile couple wanting to adopt a baby from Russia, and this makes it essential that all social workers be aware of the legal issues particular to Canada's immigrant and refugee community. Chapter 10 discusses Canada's Immigration and Refugee Protection Act and examines the classes of immigration, including the sponsorship of family members, the requirements to become a Canadian citizen, the processing of refugee protection claims with the Immigration and Refugee Board, and contemporary issues, such as international adoption, live-in caregivers, mail-order brides, sex-trade workers, and national security.

Social Workers in the Courts

A broad range of circumstances place social workers and their clients in contact with the law. In many of these circumstances, social workers may remain well outside the process and be free of the expectation to engage with the court system in any way. In these situations, social workers may act as support persons and advisors, assisting the client with the emotional challenges that their legal situation invokes. However, increasingly we are seeing that social workers and other therapists and counsellors are being drawn into the court process. Social work records are often sought by lawyers on both sides to support their case. Therefore, social workers must ensure that their records accurately reflect encounters with the client and encounters with others in relation to the client, yet are written in a way that protects both their client and themselves from unintended negative consequences. Social workers must also know how to respond to police and court demands for access to records in an ethical and legal manner while ensuring that they protect the privacy of clients and comply with legal obligations.

In addition, social workers are frequently called upon to write reports for the courts addressing issues such as the suitability of a particular individual to parent, the harms experienced by a victim of violence, or factors that may mediate the sentence of someone who has been convicted of a criminal offence. In these circumstances, social workers may also be called to court to testify as a 'fact witness' with respect to information on a client or other person or as an 'expert witness' offering opinion testimony. Chapter 11 reviews essential elements of social work practice records, means of managing access to records, preparation of court reports, and practical advice for testifying in court.

Liability for Social Workers

Social work is a self-regulated profession. Provincial colleges created by legislation administer the registration requirements for practitioners, establish the ethical and professional standards of practice, and implement the mechanisms for professional discipline. Chapter 12 provides an overview of the practice standards for the profession developed through legislation, case law, and the Canadian Association of Social Workers' *Code of Ethics*. Specific duties central to the therapeutic encounter are examined, including the duty to ensure competence in service provision, the duty to obtain informed consent, the duty to maintain confidentiality, and the duty to warn third parties of harm. The chapter concludes with a discussion on how social workers can minimize liability by having a working knowledge of the law, the mechanics of obtaining practice insurance, and the processes and possible outcomes before the colleges and the courts if a disciplinary action is launched.

Although we intend this book to be a valuable resource for social workers in the field, we must acknowledge that information provided is only as current as was available at the time of writing. Therefore, social workers are urged to maintain their awareness of legislative changes and new precedent-setting cases. Furthermore, we caution that this book is intended only as an informational resource summarizing legal issues and is not meant as legal advice. Social workers should consult legal counsel, and should advise their clients to do so as well, for specific legal advice with respect to the unique circumstances of each situation.

Key Terms

Administrative Boards and Tribunals
Charged with delegated authority from federal and provincial legislatures to pass subordinate legislation (regulations) without having to go through the traditional legislative process; may also hear cases and interpret and apply laws

Amicus Curiae
A friend of the court that is not a party to a case but is appointed by the court to make written submissions because of a valued expertise or perspective

Bill
Proposal for a law that must pass through three readings in the legislature and receive royal assent before officially becoming a law; there are public bills and private bills

Charter of Rights and Freedoms
Outlines the fundamental human rights that are guaranteed to all Canadians, which may not be violated by Canadian laws, government or bodies connected to the government unless the limits placed on the rights are shown to be reasonable, prescribed by law, and justified in a free and democratic society

Civil Code
The legal model in Quebec that is based on a set of rules used to deal with disputes; unlike common law, courts look first to this code before considering past cases

Common Law
A process by which each decision of the court rests upon previous decisions called precedents

Constitution
The supreme law of Canada outlining the basic principles of democratic government, defining the three branches of government (executive, legislature, judiciary) and affirming the federal legal system that divides powers between the federal government and the provinces/territories

Executive
Made up of the prime minister and other ministers; the executive is responsible for administering and enforcing laws and is accountable to the legislature

Intervener
A party with an interest in a case that demonstrates it can make useful submissions to the court different from the other parties and is granted leave to intervene as a party to the case

Judiciary
Judges in the various courts who apply and interpret laws for the facts of each case

Legislature
Also referred to as Parliament; provincial and federal legislatures hold the power to make, change, and repeal laws

Private Law
Also referred to as civil law; laws that govern the relationship between individuals, including family law, contract law, and tort law

Public Law
Laws that govern the relationship between individuals and society, including criminal law, constitutional law, and administrative law

Discussion Questions

1. Why is it important for social workers to be knowledgeable about the law?
2. Describe the legal framework within which social workers practice.
3. What fundamental freedoms are protected under the Charter and can they ever be violated?
4. How are laws enacted? How can you as a social worker influence the law-making process?
5. Are there any opportunities for social advocates to be heard on controversial issues before the courts? Explain.

Relevant Legislation

Federal

Canadian Charter of Rights and Freedoms: Part 1 of the Constitution Act, 1982, being Schedule B to the Canada Act (uk), c. 11
http://laws.justice.gc.ca/en/charter/

References

Canadian Association of Social Workers (CASW) (2003), 'Regulation of Social Work in Canada' (accessed at http://www.casw-acts.ca/canada/regulation_e.htm).

——— (2005), *Code of Ethics* (Ottawa: Canadian Association of Social Workers).

Canadiana (2005), *Canada in the Making: Common Law and Civil Law* (accessed at http://www.canadiana.org/citm/specifique/lois_e.pdf).

Department of Justice (2003), 'Canada's Court System' (accessed at http://www.justice.gc.ca/en/dept/ pub/trib/page1.html).

——— (2005), 'Canada's System of Justice' (accessed at http://www.justice.gc.ca/en/dept/pub/just/ index.html).

EGALE (2000), *INFOEGALE a newsletter for EGALE Canada* (accessed at http://www.egale.ca).

——— (2005), 'About Egale Canada', as presented to the House of Commons Subcommittee on Solicitation Laws, 18 April 2005 (accessed at http://www.egale.ca).

Government of Canada (2007), 'How a Bill Becomes Law – Canada' (accessed at http://dsp-psd.pwgsc.gc.ca/Reference/queens-e.html).

Halpern v. Toronto (City) (2000) CarswellOnt 4504.

Isaac, T. (2004), *Aboriginal Law, Commentary, Cases and Materials*, 3rd ed. (Saskatoon: Purich Publishing).

Kyle, R. (2009), 'Aboriginal Peoples (First Nations)' in Miller Thomson LLP, *Business Laws of Canada* (Toronto: Thomson Reuters).

Minister of Public Works and Government Services Canada (1995), *Federal Policy Guide: Aboriginal Self-Government* (Ottawa).

Multani v. Commission scolaire Marguerite-Bourgeoys (2006), 1 S.C.R 256.

Parliament of Canada (2006), 'Legislative Process' (accessed at http://www.parl.gc.ca).

Peixeiro v. Haberman, 1994 CarswellOnt 580.

Reference re Workers' Compensation Act, 1983 (Newfoundland) (Application to Intervene) (1989), 2 S.C.R. 335.

Rules of the Supreme Court of Canada, S.O.R./2002-156.

Waddams, S. (2004), *Introduction to the Study of Law* (Toronto: Thomson Canada).

CHAPTER TWO

Human Rights Law

OBJECTIVES

- To develop an understanding of the different forms that discriminatory actions may take
- To outline the sources of law pertaining to discrimination in Canada
- To describe the areas where discrimination is prohibited
- To discuss the prohibited grounds of discrimination
- To review the process for filing a human rights complaint and the potential outcomes

CASE EXAMPLE

Nancy is a 30-year-old woman with three small children—Angie (1 year), Justin (3 years), and Sophia (6 years). After 8 years, her husband, Bob, suddenly ended the marriage for a new relationship, leaving Nancy with the children and no knowledge of his whereabouts. Now that Nancy is a single mom she wants to rent a smaller apartment to cut down her costs. She has located the perfect place that is close to the restaurant where she works, the public school and the daycare her children attend, and where she knows some of the neighbours who could assist her with the child care. She has the money to make a deposit but the landlord refuses to rent to her. He has told her that he does not rent apartments to single mothers because he can't be sure they'll be able to make their rent payments. The owner of the restaurant where Nancy works mentioned to her that he thinks this is against the law. Nancy really wants to rent the apartment but doesn't know what to do.

Nancy has walked into a community social work agency looking for help.

- Is the landlord's refusal to rent the apartment to Nancy discrimination?
- Is apartment rental an area that is protected under human rights law?
- Is single motherhood a ground of discrimination prohibited under human rights law?
- Where can Nancy go to file a complaint?
- What procedures will be available to Nancy once she files a complaint?
- If the matter goes before a tribunal, what remedies may Nancy receive?

What Is Discrimination?

Social workers do not provide legal advice on any issue, including human rights, nevertheless, social workers must be aware of the rights to which all people in Canada are entitled in order to advocate for the rights of others, assist clients to advocate on their own behalf, and ensure their own social work practices respect and abide by human rights laws. Human rights are different than other civil liberties because, without laws protecting and promoting human rights, discrimination could be practised in so many of the daily activities of people, corporations, and even the government (Tarnopolsky and Pentney, 2004). Discrimination can generally be defined as:

> a distinction, whether intentional or not but based on grounds relating to personal characteristics of the individual or group, which has the effect of imposing burdens, obligations or disadvantages on such individual or group not imposed upon others, or which withholds or limits access to opportunities, benefits and advantages available to other members of society. Distinction based on personal characteristics to an individual solely on the basis of association with a group will rarely escape the charge of discrimination, while those based on an individual's merits and capacities will rarely be so classed (*Andrews v. Law Society of British Columbia* (1989), 56 D.L.R. (4th) 1 at 18).

Recently, Madam Justice Abella of the Supreme Court of Canada in considering the definition of discrimination from the Andrews case further clarified:

> The goal of preventing discriminatory barriers is inclusion. It is achieved by preventing the exclusion of individuals from opportunities and amenities that are based not on their actual abilities, but on attributed ones. The essence of discrimination is in the arbitrariness of its negative impact, that is, the

arbitrariness of the barriers imposed, whether intentionally or unwittingly.

What flows from this is that there is a difference between discrimination and a distinction. Not every distinction is discriminatory. . . . It is the link between that group membership and the arbitrariness of the disadvantaging criterion or conduct, either on its face or in its impact that triggers the possibility of a remedy (*McGill University Health Centre (Montreal General Hospital) v. Syndicat des Employes de l'Hopital general de Montreal* (2007), 1 S.C.R. 161 at paras. 48–9).

The personal characteristics that give rise to discrimination are fluid. However, the human rights laws in Canada specify both certain areas where discrimination is not permitted and certain prohibited grounds of discrimination. Discriminatory actions can be divided into four categories: direct discrimination, adverse-effect discrimination, systemic discrimination, and harassment (Zinn, 2008).

Direct Discrimination

Direct discrimination occurs when a rule, practice, preference, or restriction makes a distinction that on its face discriminates on a prohibited ground (described later in this chapter) because it is based on a group stereotype. Examples of direct discrimination include a company rule that no women may be employed or a night club charging double to its African-American patrons. If the reason for differential treatment is a prohibited ground then, whether the rule or practice was intended to discriminate or not, it will be considered direct discrimination. No harm needs to be suffered in order to establish a case of direct discrimination (Zinn, 2008).

Adverse-effect Discrimination

Identical treatment does not necessarily mean equal treatment; thus a rule, practice, preference, or restriction that is not discriminatory on its face may still be discriminatory because of its effect. The Supreme Court of Canada, in a case of discrimination in employment, defined adverse-effect discrimination:

> It arises where an employer for genuine business reasons adopts a rule or standard which is on its face neutral, and which will apply equally to all employees, but which has a discriminatory effect on a prohibited ground on one employee or a group of employees in that it imposes, because of some special characteristic of the employee or group, obligations, penalties, or restrictive conditions not imposed on other members of the work force. . . . An employment rule honestly made for sound economic or business reasons, equally applicable to all to whom it is intended to apply, may yet be discriminatory if it affects a person or group of persons differently from others to whom it may apply (*Ontario Human Rights Commission v. Simpsons-Sears* (1985), 2 S.C.R. 536, at para. 18).

In cases where adverse-effect discrimination occurs, the court will not hold a respondent liable for discrimination if he or she has made reasonable efforts to accommodate the complainant. The Supreme Court has described the duty as follows:

> The duty in a case of adverse effect discrimination . . . is to take reasonable steps to accommodate the complainant, short of undue hardship: in other words, to take such steps as may be reasonable to accommodate without undue interference in the operation of the employer's business and without undue expense to the employer. . . . The employer must take reasonable steps towards that end which may or may not result in full accommodation. Where such reasonable steps, however, do not fully reach the desired end, the complainant, in the absence of some accommodating steps on his own part . . . must either sacrifice his religious principles or his

employment (*Ontario Human Rights Commission v. Simpsons-Sears*, at para. 18).

In the preceding case, the employer, Simpsons-Sears Limited, had a policy that said that all full-time employees had to be available to work on Fridays and Saturdays. The rule applied equally to all employees, but Ms Theresa O'Malley, one of their employees, was a member of the Seventh-Day Adventist Church, could not work on the Sabbath, and therefore was not available to work on Friday evenings and Saturdays. Ms O'Malley was terminated. The court held Simpsons-Sears Limited liable for adverse-effect discrimination because Ms O'Malley could not comply with the policy due to her religious beliefs, and the employer had not shown a reasonable effort to accommodate.

Another example of an adverse-effect discrimination case is the recent Canadian Human Rights Tribunal decision in *Sangha v. Mackenzie Valley Land and Water Board* (2006). In that case, the complainant, a Canadian immigrant, had, in addition to numerous other qualifications, a PhD in environmental sciences from the Technical University of Berlin and had co-authored two books in the area. After immigrating to Canada, he applied for a position at the Land and Water Board as a regulatory officer and although he was rated very highly in the interview was turned down because he was overqualified for the job. Expert evidence was presented to the Tribunal that most Canadian immigrants are highly educated but because of job market forces, applying for jobs for which one is overqualified is a disproportionately immigrant experience. The Tribunal held that a rule not to employ overqualified candidates appears to be a neutral rule but it has an adverse discriminatory effect on immigrant applicants.

Systemic Discrimination

Systemic discrimination is hard to define and hard to identify. Adverse-effect discrimination and systemic discrimination are both unintentional, but whereas adverse-effect discrimination arises from a particular policy or practice that has a discriminatory effect, systemic discrimination has its roots in long-standing stereotypes and value assumptions that create the discriminatory effect (Zinn, 2008). The Supreme Court of Canada addressed the definition of systemic discrimination in *Canadian National Railway Co. v. Canada* (1987). In that case an employer had been found guilty of systemic discrimination against women in its hiring and promotion of blue-collar workers. The Supreme Court of Canada commented:

> systemic discrimination in an employment context is discrimination that results from the simple operation of established procedures of recruitment, hiring and promotion, none of which is necessarily designed to promote discrimination. The discrimination is then reinforced by the very exclusion of the disadvantaged group because the exclusion fosters the belief, both within and outside the group, that the exclusion is the result of 'natural' forces, for example, that women 'just can't do the job'.
>
> . . . systemic discrimination is often unintentional. It results from the application of established practices and policies that, in effect, have a negative impact upon the hiring and advancement prospects of a particular group. It is compounded by the attitudes of managers and co-workers who accept stereotyped visions of the skills and 'proper role' of the affected group, visions which lead to the firmly held conviction that members of that group are incapable of doing a particular job, even when that conclusion is objectively false (*Canadian National Railway Co. v. Canada (Canadian Human Rights Commission)* (1987), 1 S.C.R. 1114, at paras. 36 and 42).

It is often challenging to find sufficient evidence to support a claim of systemic discrimination. Evidence that may be brought forward includes: attitudes of supervisors; records of incidents that have occurred; statistical patterns, such as a disproportionate number of employees of an ethnic minority hired compared to the representation of that minority group within the geographical area; and in some cases the unlikelihood that anything but discrimination had occurred, for example, a business with thousands of employees all of whom are men (*Lasani v. Ontario*, 1993).

Combatting systemic discrimination often requires systemic remedies, such as affirmative action programs. Human rights legislation across Canada allows for distinctions to be made on the prohibited grounds if the distinction ameliorates the disadvantage faced by historically disadvantaged communities. For example, the Ontario Human Rights Commission Policy on Scholarships and Awards (1997) provides that benefactors who distribute academic scholarships and awards are permitted to establish qualifications that are discriminatory, if hardship or economic disadvantage is linked to the criteria for eligibility.

Harassment

Harassment can take many forms, for example, unwelcome physical contact, relentless racial jokes, or *Playboy* centrefolds posted up in a lunchroom. Generally, harassment can be divided into two categories. The first is *quid pro quo*, where a benefit is contingent upon participation in an activity. This type of harassment most often manifests in cases of sexual harassment at work. For instance, a promotion may be dependent on dating the supervisor. The second category of harassment is conduct that creates a 'hostile environment' that an individual is required to endure to continue working in the place of employment, to continue residing in the place of accommodation, or to continue gaining access to a facility or service. Racial, ethnic, gender, or religious harassment often takes the form of a hostile environment. In August 2004, a female firefighter in Burnaby, British Columbia, complained of 11 years of sexual harassment, including sexist jokes, offensive pictures of women, and a cartoon of her performing oral sex on the fire chief (CBC, 2004). Not only was she found to suffer from a hostile work environment, but the two male firefighters who supported her claims also won the right to have their own complaints of a poison work environment heard by the Human Rights Tribunal (CBC, 2005). Note that an isolated incident, such as a racial comment, will not constitute hostile environment harassment; there must be a pattern of conduct that the complainant is enduring over time (Zinn, 2008).

In an employment context, the respondents to harassment complaints have been found to have several obligations, the basis of which is the responsibility to provide an environment free of harassment or the fear of harassment. In addition, employers must respond to harassment when it occurs and may be liable for harassment by supervisors, co-workers, and perhaps even customers or clients if they fail to promptly respond to harassment allegations or ought to have been aware of the harassment (Zinn, 2008).

Some jurisdictions have specific legislative provisions addressing harassment. However, the Supreme Court of Canada has held that if the human rights legislation in a jurisdiction does not include a specific prohibition against harassment it will not preclude the filing of a human rights complaint for harassment with respect to prohibited grounds of discrimination (R. v. Robichaud, 1987).

What Are the Sources of Law on Discrimination?

Human rights in Canada are governed by the Canadian Charter of Rights and Freedoms as well as international, federal, and provincial human rights statutes.

International Human Rights Laws

The primary source of international human rights law is the group of instruments known as the International Bill of Human Rights that includes the Universal Declaration of Human Rights 1948 (UDHR). The UDHR sets out the basic civil, political, economic, social, and cultural rights that all people should enjoy (OHCHR, 2008). In addition to adopting the UDHR, Canada is also a party to, among others, six major international conventions: the International Covenant on Economic, Social, and Cultural Rights, the International Covenant on Civil and Political Rights, the Convention on the Elimination of all Forms of Discrimination Against Women, the Convention Against Torture, the Convention for the Elimination of Racial Discrimination, and the Convention on the Rights of the Child. The essence of international human rights obligations is that the states to which they apply undertake to give effect to their obligations in domestic law (Freeman and Van Ert, 2004). The Charter of Rights and Freedoms, together with the federal and provincial human rights statutes, are the primary means by which Canada's obligations under international human rights laws are given legal effect. The Federal-Provincial-Territorial Continuing Committee of Officials on Human Rights meets regularly to coordinate and collaborate on the ratification and domestic implementation of international human rights instruments (Canadian Heritage, 2008).

The Charter of Rights and Freedoms

As discussed in Chapter 1, the Canadian Charter of Rights and Freedoms is the part of the Canadian Constitution that ensures that Canadian laws and acts of the Canadian government or bodies created, supported, or connected with the Canadian government do not violate the rights and freedoms that Canadians believe are necessary in a free and democratic society. The Charter rights include democratic rights (for example, the right to vote), legal rights (for example, the right to be presumed innocent), mobility rights (for example, the right to reside in any province), language rights (for example, the right to be educated in English or French), equality rights (for example, the right to equal treatment before the law), and the fundamental freedoms of religion, thought, expression, peaceful assembly, and association (CRIC, 2005). From abortion to assisted suicide to homosexuality to pornography—the rights and freedoms accorded to Canadians through the Charter have been a source and forum for considerable controversy and social progress. The vast reach of the Charter is beyond the scope of this chapter. Of particular importance to our discussion of discrimination are the equality rights under section 15 of the Charter, which provides as follows:

1. Every individual is equal before and under the law and has the right to the equal protection and equal benefit of the law without discrimination and, in particular, without discrimination based on race, national or ethnic origin, colour, religion, sex, age, or mental or physical disability.
2. Subsection (1) does not preclude any law, program, or activity that has as its object the amelioration of conditions of disadvantaged individuals or groups including those that are disadvantaged because of race, national or ethnic origin, colour, religion, sex, age, or mental or physical disability.

The Supreme Court of Canada has stated that the purpose of section 15 of the Charter is to protect those groups who suffer social, political, and legal disadvantages in society (*Andrews v. Law Society of British Columbia*, 1989). However, it is understood that the grounds of discrimination under section 15(1) are not exhaustive but rather are intended to show the factors that would deny persons the equal protection and benefit of the law (Rapaport, 1988). For instance, the courts have held that although not specifically enumerated, sexual orientation is a prohibited ground of discrimination protected under this section. Generally, any person in Canada whether or not a citizen is protected by the equality rights of the Charter. However, the Charter does not mandate that all people must always be treated equally. For instance, the Charter allows for certain laws or programs that favour disadvantaged individuals or groups such as, for example, programs aimed at improving employment opportunities

for women. In addition, the Charter provides that a law may infringe the rights and freedoms in the Charter so long as it is reasonable and justified (DCH, 2003). However, there are very few cases where an infringement of the equality rights under section 15 of the Charter has been found to be justified. When interpreting and applying the equality guarantee of the Charter the courts have referred closely to the human rights statutes and the case law that has developed around those statutes as discussed below (Sharpe, Swinton, and Roach, 2002).

The Human Rights Statutes

As stated in Chapter 1, the Charter sets out the minimum level of rights only, the federal or provincial legislatures are always free to add to these rights through legislation (also called statutes). Federal and provincial human rights statutes protect individuals against discrimination by private persons and corporations. The extent of the protection provided depends on whether the federal or provincial laws apply and the province in which an individual resides (Zinn, 2008). Areas that fall under authority of the federal government are governed by the Canadian Human Rights Act, the Canadian Human Rights Commission, and the Federal Human Rights Tribunal, while the provincial human rights cases are governed by the provincial human rights codes, the provincial human rights commissions, and/or provincial human rights tribunals.

Each of the federal and provincial human rights commissions/tribunals has developed its own jurisprudence, policy, and procedure (Zinn, 2008). However, there are considerable similarities between the jurisdictions. The purpose of this chapter is to provide an overview, so discussion of specific jurisdictions will only be provided as examples; when dealing with a particular human rights matter, contact the human rights commission/tribunal in your area. Table 2.1 lists the provinces and territories, their respective human rights statutes, and the contact information for the human rights commissions/tribunals.

Table 2.1   Legislation and Agencies Governing Human Rights Claims by Jurisdiction

Jurisdiction	Legislation	Agency	Time Limit to Bring a Complaint	Persons Who Can File a Complaint
Federal	Canadian Human Rights Act, R.S. 1985	Canadian Human Rights Commission 344 Slater Street, 8th Floor, Ottawa, ON K1A 1E1, Canada Tel: (613) 995-1151 Toll-Free: 1-888-214-1090 TTY: 1-888-643-3304 Fax: (613) 996-9661 E-mail: info.com@chrc-ccdp.ca Website: http://www.chrc-ccdp.ca/	1 year	Canadian citizens, permanent residents, or persons legally present in Canada. Usually the victim files, but can also be filed by a third party such as a relative or collective bargaining unit with the consent of the victim, or the citizen itself can initiate the complaint.
Alberta	Human Rights, Citizenship and Multiculturalism Act, R.S.A. 2000	Alberta Human Rights and Citizenship Commission 800 Standard Life Centre, 10405 Jasper Ave., Edmontcn, AB T5J 4R7 Tel: (780) 427-3116 Fax: (780) 422-3563 E-mail: humanrights@gov.ab.ca Website: www.albertahumanrights.ab.ca	1 year	Any person except the Commission itself or a member of the Commission or any director or other employees of the Commission.
British Columbia	Human Rights Code, R.S.B.C. 1996	BC Human Rights Tribunal 1170 – 605 Robson Street, Vancouver, BC V6B 5J3 Tel: (604) 775-2000 Toll-Free: 1-888-440-8844 (in B.C. only) TTY: (604) 775-2021 Fax: (604) 775-2020 E-mail: BCHumanRightsTribunal@gov.bc.ca Website: www.bchrt.bc.ca	6 months	Any person or group of persons. Complaints may be made on behalf of others but the panel may refuse to proceed when the victim does not wish to proceed, or when proceeding with the complaint is not in the interest of the group or class on behalf of which the complaint is made.
Manitoba	Human Rights Code, C.C.S.M. 1987	Manitoba Human Rights Commission 7th Floor - 175 Hargrave Street, Winnipeg, MB R3C 3R8 Tel: (204) 945-3007 Toll-Free: 1-888-884-3007 TTY: (204) 945-3442 Fax: (204) 945-1292 E-mail: hrc@gov.mb.ca Website: www.gov.mb.ca/hrc	6 months	Any person; if an individual besides the victim makes a complaint, the executive director may refuse to accept the complaint unless the victim consents; the Commission can initiate a complaint itself.
New Brunswick	Human Rights Act, S.N.B. 1985	New Brunswick Human Rights Commission PO Box 6000, Fredericton, NB E3B 5H1 Tel: (506) 453-2301 Fax: (506) 453-2653 E-mail: hrc.cdp@gnb.ca Website: English: www.gnb.ca/hrc-cdp/index-e.asp French: www.gnb.ca/hrc-cdp/index-f.asp	1 year	Any person claiming to be aggrieved because of an alleged violation.

Table 2.1   Legislation and Agencies Governing Human Rights Claims by Jurisdiction *(Continued)*

Jurisdiction	Legislation	Agency	Time Limit to Bring a Complaint	Persons Who Can File a Complaint
Newfoundland and Labrador	The Human Rights Code, R.S.N.L. 1990	Newfoundland Human Rights Commission PO Box 8700, St. John's, NF A1B 4J6 Tel: (709) 729-2709 Fax: (709) 729-0709 E-mail: humanrights@mail.gov.nl.ca Website: http://www.gov.nf.ca/hrc/	6 months	A person who has reasonable grounds for believing that a person has contravened the Code; if an individual besides the victim makes a complaint, the executive director may refuse to act without the consent of the victim.
Nova Scotia	Human Rights Act, R.S.N.S. 1989, amended 1991, 2007	Nova Scotia Human Rights Commission 6th Floor, Joseph Howe Building, 1690 Hollis Street PO Box 2221, Halifax, NS B3J 3C4 Tel: (902) 424-4111 Fax: (902) 424-0596 E-mail: hrcinquiries@gov.ns.ca Website: www.gov.ns.ca/humanrights	1 year	The person aggrieved by the discriminatory conduct, the Commission itself.
Ontario	Human Rights Code, R.S.O. 1990	Ontario Human Rights Tribunal 255 Bay Street, 14th Floor, Toronto, ON M7A 2A3 Tel (Toll-Free): 1-866-598-1322 Tel (Toronto): 416-326-1312 TTY (Toll-Free): 1-866-607-1240 TTY: 416-326-2027 Fax (Toll-Free): 1-866-355-6099 Fax: 416-326-2199 E-mail: HRTO.Registration@ontario.ca Website: http://www.hrto.ca	6 months	Any person except the Tribunal or Commission, including a person or organization acting on behalf of the victim if the victim consents.
Prince Edward Island	Human Rights Act, R.S.P.E.I. 1988	Prince Edward Island Human Rights Commission 53 Water Street, PO Box 2000, Charlottetown, PEI C1A 7N8 Tel: (902) 368-4180 Toll-Free: 1-800-237-5031 Fax: (902) 368-4236 E-mail: peihr@isn.net Website: http://www.gov.pe.ca/humanrights	1 year	Any person, except the Commission or an employee of the Commission.
Quebec	Charter of Human Rights and Freedoms, R.S.Q. 1975	Quebec Commission des droits de la personne et des droits de la jeunesse 360, rue Saint-Jacques, 2eme étage, Montreal, PQ H2Y 1P5 Tel: (514) 873-5146 Toll-Free: 1-800-361-6477 TTY: (514) 873-6032 Fax: (514) 873-6032 E-mail: wesmestre@cdpdj.gc.ca Website: http://www.cdpdj.qc.ca/	2 years	Any person or member of a group who has encountered discriminatory conduct, or by an organization dedicated to the defence of human rights and freedoms or the welfare of a group of persons. Written consent of the victim is required except for in the case of the exploitation of aged persons or handicapped persons.

Table 2.1 Legislation and Agencies Governing Human Rights Claims by Jurisdiction (Continued)

Jurisdiction	Legislation	Agency	Time Limit to Bring a Complaint	Persons Who Can File a Complaint
Saskatchewan	Human Rights Code, S.S., 1979, 1980–81, 1989–90, 1993, 2000, and 2007	Saskatchewan Human Rights Commission 8th Floor, Sturdy Stone Building, 122–3rd Avenue North, Saskatoon, SK S7K 2H6 Tel: (306) 933-5952 Toll-Free: 1-800-667-9249 TTY: (306) 373-2119 Fax: (306) 933-7863 E-mail: shrc@shrc.gov.sk.ca Website: http://www.shrc.gov.sk.ca/	2 years	Any person, but only with the consent of the victim; the Commission itself.
Northwest Territories	Human Rights Act, S.N.W.T 2002	Northwest Territories Human Rights Commission PO Box 1860, Yellowknife, NWT X1A 2P4 Tel: (867) 669-5575 Toll-Free: 1-888-669-5575 Fax: (867) 873-0357 E-mail: info@nwthumanrights.ca Website: http://www.nwthumanrights.ca	2 years	Any aggrieved person or group; the Commission itself.
Nunavut	Human Rights Act, 2002, Bill 12	Nunavut Fair Practices Officer, The Government of Nunavut Department of Justice PO Box 2528, Iqaluit, Nunavut X0A 0H0 Tel: (867) 979-2043 Fax: (867) 979-6050 E-mail: billr@nunanet.com	none	Any person or group of persons. Complaints may be made on behalf of others but the panel may refuse to proceed when the victim does not wish to proceed or when proceeding with the complaint is not in the interest of the group or class on behalf of which the complaint is made.
Yukon Territory	Human Rights Act, R.S.Y. 2002	Yukon Human Rights Commission 101 - 9010 Quartz Road, Whitehorse, YK Y1A 2Z5 Tel: (867) 667-6226 Toll-Free: 1-800-661-0535 Fax: (867) 667-2662 E-mail: humanrights@yhrc.yk.ca Website: www.yhrc.yk.ca	6 months	Any person; the complaint will be dismissed if the victim asks that the investigation not proceed.

In Which Areas Is Discrimination Prohibited?

Generally, human rights statutes prohibit discrimination in employment, services and facilities, contracts, and accommodation.

Employment

Most human rights laws have developed in the area of employment. Every province and territory has legislation prohibiting discrimination with respect to employment covering:

- pre-employment—advertisements, interviews, and applications;
- employment—transfers, promotions, pensions, benefits, and work environment; and
- post-employment—layoff, termination, and retirement.

Employment in the human rights context can cover a broad range of relationships beyond the traditional master–servant relationship. Some provinces have clearly specified the scope of employment relationships in their statutory definitions of employment. For example, in Nunavut and Manitoba, employment includes work that is paid or unpaid. In Manitoba, employment is defined to include work that is actual or potential, full-time or part-time, permanent, seasonal, or casual. In addition, the Northwest Territories, Manitoba, New Brunswick, Nova Scotia, and Prince Edward Island all specifically include independent contractors in their definitions of employment. In jurisdictions where the human rights legislation does not clearly define employment there is often litigation on whether the employment relationship is governed by the human rights legislation. Many of the provincial tribunals have adopted very liberal interpretations of the employment relationship within the human rights context. For example, in Ontario, short-term agreements can give rise to a complaint (*Roberts v. Club Expose*, 1993); in British Columbia,

the definition of employment includes volunteers (*Re Thambirajah and Girl Guides of Canada*, 1995); and in Newfoundland it was held that the Ministry of Health, although it did not directly employ the complainant, was still an employer for the purpose of human rights because it participated in the formation and conduct of the relationship, funded the relationship, and could terminate it.

In addition to employers, in unionized workplaces the union may also be held liable for human rights violations. Unions may be liable with respect to membership rights and where collective agreements have a discriminatory clause and/or a discriminatory effect on the employees. A union may also be held liable for the discriminatory actions of one of its organizers or employees. While some jurisdictions limit human rights protection to unions and similar other organizations, most jurisdictions provide human rights protection in a wide range of vocational associations, occupational associations, professional associations, self-governing professions, and business associations (Zinn, 2008).

All human rights legislation in Canada provides a defence to employers for discrimination called the 'bona fide occupational requirement' defence. For instance, a police service can require that someone who is hired to be an officer pass a fitness requirement. The Supreme Court of Canada has set out a three-stage test for determining whether an employer has successfully established the *bona fide* occupational requirement defence:

A three-step test should be adopted for determining whether an employer has established, on a balance of probabilities, that a prima facie discriminatory standard is a bona fide occupational requirement (BFOR). First, the employer must show that it adopted the standard for a purpose rationally connected to the performance of the job. The focus at the first step is not on the validity of the particular standard, but rather on the validity of its more general purpose. Second, the employer must establish that it adopted the particular standard in an honest and good faith belief that it was necessary to the fulfilment of that legitimate work-related purpose. Third, the employer must establish that the standard is reasonably necessary to the accomplishment of that legitimate work-related purpose. To show that the standard is reasonably necessary, it must be demonstrated that it is impossible to accommodate individual employees sharing the characteristics of the claimant without imposing undue hardship upon the employer (*British Columbia (Public Service Employee Relations Commission) v. BCGSEU*, 1999).

Courts and tribunals will look to a variety of factors when determining whether an employer has suffered undue hardship in accommodating, including but not limited to, the financial cost to the employer, disruption of a collective agreement, problems of morale of other employees and the interchangeability of the work force and facilities (*Central Alberta Dairy Pool v. Alberta*, 1990).

Services and Facilities

All jurisdictions demand equal access to and treatment in services and facilities. Most jurisdictions, except for Ontario, Nova Scotia, and the Yukon Territory, limit the prohibition against discrimination to services and facilities that are 'customarily available to the public', including but not limited to (Zinn, 2008):

- insurance coverage;
- police services;
- university and public school education;
- private clubs;
- specialty driver's licences and taxi services;
- restaurants, hotels, and stores;
- amateur hockey teams and associations;
- rental apartments;
- access to medical services;
- unemployment insurance benefits;
- services on Native reserves;
- National Revenue Services; and
- union organizing.

Accommodation

All jurisdictions provide some protection from discrimination with respect to access to residential and commercial premises and the sale and purchase of land. For example, discrimination has been found where landlords favour older people over younger people, because they are less noisy (*Velenosi v. Dominion Management*, 1989), where landlords favour women over men because they are tidier (*Blackburn v. Lam*, 1990), where a person is denied tenancy because they have a child (*Westbury v. Trump Investments Ltd.*, 1992), and where directors have refused to allow a shareholder to transfer ownership of shares in a property to persons of certain ancestry (*Harker v. Popular Roost Resort Ltd.*, 1986). Some jurisdictions have detailed legislative provisions specifically prohibiting discrimination with respect to commercial and dwelling units; others, such as Ontario and Nova Scotia, simply refer to 'accommodation' but in such jurisdictions it is clear that the term 'accommodation' encompasses both residential and commercial premises.

Contracts

Four jurisdictions have specific provisions in their human rights legislation prohibiting discrimination in respect of contracts. In Ontario, every person has a right to contract on equal terms without discrimination on any prohibited grounds, while Saskatchewan, Manitoba, and the Yukon protect against discrimination in contracts offered to the public. In other jurisdictions that do not have specific statutory provisions protecting human rights in contracts, discrimination is nevertheless prohibited as an implied contract term; that is, discriminatory behaviour could be a breach of the contract itself or of public policy (Zinn, 2008).

What Are Prohibited Grounds of Discrimination?

When human rights codes were first enacted, they provided protection against racial and religious discrimination, but as awareness about discrimination has grown, so too has the list of prohibited grounds of discrimination (Sharpe, Swinton, and Roach, 2002). The prohibited grounds of discrimination include race, colour, place of origin, religion, creed, sex, age, marital/family status, sexual orientation, disability, and criminal record. The prohibited grounds are fairly uniform across the country but there are some jurisdictional distinctions in the grounds available and in their interpretation and application. Table 2.2 is a quick reference chart summarizing the prohibited grounds of discrimination in each jurisdiction.

Race, Colour, and Place of Origin

The human rights legislation in all jurisdictions include race and colour as prohibited grounds of discrimination. Most jurisdictions list national or ethnic origin as a prohibited ground. Some even include citizenship or nationality as a prohibited ground. However, the exact terminology used in the human rights legislation has not been determinative in human rights cases—the term 'race' has been taken to include colour, ethnic origin, national origin, nationality, and descent (Tarnopolsky and Pentney, 2004).

Discrimination on the basis of race can be difficult to identify and prove. In some instances racial discrimination may be overt, such as a nightclub charging twice the usual cover charge to black patrons. However, people are generally aware that they cannot discriminate on the basis of race and as a result racial discrimination is often covert and subtle leaving complainants only a body of circumstantial evidence to substantiate their allegations (Zinn, 2008).

Respondents to claims of race discrimination will have a difficult time demonstrating *bona fide* justifications for their actions. Respondents may defend themselves by providing a 'rational and credible' explanation for the alleged discrimination, but complainants will most often succeed if they can prove that race was at least one motivating factor behind the respondent's actions (Zinn, 2008).

Religion and Creed

All human rights legislation in Canada prohibits discrimination based on religion. It is well established under human rights law that 'religion' and 'creed' are synonymous (Tarnopolsky and Pentney, 2004). Like racial discrimination discussed above, discrimination on the basis of religion is more likely to be covert and subtle. It often manifests itself as adverse-effect discrimination, where policies or practices that are not discriminatory on their face adversely interfere with the religious rights of persons from particular faiths—like the case discussed earlier where an employment policy requiring employees to work Saturdays adversely effected Ms O'Malley's religious observance of the Sabbath on that day (*Ontario Human Rights Commission v. Simpsons-Sears*, 1985), or cases of school policies banning all headgear, adversely effecting those students whose religious faith requires that they cover their heads (*Sehdev v. Bayview Glen Junior Schools*, 1988).

In many jurisdictions employers may be permitted to discriminate on the basis of religion if they can establish that the discriminatory rule, policy, or practice is a *bona fide* occupational requirement (Tarnapolsky and Pentney, 2004). For example, parochial schools requiring their teachers to be of a particular religious persuasion or to practise by the school's denomination (*British Columbia v. BCGSEU*, 1999). However, even where the employment policy is rationally connected to job performance and is imposed in good faith, the respondents to a religious discrimination complaint still have a duty to accommodate religious needs of others to the point of undue hardship. The Canadian courts have generally respected hiring practices of religious minorities and as such it is easier for a respondent to establish undue hardship in cases of religious discrimination than on other prohibited grounds like gender.

Sex

Sex is a prohibited ground of discrimination in every Canadian jurisdiction. Generally, 'sex' refers

Table 2.2   Prohibited Grounds of Discrimination***

Ground	Federal	Alberta	British Columbia	Manitoba	New Brunswick	Newfoundland	Nova Scotia	Ontario	Prince Edward Island	Quebec	Saskatchewan	Northwest Territories	Nunavut	Yukon Territory
Places of Origin	●	●			●			●			●	●	●	
Creed			●		●	●	●	●		●	●	●	●	●
Social Conditions					●					●		●		
Social Origin						●								
Source of Income*****		●			●			●		●		●		●
Language										●				
Civil Status										●				
Sexual** Orientation	●	●	●	●	●	●	●	●	●	●	●	●	●	●
Gender Identity			●		●							●		
Family Status	●	●		●				●	●	●	●	●	●	●
Family Affiliation												●		
Political Beliefs****					●	●	●		●	●			●	
Ancestry		●	●		●	●		●			●	●	●	●
Physical Disability	●	●	●	●	●	●	●	●	●	●	●	●	●	●
Mental Disability	●	●	●	●	●	●	●	●	●	●	●	●	●	●
Criminal Conviction	●		●		●		●		●	●				●
Marital Status	●	●	●	●	●	●	●	●	●		●	●	●	●
Pregnancy/Childbirth*	●	●		●								●		
Sex/Gender	●	●	●	●	●	●	●	●	●	●	●	●	●	●
Age	●	● (18+)	● (19+)	●	●	●	● (19+)	● (18+)	●	●	● (18+)	●	●	●
Religion	●	●	●	●	●	●	●	●	●			●	●	●
Nationality/Citizenship			●		●			●			●		●	
Colour	●	●	●	●	●	●	●	●	●		●	●	●	●
National/Ethnic Origin	●				●	●	●	●	●				●	●
Race	●	●	●	●	●	●	●	●	●		●	●	●	●
Actual or Presumed Association with a Protected Group				●			●							●

Source: Reproduced with permission from *Canadian Labour Law Reporter*, published by and copyright © CCH Canadian Limited, Toronto, Ontario.

*In Alberta discrimination on the basis of pregnancy is deemed to be discrimination on the basis of sex. In Ontario, Manitoba, Nova Scotia, and the Yukon Territory discrimination on the basis of pregnancy is included in discrimination on the basis of sex.

**The Supreme Court decision in *Vriend v. Alberta* 'read in' sexual orientation as a prohibited ground of discrimination in Alberta.

***Harassment is banned on all proscribed grounds of discrimination except in New Brunswick and Nova Scotia where it only refers to sexual harassment.

****In New Brunswick, political activity is a prohibited ground of discrimination as well as political belief.

*****In Saskatchewan, receipt of social assistance is a prohibited ground of discrimination.

to gender and the personal attributes attached to each gender. Every jurisdiction now also recognizes pregnancy and pregnancy-related conditions as gender attributes to be protected under the prohibition against sex discrimination, with the exception of Quebec where pregnancy is a prohibited ground on its own (Zinn, 2008). The Supreme Court of Canada in a unanimous decision affirmed this interpretation:

> That those who bear children and benefit society as a whole thereby should not be economically or socially disadvantaged seems to bespeak the obvious. It is only women who bear children; no man can become pregnant. As I argued earlier, it is unfair to impose all of the costs of pregnancy upon one-half of the population. . . . Distinctions based on pregnancy can be nothing other than distinctions based on sex or, at least, strongly, 'sex-related' (*Brooks v. Canada Safeway Ltd.*, (1989) 1 S.C.R. 1219, at para. 43).

On the same reasoning, it has been held that discrimination on the basis that an individual is breastfeeding is a form of sex discrimination (*Poirier v. British Columbia (Ministry of Municipal Affairs, Recreation and Housing)*, 1997). Most recently, the Canadian Human Rights Tribunal in upholding a female employee's right to have her breastfeeding needs accommodated in the workplace, stated:

> In their working lives, women face particular challenges and obstacles that men do not. A woman who opts to breastfeed her baby takes on a child-rearing responsibility which no man will truly ever face. In order for a working mother to bestow on her child the benefits that nursing can provide, she may require a degree of accommodation. Otherwise, she may end up facing a difficult choice that a man will never have to address. On the one hand, stop nursing your child in order to continue working and make a living for yourself and your family. On the other hand, abandon your job to ensure that your child

will be breastfed. This dilemma is unique to women employees and results in their being differentiated adversely, in the course of their employment. It has the potential to create precisely the type of obstacle that would deny women an 'opportunity equal to others, to make for themselves the lives they are able and wish to have' (*Cole v. Bell Canada*, 2007 CarswellNat 2701 (C.H.R.T.) at para. 61).

In addition, sex is not necessarily an either/or characteristic and may be defined by factors other than physical gender. Transsexualism has emerged as another form of sex discrimination (Zinn, 2008). For example, the British Columbia Human Rights Tribunal found that a night club had discriminated on the ground of sex against a preoperative male-to-female transsexual by denying her access to the women's washroom (*Re Sheridan and Sanctuary Investments Ltd.*, 1999). In coming to this finding the tribunal noted that sex discrimination applies to more than just the objective sex of an individual, there is also a subjective identification of gender and one's objective sex and subjective sexual identity may be incongruent. The tribunal held that the prohibition against sex discrimination should also protect those who experience discrimination because they fall outside the traditional male/female categories. As stated by the Quebec Human Rights Tribunal, '[Sex] is the result of a juxtaposition of genetic, hormonal, anatomical, psychological and psychosocial elements. . .' (*Re Québec and Maison des jeunes A-Ma-Baie Inc.*, 1998).

Age

The federal government and all the provinces and territories protect against discrimination on the basis of age but the definition of age and the nature of the protection afforded differs in each jurisdiction (CLLR, 2005). Some jurisdictions have specified a minimum age required in order to obtain protection against discrimination; some have set specific age limits for human rights protection with respect to employment; others have set no age limits at all. Historically, some provinces had set an upper age limit on the prohibition against discrimination based on employment. In recent years there has been considerable opposition to mandatory retirement and as of May 2008 all such upper age limits have been removed (Zinn, 2008). Table 2.3 shows the age limits for protection under human rights legislation in the various jurisdictions both generally and specifically in respect of employment.

All provinces provide protection from discrimination on the basis of age in employment. For example, discrimination on the basis of age is prohibited in advertising job vacancies and recruiting new employees. A job applicant cannot be asked to disclose his or her age on a job application or during an interview. In addition, cases of age discrimination have been addressed in relation to seniority plans, vacation, termination, and mandatory retirement. Most jurisdictions provide protection from discrimination on the basis of age with respect to accommodation, facilities, and services generally available to the public. Some even protect from discrimination on the basis of age with respect to residential and commercial tenancies and the purchase and sale of property.

There are some exceptions to these general rules that are of note when addressing age discrimination. First, as with all the prohibited grounds of discrimination, age-based discrimination may be allowed if there is a *bona fide* justification for the differentiation. For example, an insurance company may charge higher premiums for a young male driver because young male drivers are more often involved in serious accidents than other drivers. The Supreme Court of Canada held that although this was discriminatory on its face, insurance premiums differentiated on the basis of age were *bona fide* because they were based on sound and accepted insurance practices and there was no practical alternative at the time to the use of a statistical basis of risk classification (*Zurich Insurance Co. v. Ontario*, 1992). The *bona fide* requirement exception often arises with respect to age in the employment context. Case law has developed allowing for age distinctions where the employer is able to establish a *bona fide* occupational justification or qualification by presenting evidence on the duties to be performed,

Table 2.3   Age Limits for Protection from Age Discrimination

Jurisdiction	Employment		General Application	
	Minimum	Maximum	Minimum	Maximum
Federal	none	none	none	none
Alberta	18	none	N/A	N/A
British Columbia	19	none	N/A	N/A
Manitoba	18	none	18	none
Newfoundland and Labrador	19	none	N/A	N/A
New Brunswick	19	none	19	none
Nova Scotia	none	none	none	none
Northwest Territories	none	none	none	none
Nunavut	none	none	none	none
Ontario	18	none	18	none
Prince Edward Island	none	none	none	none
Quebec	none	none	none	none
Saskatchewan	18	none	18	none
Yukon Territory	none	none	none	none

Source: Reproduced from *The Law of Human Rights in Canada: Practice and Procedure* by Russel Zinn with the permission of Canada Law Book, A Division of The Cartwright Group Ltd. (1-800-263-3269, www.canadalawbook.ca).

the conditions existing in the workplace, and the relationship between an individual's age and the ability to safely perform the duties of the position. Second, the human rights legislation in particular provinces provide for specific cases when age discrimination is acceptable such as seniors' residences, or renting to a boarder in your own private residence (Zinn, 2008).

Although legislation may protect from discrimination on the basis of age, the Supreme Court of Canada has commented that age distinctions are a common and necessary means of ordering society and since everyone will at some time or other experience being young and old, an age-based distinction may not be arbitrary marginalization of a group; the use of an age-based distinction does not automatically show a disadvantage that suggests discrimination (*Gosselin v. Québec*, 2002).

Disability

The human rights legislation in every jurisdiction protects against discrimination on the basis of disability, although the jurisdictions refer to the prohibited ground in different ways. Regardless of the terminology used, in all jurisdictions both physical and mental disabilities are afforded certain human rights protection (Zinn, 2008).

The more complex issue is what constitutes a physical or mental disability. In some jurisdictions illnesses or impediments are enumerated in the legislation. Where they are not enumerated, a determination must be made whether the condition complained of is in fact a disability within the meaning of the legislation and case law in the jurisdiction, considering also the nature and duration of the condition and severity of the limitations that it imposes. For example, complainants have been successful in establishing that the following conditions constitute disabilities meriting human rights protection: epilepsy, cancer, alcoholism, drug dependency, depression, acne, arthritis, chronic fatigue syndrome, gambling, among many others (Zinn, 2008).

Beyond the concrete classifications of disabilities discussed above, the Supreme Court of

Canada has recognized that a handicap or disability is more than a diagnosis, etiology, or prognosis of disease. The court in *Montreal v. Quebec* (2000) emphasized that the definition of 'handicap' under human rights legislation is to be multidimensional with an emphasis on human dignity, respect, and the right to equality rather than on the biomedical condition. Accordingly, discrimination on the basis of disability is prohibited not only when it is real but also when it is perceived.

Generally speaking, only disabilities that affect or are perceived to affect a person's ability to carry out life's important functions, including specific aspects of a job position, will be found to be a disability for the purpose of human rights protection (Zinn, 2008). In the contexts of employment and the provision of services, disabilities must be accommodated to the point of undue hardship.

Marital and Family Status

All Canadian jurisdictions include marital status and family status as a prohibited ground of discrimination (Zinn, 2008). The terms 'marital status' and 'family status' are not always defined. Generally, it is agreed that marital status refers to the status of being married, single, widowed, divorced, or separated, including common-law relationships and same-sex couples. Family status refers to the parent–child relationship, which has been interpreted liberally to include adoptive parents and foster parents (Zinn, 2008).

The Supreme Court of Canada has held that protection against discrimination on the basis of marital and family status extends to marital and family identity. The court concluded 'that the enumerated grounds of marital and family status are broad enough to encompass circumstances where the discrimination results from the particular identity of the complainant's spouse or family member' (*B. v. Ontario*, 2002 at para. 46). What this means is that you cannot discriminate against someone because of who they are related to—if you don't like their spouse or sibling, for example.

Cases of discrimination based on marital and family status arise in the context of employment (for example, refusing employment to a divorcee because of perceived instability), accommodation (for example, refusing tenancy to a single mother), and less often in the provision of services (for example, denying parents with young children entry into a restaurant dining room).

Sexual Orientation

The jurisprudence on sexual orientation has been an area of great and rapid change. Sexual orientation was slow to receive protection as a prohibited ground of discrimination under Canadian law, and until recently only a few jurisdictions extended such protection. In the past, some jurisdictions attempted to carve out protection for homosexuals under other prohibited grounds of discrimination such as sex, marital status, or family status but these attempts generally met with failure (Zinn, 2008). In 1995, the Supreme Court of Canada held that sexual orientation was an analogous ground of discrimination under section 15 of the Canadian Charter of Rights and Freedoms (*Egan v. Canada*, 1995). Today, all jurisdictions, except for Alberta, expressly prohibit discrimination on the basis of sexual orientation in their human rights statutes. However, by virtue of the Supreme Court of Canada judgment in *Vriend v. Alberta* (1998), all human rights statutes must be taken to include sexual orientation as a prohibited ground of discrimination and where such protection is not expressly provided the protection will be 'read in'.

None of the human rights legislation defines sexual orientation *per se*, but sexual orientation has been taken to denote an individual's orientation or preference in terms of sexual relationships with others and includes heterosexuality, homosexuality, and bisexuality (Zinn, 2008). The Supreme Court of Canada has described sexual orientation as a 'deeply personal characteristic that is either unchangeable or changeable only at unacceptable personal cost' (*Vriend v. Alberta*, 1998).

Cases in relation to discrimination on the basis of sexual orientation manifest in a variety of areas. There have been a number of cases where individuals have initiated complaints to human rights commissions to gain access to company or collective agreement benefits for their same-sex partners. In fact, to date there have been few cases of discrimination on the basis of sexual orientation in the employment relationship that do not relate to employment benefits (Zinn, 2008). In 1999 the Supreme Court of Canada conclusively settled this issue by deciding that denying homosexual couples the same rights as heterosexual couples is an infringement of the equality rights under the Canadian Charter of Rights and Freedoms (*M. v. H.*, 1999). Discrimination on the basis of sexual orientation also manifests in access to services and facilities (for example, refusing to provide artificial insemination services to lesbians) as well as accommodation (for example, refusing to rent a house to a gay couple).

Note that the courts in some jurisdictions, such as British Columbia, have made it expressly clear that one cannot avail themselves of protection against discrimination on the basis of sexual orientation unless one is either of that sexual orientation or perceived to be so. For example, in one case a boy was being harassed by students at his school who were calling him 'homo', 'queer', and 'gay'. He was not homosexual and the other students did not actually believe that he was homosexual; as such the court held that, as repugnant as the behaviour was, it was not prohibited under the human rights legislation (*North Vancouver School District No. 44 v. Jubran*, 2003).

Social Condition

Socioeconomic status has received disparate protections across Canadian jurisdictions. Alberta, British Columbia, Manitoba, Nova Scotia, Prince Edward Island, the Yukon, and Nunavut prohibit discrimination on the basis of 'source of income' (for example, discriminating against someone because they are a welfare recipient). Ontario and Saskatchewan specifically prohibit discrimination on the basis of 'receipt of public assistance'. Newfoundland prohibits discrimination on the basis of 'social origin', which refers to a person's background (for example, derogatory remarks about a community in which one was raised). New Brunswick, the Northwest Territories, and Quebec prohibit discrimination on the basis of the broader category of 'social condition', which refers to the place an individual holds in society as determined by a number of elements including family background, employment, and physical ability. Federal human rights legislation is now the only jurisdiction that affords no protections from discrimination in relation to socioeconomics. Of the jurisdictions that do afford some source of protection, all, except for Ontario and British Columbia, provide such protection in all areas including employment, services, contracts, and accommodation. In Ontario discrimination on the basis of receipt of public assistance is only prohibited in relation to the occupancy of accommodation and in British Columbia discrimination on the basis of lawful source of income is only prohibited with respect to discrimination in tenancy premises (Zinn, 2008).

Criminal Record

Although it is generally thought that once a person has served their jail time they have paid their debt to society, human rights legislation actually provides minimal protection for individuals being discriminated against because they have been charged with an offence or previously convicted.

British Columbia is the only jurisdiction that provides protection against discrimination for individuals charged with an offence. British Columbia, Ontario, Prince Edward Island, Quebec, the Northwest Territories, Nunavut, and the federal tribunal are the only jurisdictions that provide protection against discrimination for individuals convicted of an offence. However, this discrimination protection does not always extend to all areas typically protected under human rights legislation. Most jurisdictions that afford the protection do so only for discrimination with respect to employment; the federal legislation and the human rights acts in the Northwest Territories and Nunavut are the only ones that afford

protection from discrimination based on criminal records with respect to accommodation, facilities, and services (Zinn, 2008).

Of those jurisdictions where human rights protection is available for criminal convictions most restrict the protection to convictions for which pardons have been granted. Pardons were created by Parliament to reduce the negative effects of convictions. Persons who have been convicted of an offence may receive either an official or administrative pardon under the Criminal Records Act. A convicted person may apply for an official pardon either three or five years after completing their sentence depending on the nature of the offence. Once an official pardon has been granted, the record of the offence is not to be disclosed by the RCMP, unless the conviction was of a listed sexual offence (for example, sexual interference with a person under 14, sexual assault, child pornography) or when an inquiry is made in respect of an applicant for a volunteer or paid position of authority or trust relative to children or other vulnerable persons. The other type of pardon available is the administrative pardon under which offences will be automatically removed from the record one year after an absolute discharge and three years after a conditional discharge. In the human rights context this means that in the years prior to an official or administrative pardon being granted to an offender, in most jurisdictions there is no human rights protection available if persons are discriminated against based on their criminal record (Zinn, 2008).

What Is the Human Rights Complaint Process and Procedure?

A defining feature of the human rights complaint procedure is that, with the exception of Quebec, human rights protection is afforded through an administrative procedure rather than through judges in courts (Sharpe, Swinton, and Roach, 2002). Generally, human rights legislation creates a commission mandated to deal with human rights complaints. The human rights complaint process differs from jurisdiction to jurisdiction but typically involves several stages as follows.

Filing a Complaint

In all jurisdictions, a human rights action can be commenced by filing a complaint with the human rights commission, except for British Columbia, Ontario, and Nunavut where complaints must be filed directly with the tribunal. There are generally time limitations on the opportunity to file a human rights complaint and these time restrictions vary from jurisdiction to jurisdiction, ranging from 6 months to no time limitation at all; the time to file a complaint in each jurisdiction is listed in Table 2.1.

Who can file a human rights complaint also varies by jurisdiction. In some jurisdictions only the aggrieved person may file a complaint; in other jurisdictions any person may file a complaint if they have the consent of the victim or if the victim does not object; and in yet other jurisdictions a complaint may be filed by any person at all. In addition to individual complaints, some human rights commissions also recognize complaints brought by a group and others even maintain the right to initiate human rights complaints themselves. Table 2.1 provides a summary list of who may file a complaint in each jurisdiction. Upon receipt of a complaint the respondents are notified and given an opportunity to send in a response/defence.

Settlement

Every human rights commission/tribunal encourages parties to attempt to reach a settlement. Settlement provides a faster, less costly, more cooperative method of resolving complaints than investigations or tribunal hearings. The settlement option is generally introduced to parties before an investigation is commenced. Some jurisdictions offer mediation and conciliation services to the parties. Mediation and/or conciliation are voluntary and if agreed to by the parties, involve both

parties meeting with a neutral person who mediates the dispute by assisting the parties to discuss their interests and objectives and to generate options to resolve the complaint. Information provided by parties in the context of mediation or conciliation is generally without prejudice, meaning that the information will not be used for any purpose but the mediation/conciliation. In those jurisdictions that do not offer formal mediation or conciliation services the commissions nevertheless endeavour to informally assist complainants and respondents to reach settlements. Settlements can take place at any stage of the process before the human rights tribunal renders a decision. The federal human rights statute also requires that the terms of settlements reached at any time before the commencement of the tribunal hearing be approved by the commission in order to be binding upon the parties.

Investigation

In most jurisdictions complaints not previously settled between the parties must be investigated. Investigations are generally conducted at no cost to the complainant (Sharpe, Swinton, and Roach, 2002). 'Investigations' involve analysis of the merits of the case from a basic reading of the complaint in the intake form to more formal and intrusive procedures like interviews or requests for production of relevant documents (Tarnopolsky and Pentney, 2004). Once an investigation of the matter is completed, a referral of the matter by the investigators to a tribunal may be either mandatory or permissive, depending upon the jurisdiction.

Tribunal Hearing

Cases that have not been informally settled by the parties or, depending on the jurisdiction, dismissed by the commissions are referred to a judicial style board of inquiry or tribunal (Sharpe, Swinton, and Roach, 2002). The composition of the tribunal varies from one jurisdiction to another. In respect of size, adjudicative panels may range from one member to an indeterminate number. In terms of qualifications, some jurisdictions require tribunal members to be lawyers, others require members to possess experience with human rights issues, while yet others specify no qualifications at all (Tarnopolsky and Pentney, 2004).

Remedies

The human rights tribunals exercise broad remedial powers (Sharpe, Swinton, and Roach, 2002). The purposes underlying remedies for discriminatory conduct are twofold: to prevent further discrimination and to put the complainant in the position they would have been in except for the discriminatory conduct. There are specific provisions in the human rights legislation of each jurisdiction that set the limits of the remedial powers for each tribunal (Zinn, 2008). The remedial powers generally available to tribunals include the following non-monetary and monetary remedies.

Non-monetary Remedies

There are many different non-monetary remedies that can be ordered: cease and desist orders; mandatory adoption of plans to prevent future discrimination; written apologies to the complainant; notices posted in places of employment describing changes to eliminate discrimination, copies of the tribunal decision, copies of the human rights legislation, or new company human rights policies; human rights sensitivity training for staff; reinstatement of employees; and amendments to collective agreements (Zinn, 2008).

Monetary Remedies

There is a disparity in the monetary damages ordered by tribunals according to the type of discriminatory conduct and the result. For example, in cases where an individual is not hired for a position or is terminated from one because of discrimination, the damages may be hundreds of thousands of dollars; whereas if an individual suffers no loss of earnings and only humiliation or loss of dignity, the damage awards are often minimal even where the discriminatory conduct is extreme. Monetary remedies that may be ordered include damages for lost wages or lost opportunities of employment, lost entitlements to profit-sharing plans, lost benefits, lost stock options, and future medical expenses. Tribunals may also award damages for mental anguish but there are some jurisdictions that have placed a cap on the amount of damages that may be awarded for mental anguish. For example, in Saskatchewan the board of adjudication may only award up to $5,000. In addition, in only four jurisdictions, Quebec, Manitoba, the Yukon, and the Northwest Territories, are the tribunals granted explicit authority to award exemplary or punitive damages (Zinn, 2008). In the context of monetary damages, whatever they may be, complainants are required to mitigate their damages. This means they must put in reasonable effort to minimize the monetary loss suffered because of the discriminatory act by, for example, searching for alternative employment. A wronged party is only entitled to receive compensation for losses that could not be avoided. However, the onus is on the respondent to show that the complainant has failed to mitigate and the standard to establish such failure is actually quite high.

Appeal or Judicial Review

There are two options available to a party dissatisfied with a decision of a human rights tribunal—appeal the decision or make an application for judicial review. Appeals are only available in jurisdictions, such as Alberta, Newfoundland, Nova Scotia, Ontario, Saskatchewan, Nunavut, and the Yukon, where the human rights legislation provides for appeal. Courts have great remedial powers on appeal and may overturn the impugned decision for any error of law or fact (Zinn, 2008). In contrast, applications for judicial review are generally always available. Judicial review is not the same as an appeal. In an appeal the court may substitute the decision of the tribunal with its own appraisal of the merits of the case. In judicial review the courts may not substitute their appraisal of the merits if all action taken by the tribunal was lawful (Jones and de Villars, 2004). Judicial review is the power of the courts to determine whether human rights tribunals have acted within the powers that have been delegated to them under the law. In cases of judicial review the intervention of the courts is restricted to errors of law and egregious errors of fact. Note that some jurisdictions, such as Manitoba and Newfoundland, have what is called a privative clause in their legislation. Privative clauses may provide that the decisions of a tribunal are final and conclusive from which no appeal lies and all forms of judicial review are excluded or may allow for judicial review and appeal only in certain circumstances.

CASE EXAMPLE REVIEWED

We return now to the case of Nancy and how the legislation discussed in this chapter answers questions directly related to her situation.

Is the landlord's refusal to rent the apartment to Nancy discrimination?

Yes. The landlord is making a distinction based on the personal characteristics of Nancy as an individual and single mothers as a group, imposing disadvantages on Nancy not imposed upon others who are not single mothers and withholding access to opportunities available to other members of society. The landlord's practice of not renting to single mothers is a distinction which is arbitrary and discriminatory on its face and thus constitutes direct discrimination.

Is apartment rental an area that is protected under human rights law?

Yes. Human rights statutes prohibit discrimination in the area of accommodation. Accommodation includes access to residential premises such as apartment rentals.

Is single motherhood a ground of discrimination prohibited under human rights law?

Yes, depending on the jurisdiction in which Nancy resides. Single motherhood falls under the prohibited ground of discrimination termed 'marital and family status'.

Where can Nancy go to file a complaint?

Nancy may contact the human rights commission or tribunal in her area to file a human rights complaint. Nancy does not need the assistance of a lawyer to file a complaint. She need only call the commission/tribunal and an intake officer will assist her with filing a complaint. There is no cost for this service.

What procedures will be available to Nancy once she files a complaint?

Once Nancy files a complaint the landlord will be notified and given a chance to respond. Because Nancy's interest is in securing the apartment she may want to consider availing herself of any settlement services available. If the landlord wants to avoid the investigation he may be willing to rent her the apartment and the commission staff will be able to assist her in determining his position and his interests. If the landlord stands his ground then he will be subject to an investigation of the complaint.

CASE EXAMPLE REVIEWED *(Continued)*

If the matter goes before a tribunal, what remedies may Nancy receive?

Proceeding through an investigation and tribunal hearing takes time, so once Nancy is at the point of considering what remedies to ask for from the tribunal she will likely have secured another apartment. The monetary damages available may not be large. There will be a duty to mitigate on Nancy's part, meaning she will need to put in her best efforts to secure an apartment at the same rent. She may have some argument for recovery of any difference in the rent and perhaps even damages for mental anguish, however small.

Key Terms

Adverse-effect Discrimination
Where a rule or standard is neutral on its face and applies equally to everyone but actually has a discriminatory effect on an individual or group because it imposes, due to special characteristics of the individual or group, penalties or restrictions not imposed on others

Bona Fide Occupational Requirement
A defence that an employer can use to justify a discriminatory standard where the employer must establish that the standard was adopted for a purpose rationally connected to the performance of the job, the standard was adopted in an honest and good faith belief that it was necessary to fulfill the legitimate work-related purpose, and the standard is reasonably necessary to accomplish the legitimate work-related purpose by demonstrating that it is impossible to accommodate individual employees without imposing undue hardship on the employer

Direct Discrimination
Where a rule, practice, preference, or restriction makes an arbitrary distinction that on its face discriminates on a prohibited ground

Discrimination
An intentional or unintentional restriction, preference, or distinction based on grounds relating to personal characteristics of the individual or group that arbitrarily imposes burdens, obligations, or disadvantages on the individual or group not imposed on others, or withholds or limits access to opportunities, benefits, and advantages available to other members of society

Harassment: Hostile Environment
Conduct that an individual is required to endure to continue working in a place of employment, residing in a place of accommodation, or accessing facilities or services; racial, ethnic, gender, and religious harassment often take this form

Harassment: *Quid Pro Quo*
Where a benefit is contingent upon participation in an activity; sexual harassment often takes this form

Prohibited Grounds of Discrimination
Grounds of discrimination include race, colour, place of origin, religion, creed, sex, age, marital and family status, sexual orientation, disability, and criminal record

Systemic Discrimination
Discrimination that stems from long-standing stereotypes and value assumptions that create a discriminatory effect

Discussion Questions

1. Describe the different types of discriminatory actions and give an example of each.
2. Identify the general areas where discrimination is prohibited.
3. Name one prohibited ground of discrimination that you think is controversial. Discuss the arguments for and against the prohibited ground that you have chosen.
4. Is there a ground of discrimination you feel should be prohibited that is not? Explain.
5. A client has just disclosed to you a situation with his employer where his human rights have been violated. Where do you direct your client for help? What do you tell your client about the process for enforcing his rights?

Relevant Legislation

International

Universal Declaration of Human Rights, G.A. res. 217A (III), UN Doc A/810 at 71 (1948).
http://www.un.org/Overview/rights.html

International Covenant on Economic, Social and Cultural Rights, G.A. res. 2200A (XXI), 21 UN GAOR Supp. (No. 16) at 52, UN Doc. A/6316 (1966), 999 U.N.T.S. 171, entered into force 23 March 1976.
http://www.unhchr.ch/html/menu3/b/a_cescr.htm

International Covenant on Civil and Political Rights, G.A. res. 2200A (XXI), 21 UN GAOR Supp. (No. 16) at 52, UN Doc. A/6316 (1966), 999 U.N.T.S. 171, entered into force 23 March 1976.
http://www.unhchr.ch/html/menu3/b/a_ccpr.htm

Convention on the Elimination of All Forms of Discrimination against Women, G.A. res. 34/180, 34 UN GAOR Supp. (No. 46) at 193, UN Doc. A/34/46, entered into force 3 September 1981.
http://www.unhchr.ch/html/menu3/b/e1cedaw.htm

Convention against Torture and Other Cruel, Inhuman or Degrading Treatment or Punishment, G.A. res. 39/46, [annex, 39 UN GAOR Supp. (No. 51) at 197, UNDoc. A/39/51 (1984)], entered into force 26 June 1987.
http://www.unhchr.ch/html/menu3/b/h_cat39.htm

International Convention on the Elimination of All Forms of Racial Discrimination, G.A. res. 2106 (XX), Annex, 20 UN GAOR Supp. (No. 14) at 47, UNDoc. A/6014 (1966), 660 U.N.T.S. 195, entered into force 4 January 1969.
http://www.unhchr.ch/html/menu3/b/d_icerd.htm

Convention on the Rights of the Child, G.A. res. 44/25, annex, 44 UN GAOR Supp. (No. 49) at 167, UNDoc. A/44/49 (1989), entered into force 2 September 1990.
http://www.unhchr.ch/html/menu3/b/k2crc.htm

Federal and Constitutional

Canadian Charter of Rights and Freedoms: Part 1 of the Constitution Act, 1982, being Schedule B to the Canada Act (UK), c. C-12
http://laws.justice.gc.ca/en/charter/

Canadian Human Rights Act, R.S.C. 1985, c. H-6
http://laws.justice.gc.ca/en/H-6/text.html

Criminal Code, R.S.C. 1985, c. C-46
http://laws.justice.gc.ca/en/C-46/

Criminal Records Act, R.S.C 1985, c. C-47
http://laws.justice.gc.ca/en/index.html

Alberta

Human Rights, Citizenship and Multiculturalism Act, R.S.A. 2000, c. H-14
http://www.qp.gov.ab.ca/index.cfm

British Columbia

Human Rights Code, R.S.B.C. 1996, c. 210
http://www.qp.gov.bc.ca/statreg/list_statreg_h.htm

Manitoba

Human Rights Code, C.C.S.M. c. H-175
   http://web2.gov.mb.ca/laws/statutes/ccsm/index.
   php

New Brunswick

Human Rights Act, S.N.B. 1985, c. 30, s. 1, c. H-11
   http://www.gnb.ca/0062/acts/acts-e.asp#
   GlossH

Newfoundland and Labrador

The Human Rights Code, R.S.N.L. 1990, c. H-14
   http://www.gov.nf.ca/hoa/sr/

Nova Scotia

Human Rights Act, R.S.N.S. 1989, c. 214, amended
   1991, c. 12
   http://www.gov.ns.ca/legi/legc/

Ontario

Human Rights Code, R.S.O. 1990, c. H.19
   http://www.e-laws.gov.on.ca/DBLaws/Statutes/
   English/90h19_e.htm

Prince Edward Island

Human Rights Act, R.S.P.E.I. 1988, c. H-12
   http://www.gov.pe.ca/law/statutes/index.php3

Quebec

Charter of Human Rights and Freedoms, R.S.Q.,
   c. C-12
   http://www2.publicationsduquebec.gouv.qc.ca

Saskatchewan

The Saskatchewan Human Rights Code, S.S. 1979,
   c. S-24.1, as am. by S.S. 1980–81, c. 41 and 81;
   S.S. 1989–90, c.23; S.S. 1989–90, 1993, c.55
   and 61; and S.S. 2000 c.26
   http://www.qp.gov.sk.ca

Northwest Territories

Human Rights Act, S.N.W.T. 2002, c. 18
   http://www.justice.gov.nt.ca/Legislation/

Nunavut

Human Rights Act, 2002, Bill 12
   http://www.nunavutcourtofjustice.ca/library/
   statutes.htm

Yukon Territory

Human Rights Act, R.S.Y. 2002, c. 116
   http://www.canlii.org/yk/sta/tdm.html

References

Andrews v. Law Society of British Columbia (1989), 1 S.C.R. 143,
   56 D.L.R. (4th) 1.
B. v. Ontario (Human Rights Commission) (2002), 3 S.C.R. 403.
Blackburn v. Lam (1990), 12 C.H.R.R. D/289 (Ont. Bd. Inq.).
*British Columbia (Public Service Employee Relations Commission)
   v. BCGSEU* (1999), 3 S.C.R. 3.
Brooks v. Canada Safeway Ltd. (1989), 1 S.C.R. 1219.
Canadian Heritage (2008), *How Canada Works with the United
   Nations* (accessed at http://www.pch.gc.ca/pgm/pdp-hrp/
   inter/un-eng.cfm).
Canadian Labour Law Reporter (CLLR) (2005) (Toronto: CCH
   §7100 to 7460).
*Canadian National Railway Co. v. Canada (Canadian Human
   Rights Commission)* (1987), 1 S.C.R. 1114.
CBC (2004), 'Woman Firefighter Files Harassment Complaint',
   31 August 2004 (accessed 14 August 2005 at http://
   vancouver.cbc.ca/regional/).

——— (2005), 'Human Rights Victory for Firefighter Whistle-
   blowers', 11 February 2005 (accessed 14 August 2005 at
   http://vancouver.cbc.ca/ regional/).
Central Alberta Dairy Pool v. Alberta (Human Rights Commission)
   (1990), 2 S.C.R. 489.
Centre for Research and Information on Canada (CRIC) (2005),
   Canadian Charter of Rights and Freedoms (accessed
   16 January 2005 at http://www.cric.ca/ en_html/guide/
   charter/charter.html).
——— (2002), *The Charter: Dividing or Uniting Canadians?*
   (accessed at http://www.cric.ca/pdf/ cahiers/cricpapers_
   april2002.pdf).
Cole v. Bell Canada, 2007 CarswellNat 2701 (C.H.R.T.) at para. 61.
Department of Canadian Heritage (DCH), Human Rights Program (2003), *Your Guide to the Canadian Charter of Rights
   and Freedoms* (accessed at http://www.canadianheritage.
   gc.ca/progs/pdp-hrp/ canada/guide/equality_e.cfm).

Egan v. Canada (1995), 2 S.C.R. 513.

Freeman, M. and Van Ert, G. (2004), *International Human Rights Law* (Toronto: Irwin Law).

Gosselin v. Quebec (Attorney General) (2002), 4 S.C.R. 429.

Harker v. Popular Roost Resort Ltd. (1986), 7 C.H.R.R. D/3469 (B.C.C.H.R.).

Jones, D.P. and de Villars, A.S. (2004), *Principles of Administrative Law*, 4th ed. (Toronto: Thomson Canada).

Lasani v. Ontario (Ministry of Community and Social Services) (1993), 21 C.H.R.R. D/415 (Ont. Bd. Inq.).

M. v. H. (1999), 2 S.C.R. 3.

McGill University Health Centre (Montreal General Hospital) v. Syndicat des Employes de l'Hopital general de Montreal (2007), 1 S.C.R. 161.

Montreal (Ville) v. Québec (Commission des droits de la personne et des droits de la jeunesse) (2000), 1 S.C.R. 665.

North Vancouver School District No. 44 v. Jubran (2003), 3 W.W.R. 288 (B.C.S.C.).

Office of the High Commissioner for Human Rights (OHCHR) (2008), *International Human Rights Law* (accessed at http://www.ohchr.org/EN/ProfessionalInterest/Pages/InternationalLaw.aspx).

Ontario Human Rights Commission (1997), *Policy on Scholarships and Awards* (accessed at http://www. ohrc.on.ca).

Ontario Human Rights Commission v. Simpsons-Sears (1985), 2 S.C.R. 536.

Poirier v. British Columbia (Ministry of Municipal Affairs, Recreation and Housing) (1997), 29 C.H.R.R. D/87 (B.C.H.T.).

Rapaport, F. (1988), 'Part IV: Equality Rights', in *Human Rights*, vol. 14: *Canadian Encyclopaedic Digest*, 3rd ed. (Toronto: Carswell).

R. v. Robichaud (1987), 2 S.C.R. 84.

Re Québec (Commission des droits de la personne et des droits de la jeunesse) and Maison des jeunes A-Ma-Baie Inc. (1998), 33 C.H.R.R. D/263 (Que. H.R.T.).

Re Sheridan and Sanctuary Investments Ltd. (1999), 33 C.H.R.R. D/464 (B.C.H.R.T.).

Re Thambirajah and Girl Guides of Canada (1995), 26 C.H.R.R. D/1 (B.C.C.H.R.).

Roberts v. Club Expose (1993), 21 C.H.R.R. D/60 (Ont. Bd. Inq.).

Sangha v. Mackenzie Valley Land and Water Board (2006), 56 C.H.R.R. D/264 (C.H.R.T.), revd 2007 FC 856.

Sehdev (Litigation Guardian of) v. Bayview Glen Junior Schools Ltd. (1988), 9 C.H.R.R. D/4881 (Ont. Bd. Inq.).

Sharpe, R.J., Swinton, K.E., and Roach, K. (2002), *The Charter of Rights and Freedoms*, 2nd ed. (Toronto: Irwin Law).

Tarnopolsky, W.S. and Pentney, W.F. (2004), *Discrimination and the Law* (Scarborough, ON: Thomson Carswell).

Velenosi v. Dominion Management (1989), 10 C.H.R.R. D/6413 (Ont. Bd. Inq.), rev'd 5 O.R. (3d) 32 (Div. Ct.), rev'd 148 D.L.R. (4th) 575 (C.A.).

Vriend v. Alberta (1998), 1 S.C.R. 493.

Westbury v. Trump Investments Ltd. (1992), 17 C.H.R.R. D/516 (B.C.C.H.R.).

Zinn, R.W. (2008), *The Law of Human Rights in Canada* (Aurora: Canada Law Book).

Zurich Insurance Co. v. Ontario (Human Rights Commission) (1992), 2 S.C.R. 321.

CHAPTER THREE

Family Law

OBJECTIVES

- To highlight the legal rights and obligations attached to marriage
- To illustrate when a divorce can be obtained
- To discuss various methods of dispute resolution in separation and divorce
- To review the law on property division, custody, and support
- To introduce alternative family forms
- To explore considerations when working with Aboriginal persons

CASE EXAMPLE

Grace and Jeff were married for 20 years. Grace is 55 and employed as a dental assistant; she works part-time and earns $30,000 a year. Jeff is 57, a doctor, and earns $250,000 a year. They have three children, David (19 years), Mathew (16 years), and Leslie (11 years). Throughout their lives Jeff has worked long hours in the hospitals. Jeff and Grace increasingly grew apart from each other emotionally and, 15 years into the marriage, Jeff began having an affair. Grace found out about the affair, was crushed, and immediately asked Jeff to move out of the house. Jeff and Grace have been living separately for a year. All three children are living with their mother in the family home. This fall, David will be attending university to study Engineering. Mathew and Leslie both attend private schools. Grace and Jeff argue every time they meet. Jeff is worried that Grace will keep him from the children as revenge for having the affair. He doesn't mind having the children live with Grace, but he wants to be actively involved in their lives. Grace wants to divorce Jeff, but she is worried because Jeff owns the house and she relies on his income to provide for the children and pay their school tuition. Grace's boss at the dental clinic where she works has noticed that Grace is not herself lately and suggested that if she needed to talk to someone about any personal issues she could call their employee assistance provider to speak to a counsellor. Grace took her boss's advice and has now come to a social worker with her concerns. Although it is clear that Grace must consult a lawyer, it will be useful if the social worker who is helping to support Grace can make her aware of the challenges she may face and the choices that may be available to her within the parameters of the law.

- Can Grace divorce Jeff?
- Would Grace and Jeff be good candidates for mediation to determine division of property, custody, and support?
- Does Grace have any legal rights to the family home?
- Can Grace prevent Jeff from having custody of or access to the children because he had an affair? What type of custody arrangement would be best for Grace and Jeff?
- If Grace divorces Jeff and he refuses to give her any money, will she have to support herself and her children?

Marriage

When parties enter into a marriage, they are entering into a social contract. However, marriage is not *just* a social contract; marriage is also a status that is conferred by the state. Thus, irrespective of the wishes of the two individuals who choose to enter into a marriage contract, the law of marriage governs the creation and dissolution of marriages and attaches certain legal rights and obligations to marriage (Payne and Payne, 2001).

There are both federal and provincial laws that govern marriage. In order for a marriage to be valid, people entering into it must have the capacity to get married and must comply with the solemnization requirements of the place where the marriage ceremony is being conducted. If elements of either of these requirements are not met, the marriage may be considered void or voidable. A marriage that is void is automatically invalid without having to go to court. A marriage that is voidable is valid until one or both parties, as the case may be, go to court to obtain an annulment (Kruzick and Baron, 2004).

Who Can Get Married?

The capacity to enter into a marriage is composed of several elements as follows.

Age

A marriage where one or both parties are under the age of 7 is automatically invalid. However, if one of the parties to the marriage is a boy between the ages of 7 and 14 or a girl between the ages of 7 and 12, the young person may be advised that he or she has the right to decide whether or not to have the marriage annulled based on his or her age.

Sexual Orientation

Historically, under the common law, marriage has been defined as the voluntary union for life of one man and one woman to the exclusion of all others. Same-sex couples challenged this definition of marriage as a violation of the equality rights under the Canadian Charter of Rights and Freedoms. In *Reference re Same-Sex Marriage* (2004), the Supreme Court of Canada considered the issue of same-sex marriage and held that proposed federal legislation extending 'marriage' to same-sex couples is consistent with the equality rights guaranteed under section 15(1) of the Canadian Charter of Rights and Freedoms. The Supreme Court further clarified that while the definition of marriage is within the exclusive jurisdiction of the Canadian Parliament, the provinces retain responsibility for licensing and registration, and must give all couples access to the administrative aspects of marriage. Nevertheless, several provinces objected, indicating that they would not change provincial legislation to comply with the Supreme Court decision. Consequently, on 28 June 2005, with a vote of 158 to 133, the Canadian legislature passed a bill to enact legislation known as the Civil Marriage Act on same-sex marriages. The bill received royal assent a month later on 20 July 2005 and the Civil Marriage Act became law. Canada became the third country to recognize gay marriage, following the Netherlands and Belgium. Consequently same-sex couples throughout Canada now have the right to marry.

Relationship

Marriages between individuals who are too closely related by blood or through marriage are banned (Kruzick and Baron, 2004). It is commonly believed that as a result of this restriction, cousins cannot marry. However, it is legal to marry your cousin in Canada. In fact, the US is the only Western country with cousin-marriage restrictions.

Monogamy

A person may only be married to one other person at any given time. If a person desires to enter into a second marriage, then he or she must show that the first marriage was void or ended by virtue of death or divorce (Kruzick and Baron, 2004). Marriage to more than one person at the same time is a criminal offence called bigamy under section 290 of the Criminal Code of Canada. Nevertheless, recent media stories have raised the issue of religious groups who engage in polygamous practices and the reluctance of law enforcement agencies to prosecute (CBC, 2003; Macqueen, 2007). While polygamous marriage is indeed illegal in Canada, authorities such as the Attorney General of British Columbia have elected not to prosecute based on the fear that such prosecution may be found to be a violation of the Charter (Kaufman, 2005).

Ability to Consummate

If at the time of a marriage one of the parties is unable to consummate the marriage, then the other party may, if he or she wishes, have the marriage annulled. Consummation occurs when the spouses engage in complete sexual intercourse after the marriage ceremony. An inability to consummate a marriage may be based on a physical or mental condition. However, the use of contraceptives or a capricious refusal to engage in intercourse will not be sufficient to establish an inability to consummate (Kruzick and Baron, 2004).

When Is There Valid Consent to Marry?

It is important for social workers to be aware that clients who feel they have been trapped or tricked into marriage may, in fact, have a marriage that is invalid or for which they may obtain an annulment if they did not enter into the marriage with free and informed consent. There are several circumstances in which a person's consent may not be viewed as valid.

Understanding

Each party to a marriage must, at the time of the ceremony, understand the nature of marriage and the obligations it entails. If one party does not

have the requisite understanding, the marriage will be void. Lack of understanding may result from medical mental incapacity or from mental incapacity resulting from the use of drugs or alcohol (Kruzick and Baron, 2004).

Duress

If a person is under duress at the time of marriage, then his or her consent to the marriage may be negated and the marriage may be annulled at his or her option. Duress is established when it is shown that due to external circumstances for which the person is not responsible, he or she was in reasonable fear to a level that would remove consent to the marriage (Kruzick and Baron, 2004).

Mistake and Fraud

There are two types of mistakes or fraud that will render a marriage invalid. The first type is regarding the identity of the other party to the marriage at the time of the ceremony; that is, the person identified him- or herself as someone else. However, this does not extend to the personal characteristics of an individual. For example, a mistake or fraud as to the wealth of the other party would not void the marriage. The second kind of mistake that will void a marriage concerns the nature of the ceremony; this typically arises when one party is unfamiliar with the language or customs through which the marriage ceremony is being conducted and does not realize that they were, in fact, married (Kruzick and Baron, 2004).

Divorce

According to Statistics Canada, in 2004 a total of 69,644 couples in Canada had a divorce finalized, with the average duration of marriage being 14.5 years and the average age at divorce being 43.8 for men and 41.2 for women. It is interesting to note that divorce rates do vary by province. For example, as of 2004 in Newfoundland and Labrador only 21.6 per cent of marriages were expected to end in divorce within 30 years of marriage, while 48.4 per cent of couples in Quebec are expected to divorce within this time span (Statistics Canada, 2008).

Although divorces have decreased since 2000 (Statistics Canada, 2008), the divorce rate has risen considerably in the last century. There are many reasons for this, including growing individualism that has discouraged staying in a marriage out of a sense of duty, the growth of the number of women in the labour force that has made divorce more economically feasible, the reduction in family size that has made the logistics of divorce easier, and the general liberalization of divorce in society (Baker, 1993). The law of divorce is grounded in the Divorce Act. The Divorce Act is federal legislation, so the legal rules for obtaining a divorce are the same in all provinces and territories in Canada.

When Can a Spouse Obtain a Divorce?

Canada has a no-fault–based system of divorce. Spouses may obtain a divorce for any reason or for no reason at all. The only ground for divorce under the Divorce Act is marriage breakdown. To prove marriage breakdown, the spouse seeking the divorce must prove one or more of the following:

1. They have been living separate and apart for at least one year immediately before and at the time of the granting of the divorce judgment.
2. The other spouse has committed adultery.
3. The other spouse has inflicted physical or mental cruelty making continued cohabitation intolerable.

Separation

Spouses must be separated for one year before the divorce can be granted. So long as the spouses are separated, they may commence the divorce process before a year passes, but the divorce will not be granted until there is a full year of separation. In order to prove separation the law requires a unilateral or mutual intention to separate. The decision to separate may be made by one spouse and does not at any time require the agreement of the other spouse. However, at least one spouse must have an intention to withdraw from the marriage—spouses may travel for work or pleasure and be physically apart for extended periods of time but this alone is not enough for legal separation. In addition, so long as there is an intention to separate, a physical separation is not required. A couple may be 'separated' under the same roof where there is evidence that they are living separate and apart. For example, there may be virtually no communication between the spouses—they may eat separate meals, sleep in separate bedrooms, and participate in separate social activities (MacDonald, Baron, and Kruzick, 2004). It is important to note that the Divorce Act encourages reconciliation. Spouses may attempt to reconcile by cohabiting for a single period of, or several periods amounting to, 90 days without stopping the clock on the one year of separation required for marriage breakdown.

Adultery

Adultery may only be used to obtain a divorce by the spouse who has been wronged. The spouse who committed the adultery may not use the adultery to establish marriage breakdown for a divorce petition. Furthermore, the wronged spouse may not use the adultery to support a divorce proceeding if he or she has condoned the offence by continuing to cohabit for a substantial period of time following the adultery, or has encouraged or promoted the adultery (MacDonald, Baron, and Kruzick, 2004).

If adultery is introduced as the basis of marriage breakdown, the spouse commencing the proceeding on this ground must prove the adultery. Proving adultery is harder in some jurisdictions than in others. For example, the Evidence Act in Ontario, Alberta, Nova Scotia, Prince Edward Island, Nunavut, the Yukon, and the Northwest

Territories prohibits asking a witness in a divorce proceeding any question that would show that he or she is guilty of adultery unless that person has consented to the question or has already given evidence denying the affair. In contrast, the Evidence Act in Manitoba and Newfoundland provides that no witnesses will be excused from answering any question by reason of it tending to show that he or she has been guilty of adultery.

Physical or Mental Cruelty

A spouse's conduct in a marriage is considered cruel if it causes 'wanton, malicious or unnecessary infliction of pain, or suffering upon the body, the feelings or emotions of the other, and is of such a kind as to render intolerable the continued cohabitation of the spouses' (MacDonald, Baron, and Kruzick, 2004). Whether the conduct amounts to cruelty will depend on the subjective temperament, sensibility, and state of health of the victim as well as whether such conduct would be considered grave on an objective standard (that is, whether the conduct would be considered grave by a reasonable person). Isolated acts that alone do not reach the standard of cruelty may meet this test if the cumulative effect of a continued course of conduct renders cohabitation intolerable.

Can the Court Refuse to Grant a Divorce?

Even if marriage breakdown is proven, under the Divorce Act the court has a duty to refuse to grant the divorce if it is not satisfied that reasonable arrangements have been made for the support of any children of the marriage. In such cases, the court will often stay the granting of the divorce until adequate arrangements have been made. In some cases it may be possible that a court will grant the divorce if the spouses provide a written undertaking that they will abide by any terms imposed by the court regarding the support and maintenance of the children (MacDonald, Baron, and Kruzick, 2004).

Same-Sex Spouses and Divorce

The Divorce Act applies to couples who are married but it previously defined a 'spouse' as either of a man or woman who is married to each other. The Civil Marriage Act enacted by the Canadian legislature in July 2005 (discussed earlier in this chapter) amended the definition of 'spouse' in the Divorce Act, making it gender-neutral. Therefore, same-sex couples now have the legal right to both get married and divorced.

Choice of Process for Property Division, Custody, and Support

Once a couple separates, they eventually turn their minds to the division of their property, who will have care and custody of the children, and what, if any, support payments need to be made between the spouses to support their children and each other financially. There are several different ways that decisions regarding property division, custody, and support may be made by the parties. The next sections of this chapter outline the processes available as well as the laws that guide and govern in each. These processes are shown in Figure 3.1 and the laws that apply to property division, custody, and support under each jurisdiction are listed in Table 3.1.

Domestic Contracts

Although family law generally defines substantive norms for marriage, marital partners can, if they wish, define the obligations flowing from their marital bond through a domestic contract. This has been termed by some commentators as 'marriage à la carte' (Bailey, 2004). Domestic contracts include marriage contracts (also known as prenuptial agreements) and separation agreements. Marriage contracts are agreements between parties who are already married or about to be married to

Figure 3.1   The Process on Relationship Breakdown

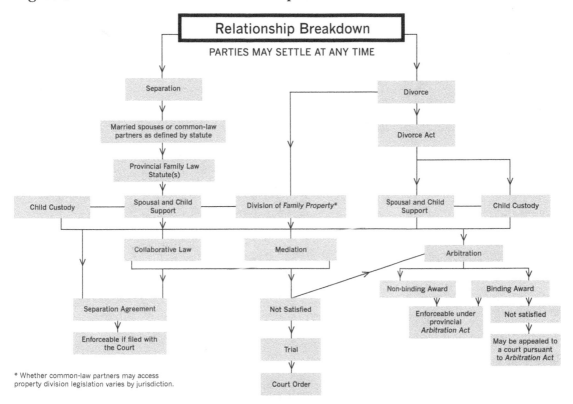

each other. They may address any issue that might arise during the course of the marriage or on the breakdown of the marriage, except custody/access and limitations on a spouse's rights regarding the matrimonial home. Separation agreements are entered into by parties following relationship breakdown and may deal with any and all matters that are relevant to the settlement of their affairs and may include a release from any other claims against each other (Sadvari, 2004).

Domestic contracts are formal legal agreements. Most of the family law statutes require that for the contracts to be recognized by law they must be properly drafted and endorsed by the parties. For example, in Ontario the domestic contracts must be in writing, signed by both parties, and witnessed. Once validly entered, domestic contracts can be reopened by the courts (that is, changed by the courts) only in exceptional circumstances.

In 2003, the Supreme Court in *Miglin v. Miglin* established a two-part test to be met before a court can open a domestic contract: 1) there must be evidence that one party was particularly vulnerable and unable to negotiate a fair deal or 2) there must be a significant departure from the financial circumstances under which the agreement was signed that could not have been reasonably foreseen by the parties when they signed the deal. The court went on to discuss the concept of the unforeseeable significant departure and stated:

It will be unconvincing, for example, to tell a judge that an agreement never contemplated that the job market might change, or that parenting responsibilities under an agreement might be somewhat more onerous than imagined, or that a transition into the workforce might be challenging. Negotiating

Table 3.1   Family Law Legislation by Jurisdiction

Jurisdiction	Marriage	Separation	Child and Spousal Support	Child Custody	Property Division	Enforcement
Federal	Provincial Power	Divorce Act, R.S., 1985, c. 3 (2nd Supp.)	Divorce Act, R.S., 1985, c. 3 (2nd Supp.)	Divorce Act, R.S., 1985, c. 3 (2nd Supp.)	Provincial Power	Family Orders and Agreements Enforcement Assistance Act, R.S., 1985, c. 4 (2nd Supp.)
British Columbia	Marriage Act, R.S.B.C. 1996, c. 282	Family Relations Act, R.S.B.C. 1996, c. 128	Family Relations Act, R.S.B.C. 1996, c. 128	Family Relations Act, R.S.B.C. 1996, c. 128	Family Relations Act, R.S.B.C. 1996, c. 128	Family Maintenance Enforcement Act, R.S.B.C. 1996, c. 127 Interjurisidictional Support Orders Act, S.B.C. 2002, c. 29
Alberta	Marriage Act, R.S.A. 2000, c. M-5	Domestic Relations Act, R.S.A. 2000, c. D-14	Domestic Relations Act, R.S.A. 2000, c. D-14 Maintenance Order Act, R.S.A. 2000, c. M-2	Domestic Relations Act, R.S.A. 2000, c. D-14 Provincial Court Act, RSA 2000, P-31	Matrimonial Property Act, M-8 R.S.A. 2000	Interjurisdictional Support Orders Act, 2002, c. I-3.5 Maintenance Enforcement Act, R.S.A. 2000, c. M-1
Saskatchewan	Marriage Act, 1995, c. M-4.1 of the Statutes of Saskatchewan, 1995 (effective 21 February 1997) as amended by the Statutes of Saskatchewan, 2004, c. 66	Family Maintenance Act, 1997, c. F-6.2 of the Statutes of Saskatchewan, 1997 (effective 1 March 1998) as amended by the Statutes of Saskatchewan, 2001, c. 51; 2002, c. I-10.03 and 5; and 2004, c. 66	Family Maintenance Act, 1997, c. F-6.2 of the Statutes of Saskatchewan, 1997 (effective 1 March 1998) as amended by the Statutes of Saskatchewan, 2001, c. 51; 2002, c. I-10.03 and 5; and 2004, c. 66	The Children's Law Act, 1997, c. C-8.2 of the Statutes of Saskatchewan, 1997 (effective 1 March 1998) as amended by the Statutes of Saskatchewan, 2001, c. 34; and 2004, c. 66	Family Property Act, c. F-6.3* of the Statutes of Saskatchewan, 1997 (effective 1 March 1998) as amended by the Statutes of Saskatchewan, 1998, c. 48; 2000, c. 70 and 2001, c. 34 and 51. Formerly The Matrimonial Property Act, 1997, being c. M-6.11 of the Statutes of Saskatchewan, 1997	Inter-jurisdictional Support Orders Act, c. I-10.03 of The Statutes of Saskatchewan, 2002 (effective 31 January 2003)

Table 3.1 Family Law Legislation by Jurisdiction (Continued)

Jurisdiction	Marriage	Separation	Child and Spousal Support	Child Custody	Property Division	Enforcement
Manitoba	Marriage Act, C.C.S.M. c. M50	Family Maintenance Act, C.C.S.M. c. F20	Family Maintenance Act, C.C.S.M. c. F20	Family Maintenance Act, C.C.S.M. c. F20	Family Property Act, C.C.S.M. c. F25; Common Law Partners Property and Related Amendments Act, S.M. 2002, c. 48	Interjurisdictional Support Orders Act, C.C.S.M. c. 160; Child Custody Enforcement Act, C360 R.S.M. 1987
Ontario	Marriage Act, R.S.O. 1990, c. M.3	Family Law Act, R.S.O. 1990, c. F.3	Family Law Act, R.S.O. 1990, c. F.3	Children's Law Reform Act, R.S.O. 1990, c. C12	Family Law Act, R.S.O. 1990, c. F.3	Family Responsibility and Support Arrears Enforcement Act, 1996, S.O. 1996, c. 31
Quebec	c. C-1991, r.2.1, Rules respecting the solemnization of civil marriages and civil unions, Civil Code of Québec, (1991), c. 64, ss. 40–3; 1999, c. 6, s. 22	Civil Code of Québec, S.Q. 1991, c. 64, Art. 118 (C.C.Q.)	Civil Code of Québec, S.Q. 1991, c. 64, Art. 585 (C.C.Q.)	Civil Code of Québec, S.Q. 1991, c. 64, Art. 605 (C.C.Q.)	Civil Code of Québec, S.Q. 1991, c. 64, s. 414 (C.C.Q.)	Act to Facilitate the Payment of Support, R.S.Q., c. P-2.2; Regulation Respecting Collection of Support, O.C. 1531-95; Reciprocal Enforcement of Maintenance Orders Act, R.S.Q. 1977, c. E-19, as amended by 1982, c. 32; 2002, c. 6
Nova Scotia	Solemnization of Marriage Act, c. 436 of the R.S.N.S., 1989, amended 1992, c. 16, s. 129; 1996, c. 23, ss. 40–3; 1999, c. 4, ss. 31, 32	Maintenance and Custody Act, c. 160, R.S.O. 1989, 1990, c. 5, s. 107; 1994–5, c. 6, s. 63; 1997 (2nd Sess.), c. 3; 1998, c. 12, s. 2; 2000, c. 29, ss. 2–8	Maintenance and Custody Act, c. 160, R.S.O. 1989, 1990, c. 5, s. 107; 1994–5, c. 6, s. 63; 1997 (2nd Sess.), c. 3; 1998, c. 12, s. 2; 2000, c. 29, ss. 2–8	Maintenance and Custody Act, c. 160, R.S.O. 1989, 1990, c. 5, s. 107; 1994–5, c. 6, s. 63; 1997 (2nd Sess.), c. 3; 1998, c. 12, s. 2; 2000, c. 29, ss. 2–8	Matrimonial Property Act, amended 1995–6, c. 13, s. 83, c. 275 of the R.S.N.S. 1989	Maintenance Enforcement Act, c. 6 of the Acts of 1994–5, amended 1995–6, c. 28; 1998, c. 30; 1998, c. 12, s. 11; 2002, c. 9, ss. 58 & 59; Reciprocal Enforcement of Custody Orders Act, c. 387, R.S.N.S., 1989
New Brunswick	Marriage Act, R.S.N.B. 1973, c. M-3	Family Services Act, S.N.B. 1983, c. 16, s. 1, c. F-2.2	Family Services Act, S.N.B. 1983, c. 16, s. 1, c. F-2.2	Family Services Act, S.N.B. 1983, c. 16, s. 1, c. F-2.2	Family Services Act, S.N.B. 1983, c. 16, s. 1, c. F-2.2	Interjurisdictional Support Orders Act, c. I-12.05

Table 3.1   Family Law Legislation by Jurisdiction (Continued)

Jurisdiction	Marriage	Separation	Child and Spousal Support	Child Custody	Property Division	Enforcement
Prince Edward Island	Marriage Act, R.S.P.E.I. 1988, c. M-3	Family Law Act, 1995 c. 12, R.S.P.E.I. 1988, c. F-2.1	Family Law Act, 1995 c. 12, R.S.P.E.I. 1988, c. F-2.1	Family Law Act, 1995 c. 12, R.S.P.E.I. 1988, c. F-2.1; Custody Jurisdiction and Enforcement Act, R.S.P.E.I. 1988, c. C-33	Family Law Act, 1995 c. 12, R.S.P.E.I. 1988, c. F-2.1	Custody Jurisdiction and Enforcement Act, R.S.P.E.I. 1988, c. C-33; Maintenance Enforcement Act, R.S.P.E.I. 1988, c. M-1; Interjurisdictional Support Orders Act, 2002 c. 14 R.S.P.E.I. 1988, c. I-4.2
Newfoundland and Labrador	Solemnization of Marriage Act, RSNL1990 S-19	Family Law Act, RSNL1990 F-2	Family Law Act, RSNL1990 F-2	Children's Law Act, RSNL1990 C-13	Family Law Act, RSNL1990 F-2	Support Orders Enforcement Act, RSNL1990 S-31; Interjurisdictional Support Orders Act, SNL2002 I-19.2
Yukon	Marriage Act, R.S.Y. 2002, c. 146	Family Property and Support Act, R.S.Y. 2002	Family Property and Support Act, R.S.Y. 2002, c. 83	Children's Act, R.S.Y. 2002, c. 31	Family Property and Support Act, R.S.Y. 2002, c. 83	Maintenance Enforcement Act, R.S.Y. 2002, c. 145
Northwest Territories	Marriage Act, R.S.N.W.T. 1988, c. M-4	Family Law Act, S.N.W.T. 1997, c. 18	Family Law Act, S.N.W.T. 1997, c. 18	Children's Law Act, S.N.W.T. 1997, c. 14	Family Law Act, S.N.W.T. 1997, c. 18	Maintenance Orders Enforcement Act, R.S.N.W.T. 1988, c. M-2
Nunavut	Marriage Act, R.S.N.W.T. 1988, c. M-4	Family Law Act (Nunavut), R.S.N.W.T. 1997, c. 18	Family Law Act (Nunavut), R.S.N.W.T. 1997, c. 18	Children's Law Act (Nunavut), R.S.N.W.T. 1997, c. 14	Family Law Act (Nunavut), R.S.N.W.T. 1997, c. 18	Maintenance Orders Enforcement Act (Nunavut), R.S.N.W.T. 1988, c. M-2

parties should know that each person's health cannot be guaranteed as a constant. An agreement must also contemplate, for example, that the relative values of assets in a property division will not necessarily remain the same. Housing prices may rise or fall. A business may take a downturn or become more profitable. Moreover, some changes may be caused or provoked by the parties themselves. A party may remarry or decide not to work. Where the parties have demonstrated their intention to release one another from all claims to spousal support, changes of this nature are unlikely to be considered sufficient to justify dispensing with that declared intention (para. 83, [2003] 1 S.C.R. 303).

Thus, anyone entering into a domestic contract should do so on the assumption that the deal they are making is final. If a spouse is not upholding his or her end of the bargain, the domestic contracts may be enforced by commencing legal action in the same way as with any other contract but, more importantly, if the domestic contract is registered with the court it will be subject to the enforceability statutes applicable in the jurisdiction. For a listing of the enforcement statutes in each jurisdiction, see Table 3.1.

Mediation

Family law lawyers have a duty to discuss with their clients the possibility of reconciliation, to inform their clients of marriage-counselling facilities in the area, and if reconciliation is not possible, to suggest the use of mediation to come to an amicable agreement on support and custody matters. In fact, before a petition for a divorce can be filed, the lawyer representing the petitioning spouse must certify that reconciliation and mediation have been discussed with their client unless it would have been inappropriate to do so under the circumstances, such as in cases of domestic abuse (MacDonald, Baron, and Kruzick, 2004).

Family mediation is a cooperative dispute-resolution process in which an impartial third party, the mediator, assists the parties to reach mutually acceptable solutions to one or more of the issues between them (Noble, 1999). The mediator facilitates discussion by exploring underlying motives, exposing the interests that underlie the positions being taken, and suggesting creative options for settlement that meet the needs of both parties (Siegel, 2004). Mediation advocates believe that voluntary settlements, worked out on an emotional as well as intellectual level, are not only more humane than those forced by litigation but are also more practical, economical, and likely to endure (Irving and Benjamin, 2002). There are several different styles and techniques that a mediator may employ to foster settlement. For example, transformative mediation focuses on empowerment of individuals and recognition of individual strengths and weaknesses, whereas evaluative mediation is conducted like a pretrial, where the lawyers present their clients' arguments to the mediator who then provides his or her view on the likely outcome if the dispute is litigated.

Participation in mediation is voluntary, but mediation is not always a suitable solution. Mediation may not be advisable if there is a significant power imbalance between the parties or a history of abuse, such as in cases of domestic violence (Regehr, 1994; Siegel, 2004). Parties will also not be candidates for mediation if they do not intend to make full and frank disclosure, do not show respect for the mediation process, or have no intention of abiding by the agreements made.

If mediation is appropriate in the circumstances, then the parties must give careful consideration to whether they would like to participate in closed or open mediation. Closed mediation is the norm. At the conclusion of closed mediation, the mediator will prepare a report that either sets out the settlement agreement between the parties or, alternatively, states that no settlement could be reached. Anything said in the course of a closed mediation is not admissible as evidence in any proceeding without the consent of both parties. In contrast, in an open mediation the mediator's report at the conclusion of the mediation may include anything that the mediator considers relevant and anything said in the mediation may be admitted as evidence in proceedings regardless of whether the parties consent. There are advantages and disadvantages to both forms of mediation. Generally, critics of closed mediation argue that parties will be less motivated to adopt reasonable attitudes because their positions won't be revealed in court; critics of open mediation argue that knowing that what is said can be revealed in court will inhibit full and frank disclosure (Siegel, 2004). Regardless of whether parties use closed or open mediation, it will only succeed if both parties are open to the process and approach the dispute resolution in good faith.

Mediators are most frequently lawyers or social workers with specialized training. Individuals interested in learning more about mediation or locating a mediator should consult the Family Mediation Canada website at http://www. fmc.ca.

Collaborative Family Law

Collaborative family law is another dispute-resolution process available to couples following relationship breakdown. Whereas in mediation a settlement is developed with the assistance of a neutral third party, in collaborative family law it is only the parties and their lawyers who commit themselves to reaching a negotiated outcome. The cardinal rule of collaborative family law is that the parties agree that litigation will not be commenced during the course of the negotiation and if they are unable to resolve the dispute the lawyers must withdraw from representing their clients in any subsequent litigation (MacDonald, 2002). Fundamental to the collaborative law process is the execution of a participation agreement, which is a contract entered into by the parties whereby they agree to abide by the principles of collaborative practice, including that negotiations will be dignified and respectful, all important information will be exchanged, and all members of the team will endeavour to reach a comprehensive agreement that is mutually acceptable (Collaborative Practice Toronto, 2005). Like mediation, collaborative family law is less costly

and more amicable than proceeding through litigation. Most lawyers who practise collaborative family law have specialized training. Individuals interested in learning more about collaborative family law or locating a lawyer who engages in this practice should consult the Collaborative Family Law Association website at http://www. collaborativefamilylawassociation.com.

Arbitration

Whereas mediation and collaborative family law leave decision-making in the hands of the parties, in arbitration an independent arbiter decides the rights and obligations of the parties. There are several advantages to arbitration over litigation. First, the parties are directly involved in the appointment of the arbitrator. Whereas in litigation the parties have no choice as to the judge assigned to hear the matter, in arbitration the parties may select their arbitrator based on the nature of the dispute and the arbitrator's qualifications and expertise. Second, an arbitration hearing can be tailored to the needs and desires of the parties. The parties may choose whether they want an arbitration hearing that is formal and adversarial, such as a court case, or informal, such as a roundtable conference. Third, in arbitration the parties have the power to define the limits of the arbitrator's decision-making power. Fourth, arbitration hearings are conducted in private; only the parties, their counsel, and witnesses may attend. Last, arbitration hearings are faster than proceeding through court and even though the parties themselves must pay for the arbitrator, on the whole arbitration is less expensive than the courts (Payne and Payne, 2001).

If parties choose to proceed with arbitration they must decide whether they intend the arbitration to be non-binding or binding. In non-binding arbitration, if the parties are not satisfied with the outcome they may proceed to litigation. In binding arbitration, the parties may only proceed to the courts on grounds of appeal available under their provincial arbitration legislation. In either case, if the parties are satisfied with the arbiter's decision they may register the arbitration award with a court to avail themselves of the protections under the applicable enforcement statute.

Litigation

If the parties do not have an agreement, are unable to reach a settlement through mediation or collaborative law, and do not want to proceed through arbitration, then the only alternative left is to obtain relief through the court process by commencing a legal action.

Division of Property

The purpose of law on the division of property upon marriage breakdown is to ensure that the contributions of both spouses to the marriage are recognized and that the spouses share equally in the financial gains made over the course of the marriage. While division of property does not fall within the purview of social work, inadequate financial resources to care for themselves and their children is often cited as a primary reason that people remain in abusive and intolerable marriages. Encouraging clients to determine and execute their rights to property can often lead to increased choices and empowerment.

How Is 'Property' Defined for the Purpose of Family Law in the Provinces and Territories?

Each province and territory has its own legislation governing the division of property in a divorce. Even if a couple applies for a divorce under the federal Divorce Act, the division of property will still be governed by provincial legislation. Provincial legislation differs markedly in this area and thus social workers must advise their clients to seek legal advice on the processes in the jurisdiction in which they reside. Some provinces, like British Columbia and Alberta, use the term 'assets' and define assets by reference to who uses the asset and for what purpose. In such jurisdictions

'family assets' subject to property division upon relationship breakdown are those assets owned by one or both spouses and used by a spouse or minor child for a family purpose. In contrast, the legislation in other provinces, like Ontario and Manitoba, define property broadly to mean 'any interest, present or future, vested or contingent, in real or personal property'. For the purpose of this chapter the terms 'assets' and 'property' will be used interchangeably and will encompass what is typically known as real property (for example, land and buildings) as well as personal property (for example, cash, investments, vehicles, and pension entitlements).

What Property Will Be Subject to Division Upon Marriage Breakdown?

The primary areas of concern when determining what property will be subject to division upon relationship breakdown are whether the property was acquired before or during the marriage, the matrimonial home (no matter when or how acquired), and business assets owned by one spouse.

Property Brought into the Marriage versus Acquired During the Marriage

In six jurisdictions (Alberta, Manitoba, Newfoundland, Prince Edward Island, Saskatchewan, and Ontario) the family law legislation stipulates that property brought into the marriage is not divisible between the spouses on marriage breakdown (CCH, 1976). For example, if Bob had $50,000 in the bank and a car worth $20,000 when he entered the marriage, then upon marriage breakdown $70,000 of the value of the couples' property would be earmarked for Bob only and would not be subject to division. Note that other jurisdictions, such as British Columbia, leave the exclusion of property brought into the marriage from division upon marriage breakdown to the discretion of the courts.

Generally, all property acquired during the course of the marriage will be subject to division upon marriage breakdown, except in Alberta, Manitoba, Newfoundland, Nova Scotia, and Ontario, where generally any gift or inheritance acquired during the course of the marriage is not divisible between the spouses (CCH, 1976). The scope of property subject to division is broad, including even employment benefits such as pensions. For example, some jurisdictions provide that pensions up to certain limits may be assigned to a former spouse, and other jurisdictions even set out detailed methods for the division, calculation, and payment of pension benefits to spouses (Canadian Institute of Actuaries, 2003).

The Matrimonial Home

The 'matrimonial home', 'family home', 'marital home', or 'family residence' is often the largest asset owned by a couple and is the asset that has the greatest emotional connection to the marriage and previous family life. In most jurisdictions, including Manitoba, New Brunswick, Newfoundland, Nova Scotia, Ontario, Prince Edward Island, and Saskatchewan, regardless of who technically owns the matrimonial home, both spouses upon marriage breakdown have an automatic and equal right to the home and either or both spouses can apply to the court for an order giving one of them exclusive possession of the matrimonial home upon separation. There are a number of factors that will be considered by the court when determining exclusive possession, including the best interests of the children and the individual economic circumstances of each spouse (Fodden, 1999). Furthermore, pending the final division of property, neither spouse can sell the house or have an encumbrance (such as a mortgage) placed on the title without the other's agreement or a court order. Some provinces, such as Manitoba and Saskatchewan, also have legislation explicitly addressing the family farm.

Business Assets

Some provinces, such as British Columbia, Nova Scotia, and Newfoundland, classify property into family and non-family assets and specifically exclude business assets from marital property subject to division (CCH, 1976). However, these provinces do allow a court, when determining property division, to take into consideration the contributions of the non-owning spouse towards the maintenance and operation of a business. These issues of business assets are of particular interest in farming communities where the family home and business are often intertwined. In the 1974 case of *Murdoch v. Murdoch*, Jean Murdoch was denied a portion of the family farm because it was determined that a wife's labour did not constitute a financial contribution to the farming business owned by her husband. Four years later in *Rathwell v. Rathwell* (1978) it was determined that both spouses had made direct financial contributions to the family farming business. Acquiring the assets can be difficult, however, because courts will often be prohibited from making orders that would require or result in the sale of a business or farm or would seriously impair its operation, unless there is no other reasonable way to satisfy the award.

How Is Property Divided by the Courts?

Generally, couples who do not have a prenuptial agreement addressing property division, or who have not come to a settlement agreement between themselves, bring an application to court for the division of property. The spouses are required to submit, to the court and to each other, financial statements indicating all their assets, property, and liabilities both at the date of marriage and at the date of separation. Once the property has been identified, it is valued according to 'fair market value' at that time. The courts then divide the value of the property (or the increase in value of the property over the course of the marriage) between the spouses, based on a formula for division provided in the legislation in their jurisdiction. For example, in Ontario if the net worth of one spouse has increased more than the net worth of the other spouse, the court will order the wealthier spouse to make what is known as an 'equalization payment' equal to half the difference of the two amounts to the poorer spouse. It is important to note that not all jurisdictions provide for monetary equalization payments; some instead make equalization-type distributions by providing parties with an interest in specific property (Cornet and Lendor, 2002). However, the courts in every province and territory have the power to order that an unequal division of property take place if equal division would be 'unjust', 'unconscionable', 'unfair', and/or 'inequitable' (CCH, 1976).

Custody and Access

Orders for custody of and access to the children can be sought by divorcing couples under the federal Divorce Act or by separated spouses (or unmarried couples as discussed later in this chapter in 'Alternative Family Forms') under provincial law. Table 3.1 lists the custody and access legislation applicable in each jurisdiction. In most jurisdictions, either or both spouses or any other person, including grandparents, may apply for custody of or access to a child. However, in some provinces third parties must obtain leave of the court to pursue an application for custody or access. There are a range of custody orders available with the determinative criterion for selection between them being the best interests of the child.

In 2002 a federal bill, known as Bill C-22, was introduced into the legislature. This bill proposed changes to the federal Divorce Act, including replacing the custody and access model, which has been perceived to be win–lose, with a cooperative model based on parental responsibility where custody and access orders would be replaced with parenting orders that set out the time-sharing and responsibilities of each parent (Carson and Vallance, 2004). Bill C-22 received its second reading in 2003 and was then sent to committee for further review where the bill died. At the time of this writing, no further action has been taken on Bill C-22.

What Custody Orders Are Available?

The specific definition or use of the term 'custody' varies from statute to statute, but, except for Quebec where parental authority is distinguished from physical custody, the term 'custody' usually refers to all the rights and obligations related to the care and control of a child, which includes both legal custody (the responsibility to make all important decisions about a child's care and upbringing) and physical custody (the responsibility for the everyday physical care and control of the child) (Federal–Provincial–Territorial Family Law Committee, 2002). There are several custody arrangements that may be rendered by a court (or negotiated between the parties themselves as discussed earlier), including sole custody, joint custody, shared custody, and split custody.

Sole Custody

In sole custody, one parent has the legal right and responsibility to care for and make all the decisions regarding the children. For example, the parent with sole custody will make the decisions about the child's education, religion, health care, and general upbringing (PLEIS-NB, 2001). The non-custodial parent still has a right to be given information on the education, health, and welfare of the child. Sole custody is the most common custody order. Statistics show that only 10 per cent to 12 per cent of children are under the sole custody of their father (Vanier Institute of the Family, 2005).

Joint Custody

Joint custody has nothing to do with where the children live or how much time the children spend with each parent. The essence of joint custody is that both parents continue to share the responsibility of making significant decisions about the child. The living arrangements in cases of joint custody vary markedly. The children may move freely between each parent's home; the children may spend certain amounts of time living with each parent; the children may have a primary residence with one parent where they live most of the time and may even only visit the other parent a few times a year if he/she lives far away. Regardless of the living situation, in joint custody, both parents have a right to be informed about the child and to be involved in the parenting of the child. Statistics show that approximately 42 per cent of custody orders are for joint custody (Vanier Institute of the Family, 2005). While in theory joint custody seems fair and equitable, it can be highly problematic in situations of spousal violence or excessive conflict because decisions regarding the child can be hampered and stalled to an extent that is damaging to the child (Regehr, 1994). If the parents have incompatible parenting styles and are unable to agree on decisions about the children, then they may be better suited for a sole custody arrangement (NAWL, 2002).

Shared Custody

Shared custody is a joint custody arrangement where the children spend at least 40 per cent of their time with each parent. Shared custody arrangements may take different forms—the children may move between houses during the week, spend alternate weeks with each parent, or even alternate months with each parent. Often when there is shared custody, child support payments are reduced or not ordered since expenses for any one parent are usually lower because the children are with the other parent at least 40 per cent of the time (NAWL, 2002). In a recent decision the Supreme Court of Canada established a discretionary approach to the determination of child support in shared parenting situations referring to section 9 of the Federal Child Support Guidelines (see discussion on Child Support later in this chapter) (*Contino v. Leonelli-Contino*, 2005). The Supreme Court clarified that the starting point will be a straight set-off of the table amounts of support (discussed later) of each parent; but this will not be the final amount where one parent brings evidence that because of increased costs created by the shared custody, a disproportionate assumption by one parent of child-related expenses, or

a disparity in the standard of living between the households the set-off amount is too little or too much (Shaffer and Bala, 2007). Shared custody is relatively uncommon because it requires parents who are very involved in their children's lives, who can communicate and cooperate with each other, and who can live close together, often in the same neighbourhood or school district).

Split Custody

In split custody each parent has at least one child living with him or her. In split custody arrangements, the parents may have sole custody of the children residing with them or may have joint custody of all the children. Split custody will affect the amount of child support that is awarded. The income of both parents will be taken into account and will be set off against each other, meaning that the difference in support owed to each other will be determined and that difference will be the amount of support payable (NAWL, 2002). The split-custody arrangement is more common when there are teenagers instead of young children. When there are younger children involved, the courts prefer to keep children together if possible and will do so absent of compelling reasons such as where siblings have a hostile relationship or where neither parent would be able to care for all the children at once (Folberg, 1984).

What Does It Mean to Have Access to a Child?

When a child is in the custody of one parent it is common for the other parent to receive access to the child. There is no authoritative definition of access. Access may range from only provision of information about the child, to periodic visitation with the child, to the child residing with the access parent for long periods of time during which the access parent may have nearly full authority over the life of the child and as such may be indistinguishable from a custodial parent. The more the rights and responsibilities of the access parent approach that of the custodial parent, the more likely it is for conflicts of authority to develop between the parents. The courts are still working on the boundaries of the respective roles assumed by access and custodial parents (Fodden, 1999). As with custody, orders for access are based on the best interests of the child.

How Are the Best Interests of the Child Determined?

The paramount test for determining the appropriate arrangements for child custody and access in all Canadian jurisdictions is the 'best interests of the child'. Several provinces and territories, including British Columbia, New Brunswick, Newfoundland, Ontario, Saskatchewan, and the Yukon, have statutorily designated particular factors that courts must take into account when determining the best interests of the child. Factors to be considered when determining best interests may include the emotional ties between the child and the parent claiming custody, the length of time the child has lived in a stable home, plans for the care and upbringing of the child, and the views and preferences of the child. Note that most family law legislation in Canada stipulates that the conduct of a party is only relevant insofar as it affects parenting ability (Payne and Payne, 2001). For example, if two people divorce because one had an affair, the affair will likely not be relevant to the question of which parent should have custody of the children (NAWL, 2002).

In many provinces and territories, such as British Columbia, Manitoba, Saskatchewan, Ontario, Nova Scotia, the Yukon, and the Northwest Territories, the courts may order investigations, assessments, and reports to be undertaken by independent experts to assist in determining the best interests of the child. Generally, courts may order an assessment at the request of any party to the proceeding or on its own initiative. Where possible, courts will attempt to appoint an assessor that is agreed upon between the parties, but a failure to agree will not preclude the court from appointing an assessor (Payne and Payne, 2001). Refusal of either parent to submit to a court-ordered assessment may result in an adverse inference against that parent when deciding who will get custody. Assessors are usually psychiatrists, psychologists, or social workers. The assessor will observe and interview the parents, the child, extended family members (for example, grandparents), and other individuals in the child's life (for example, teachers) (Government of Manitoba, 2002). Following the assessment, the assessor files a report with the court and provides a copy to the parties. The assessor may be called upon to testify in the family court proceeding but this does not preclude the parties from submitting other expert evidence. Note that the cost of the assessor must be borne by the parties in proportions ordered by the court but a court may relieve a party from financial responsibility if payment would cause serious financial hardship.

Can a Custody Order Be Changed?

If there is a significant change in the circumstances of either parent since the original custody order rendered by the court, then either parent may apply to the court to have the custody order changed. For example, if one parent wants to move with the children to another province, the other parent may make an application to the court to have the custody order changed or the custodial parent ordered to remain in the province. Courts may require custodial parents to obtain the other parent's consent or give the other parent notice before moving the child; indeed, such consent will always be required in cases of joint custody (Government of Manitoba, 2002). Notice of an intended move often precipitates applications for changes in custody. How a court decides the change will depend on what is in the best interests of the child. It is important to note that an application to change a custody order is not a mechanism to appeal an order that a parent is not happy with. A judge, when changing a custody order, will not retry the case but rather will only consider the evidence on the change in circumstances to determine whether the variation in custody is in the best interests of the child (PLEIS-NB, 2001).

How Do You Enforce a Custody Order?

Once a custody order exists, the parents may use the family law system to deal with violations of the order. If a parent is not abiding by the terms of the custody order (for example, a parent wrongfully denying access to the child), there are a few remedies available. First, an application may be made to a court to have the non-compliant parent found in civil contempt. For contempt to be a viable option, the access order must be one for specified periods of access. Once an individual has been found in contempt of an access order, the court may impose periods of incarceration, suspended sentences, fines, stays of ongoing litigation, compensatory access, supervised access, and suspension of maintenance or other payments pending resumption of access (Federal–Provincial–Territorial Family Law Committee, 2002). However, courts have held that a contempt proceeding should be a last resort where there are other means to ensure compliance.

A second option for parents seeking to enforce a custody order is to make an application to the courts for an enforcement order under the enforcement legislation in the jurisdiction. For a list of enforcement statutes applicable in each jurisdiction, see Table 3.1. These enforcement acts contain a wide range of remedies that can be used to enforce access or custody orders, including posting of a bond, signing of a recognizance, authorization for a person to apprehend and deliver a child to another person, or the transfer of property or maintenance payments to a trustee. Access enforcement is not easily resolved because allegations range from complete denial of contact with the child to the child not being provided at expected or agreed upon times. Identifying effective solutions is sometimes difficult, given the wide range of circumstances in each case. As such, parents should be encouraged to work out access issues through mediation and negotiation where possible (Federal–Provincial–Territorial Family Law Committee, 2002).

Cases of more serious non-compliance are situations of child abduction. If the child is taken, whether willingly or unwillingly, to another province, the courts in that province may act to enforce a custody order obtained in any other Canadian jurisdiction and may make an enforcement order. In such cases, the abducting parent may or may not be arrested, but police officers or child-care authorities in the province where the enforcement order is made will be able to find and return the child to the parent with legal custody. If the custodial parent thinks a child may be taken out of the country, then the custodial parent may bring an application to court to prevent the other parent from taking the child by ordering him or her to surrender his or her passport and travel documents. If a child under the age of 16 is taken out of the country by the non-custodial parent to a country which has signed the Hague Convention on Civil Aspects of International Child Abduction, the custodial parent may apply for the custody order to be enforced and the child returned. Aside from the enforcement available through the family regime, it is important to note that child abduction is a crime under sections 282 and 283 of the Criminal Code. A parent, or anyone else, who removes and hides a child under the age of 14 without the consent of the custodial parent, commits a criminal offence and the police may charge the abducting parent and issue a Canada-wide warrant for his or her arrest. This enables the police to find and return the child more quickly than by using family court procedures. If the charge is treated as a summary conviction offence, the abducting parent could be jailed for six months and/or pay a fine; if the charge is treated as an indictable offence, the abducting parent could face up to 10 years in prison (PLEIS-NB, 2001).

Child Support

Both federal and provincial legislative regimes provide that parents owe an obligation to support their children. Generally, the legislation provides broad definitions of child and parent to identify the boundaries of child support rights and obligations. These definitions take a variety of forms. Support must be provided for children under the age of majority as determined by the province of ordinary residence. In addition, the federal Divorce Act and provincial legislation empower the courts to order support for children over the age of majority in circumstances where the child is unable, by reason of illness, disability, pursuit of reasonable education, or other cause, to withdraw from the charge of the parents or to obtain the necessaries of life. Child support obligations may be imposed on a 'parent', which generally means the father or mother of a child either naturally or through adoption, or a person who has demonstrated a settled intention to stand in the place of the parent of a child (for example, a stepparent) (Payne and Payne, 2001). When determining the appropriate amount of child support, there are two primary considerations: the federal or provincial child support guidelines and adjustments to the guideline amount of support.

What Are the Child Support Guidelines?

A fundamental change in Canadian law on child support occurred in 1997 when the *Federal Child Support Guidelines* were introduced. The Divorce Act provides that the federal guidelines are to be used unless the province in which both spouses reside at the time of application has passed its own set of comparable guidelines. Most jurisdictions mirror the *Federal Child Support Guidelines* in their legislation. The heart of the guidelines are the tables that prescribe the amount of child support that must be paid per child, according to the paying parent's annual income and the number of children in the family to whom the order relates. The table amounts of support under the guidelines were developed based on studies conducted of the average costs of raising children (Department of Finance, Canada, 1996). The Canadian minister of justice was required to review the operation of the guidelines and present a report

to Parliament within five years of the *Federal Child Support Guidelines* coming into force. In 2002 the government released its report and concluded the guidelines to be a success:

> The Government of Canada took a huge step in reforming the child support system when it implemented the Child Support Initiative. The Initiative has been a solid success. Fair, consistent and predictable amounts of support for children whose parents are separated or divorced have been established across the country, and every effort is being made to ensure children receive that support in full and on time. The Guidelines have helped reduce conflict and tension between parents by making the calculation of child support more objective, and by improving the efficiency of the legal process to such an extent that most parents are now setting child support amounts without going to court (Department of Justice, 2002, p. v).

When Can the Guideline Amounts of Child Support Be Adjusted?

Not all families and children are alike and there is thus a degree of flexibility to the guideline amounts of support to ensure that child support awards are equitable in individual situations. The guideline amounts of support may be adjusted to account for:

- special and extraordinary child-care, education, and health expenses identified under section 7 of the guidelines;
- the payor earning in excess of $150,000;
- specific custody and living arrangements related to the child (for example, shared or split custody arrangements); and
- circumstances where the guideline amount will cause undue hardship to either parent or the child (for example, incurring high levels of debt to support the family, significant access expenses such as travel costs, or legal duties to support others).

Retroactive Child Support

The law in Canada on retroactive child support has been inconsistent with some provinces taking a more liberal approach to retroactive awards than others (Shaffer and Bala, 2007). In 2006, the Supreme Court of Canada considered the matter of retroactive child support in four cases that originated from Alberta (*D.B.S. v. S.R.G.*, 2006). The Supreme Court held that courts have jurisdiction to make retroactive orders. However, that these are not retrospective in the true sense in that they do not impose legal obligations on the payor that did not exist at that time. Rather the retroactive support order is designed to address the payor who has not been fulfilling existing child support obligations. The Supreme Court identified four factors to be considered:

- whether the recipient has a reasonable excuse for why support was not sought earlier;
- blameworthy conduct of the payor;
- the circumstances of the child; and
- hardship to the payor occasioned by a retroactive award.

The factors are to be weighed to strike a balance between the payor's interest in certainty and fairness to the children. To the extent that retroactive support is awarded, the start date will be the date that effective notice was given by the recipient parent that support should be paid or if already being paid should be adjusted. There are two exceptions: the order is made more than three years after the effective notice (i.e., the recipient parent did not move forward with efforts to enforce the support claim) or the payor has engaged in blameworthy conduct (i.e., payor lies about an income increase). The Supreme Court emphasized that enforcement of the payor's child support obligation lies with *both* parents. Some commentators have criticized this judgment arguing that it places too much emphasis on the delay of a recipient parent in requesting support. Effectively, this means that legitimate support entitlements of children will be compromised by parental conduct. This is contrary to the very policy underlying child support—that children have a right to be supported by their parents and this entitlement should not be jeopardized by parental misconduct (Shaffer and Bala, 2007). Commentators further suggest that the result of this decision will be that professionals engaged in dealing with issues of retroactive support will spend more time assessing blame and looking at parental conduct.

Spousal Support

The Supreme Court of Canada has held that a former spouse has an obligation to pay spousal support if the other spouse is experiencing economic need at the point of marriage breakdown (*Bracklow v. Bracklow*, 1999). Separated spouses may seek spousal support under provincial legislation or by way of corollary relief under the federal Divorce Act (Payne and Payne, 2001). Note that if both child support and spousal support is being sought, the federal and provincial legislation give child support priority over spousal support (Barr, 2003).

How Are Spousal Support Amounts Determined?

The federal Divorce Act sets out the following four objectives for courts determining spousal support orders:

1. recognize any economic advantages or disadvantages to the spouses arising from the marriage or its breakdown;
2. apportion between the spouses any financial consequences arising from the care of any child of the marriage over and above any obligation for the support of any child of the marriage;
3. relieve any economic hardship of the spouses arising from the breakdown of the marriage; and
4. insofar as practicable, promote the economic self-sufficiency of each spouse within a reasonable period of time.

The Supreme Court has emphasized the Divorce Act does not mandate one model of support—it must retain flexibility so that judges may exercise their discretion as they balance the support objectives and apply them to the facts of each case (*Bracklow v. Bracklow*, 1999). To achieve these objectives when rendering spousal support orders, the courts are to consider the conditions, means, needs, and other circumstances of each spouse, including the length of the marriage, the functions performed by each spouse during the marriage, and any existing agreements or orders for support. In a recent decision, the Supreme Court of Canada confirmed that marital misconduct of a spouse cannot be the basis for spousal support but clarified that emotional suffering arising from a spouse's wrongdoing can be a factor when determining how much support should be paid and will not be rendered irrelevant just because of its genesis in the other spouse's conduct (*Leskun v. Leskun*, 2006).

The provincial and territorial legislation differ markedly in language from the Divorce Act and from each other in their specific provisions respecting spousal support (Payne and Payne, 2001). Several provinces, such as New Brunswick, Nova Scotia, and Prince Edward Island, provide detailed lists of several factors for courts to take into account when determining the right to, duration, and amount of spousal support. For example, the role of each spouse in the family, implied or express agreements to support each other, custody obligations, economic circumstances, physical or mental disability, and the contribution of one spouse to the education or career potential of the other. Other provinces, such as Saskatchewan, Ontario, Newfoundland, and the Northwest Territories, provide both detailed criteria and general objectives to be achieved when weighing those factors much like the objectives for spousal support outlined in the Divorce Act.

Differences between the Divorce Act and the provincial/territorial legislation are more in form than in substance. Judges are unlikely to allow the spousal support ordered to depend on whether a person pursues their right to support under the federal law or the applicable provincial statute (Payne and Payne, 2001). Generally, all determinations of the right to, amount, and duration of spousal support orders will weigh the needs, means, capacities, and economic circumstances of each spouse. However, there is one difference between federal and provincial regimes for spousal support—the courts hold different powers for what type of order may be granted, which is described in a section that follows.

Spousal Support Advisory Guidelines

Concerns have arisen over the years that the discretionary nature of the law of spousal support has generated wide variation in outcomes and thus a level of uncertainty that has impeded settlement (Rogerson and Thompson, 2008). In July 2008 the Department of Justice, Canada, released the final *Spousal Support Advisory Guidelines*, with the intention of bringing more certainty and predictability to the determination of spousal support under the federal Divorce Act. These guidelines emulate the *Federal Child Support Guidelines* that structure the determination of child support payments under the Divorce Act. However, unlike the child support guidelines, the spousal support guidelines have not been legislated by the federal government and operate on an advisory basis only. The spousal support guidelines do not deal with entitlements to support but rather with the amount and duration of support once an entitlement has been found. Therefore, there must be a finding or agreement on entitlement before the guidelines can be applied. The guidelines propose two basic formulas for the determination of amount and duration of support: the without-child support formula and the with-child support formula. The dividing line between the two is the absence or presence of a dependent child or children of the marriage, and a concurrent child support obligation, at the time that spousal support is determined. Both formulas use income-sharing as the method for determining the amount of spousal support and produce ranges for the amount and duration of support. The precise number chosen within that range will be subject to negotiation or adjudication, and be determined with reference to the facts of a particular case. It is important to note that since the *Spousal Support Advisory Guidelines* have been developed specifically under the federal Divorce Act, any use of the guidelines in the provincial or territorial context will have to take into account the distinguishing features of the legislation in each jurisdiction, including matters of entitlement. In addition, prior agreements may limit the application of the guidelines as the guidelines cannot be used to override existing agreements.

Since the *Spousal Support Advisory Guidelines* are not legislated, they do not have the binding force of law—lawyers and judges may apply them at their discretion to the extent that they find them useful. In 2005 a draft of the guidelines were released. They have been warmly received in the legal community and since the release of the draft have been considered in more than 425 judicial decisions across the country and are being widely used in settlement negotiations (Rogerson and Thompson, 2008). The guidelines have received strong endorsements from Courts of Appeal in British Columbia, Ontario, and New Brunswick and have been referred to with approval in Alberta and Nova Scotia. At the time of this writing the guidelines have not yet been considered by the Supreme Court of Canada.

What Spousal Support Orders Are Available?

Support orders may be made on an interim basis until court proceedings are completed or settlement is reached, at which time a final support order will be rendered. Support orders that may be granted depend on whether the support is awarded under federal or provincial legislation. If an application for spousal support is brought under the Divorce Act, then the court will be empowered to grant orders for periodic support, lump sum support, or both, and security for support payments, but it may not order any

transfer of property in lieu of support payments. In contrast, if an application for spousal support is made under provincial legislation, the court has wide authority to order periodic payments, lump sum payments, transfers or settlements of property, exclusive possession of the matrimonial home, security for support payments, and designations of spouses as beneficiaries under life insurance policies and pension plans (Payne and Payne, 2001). Interim and final support orders can be varied if there is a significant change in circumstances, such as illness, loss of employment, receipt of a significant promotion, or unanticipated receipt or loss of income or assets. Variation orders may increase the amount of support, decrease the amount of support, terminate the support, or change other details, such as how often the support is paid (NAWL, 2002).

Enforcement of Support Orders

Once a person is obligated to pay child support or spousal support, what happens if the person does not comply with the obligation to pay? The enforcement of support orders is regulated primarily by provincial and territorial legislation (see Table 3.1). Generally, orders for support are registered with provincial or territorial agencies that monitor the payments and take any actions necessary to enforce orders that have fallen into default (Payne and Payne, 2001). Several provinces have even set up systems for automatic deductions of child and spousal support payments from an employee's paycheque. In addition, there are numerous remedies that may be obtained from the courts to enforce support orders, including seizure of assets, garnishment of wages or bank accounts, and committal or contempt of court hearings (Barr, 2003). The Supreme Court of Canada has also signalled its support for courts to take more aggressive and creative approaches to the enforcement of family obligations, recognizing that defiance of support orders is a problem that undermines respect for the administration of justice and harms the intended recipients who are often vulnerable persons (Shaffer and Bala, 2007).

Alternative Family Forms

Although the majority of this chapter has focused on the traditional family form of marriage, it must be recognized that the boundaries of families are fluid and have been for several decades (Eichler, 1983). The question of whom and what constitutes a family and how familial relationships will be governed by law have become increasingly complex.

What Is a Common-law Relationship?

A common-law relationship has become, for many individuals, an alternative to marriage. In fact, while marriage rates are decreasing, common-law unions in Canada are on the rise (Vanier Institute of the Family, 2000). Common-law relationships range from short-term arrangements with little or no commitment to lifelong commitments. Census figures released by Statistics Canada (2006) revealed that 11 per cent of Canada's children live in a common-law home.

In Quebec, the ratio was closer to 25 per cent. There are a number of different reasons why partners may choose to live common-law instead of getting married and these include rejection of the institution of marriage, absence of incentives to marry, or sometimes even a desire not to lose legal entitlements that are accorded to those who are single (Holland, 1990–1).

Common-law is also often referred to as cohabitation and generally means to live together in a conjugal relationship outside of marriage. Legally, what constitutes a common-law relationship is defined on a statute-by-statute basis and ranges from cohabitation in a relationship of some permanence of parents of a child to cohabitation for not less than three years. Table 3.2 provides legal definitions of common-law relationships by jurisdiction. There is a distinction between common-law relationships and common-law marriage. These terms are often used interchangeably, but a common-law marriage is different in how it is formed and the rights that attach to it. Common-law marriages result from marriage ceremonies in circumstances

Table 3.2 Legal Definitions of Common-Law Relationships

Jurisdiction	Legal Definition of Common-Law Relationships
Federal	Does not apply to federal statutes as it is a provincial power.
British Columbia	For all purposes, a spouse is defined as a person who has lived with another person in a marriagelike relationship for a period of at least two years.
Alberta	Recognizes 'adult interdependent relationships' for most purposes.
Saskatchewan	Common-law couples are included in the family property division regime, where a 'spouse' is defined as a person who has cohabited with another person as spouses continuously for a period of not less than two years or in a relationship of some permanence, if they are the parents of a child.
Manitoba	Under the Family Property Act, common-law partners may register their common-law relationship under section 13.1 of the Vital Statistics Act, or simply cohabit in a conjugal relationship for a period of at least three years to access the family property division regime. Under the Family Maintenance Act the definition of common-law partners includes those living together for at least one year if they are parents of a child.
Ontario	Common-law spouses are excluded from the property division regime, but for other purposes, the definition of spouse includes those who have cohabited continuously for a period of not less than three years, or who are in a relationship of some permanence, if they are the natural or adoptive parents of a child.

Table 3.2   Legal Definitions of Common-Law Relationships *(Continued)*

Jurisdiction	Legal Definition of Common-Law Relationships
Quebec	Common-law couples are included in the division of property regime. Article 521.1 of the amended Civil Code defines 'civil union' as a commitment by two persons eighteen years of age or over who express their free and enlightened consent to live together and to uphold the rights and obligations that derive from that status. A civil union may only be contracted between persons who are free from any previous bond of marriage or civil union and who in relation to each other are neither an ascendant or a descendant, nor a brother or a sister. Those in civil unions can opt into family property regimes.
Nova Scotia	'Common-law partner' means another individual who has cohabited with the individual in a conjugal relationship for a period of at least two years. Common-law spouses may opt into the family property division regime.
New Brunswick	Generally 'common-law partner' means a person who cohabits in a conjugal relationship with another person if the persons are not married to each other. For the purposes of support, 'common-law' is defined as two persons, not being married to each other, who have lived together continuously for a period of not less than three years in a family relationship in which one person has been substantially dependent upon the other for support, or in a family relationship of some permanence where there is a child born of whom they are the natural parents.
Prince Edward Island	Common-law spouses are excluded from the property division regime, but otherwise, a 'common-law partner' is either of two persons who have cohabited outside marriage continuously for a period of not less than three years, or are in a relationship of some permanence, if they are the natural or adoptive parents of a child.
Newfoundland and Labrador	Common-law spouses are excluded from the property division regime, but for other purposes, 'partner' means either of two persons who have cohabited in a conjugal relationship outside of marriage for a period of at least two years or for a period of at least one year, where they are, together, the biological or adoptive parents of a child.
Yukon	Common-law spouses are included in the property division regime, and either of a man and a woman who, not being married to each other and not having gone through a form of marriage with each other, have cohabited in a relationship of some permanence, may, during cohabitation or not later than three months after the cohabitation has ceased, apply to a court for an order for support.
Northwest Territories	For all purposes, 'spouse' includes those who have lived together for a period of at least two years, or the relationship is one of some permanence and they are together the natural or adoptive parents of a child.
Nunavut	For all purposes, 'spouse' includes those who have cohabited outside marriage, if they have cohabited for a period of at least two years, or have cohabited in a relationship of some permanence and are together the natural or adoptive parents of a child.

where compliance with statutory requirements is impossible, for example, in situations of war. Individuals who are married at common-law have all the same rights and responsibilities as married couples, but this is not so for those who are in a common-law relationship.

What Is the Legal Difference Between a Common-Law Relationship and Marriage?

Traditionally, courts and legislatures have not accorded cohabiting couples the status and rights that have been given to married spouses and their children. However, over the past 30 years there has been an increased legal recognition of common-law relationships, and the courts and legislatures have begun to extend property rights, support obligations, and statutorily defined benefits to cohabiters (Holland, 1990–1).

As discussed earlier, matrimonial property legislation differs across Canada, but all such legislation does not apply to individuals in common-law relationships. Some jurisdictions, including British Columbia, Saskatchewan, Quebec, Nova Scotia, the Northwest Territories, the Yukon, and Nunavut, have extended their property division regimes to the dissolution of common-law relationships. However, the Supreme Court of Canada has held that even in jurisdictions where matrimonial property legislation does not apply to common-law couples, common-law spouses may still be able to establish entitlements to property (*Becker v. Pettkus*, 1980).

In most jurisdictions the concept of illegitimacy with respect to children has been abolished. Whether born inside or outside a marriage, children are treated similarly in relation to child custody, access, and support (Payne and Payne, 2001). Similarly, support obligations under family law legislation are generally applicable to cohabiters who meet the jurisdictional thresholds to be recognized at law (CCH, 1976).

Aboriginal Family Law

Family law in Aboriginal communities may be governed by federal laws, provincial laws, customary Aboriginal laws, and First Nations self-government agreements. It is important when working with Aboriginal persons to have an appreciation for the relationship among these various laws and to recognize that outside of the legal mechanisms the services of elders, community leaders, or bands may be available and useful in helping Aboriginal persons work out arrangements following marriage breakdown (Legal Services Society, 2008).

Marriage and Divorce

Aboriginal marriages and divorces are governed by the federal and provincial laws that are applicable to all other citizens in Canada. There are two exceptions to this general rule. First, Aboriginal customary marriages and divorces have been recognized at law. From the case law it appears that an Aboriginal customary marriage may be recognized as a legal marriage if it meets the criteria of a common-law marriage in that it is voluntary, the individuals intend to make a lifelong commitment, and it is not polygamous. Second, the First Nations may also have some jurisdiction over marriage and divorce through the self-government agreements negotiated among Canada, the relevant province or territory, and a First Nation community. All self-government agreements include provisions governing the relationship of laws. Social workers working with a member of a First Nation community in relation to issues of marriage or divorce must first determine if that First Nation is a party to a self-government agreement, if there are any First Nation laws governing marriage and divorce, and what priority those First Nation laws hold in relation to federal and provincial laws (O'Donnell, 2004).

Division of Property

Provincial and territorial matrimonial property legislation cannot apply to alter any interests granted to individuals under the Indian Act in unsurrendered reserve lands unless the application of the provincial law to a given reserve has been negotiated through self-government or land claims agreements. There are no Indian Act provisions addressing the issue of matrimonial real property rights on reserves. The only way for a reserve to communally escape the silence of the Indian Act on matrimonial real property is through negotiation of an agreement for the reserve to come under the First Nations Land Management Act or, if available to the reserve, to negotiate a self-government or claims agreement. Those reserves under the First Nations Land Management Act regime are required to adopt a law respecting the division of matrimonial real property on marriage breakdown as part of a comprehensive land code, for which responsibility lies with the First Nation's leadership. The result of these different regimes is that matrimonial real property division is being addressed in some reserve communities but not in others. Consequently, the effect of the current legal system as it relates to the area of division of real property interests upon marriage breakdown is that most First Nations women living on reserves suffer a lack of basic legal remedies. However, although the provincial and territorial legal remedies in respect of real property interests are not available, in jurisdictions where monetary equalization payments are made, if both spouses are band members the courts may include a valuation of the interest in the reserve land when calculating the equalization payments. Furthermore, provincial laws dealing with the division of personal property upon marriage breakdown as well as laws with respect to real property that is located off the reserve do apply to First Nations people on reserve regardless of their status or band membership (Cornet and Lendor, 2002).

Child Custody and Access

As previously discussed, the test in cases of child custody is what is in the best interests of the child. If the child is Aboriginal, the importance of preserving the child's cultural identity and link to the Aboriginal community is one factor to be considered in determining the custody and access arrangements that are in the best interests of the child (Barr, 2003). However, the weight accorded to this factor in determining the child's best interest will depend on the facts of the particular case. For example, in *Racine v. Woods* (1983) the natural Aboriginal mother of a child who had been apprehended argued that adoption of her child by non-Native parents would interfere with her child's exposure to her Native culture. The Supreme

Court of Canada stated: '[W]hen the test to be met is the best interests of the child, the significance of cultural background and heritage as opposed to bonding abates over time. The closer the bond that develops with the prospective parents, the less important the racial element becomes' (*Racine v. Woods*, 1983). In that case the Supreme Court ruled in favour of the family bond the child had developed with the non-Native family. In dealing with custody cases when Aboriginal culture is a relevant factor it is important to note that courts have and will also consider the Royal Commission on Aboriginal Peoples (1996), the landmark case on Aboriginal peoples called *Delgamuukw v. British Columbia* (1997), and evidence from chiefs in the Aboriginal community on Aboriginal customary practices (Barr, 2003). In addition, although individuals who are not band members are not usually entitled to live on the reserve, if a parent is of Aboriginal heritage, lives on a reserve, and has custody of the children, the children may continue to live on the reserve, even if they are not band members (Legal Services Society, 2004). Note that in rare cases band council resolutions may restrict a non-Aboriginal or non-band member parent from going onto the reserve to see his or her children and in such instances the non-Aboriginal or non-band parent may want to secure an agreement or access order that will allow him or her to take the children off the reserve for access visits (Legal Services Society, 2008).

Child Support

The laws with respect to child support discussed earlier in this chapter are applicable to Aboriginal persons as well. The major difference in Aboriginal family law is the applicability of section 19 of the *Federal Child Support Guidelines*, which provides that when calculating the income of a spouse the courts may impute income as appropriate under the circumstances, including if the paying spouse is exempt from paying federal and provincial income tax. The premise of section 19 of the *Federal Child Support Guidelines* is that the apportionment of support responsibility between the parents is based on before-tax income; thus, if the paying parent is exempt from paying income tax, the court will 'gross up' the income before applying the table amount in the *Federal Child Support Guidelines* so that the children are not precluded from benefiting from the full financial means of the parent(s) (Barr, 2003). In Aboriginal communities, status Indians may be exempt from federal and provincial income tax if their income is earned on the reserve and in such cases would be subject to the gross up. For example, in *Le Bourdais v. Le Bourdais* (1998), Mr Le Bourdais was a status Indian who lived and worked on the Indian reserve; although he claimed that his income was $61,400 a year, the court ordered that, because he was exempt from paying federal and provincial income taxes, for the purpose of calculating child support his income would be grossed up to $104,000. It is thus important to determine the paying parent's tax status when assessing the amount of child support that will be payable.

Spousal Support

As with child support, the main factor to consider in relation to Aboriginal persons is the tax-exempt status of the persons liable for or claiming spousal support. Courts will take into account the availability of tax exemptions to both parties when determining how much income is available and how much income is needed in the form of spousal support (Barr, 2003). In addition, section 68 of the Indian Act provides that a spouse's treaty or annuity payments could be redirected to the other spouse for support if the Minister of Indian Affairs and Northern Development is satisfied that the person:

1. has deserted his spouse or common-law partner or family without sufficient cause;
2. has conducted himself in such a manner as to justify the refusal of his spouse or common-law partner or family to live with him; or

3. has been separated by imprisonment from his spouse or common-law partner and family.

However, the power provided for under section 68 of the Indian Act is rarely used (Barr, 2003). Even where the power is exercised, the treaty or annuity payments are only a few dollars per person per year and are thus not a significant source of support (O'Donnell, 2004).

Enforcement of Support

In Aboriginal communities the enforcement of child support and spousal support orders is affected by whether the child or spouse in whose favour the support order is made is a status Indian. Under section 89 of the Indian Act the real and personal property of an Indian on a reserve is not subject to a charge, pledge, mortgage, attachment, levy, seizure, distress, or execution in favour or at the instance of any person other than an Indian or band. Therefore, if the beneficiary of a support order is an Indian, the status Indian owing the support will not be relieved from being subject to garnishment or attachment proceedings. However, if the support order is in favour of a child or a spouse who is not an Indian, then the debtor who is a status Indian may rely on the Indian Act to resist enforcement proceedings for property located on the reserve. In such cases, the non-Indian creditor will have to resort to other methods to enforce the support order, such as seizure of assets off-reserve, contempt of court proceedings, or committal hearings (Barr, 2003).

CASE EXAMPLE REVIEWED

We return now to the case of Grace and how the legislation discussed in this chapter answers questions directly related to her situation.

Can Grace divorce Jeff?

Yes. To obtain a divorce, Grace needs to be able to establish marriage breakdown. One of the criteria for marriage breakdown is living separate and apart for one year and Grace and Jeff have met this threshold since Jeff moved out of their home a year ago.

Would Grace and Jeff be good candidates for mediation to determine division of property, custody, and support?

The fact that Grace and Jeff always argue will not itself preclude them as candidates for mediation. Whether Grace and Jeff are good candidates for mediation will depend on the nature of their relationship and their willingness to reach an agreement. If there is no significant power imbalance and if they are both willing to try to negotiate through mediation, then they may engage in the process, however heated the discussions themselves may become.

Does Grace have any legal rights to the family home?

Yes. At the time of marital breakdown both spouses have an equal right to possession of the matrimonial home regardless of who owns it. If Grace and Jeff cannot agree on what to do about the house, Grace has the right to ask the court to grant her exclusive possession of the home. Whether the court will grant her exclusive possession depends on the interests of the children and the individual economic circumstances of Grace and Jeff.

Can Grace prevent Jeff from having custody of or access to the children because he had an affair? What type of custody arrangement would be best for Grace and Jeff?

Grace may fight Jeff for sole custody, but if she does, the courts will decide the custody and access arrangements based on the best interests of the children. Jeff's affair will not impede his rights to custody or access to his children. If Grace and Jeff are able to set aside their differences when making decisions for the children, then joint custody may be the arrangement of preference as both parents want to share in the responsibility of making significant decisions for their kids. If Grace and Jeff have joint custody, the kids may still continue to live with Grace. Given the ages of the children, their views about where they would like to live will likely be given strong weight by the court.

If Grace divorces Jeff and he refuses to give her any money, will she have to support herself and her children?

No. Grace will have access to child support based on the child support guidelines in her jurisdiction. In addition to the guideline amount of support, she will be entitled to receive additional monies from Jeff for his share of the special and extraordinary expenses (David's university tuition and Mathew and Leslie's private school tuitions) as well as additional support based on Jeff's income over $150,000. Grace will also be entitled to spousal support from Jeff based on the conditions, means, and needs of each of them as determined by the courts.

Key Terms

Access
The amount of time and information given to the non-custodial parent, which can range from only having information about the child provided to the child residing with the access parent for long periods of time

Arbitration
A dispute-resolution method where an independent arbitrator, chosen by the parties, decides the rights and obligations of the parties; arbitration may be binding (parties may only turn to the court system by formally appealing the decision made by the arbitrator) or non-binding (litigation may be pursued if parties are unsatisfied with the outcome)

Best Interest of the Child
The paramount test for determining child custody and access arrangements in Canada

Child Support
The legal obligation of parents to support their children financially

Collaborative Family Law
A dispute-resolution process used after a relationship breakdown where the parties and their lawyers commit to reaching a negotiated outcome, and agree not to commence litigation during the negotiation process; the parties must enter into a participation agreement binding them to the principles of collaborative practice

Common-law Relationship
Also referred to as cohabitation; generally means living together in a conjugal relationship outside of marriage, but legally defined by statute in each jurisdiction

Custody
The rights and obligations related to the care and control of a child, which includes legal custody (decision making) and physical custody

Domestic Contract
A formal written legal agreement signed by marital partners defining the obligations flowing from the marital bond; includes marriage contracts and separation agreements

Joint Custody
Both parents have the legal right and responsibility to care for and make decisions regarding their children; does not define where the child lives or how much time a child spends with each parent

Litigation
A dispute-resolution process involving the court system and the commencement of a legal action

Marriage Breakdown
Under the Divorce Act, marriage breakdown must be proven in order to obtain a divorce, including one or more of the following: 1) living separate and apart for at least one year immediately before and at the time of the granting of the divorce judgment; 2) adultery committed by the other spouse; 3) physical or mental cruelty inflicted by the other spouse making continued cohabitation intolerable

Marriage Contract/Prenuptial Agreement
A domestic contract outlining an agreement between about to be married or already married parties that addresses any issue that may arise during the marriage or in the event of a marriage breakdown, except child custody/access and limitations on a spouse's rights to the matrimonial home

Matrimonial Home
The family residence to which both spouses have an automatic and equal right in the event of a marriage breakdown; upon separation, one or both spouses may apply to the court for exclusive possession of the matrimonial home and pending final division of property neither spouse can sell or encumber the house without the other's agreement or a court order

Mediation

A cooperative dispute resolution process where an impartial third party, a mediator, facilitates discussion between parties to assist them in reaching mutually acceptable solutions; mediation may be open (proceedings and report can be admitted as evidence regardless of whether either party consents) or closed (proceedings and report cannot be used as evidence in any proceeding without the parties' consent)

Separation

A unilateral or mutual intention to withdraw from a marriage; does not necessarily require a physical separation

Separation Agreement

A domestic contract entered into by parties after marriage breakdown that deals with matters relating to the settlement of their affairs

Sole Custody

One parent has the legal right and responsibility to care for and make all the decisions regarding the children

Shared Custody

A joint custody arrangement where the child spends 40 per cent of the time with each parent

Split Custod

A sole or joint custody arrangement where each parent has at least one child living with him or her

Spousal Support

The legal obligation of a spouse to support the other spouse financially

Discussion Questions

1. Give two examples of an individual entering a marriage without free and informed consent. Discuss the options that may be available.
2. To divorce a spouse must demonstrate marriage breakdown. How can a spouse seeking a divorce prove marriage breakdown?
3. Describe the differences between mediation, collaborative family law, arbitration, and litigation.
4. What is the principle underlying the law on division of property at marriage breakdown?
5. What is the paramount test for determining custody and access?
6. Do individuals in common-law relationships have any rights or obligations under family law? Discuss.

Relevant Legislation

Federal and Constitutional

Canadian Charter of Rights and Freedoms: Part 1 of the Constitution Act, 1982, being Schedule B to the Canada Act (UK), c. 11
http://laws.justice.gc.ca/en/charter/
Criminal Code of Canada, R.S.C. 1985, c. C-46
http://laws.justice.gc.ca/
Divorce Act, R.S.C. 1985, c. 3
http://laws.justice.gc.ca/en/D-3.4/49354.html

Family Orders and Agreements Enforcement Assistance Act, R.S., 1985, c. 4 (2nd Supp.)
http://www.canlii.org/ca/sta/f-1.4/whole.html
First Nations Land Management Act, (1999), c. 24
http://laws.justice.gc.ca/en/F-11.8/ 60534.html
Hague Convention on Civil Aspects of International Child Abduction
http://canada.justice.gc.ca/en/news/nr/1998/ abductbak.html

Indian Act, R.S., c. I-6, s. 1
http://laws.justice.gc.ca/en/index.html

Alberta
Family Law Act, Chapter F-4.5
http://www.qp.gov.ab.ca/documents/Acts/
F04P5.cfm?frm_isbn=0779740718
Interjurisdictional Support Orders Act, 2002,
c. I-3.5
http://www.canlii.org/ab/laws/sta/i-3.5/2005
0211/whole.html
Maintenance Enforcement Act, R.S.A. 2000, c. M-1
http://www.canlii.org/ab/laws/sta/m-1/2005
0211/whole.html
Marriage Act, R.S.A. 2000, c. M-5
http://www.canlii.org/ab/laws/sta/m-5/2005
0211/whole.html
Provincial Court Act, R.S.A. 2000, P-31
http://www.qp.gov.ab.ca/index.cfm

British Columbia
Family Maintenance Enforcement Act, R.S.B.C.
1996, c. 127
http://www.qp.gov.bc.ca/statreg/stat/F/ 96127_
01.htm
Family Relations Act, R.S.B.C. 1996, c. 128
http://www.qp.gov.bc.ca/statreg/stat/F/ 96128_
01.htm
Interjurisdictional Support Orders Act, S.B.C.
2002, c. 29
http://www.legis.gov.bc.ca/37th3rd/3rd_read/
gov23-3.htm
Marriage Act, R.S.B.C. 1996, c. 282
http://www.qp.gov.bc.ca/statreg/list_statreg_h.
htm

Manitoba
Child Custody Enforcement Act, C360 R.S.M. 1987
http://web2.gov.mb.ca/laws/statutes/ccsm/
c360e.php
Common Law Partners Property and Related
Amendments Act, S.M. 2002, c. 48
http://web2.gov.mb.ca/bills/37-3/b053e.php
Family Maintenance Act, C.C.S.M. c. F20
http://www.canlii.org/mb/laws/sta/f-20/2005
0211/whole.html

Family Property Act, C.C.S.M. c. F25
http://www.canlii.org/mb/laws/sta/f-25/
20050110/ whole.html
Interjurisdictional Support Orders Act, C.C.S.M.
c. I60
http://web2.gov.mb.ca/laws/statutes/ccsm/i060e.
php
Marriage Act, C.C.S.M. c. M50
http://web2.gov.mb.ca/laws/statutes/ccsm/index.
php

New Brunswick
Family Services Act, S.N.B. 1983, c. 16, s. 1, c. F-2.2
http://www.gnb.ca/acts/acts/f-02-2.htm
Interjurisdictional Support Orders Act, Chapter
I-12.05
http://www.canlii.org/nb/laws/sta/i-12.05/ 2005
0114/whole.html
Marriage Act, R.S.N.B. 1973, c. M-3
http://www.gnb.ca/0062/acts/acts-e.asp# GlossH

Newfoundland and Labrador
Children's Law Act, R.S.N.L. 1990 C-13
http://www.canlii.org/nl/laws/sta/c-13/2005
0112/ whole.html
Family Law Act, R.S.N.L. 1990 F-2
http://www.canlii.org/nl/laws/sta/f-2/20050112/
whole.html
Interjurisdictional Support Orders Act, S.N.L. 2002
I-19.2
http://www.canlii.org/nl/laws/sta/i-19.2/2005
0112/whole.html
Solemnization of Marriage Act, R.S.N.L. 1990 S-19
http://www.canlii.org/nl/laws/sta/s-19/2005
0112/whole.html
Support Orders Enforcement Act, R.S.N.L. 1990
S-31
http://www.gov.nf.ca/hoa/sr/

Nova Scotia
Matrimonial Property Act, amended 1995–96,
c. 13, s. 83, c. 275 of the R.S.N.S. 1989
http://www.canlii.org/ns/laws/sta/r1989c.275/
20050211/whole.html
Maintenance Enforcement Act, c. 6 of the Acts of
1994–5, amended 1995–6, c. 28; 1998, c. 30;

1998, c. 12, s. 11; 2002, c. 9, ss. 58, 59
http://www.canlii.org/ns/laws/sta/1994-95c.6/
20050211/part1.html
Reciprocal Enforcement of Custody Orders Act,
c. 387, R.S.N.S. 1989
http://www.gov.ns.ca/legi/legc/
Solemnization of Marriage Act, c. 436 of the
R.S.N.S. 1989, amended 1992, c. 16, s. 129;
1996, c. 23, ss. 40–3; 1999, c. 4, ss. 31, 32
http://www.canlii.org/ns/laws/sta/r1989c.436/
20050211/whole.html

Ontario

Children's Law Reform Act, R.S.O. 1990, c. C.12
http://www.e-laws.gov.on.ca/DBLaws/Statutes/
English/90c12_e.htm
Family Law Act, R.S.O. 1990, c. F.3
http://www.e-laws.gov.on.ca/DBLaws/Statutes/
English/90f03_e.htm
Family Responsibility and Support Arrears Enforce-
ment Act, 1996, S.O. 1996, c. 31
http://www.e-laws.gov.on.ca/DBLaws/Statutes/
English/90h19_e.htm
Marriage Act, R.S.O. 1990, c. M.3
http://www.e-laws.gov.on.ca/DBLaws/Statutes/
English/90m03_e.htm

Prince Edward Island

Custody Jurisdiction and Enforcement Act,
R.S.P.E.I. 1988, C-33
http://www.gov.pe.ca/law/statutes/pdf/c-33.pdf
Family Law Act, 1995, c. 12 R.S.P.E.I. 1988, F-2.1
http://www.canlii.org/pe/laws/sta/f-2.1/2005
0211/whole.html
Interjurisdictional Support Orders Act, 2002 c. 14
R.S.P.E.I. 1988, I-4.2
http://www.gov.pe.ca/law/statutes/index.php3
Maintenance Enforcement Act, R.S.P.E.I. 1988, M-1
http://www.gov.pe.ca/law/statutes/pdf/m-01.pdf
Marriage Act, R.S.P.E.I. 1988, M-3
http://www.canlii.org/pe/laws/sta/m-3/2004
1117/whole.html

Quebec

Act to Facilitate the Payment of Support, R.S.Q.,
c. P-2.2

http://www.canlii.org/qc/laws/sta/p-2.2/2005
0211/whole.html
c. C-1991, r.2.1, Rules respecting the solemnization
of civil marriages and civil unions, Civil Code of
Québec, (1991), c. 64, s. 365; 2002, c. 6, s. 22
http://www.canlii.org/qc/laws/sta/ccq/2005
0211/ whole.html
Civil Code of Québec, S.Q. 1991, c. 64, Art. 118
(C.C.Q.)
Civil Code of Québec, S.Q. 1991, c. 64, Art. 585
(C.C.Q.)
Civil Code of Québec, S.Q. 1991, c. 64, Art. 605
(C.C.Q.)
Civil Code of Québec, S.Q. 1991, c. 64, s. 414
(C.C.Q.)
Reciprocal Enforcement of Maintenance Orders
Act, R.S.Q. 1977, c. E-19, as amended by 1982,
c. 32; 2002, c. 6
http://www2.publicationsduquebec.gouv.qc.ca/
home.php#
Regulation Respecting Collection of Support, O.C.
1531-95
http://www.canlii.org/qc/laws/regu/p-2.2r.1/
20050211/whole.html

Saskatchewan

Children's Law Act, 1997, c. C-8.2 of the Statutes
of Saskatchewan, 1997 as amended by the Statutes of Saskatchewan, 2001, c. 34; and 2004,
c. 66 Family Property Act, F-6.3
http://www.canlii.org/sk/laws/sta/c-8.1/2005
0211/whole.html
Family Maintenance Act, 1997, Chapter F-6.2 of
the Statutes of Saskatchewan, 1997 as amended
by the Statutes of Saskatchewan, 2001, c. 51;
2002, c. I-10.03 and 5; and 2004, c. 66
http://www.canlii.org/sk/laws/sta/f-6.2/2005
0211/whole.html
Family Property Act, Chapter F-6.3* of the Statutes
of Saskatchewan, 1997 as amended by the
Statutes of Saskatchewan, 1998, c. 48; 2000,
c. 70 and 2001, c. 34 and 51. Formerly The
Matrimonial Property Act, 1997, being Chapter
M-6.11 of the Statutes of Saskatchewan, 1997
http://www.canlii.org/sk/laws/sta/f-6.3/2005
0211/whole.html

Interjurisdictional Support Orders Act, Chapter
I10.03 of The Statutes of Saskatchewan, 2002
http://www.qp.gov.sk.ca/

Marriage Act, 1995, Chapter M-4.1 of the Statutes
of Saskatchewan, as amended by the Statutes of
Saskatchewan, 2004, c. 66
http://www.canlii.org/sk/laws/sta/m-4.1/2005
0211/whole.html

Northwest Territories

Family Law Act, S.N.W.T. 1997, c. 18
http://www.canlii.org/nt/laws/sta/1997c.18/
20050211/whole.html

Children's Law Act, S.N.W.T. 1997, c. 14
http://www.canlii.org/nt/laws/sta/1997c.14/
20050211/whole.html

Maintenance Orders Enforcement Act, R.S.N.W.T.
1988, c. M-2
http://www.justice.gov.nt.ca

Marriage Act, R.S.N.W.T. 1988, c. M-4
http://www.canlii.org/nt/laws/sta/m-4/2005
0211/whole.html

Nunavut

Children's Law Act (Nunavut), R.S.N.W.T. 1997, c. 14
http://www.nunavutcourtofjustice.ca/library/
consol-stat/CSNu_1999_025_Childrens_Law.
pdf

Family Law Act (Nunavut), R.S.N.W.T. 1997, c. 18
http://www.nunavutcourtofjustice.ca/library/
consol-stat/CSNu_1999_069_Family_Law.pdf

Maintenance Orders Enforcement Act (Nunavut),
R.S.N.W.T. 1988, c. M-2
http://www.nunavutcourtofjustice.ca/library/
statutes.htm

Marriage Act, R.S.N.W.T. 1988, c. M-4
http://www.nunavutcourtofjustice.ca/library/
consol-stat/CSNu_1999_121_Marriage.pdf

Yukon Territory

Children's Act, R.S.Y. 2002, c. 31
http://www.canlii.org/yk/laws/sta/31/20041124/
whole.html

Family Property and Support Act, R.S.Y. 2002
http://www.canlii.org/yk/laws/sta/83/20041124/
whole.html

Maintenance Enforcement Act, R.S.Y. 2002, c. 145
http://www.canlii.org/yk/sta/tdm.html

Marriage Act, R.S.Y. 2002, c. 146
http://www.canlii.org/yk/laws/sta/146/2004
1124/whole.html

References

Bailey, M. (2004), '*Marriage à la carte*: A Comment on *Hart-shorne v. Hartshorne*', *Canadian Journal of Family Law*, 20.

Baker, M. (1993), 'Family Trends and Family Policies', *Transition*, 7.

Barr, M. (2003), 'Aboriginal Persons in Family Law Proceedings', Continuing Legal Education Society of British Columbia (accessed at http://www.cle. bc.ca/cle).

Becker v. Pettkus (1980) 2 S.C.R. 834.

Bracklow v. Bracklow (1999) 1 S.C.R. 420.

Canadian Institute of Actuaries (2003), 'The Division of Pension Benefits on Marital Break-down' (accessed at http://www.actuaries.ca).

Carson, G.L. and Vallance, I.C. (2004), 'Custody and Access', *47th Bar Admission Course Academic Phase* (Toronto: Law Society of Upper Canada).

CBC (2003), 'Polygamy in Bountiful' (accessed on 27 July 2005 at http://www.cbc.ca/fifth/polygamy/ polygamy.html).

——— (2005), 'The Supreme Court of Canada and Same-Sex Marriage' (accessed on 27 July 2005 at http://www.cbc.ca/news/background/samesexrights/).

CCH Canadian Limited (CCH) (1976 looseleaf, v. 3), *Canadian Family Law Guide*, Canada.

Collaborative Practice Toronto (2005), 'Principles of Collaborative Practice' (accessed at http://www. collaborative-familylawassociation.com/ Principles.htm).

Contino v. Leonelli-Contino (2005) 3 S.C.R. 217.

Cornet, W. and Lendor, A. (2002), 'Matrimonial Real Property on Reserve' (accessed at http://www.ainc- inac.gc.ca/pr/pub/matr/ int_e.html).

D.B.S. v. S.R.G.; L.J.W. v. T.A.R.; Henry v. Henry; Hiemstra v. Heimstra (2006) 2 S.C.R. 231.

Delgamuukw v. British Columbia (1997) 3 S.C.R. 1010.

Department of Finance, Canada (1996), 'The New Child Support Package' (accessed at http://www. fin.gc.ca/budget 96/chsup/chsupe.htm).

Department of Justice, Canada (2002), *Children Come First: A Report to Parliament Reviewing the Provisions and Operation of the Federal Child Support Guideline* (Ottawa: Her Majesty the Queen in Right of Canada).

Eichler, M. (1983), *Beyond the Monolithic Bias in Family Literature: Families in Canada Today* (Toronto: Gage).

Federal–Provincial–Territorial Family Law Committee (2002), *Final Federal–Provincial–Territorial Report on Custody and Access and Child Support: Putting Children First* (accessed at http://www.justice.gc.ca/en/ps/pad/reports/flc2002.html #exec).

Fodden, S. (1999), *Family Law* (Toronto: Irwin Law).

Folberg, J. (1984), 'Joint Custody Law: The Second Wave', *Journal of Family Law*, 23(1).

Government of Manitoba (2002), 'Family Law in Manitoba' (accessed at http:www.gov.mb.ca; justice/family/english-booklet2004.html).

Holland, W. (1990–1), 'Cohabitation and Marriage: A Meeting at the Crossroads?' *Child and Family Law Quarterly*, 7(33).

Irving, H. and Benjamin, M. (2002), *Therapeutic Family Mediation* (Toronto: Sage).

Kaufman, A. (2005), 'Polygamous Marriages in Canada', *Canadian Journal of Family Law*, 21(2): 315–44.

Kruzick, E.R. and Baron, R.E. (2004), 'Marriage and Annulment', *47th Bar Admission Course Academic Phase* (Toronto: Law Society of Upper Canada).

Le Bourdais v. Le Bourdais (1998), 36 R.F.L. (4th) 387 (B.C.S.C.).

Legal Services Society (2004), *If Your Marriage Breaks Up: Dealing with the Legal Issues*, 8th ed. (Vancouver: Legal Services Society, British Columbia) (accessed at http://www.lss.bc.ca).

——— (2008), 'Aboriginal People and Family Law Issues' (accessed at http://www.familylaw.lss.bc.ca/resources/fact_sheets/Aboriginal_people_and_family_law_issues.asp).

Leskun v. Leskun (2006), 1 S.C.R. 920.

MacDonald, J.C. (July 2002), 'Collaborative Family Law', paper presented at National Program on Family Law, Kelowna, BC.

———, Baron, R.E., and Kruzick, E.R. (2004), 'Divorce Law', *47th Bar Admission Course Academic Phase* (Toronto: Law Society of Upper Canada).

Macqueen, K. (2007), Polygamy: Legal in Canada, *Maclean's*, 25 June 2007 (accessed at http://www.macleans.ca/article.jsp?content=20070625_106285_106285).

Miglin v. Miglin, [2003] 1 S.C.R. 303.

National Association of Women and the Law (NAWL) (2002), *Understanding the Law: A Guide for Women in Nova Scotia*, 4th ed. (accessed at http://www. nawl.ca/affil/NSAWL-utl1. htm).

Noble, A. (1999), *Family Mediation: A Guide for Lawyers* (Aurora: Canada Law Book).

O'Donnell, T. (2004), 'Aboriginal Law in a Family Law Context', *47th Bar Admission Course Academic Phase* (Toronto: Law Society of Upper Canada).

Payne, J.D. and Payne, M.A. (2001), *Canadian Family Law: Law in a Nutshell* (Ottawa: Danreb Inc.).

Public Legal Education and Information Service of New Brunswick (PLEIS-NB) (2001), 'Custody and Access in New Brunswick' (accessed at http://www.legal-info-legale. nb.ca).

Racine v. Woods listed as *R. (A.N.) v. W. (L.J.)* (1983), 2 S.C.R. 173

Rathwell v. Rathwell (1978), 2 S.C.R. 436.

Reference re Same-Sex Marriage (2004), SCC 79.

Regehr, C. (1994), 'The Use of Empowerment in Child Custody Mediation: A Feminist Critique', *Mediation Quarterly*, 11(4): 361–71.

Rogerson, C. and Thompson, R. (2008), *Spousal Support Advisory Guidelines, Ministry of Justice and Attorney General* (accessed at http://www.justice. gc.ca/eng/pi/pad-rpad/res/spag/index.html).

Royal Commission on Aboriginal Peoples (1996), *Report of the Royal Commission on Aboriginal Peoples*, vol. 3: *People to People, Nation to Nation* (Ottawa: Supply and Services) (accessed at http://www.ainc-inac.gc.ca/ch/rcap/index_e. html).

Sadvari, G. (2004), 'Domestic Contracts', *47th Bar Admission Course Academic Phase* (Toronto: Law Society of Upper Canada).

Shaffer, M. and Bala, N. (2007), 'Developments in Family Law: The 2005–2007 Terms', *Supreme Court Law Review*, 38: 405.

Siegel, B.D. (2004), 'Alternative Dispute Resolution', *47th Bar Admission Course Academic Phase* (Toronto: Law Society of Upper Canada).

Statistics Canada (n.d.), 'Divorces by Province and Territory (Table): Canadian Statistics', version updated 22 March 2006 (accessed 24 October 2008 at http://www40.statcan.ca/l01/cst01/famil02.htm).

——— (2008) *Divorces in Canada, 2004*. Canadian Statistics. Statistics Canada Catalogue no. 84F0213XWE (accessed 24 October 2008 at http://www.statcan.ca).

Vanier Institute of the Family (2005), *Contemporary Family Trends* (Ottawa: Vanier Institute of the Family).

CHAPTER FOUR

Child Protection

OBJECTIVES

- To identify the circumstances under which reports of suspected abuse must be reported to child protection services
- To discuss the consequences of not reporting
- To identify the historical context of child protection legislation
- To describe the process of child welfare investigations and court interventions
- To identify special issues related to child welfare in Aboriginal children in Canada

CASE EXAMPLE

A forensic social worker, who has not had much experience in the area of child welfare, has a client, Joanna, who was found not criminally responsible (NCR) 15 years ago for the death of her infant child whom she killed while suffering from postpartum psychosis. Since that time the social worker has been seeing Joanna on a regular basis to assist her with managing the challenges of living. Joanna has suffered from depression and despondence at times over the past 15 years but has not become psychotic and is functioning quite well at this time. Her 20-year-old daughter Kelly, who was a Crown ward, has a two-year-old child whom she is having difficulty caring for because of the emotional aftermath of Kelly's own abuse and neglect, her attempts to deal with her abusive partner, and drug addiction. The social worker has concerns, based on information provided by Joanna, that Kelly is neglectful and that either she or her partner may be abusive to the child. Kelly lives in an apartment in the same building as her mother and Joanna is providing the primary care for the child. Although the social worker is pleased with Joanna's individual functioning at this time, she is unable to assess her ability to care for a small child. Child welfare has become involved and this is highly distressing for the client, who fears that another child will be taken away.

- If child welfare were not involved, would the social worker have a responsibility to report suspected child abuse or neglect?
- What is the likely process that will now occur for the client and her family?
- Does the social worker need to provide a report or records to a child welfare organization? Will child welfare share information about their investigation?
- Would this situation be different if this family was Aboriginal?

Do I Need to Report This?

Throughout Canada, legislation imposes the responsibility on individuals to report suspected child abuse or neglect perpetrated by parent, caregiver, or guardian to the relevant child welfare agency or to the police. Many provinces, such as Nova Scotia, Ontario, and Newfoundland, specifically identify the responsibilities of professionals. Other provinces, such as Saskatchewan, Prince Edward Island, and British Columbia, simply state that the responsibility is placed on all persons. The one exception to this is the Yukon, which does not have mandatory reporting but nevertheless grants civil immunity to those who report child abuse in good faith and has specific policies governing the reporting responsibilities of professionals, such as teachers (Vogl and Bala, 2004). This duty to report child abuse supersedes the ethical and legal obligation to maintain confidentiality; for instance, the Saskatchewan Child and Family Services Act states that the duty to report 'applies notwithstanding any claim of confidentiality or professional privilege'. However, it is important to note that solicitor–client privilege is exempt from this edict in every province except Newfoundland (Bessner, 1999). Thus, if a person discloses child abuse to her or his lawyer, it is not mandatory for the lawyer to report it.

An additional question often arises about who should make the report if child abuse is suspected by someone in an organization. Two coroner's inquests into deaths of children because of abuse and neglect have recommended that the duty to report information regarding a child at risk cannot be delegated to another person (Chief Coroner, 1998). That is, the common practice for school principals or social workers to report information from a teacher or of hospital social workers to report for the health care team is not acceptable. Rather, a professional suspecting abuse has a direct duty to report. Further, professionals have ongoing duties to report any new concerns that are not discharged by an earlier report to child welfare authorities. That is, if an individual has previously reported concerns about a particular child and then sees that child again with bruises, a new report must be made.

Although the expectation is on the child welfare agency, not the individual reporting, to determine whether suspicions of abuse or neglect are in fact founded, social workers should use discretion in determining which cases should be referred and which should not. The legislative requirement is that a report must be made when there are reasonable and probable grounds to suspect abuse or neglect. The process of undergoing a child-protection investigation is highly distressing for families, and an overzealous report can undermine the work that a social worker is doing with the family in other realms. In addition, an overabundance of reports that do not meet the specified criteria can overtax child welfare organizations, leaving less time for intervention with families in need and children at risk. Nevertheless, vague, unsubstantiated, or less serious concerns can provide an opportunity for consultation with child welfare professionals and may not lead to an investigation. That is, when in doubt, it is advisable to call the intake department of a local child welfare authority and ask whether the information acquired is reportable and what options exist.

Defining a Child

The first question to ask in deciding whether to report a suspicion of abuse is whether the person at risk is a child. Although the International Convention on the Rights of the Child (United Nations, 1989) defines a child as under 18 years of age, other definitions differ among provinces and territories. In PEI, for instance, a child is a person under the age of majority, or 18 years of age, except for the purposes of adoption, in which case anyone under the age of 21 is included. Conversely, Saskatchewan legislation refers to unmarried persons under the age of 16 but extends services to Crown wards age 16 and 17 years and protection to 16 or 17 year olds in dangerous situations or who are being encouraged to engage in prostitution. The complete list of definitions for each province and territory is given in Table 4.1.

Table 4.1 Child Welfare Legislation

Province/ Territory	Governing Legislation	Responsibility for Child Welfare	Court of Jurisdiction	Definition of Child	Legal Representation for Child	Services to Aboriginal Children	Consequences for Not Reporting
British Columbia	Child, Family and Community Services Act, R.S.B.C. 1996	Ministry of Children and Families, Child Protection Division	Provincial Court or Supreme Court	Under the age of 19	Court may allow child to be a party—counsel appointed by the AG from private bar	Act has provisions for Aboriginal children in planning and delivery of services; protection of heritage	Maximum fine of $10,000 and six months in jail
Alberta	Children and Youth Family Enhancement Act, R.S.A. 2004	Ministry of Children's Services, Child and Family Services Authorities	Provincial Court	Under the age of 18	The child's rights are represented by the Child and Youth Advocates Office.	Act does not provide for independent Native Child Welfare Services, however Act specifies that in making decisions Aboriginal heritage should be considered	Maximum fine of $2,000 or six months in jail for defaulting on fine. Report must be made to professional body
Saskatchewan	Child and Family Services Act, S.S. 1989–90	Department of Social Services	Provincial Court or Court of Queen's Bench	Under the age of 16, 18 for adoption	Court may hear from child but child is not party to proceedings	Aboriginal CFS provides services—band leader is party to legal proceedings	Maximum fine of $5,000 and six months in jail
Manitoba	Child and Family Services Act, C.C.S.M. 1985	Ministry of Family Services and Housing, Department of Child and Family Services	Provincial Court or Court of Queen's Bench	Under the age of 18—can be extended to 21 in special circumstances	Court may order counsel be appointed for the child	Act refers to protection of heritage, minister may enter into agreements with band	Report may be made to professional body regarding violation of statutory duty
Ontario	Child and Family Services Act, R.S.O. 1990	Ministry of Community and Social Services authorizes services by independent Children's Aid Societies	Court of Justice or the Family Court of the Superior Court of Justice	Under the age of 16, or 18 if already in care	Child frequently a party to proceedings represented by Office of the Children's Lawyer	Act provides for independent Native Child Welfare Services	Maximum fine of $1,000

Table 4.1   Child Welfare Legislation *(Continued)*

Province/ Territory	Governing Legislation	Responsibility for Child Welfare	Court of Jurisdiction	Definition of Child	Legal Representation for Child	Services to Aboriginal Children	Consequences for Not Reporting
Quebec	Youth Protection Act, R.S.Q. 1991	Department of Health and Social Services	Court of Quebec	Under the age of 18	Child must be informed of right to representation by Legal Aid program lawyers	Act does not extend child protection authority to chiefs or councils	Fine of $250–$2,500
New Brunswick	Family Services Act, S.N.B. 1980	Family and Community Services Division	Court of Queen's Bench	Under the age of 18—or 19 if disabled	Court can inform Ministry or AG that child requires representation from roster of lawyers	Service provided under agreement between FCS, Indian and Northern Affairs Canada, and Aboriginal Child Welfare Agencies	Minister may require professional body to investigate
Nova Scotia	Children and Family Services Act, S.N.S. 1990	Ministry of Community Services and independent Children's Aid Societies	Family Court or Supreme Court Family Division	Under the age of 16	Children over 12 may have representation; a guardian ad litem is appointed when child is not a party	Mi'kmaw Family and Children's Services is an independent agency that provides services to all Aboriginal members—Act states that the agency must be notified of any cases that involve Aboriginal members	Maximum fine of $5,000 and/ or one year in jail
Prince Edward Island	Child Protection Act, R.S.P.E.I. 2003	Ministry of Health and Social Services, Child and Family Services Division	Supreme Court	Under the age of 18	Child over 12 who can understand proceedings may have representation at expense of child welfare	Regional officers provide services to two First Nations communities, not specifically addressed in legislation	Maximum fine of $1,000

Table 4.1   Child Welfare Legislation (Continued)

Province/ Territory	Governing Legislation	Responsibility for Child Welfare	Court of Jurisdiction	Definition of Child	Legal Representation for Child	Services to Aboriginal Children	Consequences for Not Reporting
Newfoundland and Labrador	Child, Youth and Family Services Act, S.N. 1998	Department of Health and Community Services, Children's Services Division	Unified Family Court or Provincial Court	Under the age of 16	Presumption that child over 12 can have representation, child can meet with judge to express views	Provisions for Aboriginal agencies are not mentioned in the Act—there is one agency that functions under the Conne River Health and Social Services—elders included in child welfare committees that discuss cases	Maximum fine of $10,000 and six months in jail
Northwest Territories and Nunavut	Child and Family Services Act, R.S.N.W.T. 1997 Child and Family Services Act, R.S.N. 1997	Ministry of Health and Social Services, Department of Child and Family Services	Supreme Court or Territorial Court	Under the age of 16, or 18 if already in care	Court must ensure that child is represented by lawyer independent of parents—parents with means must pay	Act provides for agencies external to the CFS, through Community Agreements—Aboriginal must be informed of a member of their community is involved in a case	Fine of $5,000 and/ or six months in jail
Yukon	Children's Act, R.S.Y. 2002	Department of Health and Social Services	Territorial Court	Under the age of 18	Official guardian has exclusive right to determine whether child requires representation	No agreements for First Nations CFS. Kwanlin Dun First Nations and Kaska Tribal Council provide services—protocols for joint investigation and participation of First Nations representative in placement of a child	For reports of malicious information, maximum fine of $5,000 and/ or six months in jail

At times provinces have enacted special measures to accommodate unusual situations. For instance, although British Columbia legislation provides for children up to the age of 19, in practice child welfare services do not take children into care after the age of 16. Between the ages of 16 and 19, a youth agreement can be entered into with child welfare services that allows for supervised independent living, although limited resources often require that community services carry much of the burden for the needs of young people. In recent years, however, with the increase in global migration, BC has been confronted with unaccompanied minors who entered Canada illegally and have no means of support. Traditional legislation did not accommodate their needs. For example, in 1999, 134 youth arrived on the western shores of Canada in boats that originated in China. Long-existing but rarely used legislation allowed child welfare services to assume guardianship of these young people through means of written notification to the courts. As a result, child welfare services were able to provide full services to them, including medical coverage, legal costs for refugee claims, and daily sustenance needs. The immigrant services team that was set up when the boats arrived now serves youth from a broad range of nationalities (Pike, 2004).

A more challenging issue in definitions concerns the protection of unborn children. There are frequently situations where social workers are aware of pregnant women who are risking the safety and security of their unborn children through the use of drugs or alcohol, inadequate prenatal care, or exposure to illnesses such as AIDS. Many philosophical and ethical issues are raised about the woman's right to govern her own life and this has resulted in a struggle not only for professionals but also for the courts. In 1987, an Ontario child-protection agency sought a protection order on behalf of the unborn child of a woman who was about to deliver and was viewed to be incapable of obtaining proper care during delivery or providing the basic necessities of life. The judge in this case ordered the temporary wardship of the child and a psychiatric assessment of the mother under

the Ontario Mental Health Act (Vogl and Bala, 2004; *Children's Aid Society of Belleville v. Linda T. and Gary K.*, 1987). Ten years later, the Supreme Court of Canada found that in the absence of explicit legislation, child welfare agencies and the courts cannot protect unborn children (*Winnipeg Child and Family Services v. G.(D.F.)*, 1997).

Two issues are central to this decision. First, Canadian law does not recognize an unborn child as a legal person. Second, any legislation enacted to protect unborn children would contravene the rights of women under the Canadian Charter of Rights and Freedoms. Thus, while New Brunswick does extend the definition of children in the Family Services Act to 'an unborn child; a still born child; a child whose parents are not married', the legislation did not survive a court challenge. A New Brunswick Court of the Queen's Bench judge ruled in 1996 that imposing health care on a woman whose unborn child was viewed at risk violated the mother's rights under the Charter (Vogl and Bala, 2004; *Minister of Health and Community Services v. N.H.*, 1996). Consequently, child protection does not extend to unborn children in Canada and the only recourse for concerned professionals is to report the birth of a child at risk. In these circumstances, child welfare authorities can place an alert at the hospitals that a particular high-risk mother is expected to give birth and arrange for intervention before the child is released from hospital. These alerts are often placed well in advance of the birth since the infants of high-risk mothers are often delivered prematurely.

Defining a Child at Risk

According to the Department of Justice (2004), the term 'child abuse' refers to the violence, mistreatment, or neglect a child or adolescent may experience while in the care of someone they trust or on whom they depend. This definition includes physical abuse, sexual abuse and exploitation, neglect, and emotional abuse. Physical abuse involves the deliberate use of force against a child such that the child sustains or is at risk of sustaining physical injury. Neglect involves the failure to provide the necessities of life, as well as failure to protect from harm and failure to provide a child with love, safety, and a sense of worth. How these are defined within individual provinces, however, varies somewhat (Trocmé et al., 2004). Some provinces, such as Ontario, broadly define the abuser as anyone having charge of the child. British Columbia specifically refers to the child's parent. Quebec does not specify the perpetrator but rather refers to impact on the child.

A controversial issue in Canadian child welfare law is the extent to which physical discipline constitutes abuse. Section 43 of the Criminal Code has remained part of our criminal law since 1892 as a defence to the assault of certain identified classes of persons, including children, apprentices, prisoners, and sailors. All these special exemptions have been repealed from section 43 of the Criminal Code over time, with the exception of children, who can still be assaulted, providing the force is considered reasonable in the circumstances and is used for purposes of correction (Bernstein, 2004). Section 43 states: 'Every schoolteacher, parent or person standing in the place of a parent is justified in using force by way of correction toward a pupil or child, as the case may be, who is under his care if the force does not exceed what is reasonable under the circumstances.' Despite vocal criticism of this provision (see, for example, www.repeal43.org), the Supreme Court of Canada upheld the constitutionality of the physical punishment of children in a decision released on 30 January 2004. Concerns expressed against this ruling stated that the failure to protect children from harm violated several rights under the Charter, including the right to equal protection under the law, the right to security, and the right to protection from cruel and unusual punishment. Further, it is argued that the law violates the terms of the UN Convention on the Rights of the Child. Finally, research demonstrating that physical punishment has no beneficial long-term effects and is associated with long-term risk to children was cited in opposition to the law (Durrant and Ensom, 2004; Trocmé et al., 2004).

Despite this controversial ruling, there are limitations specified in the Supreme Court decision that include hitting children with objects or on the head, hitting children under the age of 2 or over the age of 13, and hitting children with disabilities. As Bernstein (2004) indicates, however, this leaves considerable room for ambiguity. For instance, what constitutes a disability? Does the definition include such things as Attention Deficit Disorder? Further, how can someone differentiate between corrective physical punishment that is accepted under the law and conduct that is not—for example, stemming from a caregiver's frustration, loss of temper, or abusive personality? Finally, how can child-protection agencies communicate to parents that this ruling does not absolve them of abuse conducted in the name of correction, if they see the court's limitations as merely inconsequential fine print?

Religious beliefs and practices that may result in physical assault on the child or physical risk to the child are a challenge to both the courts and child welfare services. One example is the use of physical punishment. A case that resulted in a great deal of media attention involved a Mexican Mennonite couple in Aylmer, Ontario, who had their seven children removed by child welfare because of the use of physical discipline. In their defence, their pastor stated that the Bible advocates physical discipline and quoted Proverbs 13:24: 'Those who spare the rod hate their children, but those who love them are diligent to discipline them' (see www.christianweek.org). Another example is the issue of medical care for children of parents who do not believe in certain types of intervention. In a 1995 case, the child of Jehovah's Witness parents was apprehended by the Children's Aid Society in order to facilitate the child obtaining a blood transfusion that was considered medically necessary by medical staff (*B. (R.) v. Children's Aid Society of Metropolitan Toronto*, 1995). The parents argued that two sections of the Charter upheld their right to refuse treatment—those guaranteeing religious freedom and their right to raise their children as they saw fit. In the end, the Supreme Court ruled that the state has the right to intervene when parental conduct falls below the standard accepted by the community (Vayda and Satterfield, 1997). Thus, child welfare now has jurisdiction to intervene when parents refuse medical care on religious grounds (this is discussed further in Chapter 6 – the law of consent and capacity).

According to the Department of Justice (2004), emotional abuse includes not only verbal threats, social isolation, intimidation, and exploitation but also exposure to spousal violence. The issue of defining exposure to domestic or spousal violence as child abuse is relatively recent and has been difficult to address from both a legislative and child welfare intervention perspective. There is certainly evidence to suggest that children exposed to such violence are at risk. For one thing, the presence of domestic violence is considered to be a strong predictor of various forms of child maltreatment (Apple and Holden, 1998; Waugh and Bonner, 2002). For instance, one study of 3,363 American parents found that 22.8 per cent of physically violent husbands and 23.9 per cent of violent wives also physically assaulted their children (Ross, 1996). Other research has demonstrated that in families reported to child protection where the woman is a victim of intimate partner violence (IPV), there is a co-occurrence rate of child abuse in 30 to 60 per cent of the cases, with a median rate of 40 per cent. In community-based studies the co-occurrence rate between IPV and child abuse is 5.6 to 11 per cent (Zolotor et al., 2007). Further, the detrimental effects of witnessing the repeated degradation and assault of a parent have been well documented in terms of threats to emotional, psychological, social, and academic well-being (Jaffe et al., 1986; Cox, Kotch, and Everson, 2003; Alaggia et al., 2007). Indeed in 63 per cent of cases, outcomes for children who witness interparental violence are equivalent to children who are physically abused themselves (Kitzmann et al., 2003). Community-based studies suggest that approximately 13 per cent of these children will develop posttraumatic stress disorder (PTSD) and about half will have at least one symptom of PTSD, such as intrusive thoughts of the event (Vickerman and

Margolin , 2007). In large part these childhood effects are the result of severe stress experienced by the abused parent and the effect that this stress has on their ability to parent (Huth-Bocks and Hughes, 2007). Yet, despite these alarming findings about the impact of witnessing violence on children, it is important not to conclude that all children exposed to IPV will have negative effects. A meta-analysis of 118 studies of children exposed to interparental violence demonstrated that 37 per cent showed outcomes that were similar to or better than non-witnesses. Thus, as in all cases of victimization, individual resilience can overcome extremely adverse conditions.

In most provinces across Canada, child welfare legislation has been amended to provide child welfare workers with the authority to intervene in cases where children are exposed to domestic violence; generally, these are not specifically stated but are included under provisions for emotional harm (Alaggia and Trocmé, 2004). Further, in Ontario a policy change within the ministries of the Solicitor General and the Attorney General directed police officers to notify Children's Aid when investigating cases of spousal violence with child witnesses (Dudding, 2005). These combined changes have resulted in a dramatic increase in reporting of emotional maltreatment cases. The Ontario Incidence Study of Reported Child Abuse and Neglect (OIS) reported an 870 per cent increase in investigations for emotional maltreatment between 1993 and 1998, largely driven by exposure to domestic violence reports (Trocmé et al., 2002). The 2003 Canadian Incidence Study of Reported Child Abuse and Neglect revealed that 34 per cent of all substantiated cases of child abuse in Canada involved some form of children witnessing IPV (Black et al., 2006; 2008). Not only have child welfare agencies been unprepared for the increase in reports of suspected child abuse, but in addition, traditional means of evaluating and intervening with children at risk have not applied to these types of cases, requiring a rethinking of approaches. One such problem is the role of the abused, non-offending parent. Most provincial legislation contains failure-to-protect sections, stemming from the notion that parents have an obligation to protect their children from foreseeable harm. Concerns have arisen about the impact of this in terms of blaming abused women for the plight of their children in Canada (Alaggia et al., 2007) and elsewhere (Waugh and Bonner, 2002). For instance, in the Quebec Incidence Study of Reported Child Abuse (EQI), failure to protect against potential physical harm—one of eight types of neglect identified by caseworkers—involved mothers in 66 per cent of the cases (Lavergne et al., 2003). Clearly, this issue requires collaboration between child welfare and other community social services, and social workers should not feel absolved of responsibility once a referral has been made. Continued efforts must be made to support the parent who is being abused by her spouse, ensure her safety, and assist her with economic and social/emotional independence from the abuser.

Consequences of Not Reporting a Child Who May Be at Risk

No professional worker relishes the notion of reporting child abuse to child welfare services. Several studies have sought to answer the question of why professionals, such as psychologists, physicians, and teachers, fail to report suspected child abuse despite clear legislative requirements that they do so. One concern raised by professionals is that overburdened child welfare services cannot improve the situation and thus the breach of confidentiality and the intrusion into the family may in fact exacerbate risks to the child (Zellman, 1990; Vulliamy and Sullivan, 2000). Other reasons for not reporting include ethical considerations about confidentiality, lack of awareness regarding definitions of abuse, reluctance to appear in court, and frustrations regarding lack of feedback from child welfare services once a report is made.

The most obvious and serious consequence to not reporting suspected child abuse is that a child continues to suffer physical maltreatment,

emotional maltreatment, sexual abuse, and/or neglect, at times to the point of death. This is indeed a serious problem in Canada. Trocmé and colleagues (2003), in reporting the results of the Canadian Incidence Study on Child Abuse and Neglect, estimated that 135,500 child-maltreatment cases were investigated in Canada in 1998. Of these, maltreatment was substantiated in 61,156 cases, 13 per cent of which involved moderate injuries or health conditions (8,221 cases) and an additional 4 per cent of which involved severe injuries or health conditions (2,621 cases).

A second consequence of not reporting is the potential liability to the social worker. Some provinces, such as Ontario, Quebec, and Alberta, impose fines on those who do not report information that a child may be at risk. Saskatchewan, Newfoundland, Nova Scotia, and British Columbia impose both fines and imprisonment to a maximum of six months or one year. Legislation in Manitoba, Alberta, and New Brunswick addresses reporting to the relevant professional association for discipline (see Table 4.1 for a summary). Bessner (1999) reviewed lawsuits that had been initiated against people who failed to report abuse or neglect and concluded that few lawsuits had been initiated. Further, of the few cases that had been prosecuted, many occurred in the 1980s and the majority of those were acquitted. In general, this was because of difficulty in meeting the standard of reasonable doubt of the offence, and the fact that the cooperation of this person may be necessary to establish the guilt of the abuser. More recently in an Alberta case (*Brown v. University of Alberta Hospital*, 1997) a radiologist was found to be liable for failure to report evidence of Shaken Baby Syndrome in a civil suit brought on behalf of an abused three-month-old child.

Conversely, a concern may exist that clients will take action against a social worker who does report them to child welfare for suspected child abuse or neglect. Because provinces and territories were anxious to ensure that professionals would report, provisions have been enacted to protect those who do. In general, these state that no legal actions or disciplinary proceedings can be taken against a reporting person unless they knowingly and/or maliciously presented false information (Bessner, 1999). To date, there has been no successful legal action against a professional who reported suspected child abuse or neglect in good faith.

The Historical Context of Child-protection Investigations

In understanding the process of child welfare intervention (or the decision to not intervene), it is first necessary to consider the history of child welfare services in Canada. During the eighteenth and nineteenth centuries, child welfare services were non-existent in Canada. In Ontario, for instance, the Orphan's Act in 1799 empowered town wardens to bind orphaned or deserted children to apprenticeships. Following this, the Apprentices and Minors Act of 1851 extended this authority to include the forced apprenticeship of any minor whose parents were in jail or dependent on public charity (CAS of Ottawa, 2004). These laws reflected the prevailing emphasis on the work ethic and only children bound into apprenticeship were offered any form of legal recognition and this was solely in exchange for their labour. In the 25 years that followed, private charitable organizations emerged in the form of orphanages and training schools that became regulated in 1874. In 1891, the Toronto Children's Aid Society was established. The powers of this agency and other subsequent child welfare organizations were enshrined in law two years later with the 1893 Children's Protection Act that allowed for the removal of children from their homes. Although governmental legislation and funding increased somewhat over the subsequent years, it was the 1954 Child Welfare Act and its subsequent regulations and amendments that marked governmental acceptance of responsibility and accountability for child welfare and the agencies designed to protect children (CAS of Brant, 2004).

As legislation governing the care of vulnerable children changed over the years, so did social attitudes and legal responses. The original mandate of the Toronto Children's Aid Society, for instance, was to 'deal with all matters affecting the moral and physical welfare of children, especially those who from lack of parental care . . . are in danger of growing up to swell the criminal classes' (Trocmé, 1991). Until the early 1960s, child welfare agencies focused on severe cases of abuse and neglect and adolescent unmanageability. The identification of the consequences of, first, physical battering (Battered Child Syndrome) and then sexual abuse expanded the mandate to protect children in part because of public outrage over the issue. Removal of children from their homes was a relatively informal process, affording little protection to vulnerable families. Many of the parents of children removed from their homes were Aboriginal or socially marginalized, such as the Doukhobors in British Columbia. As a result, during the 1970s the child welfare system came under public scrutiny and critics maintained that in spite of good intentions, many child welfare agencies were doing more harm than good. This precipitated a move towards legislation that balanced the power of the state and the safety of the child with a recognition of the importance of the family, requiring that child welfare agencies take the 'least restrictive' action. The rights of parents did not become central, however, until a 1999 decision by the Supreme Court of Canada in *New Brunswick v. G.(J.)*, which accorded parents the right to 'fundamental justice in child protection proceedings' under the Charter (Bala, 2004). Thus, abused children can only be removed from their homes under due process of law.

We have witnessed shifting attitudes towards the welfare of children, significantly affecting laws governing their care and services available. We began with orphaned children and the children of the poor being viewed as scourges on society in need of the discipline of hard work to avoid a future of criminal behaviour or reliance on social benefits. This was followed with outrage over the abuse of children and the widespread removal of children from the home. Next, the pendulum swung in favour of parental rights, due process, and family preservation. Finally, in the late-twentieth and early-twenty-first centuries, we have witnessed the advent of public inquiries into the deaths of children and the assertion that child welfare workers have not been aggressive enough in protecting children from abusive parents (Regehr et al., 2002).

In April 1996, the Child Mortality Task Force was established in Ontario to undertake a review of the children who died while receiving child welfare services during 1994 and 1995. This task force was formed in response to five coroner's inquests that were conducted to examine the deaths of children who were known to Children's Aid Societies. The more than 400 recommendations emanating from the inquests, and 16 resulting from the Child Mortality Task Force, resulted in the Child Welfare Reform Agenda, which was initiated by the provincial government (OACAS, 1998). Similar processes have occurred in other provinces. Stung by suggestions that child protection officials failed to save a little girl from neglectful parents, the New Brunswick government created an independent committee in 1997 to review deaths in the child protection system (Morris, 1997). The most specific, expressed concern was that social workers had become too family-oriented and tried at all costs to keep the family together rather than putting the needs of children first. These inquiries in Ontario and New Brunswick followed the earlier example of British Columbia, where a subsequent inquiry into the murder of five-year-old Matthew Vaudreuil produced the Gove Report on child welfare reform (Brunet, 1998).

Among other issues, these inquiries have served to highlight inherent conflicts in the roles of child protection workers. That is, child welfare workers are charged with balancing society's wish to protect children from abuse while maintaining the family as the bastion of liberty (Munro, 1996). Increasingly, child welfare workers are being held accountable for failing to manage these competing demands. While mandatory reporting laws increased at a dramatic rate, criminal and civil courts have found child welfare workers liable for breaching family members' rights to remain

together and conversely for failing to protect children at risk (Kanani, Regehr, and Bernstein, 2002). In either case, social workers are blamed. Following the criminal indictment of a child protection worker in Illinois for failure to remove a child from a dangerous situation, a state attorney proclaimed that this would 'send a message to all social workers that the state attorney's office will be reviewing their work to protect all the children of this country' (Alexander and Alexander, 1995 [original text in the *Chicago Tribune*]). Conversely, lawyers in British Columbia have charged that child welfare workers post–Gove Inquiry use an apprehend-first-and-ask-questions-later strategy: 'Social workers' intrusiveness constitutes an unlawful invasion of privacy' (Brunet, 1998).

Therefore, the 'best interest and safety of the child' principle remains central to child welfare investigation and intervention; however, social attitudes, public policies, and shifting legal precedents also have an influence. Critics of child welfare must be aware of the multiple demands and influences on those who are managing within the system.

What Happens After the Report?

From Investigation to Intervention

Reports of suspected abuse or neglect are made by members of the community to the appropriate child welfare service. In some jurisdictions, these are independent non-profit organizations operated by a board of directors (for instance, Toronto is served by Toronto Children's Aid Society, Catholic Children's Aid Society of Toronto, Native Child and Family Services, and Jewish Child and Family Services) and in others child welfare responsibilities are held by department of the provincial government (such as the Department of Social Services in Saskatchewan). The legislation of each province or territory determines the time frame in which the investigation must be completed by the responsible agency. Often, the response time is determined by the severity of the case as assessed during the intake phone call. For instance, in Ontario, the response time ranges from 12 hours to 7 days. Police are frequently notified in cases of physical abuse and must be notified in cases of child sexual abuse, because that is clearly defined as a criminal act, in order for a parallel criminal investigation to be conducted. Increasingly, risk assessments are following a highly standardized model, such as the Ontario Eligibility Spectrum and the New Brunswick Immediate Safety Assessment Instrument.

Although these models were intended as guides, they have often been interpreted as limiting the discretion of workers regarding decisions to intervene or not. Quebec legislation, for example, clearly specifies a four-step process of investigation:

1. Risk assessment at the time of the referral results in a coding of urgency. Code 1 requires immediate attention; Code 2 requires assessment within 24 hours; and Code 3 requires intervention within four working days.
2. A determination is made whether urgent measures are required as the child's security is in imminent or serious danger. Urgent measures such as removal of a child or ordering of medical treatment are limited to 24 hours but can be extended to five days with a court order.
3. A thorough investigation is conducted to determine risk. In every case the child is interviewed prior to interviewing the parent.
4. If intervention is required, the director of youth protection takes primary responsibility for the child, although custody remains with the parent, and determines appropriate interventions and whether to pursue these through voluntary agreements or through court order.

High rates of unsubstantiated cases (Trocmé et al., 2002; 2003) have led a number of jurisdictions to institute differential response systems. Alberta was the first Canadian jurisdiction to adopt a differential response model called the Alberta Response Model. Under this model, unless there is evidence of urgency or high risk, the investigation is preceded by a screening procedure that does not necessarily involve direct contact with the child (Vogl and Bala, 2004).

If a child is determined to be at imminent and serious risk, provisions exist in each Canadian jurisdiction to immediately apprehend him or her (some jurisdictions still require a warrant) followed by a court application. This was upheld by a Supreme Court decision in 2000 that ruled that the responsibility to protect a child from serious harm superseded the Charter rights of the parent (*Winnipeg Child and Family Services v. K.L.W.*, 2000). Whether or not a child at risk is apprehended, continuing child welfare involvement is frequently necessary. A parent may voluntarily agree to child welfare services. Although as has been argued on many occasions, consent is not really freely given and engagement is not truly voluntary if the consequences of not consenting are highly aversive—such as losing custody of one's child (Regehr and Antle, 1997). Alternatively, court proceedings must be initiated in order to intervene on an ongoing basis. In addition to child welfare proceedings, parents suspected of child abuse or neglect may be criminally prosecuted. This is a parallel process and is described in Chapter 9.

Going to Court

The nature of a child-protection hearing does not always require that all parties appear in court. Increasingly, courts are adopting affidavit-based proceedings and the child welfare worker is key to preparing the evidence. In Ontario, for instance, a summary judgment can be requested, whereby the court bases the decision on affidavits and documents, without an oral hearing with witnesses. The burden of proof in a child-protection hearing is generally recognized to be at the civil level (the balance of probabilities) meaning that it simply has to be proven that it is more likely that the abuse did occur than it did not, rather than at the criminal level (beyond a reasonable doubt) meaning that conclusive evidence proving guilt has been presented, although this is not explicitly stated in most Canadian jurisdictions (Bernstein and Reitmeier, 2004). The Yukon Children's Act does explicitly state: 'In proceedings under this act . . . the standard of proof shall be proof on the balance of probabilities . . . evidence sufficient to establish that the existence of the fact is more probable than its non-existence' (section 168(1)).

All jurisdictions require that soon after a child has been removed from the parent's care (usually within five to ten days) a court hearing be held, which is referred to as an interim-care hearing, a presentation hearing, or a temporary custody hearing. This first hearing (at times also called a show cause) is not a full trial and the introduction of hearsay evidence is permitted (Vayda and Satterfield, 1997). Reasonable attempts must be made to notify the parents of the hearing. This is the first opportunity for the family to hear evidence collected and challenge the intrusion of child welfare. However, because of a number of factors—timing, parents not able to retain counsel, parents overwhelmed—many do not challenge at this time and acquiesce to an interim agreement (Vogl and Bala, 2004).

A subsequent hearing is then established to determine whether the child needs protection. This may be preempted by a pretrial conference in which counsel summarize their cases, indicate the evidence they will present, and obtain the opinion of the judge regarding the probable disposition should the case go to court. The goal here is to facilitate a settlement between child welfare and the parents, without the costly and emotionally taxing burden of going to court (Vayda and Satterfield, 1997). The court may have ordered a child and/or family to undergo medical, psychological, psychosocial, or parenting-capacity assessments prior to the hearing. Evidence from these experts will be presented at the hearing and the parents' lawyer will have an opportunity to cross-examine and challenge these experts and present witnesses of their own. Other individuals, including health care and social work professionals, may be subpoenaed to testify in court regarding their interactions with the parent and/or child and the outcome of treatment. If there is a finding that the child is in need of protection, the child welfare agency must present a plan of care for the child.

Rights and Representation of Parties in the Proceedings

The rights of the family include privacy and freedom from interference, without just cause, stemming from the need of the child to grow up within the warmth, security, and affection of her or his own family (*CAS of the City of Kingston v. H. and G*, 1979). Parents, therefore, have the right to custody of their child unless they have acted in a way to lose that right. The law is directed to rule on the side of the biological parents unless there are grave reasons endangering the welfare of the child (*CAS of Ottawa v. Mugford*, 1970): 'Prima facie, the natural parents are entitled to custody unless by reason of some act, condition or circumstance affecting them, it is evident that the welfare of the child requires that the fundamental natural relations be severed' (*Hepton v. Maat*, 1957). The jurisdiction of the courts to intervene when a child is at risk derives from the doctrine of *parens patriae*—or the power of the state as parent. In Canada the legal precedent was set in 1893 in *R. v. Gyrgall*, which stated: 'The court is placed in a position by reason of prerogative of the Crown to act as supreme parent of children and must exercise that jurisdiction in the manner in which a wise, affectionate and careful parent would act for the welfare of the child' (O'Donoghue, 1985).

Parents have the right to representation in child welfare proceedings under the Canadian Charter of Rights and Freedoms. If they are unable to pay for representation, legal aid plans generally cover costs, and where they do not, the courts have invoked the Charter to assure that parents have access to a lawyer. In *New Brunswick v. G.J.* (1999), the Supreme Court ruled that a single mother receiving social benefits had the constitutional right to have her legal fees paid by the government in temporary-wardship proceedings for her child so that her right to fundamental justice was upheld. The responsibility of the lawyer representing the parents is to vigorously defend their position (Hatton, Bala, and Curtis, 2004). This will necessarily involve cross-examining experts retained by child welfare, calling experts of their own, and subpoenaing treating professionals who may support their position.

One right of the parents in a child-protection hearing is access to all information collected in the abuse/neglect investigation. This right follows the precedent of a criminal court issue decided at the Supreme Court level in *R. v. Stinchcombe* (1991). In this case it was ruled that the Crown attorney has the obligation to provide full disclosure of all evidence compiled in the case, whether it points to guilt or innocence. While it was presumed that this also applied in child-protection situations, this was confirmed in a 2002 decision in Alberta (*S.D.K. v. Alberta*, 2002). Consequently, all information except the identity of the person making the initial report of abuse must be shared with the parents and their legal representative (Vogl and Bala, 2004). A specific application can be made to withhold other information if there is evidence that the harm to the child of disclosing the information outweighs the parents' right to disclosure.

Children also have a right to representation. In 1974, the Law Reform Commission of Canada recommended that children who are subjects of family law proceedings be provided with independent legal counsel. This followed the lead of the Ontario Law Reform Commission, which recommended representation of children in child welfare proceedings. In 1991 Canada ratified the United Nations Convention on the Rights of the Child, which gives children the right to express views on legal matters affecting them, either directly or through representation. Nevertheless, there is considerable variation across Canada regarding representation of the child. In Ontario, for instance, children are represented by the Office of the Children's Lawyer. In Saskatchewan, although the court may hear from the child, the child is not a party to proceedings. In

the Northwest Territories, parents can be ordered to pay for the child's counsel.

The lawyer for the child can assume three different roles (Goldberg, 2004):

1. Amicus curiae or friend of the court. In this case the lawyer informs and advises the child about court procedures and presents the child's views to the court but does not advocate a particular position.
2. Guardian ad litem. Here the lawyer is not neutral and presents a position that she or he believes to be in the best interest of the child, which does not have to reflect the child's stated views.
3. Advocate. This is the traditional role where the lawyer represents the child's wishes and owes a duty of confidentiality to the child client.

There is, however, considerable controversy about some of the roles—in particular, guardian ad litem—as concerns arise about the ability of the lawyer to form a judgment regarding the best interest of the child and the ethical issues involved in disregarding the wishes of the client, regardless of their age. This varies across Canada: the Office of the Children's Lawyer in Ontario will not permit a guardian ad litem role; in Manitoba, only a child 12 years of age or older can instruct counsel.

Outcomes of Court

Court processes can result in several outcomes:

- *Dismissal or withdrawal of proceedings.* If the court determines that the evidence is not sufficiently strong to support the contention that the child is in need of protection, the proceeding must be dismissed. In this case, the child is returned to the person who had last custody before child welfare intervention unless a contrary custody order exists. Alternatively, a child welfare organization may obtain further information that suggests that the child is not at risk, or it may be determined that

Figure 4.1   The Progression of a Case

Note: Anytime that a child is no longer at risk, the case may be closed. In all situations the least intrusive measure must be taken. Parental cooperation can preclude court proceedings.

the situation has changed and the child is no longer at risk. In these situations, a court application can be made to have proceedings withdrawn or discontinued, at which time parents may seek to have costs reimbursed (Bernstein and Reitmeier, 2004).

- *Supervision of the parents and child in the community.* Under a supervision order, the court may impose terms and conditions on the parent regarding such things as attending for psychiatric care, taking prescribed medications, or not allowing another family member who is known or alleged to be abusive to the child access to the child or home.

- *Temporary or society wardship.* The legal guardianship of the child is placed with the child welfare organization, which assumes all rights and responsibilities for the child's well-being (in practice, the parents are often consulted about matters). This allows for the child to be placed in temporary care, such as in a foster home, group home, or with another member of the child's community, for a specified period of time. Because the presumption is that the child may be returned to the family, access with the family continues (Dewart, 1985).

- *Permanent or Crown wardship.* This outcome is only considered after all other less restrictive avenues have been exhausted; termination of parental rights is the most drastic of all state intrusions into the family. If parental rights to custody are terminated, the child can then be adopted. This requires, however, that all parental rights to contact cease; the parent loses not only the right to custody, but also the right to relationship if an adoption occurs (O'Donoghue, 1985). If it is determined that parental contact must continue for the best interest of the child, the child may remain in a foster home or group home. This is an important point for social workers providing recommendations to the court; that is, if further contact with the parent is recommended and awarded, the child cannot be adopted by another family. The exception to this occurs in British Columbia, which recognizes the possibility of open adoption; an outstanding access order does not necessarily prevent adoption (Bernstein and Reitmeier, 2004).

What Information Can/Should Be Shared?

Sharing information can be problematic. What can treating social workers and other community professionals share with child welfare? What can child welfare share with others, including the police? Obviously, investigations are hampered if community professionals cannot or do not share information with child welfare investigators, or if child welfare agencies cannot share information with the police. In addition, treatment becomes more challenging when treating social workers are unaware of the current state of the case with child welfare and the possible outcomes for the child and family in question. Many of the confidentiality policies are established by individual child welfare agencies and may not be consistent within provinces or within a particular city that has more than one child welfare agency. Some provinces, such as Manitoba, Nova Scotia, and Ontario, maintain child abuse registries that list abusers and document abusive acts; others do not.

Police access to the registries varies; in Ontario they are precluded from obtaining information on the registry (Bessner, 1999). Sharing among child welfare agencies has also been problematic and consequently Ontario is quickly moving to a central database of child welfare information.

In ideal circumstances parents will consent to the release of medical and counselling records regarding their own health and that of their children to child welfare authorities. In practice, however, this often does not occur. Consequently, records can only be obtained through court order as specified by child welfare legislation. Where a child is at risk, social workers must be aware that their records may be compelled and should ensure that they contain factual information and that all opinions are well supported by evidence. Further, clients involved in court cases related to any matter, including custody of their children, should be warned that records may be subpoenaed and used as evidence in court. This issue is discussed in greater detail in Chapter 11.

Aboriginal Child Welfare

It is not possible to discuss child welfare law in Canada without considering the unique experience of Aboriginal children. A history of state treatment of Aboriginal children is provided by the Aboriginal Justice Implementation Commission of Manitoba (Aboriginal Justice Implementation Commission, 2004), which acknowledges that since the time of earliest contact, Aboriginal people and European settlers to Canada have had vastly different experiences. Early missionaries condemned Aboriginal styles of child-rearing as negligent, irresponsible, and uncivilized. In 1920, this led to the establishment of the residential school system, whose main goal was to assimilate Aboriginal people into Euro-Canadian society. While social workers have always strived to provide the best interventions for our clients, at times dominant treatment methods have been detrimental. One clear example of this is the role social workers played in the removal of Aboriginal children from their homes to be placed in residential schools in Canada. It has been observed that social workers were some of the strongest supporters of the residential school system, and when a joint House of Commons and Senate Committee recommended closure of all residential schools in 1948, the social work professional joined with the churches in lobbying against such action. Social workers sat on admissions committees for the residential schools and by the 1960s over 80 per cent of Aboriginal children in Saskatchewan who were in residential schools were placed there by social workers (Blackstock, Brown, and Bennett, 2007). The negative aspects of residential schools including abuse, inadequate education, and shockingly high death rates are now well known.

After the Second World War, the Canadian government began to reconsider the residential school system and to develop child welfare services. At first, these services had little impact on Aboriginal communities because of their isolation. That quickly changed. In 1951 the federal government amended the Indian Act to extend provincial child-protection laws to First Nations children. Provincial governments were reluctant to assume this responsibility, in large part because of funding disagreements between the levels of government. Nevertheless, when residential schools closed and Aboriginal children were returned to reserves, high poverty levels and low levels of support services resulted in many families struggling to raise their children. In response, First Nations children were apprehended by child welfare services and many were adopted into non-Aboriginal homes (Gough, Blackstock, and Bala, 2005). In 1955 only 1 per cent of the 3,433 children in care in British Columbia were Aboriginal; by 1964, 34.2 per cent of the children were Aboriginal, representing 1,446 children. In other provinces, similar practices resulted in what is now termed 'the '60s scoop' (Aboriginal Justice Implementation Commission, 2004). There is now a large body of literature to document the destructive effects of this movement (Bennett, Blackstock, and De La Ronde, 2005).

Aboriginal control over delivery of services has been evolving over the past two decades as a result of the move to Aboriginal self-government (McKenzie and Flette, 2003). The goals of self-government are: 1) to increase local control and decision-making; 2) to recognize the diverse needs and cultures of Aboriginal people in Canada; and 3) to provide accountability to locally elected people (Durst, McDonald, and Rich, 1995).

Aboriginal child welfare services fall into one of two main categories:

- delegated agencies have authority from provincial or territorial child welfare services to provide either a full range of services or family support and guardianship services—this is the common model on reserves (Sinclair et al., 2004): Native Child and Family Services of Toronto became a mandated or delegated agency on 5 July 2004, allowing them to provide the full array of services (Murray, 2004);

- other agencies, primarily those found in urban centres, are not legally delegated to investigate abuse and provide protection services—they work in a voluntary capacity providing services to Aboriginal people in larger communities.

One example of services provided by a delegated agency occurs in western Manitoba. Similar to most jurisdictions in Canada, Manitoba has adopted a tripartite model of Aboriginal child welfare that involves: 1) federal funding; 2) provincial responsibility for standards in accordance with provincial legislation; and 3) Aboriginal administration and delivery of services (McKenzie, Seidl, and Bone, 1995). Manitoba's West Region Child and Family Services agency has provided a full range of child welfare services to nine Aboriginal communities since 1985. In 1992 it negotiated a block grant for child maintenance, child placement, and service costs for children and families funded by the federal government. The agency is governed by a board of chiefs and each of the nine communities has a local child and family committee that guide protection and prevention services. Services are highly decentralized and responsibilities are carried out by local service teams. Core values of the agency include preservation of families and communities, holistic approaches to services and Native self-determination, and full jurisdiction over child and family services (McKenzie and Flette, 2003).

Another example occurs in British Columbia, where the provincial government has delegated child welfare services to Aboriginal agencies. By 2004, 26 communities had created their own child welfare services ranging broadly in administrative structure and service delivery. In Port Alberni, for instance, Nuuchuunalth has assumed full responsibility for a wide range of services, including investigations, interventions, and care of children (Pike, 2004).

A clear difference in child welfare services provided to Aboriginal children is the involvement of the community in the child's care. In several provinces, including Alberta, Manitoba, and Ontario, provincial legislation requires that a child welfare agency commencing child welfare or adoption proceedings must notify the band. This then allows band representatives to participate in the proceedings or present an alternative plan of care. A slightly modified requirement for notification exists in Nova Scotia, where notification is given to a central Aboriginal agency. In other jurisdictions where this is not clearly stated, there has been a tendency in the courts to allow band involvement (Sinclair et al., 2004). In some situations, an alternative dispute resolution process exists in Aboriginal communities that attempts to resolve child welfare concerns through community involvement and mutual agreement.

Despite advances in policies and programs for children in Aboriginal communities, they remain shockingly overrepresented in Canada's child welfare system. Aboriginal children represent about 8 per cent of the Canadian population of children but about 35 per cent of children in the care of child welfare services. Saskatchewan reports that 61 per cent of its children in care are Aboriginal and in Manitoba the number reaches 78 per cent (Blackstock, 2003). Once they have come to the attention of child welfare authorities, Aboriginal children are two-and-a-half times more likely to be placed in the care of someone other than their parents (First Nations Caring Society, 2005). That is, the Canadian Incidence Study of Reported Child Abuse and Neglect—2003 (Trocmé et al., 2005) found that Aboriginal children living on reserves who were investigated by child welfare were placed at a rate of 15 per cent, while non-Aboriginal children were placed at a rate of 6 per cent. Increased efforts to maintain Aboriginal children within their communities have had some success in BC, where in 1998 only 2.5 per cent of Aboriginal children were reportedly placed in Aboriginal homes (Blackstock, 2003).

An additional problem related to the care of Aboriginal children is the split in funding responsibilities between the provincial and federal governments. The following description of the case of Jordan River Anderson is found on the First Nations Child and Family Caring Society of Canada webpage (2008).

Jordan was a young First Nations child who was born with complex medical needs. As his family did not have access to the supports needed to care for him at their home on reserve they made the difficult decision to place Jordan in child welfare care shortly after birth. Jordan remained in hospital for the first two years of his life as his medical condition stabilized. During this time the First Nations child and family service agency, First Nations community and family worked together to locate a medically trained foster home and to raise money to refit a van for Jordan's safe transportation. Shortly after Jordan's second birthday, doctors said he could go to a family home. This decision should have been a time of celebration but for federal and provincial governments it was a time to begin arguing over which department would pay for Jordan's at home care. The jurisdictional dispute would last over two years during which time Jordan remained unnecessarily in hospital. The costs they argued over ranged from some higher cost items such as renovations to the home for a wheelchair ramp to low cost items such as showerheads. The community initially tried to mediate a solution between the governments but when this failed they turned to legal action. Shortly after Jordan's fourth birthday in hospital, the jurisdictional dispute was settled but not in time for Jordan who sadly passed away before he could live in a family home.

Stemming from this tragic situation is Jordan's Principle. Under Jordan's Principle, if a jurisdictional dispute arises between two government parties or between two ministries of the same government regarding payment for services guaranteed to First Nations children, the agency first contacted must pay for the services without delay or disruption. After the care of the child is assured, the paying government can seek recompense through jurisdictional dispute mechanisms. In short, this principle states, first address the medical needs of the child, and worry about payment later. On 12 December 2007 Jordan's Principle was passed unanimously in the House of Commons. One month later Premier Gordon Campbell announced that the BC government supports Jordan's Principle, recognizing the culture and traditions of First Nations children, and promised to work in cooperation with First Nations across the province to bring it into effect in British Columbia.

Efforts to provide services to children in Aboriginal communities are hampered by: living costs in remote communities that are three to four times higher than in urban centres; non-existent or limited infrastructure for social service delivery; excessive travel time that limits service time; and inaccessibility of some communities (Blackstock, 2003). Further, although self-government of child welfare services in Manitoba has resulted in more community-based and culturally appropriate care, it has not led to fewer children in care. In fact, between 1987 and 1990, a 30-percent increase in children in care was reported by Aboriginal agencies (McKenzie, Seidl, and Bone, 1995).

CASE EXAMPLE REVIEWED

We return now to the case involving Joanna and Kelly and the questions facing the forensic social worker that were posed at the outset of this chapter.

If child welfare were not involved, would the social worker have a responsibility to report suspected child abuse or neglect?

The social worker may or may not believe that the child is at risk due to Kelly's drug abuse as he or she believes that Joanna is able to adequately provide care—despite her history of killing her own child. However, as the child is exposed to spousal violence in the home, a report must be made to child welfare. In addition, close monitoring must be maintained because a change in Joanna's mental state could put the child at risk.

What is the likely process that will now occur for the client and her family?

The process of a child abuse investigation is highly regulated. The timing of the investigation and the criteria for assessing risk are defined by provincial and territorial legislation. Court processes and the rights of participants in the process have been established through the development of case law. A summary of the process is shown in Figure 4.1 and a summary of relevant legislation is given in Table 4.1.

CASE EXAMPLE REVIEWED (Continued)

Does the social worker need to provide a report or records to a child welfare organization? Will child welfare share information about their investigation?

Having made a report, the social worker is obliged to share information leading to the concerns. Although the social worker must identify him- or herself when making the report, his or her identity will not be disclosed to the family. The treatment records are protected by the rules of confidentiality and thus cannot be shared without the client's consent (as specified in Chapter 11). However, the social worker may be subpoenaed to testify in a hearing or his or her records may be subject to court order (at which time the identity of the social worker will obviously become known). Means of responding to a subpoena are discussed in Chapter 11. Child welfare agencies are similarly bound by rules of confidentiality and thus without client consent or court treatment order, they will be unable to freely share the results of their investigation with the reporting professional.

Would this situation be different if this family was Aboriginal?

The duty to report child abuse applies to all children. However, if this was an Aboriginal family, Aboriginal child welfare involvement would depend on where they resided. In some areas, child welfare authority is delegated to Aboriginal child welfare agencies; in other jurisdictions Aboriginal agencies may act as a resource, augmenting other mandated services. On reserves the plight of this child and her family would be seen as a community issue. Every effort would be made to maintain the child within her community. Band leaders may be notified of any child welfare proceeding, could be involved in any court process, and may choose to provide a plan of care to the courts.

Key Terms

Advocate
Traditional role of the lawyer representing the child in a solicitor–client relationship

Amicus Curiae
Friend of the court; lawyer informs and advises the child about court procedures and presents the child's views to the court but does not advocate a particular position

Balance of Probabilities/Civil Burden of Proof
The burden of proof in child protection hearings, where it has to be proven that it is more likely than not that the abuse did occur

Child Abuse
Violence, mistreatment, or neglect a child or adolescent may experience while in the care of someone they trust or on whom they depend; includes physical abuse, sexual abuse and exploitation, neglect, and emotional abuse

Emotional Abuse
Includes verbal threats, social isolation, intimidation, exploitation, and exposure to spousal violence

Guardian Ad Litem
Lawyer presents a position that he or she believes to be in the best interest of the child, which is not necessarily the same as the child's stated views

Neglect
The failure to provide the necessities of life, to protect from harm, and/or to provide a child with love, safety, and a sense of worth

Parens Patriae
'Power of the state as parent': the ability of the courts to intervene when a child is at risk and act as the supreme parent of the child who must exercise that role in the way that a wise, affectionate, and careful parent would act for the welfare of the child

Permanent/Crown Wardship
The most drastic of state intrusions into the family where parental rights, custody, and access are terminated and legal guardianship is permanently placed with the Crown; adoption may occur with children in permanent wardship—this option is only considered after less restrictive options have been attempted

Physical Abuse
The deliberate use of force against a child such that the child sustains or is at risk of sustaining physical injury

Pretrial Conference
Meeting before a trial where lawyers summarize their cases, indicate the evidence they will present, and obtain the opinion of the judge on the probable outcome should the case go to court. The goal is to facilitate settlement between child welfare and parents before having to go to court

Temporary/Society Wardship
Legal guardianship of the child is placed with the child welfare organization, who assumes all rights and responsibilities for the child's well-being; child may be placed in temporary care in a foster home, group home, or another member of the child's community for a specified period of time; access with the family continues

Discussion Questions

1. How might reporting of suspected child abuse impact the therapeutic alliance between the social worker and the client?
2. What challenges might be raised for social workers regarding the inclusion of witnessing domestic violence as a form of child abuse?
3. How might a social worker who is not employed by child welfare support a parent who is under investigation by child welfare services?
4. What may be the implications for children and their families of specialized services for Aboriginal children vs integrated child welfare services?

Relevant Legislation

Federal
Canadian Charter of Rights and Freedoms: Part 1 of the Constitution Act, 1982, being Schedule B to the Canada Act (UK), c. 11
http://laws.justice.gc.ca/en/charter/
Criminal Code of Canada, R.S.C. 1985, c. C-46
http://laws.justice.gc.ca/

Alberta
Child, Youth and Family Enhancement Act (2004)
http://www.qp.gov.ab.ca/documents/Acts/

British Columbia
Child, Family and Community Service Act (1996)
http://www.qp.gov.bc.ca/statreg/stat/C/96046_01.htm

Manitoba
Child and Family Services Act (1985)
http://web2.gov.mb.ca/laws/statutes/ccsm/c080ei.php

New Brunswick
Family Services Act (1983)
    http://www.gnb.ca/acts/acts/f-02-2.htm

Newfoundland and Labrador
Child, Youth and Family Services Act (1998)
    http://www.gov.nf.ca/hoa/statutes/C12-1.htm

Nova Scotia
Children and Family Services Act (amended 2002)
    http://assembly.nl.ca/Legislation/sr/statutes/
    c12-1.htm

Ontario
Child and Family Services Act (R.R.O. 1990, Reg.
    70 as of July 2002)
    http://www.e-laws.gov.on.ca/html/statutes/
    english/elaws_statutes_90c11_e.htm

Prince Edward Island
Child Protection Act (2003)
    http://www.gov.pe.ca/law/statutes/pdf/c-05_1.
    pdf

Quebec
Youth Protection Act (2002)
    http://www.canlii.org/qc/laws/sta/p-34.1/2008
    0715/whole.html

Saskatchewan
Child and Family Services Act (1989–1990)
    http://www.qp.gov.sk.ca/documents/english/statutes/
    statutes/C7-2.PDF

Northwest Territories
Child and Family Services Act (1997)
    http://www.canlii.org/nt/laws/sta/1997c.13/
    20080715/whole.html

Nunavut
Child and Family Services Act (1997)
    http://www.canlii.org/nu/laws/sta/1997c.13/
    20070904/whole.html

Yukon Territory
Children's Act (2002)
    http://www.canlii.org/yk/laws/sta/31/20060728/
    whole.html

References

Aboriginal Justice Implementation Commission (2004), 'The Justice System and Aboriginal People' (accessed 8 April 2004 at www.ajic.mb. ca/volume1).

Alaggia, R., Jenney, A., Mazzuca, J., and Redmond, M. (2007), 'In Whose Best Interest? A Canadian Case Study of the Impact of Child Welfare Policies in Cases of Domestic Violence', *Brief Treatment and Crisis Intervention*, 7(4): 275–90.

—— and Trocmé, N. (2004), Proceedings from Roundtable on Child Welfare Practices in Domestic Violence Cases, University of Toronto, July 2004.

Alexander, R. and Alexander, C. (1995), 'Criminal Prosecution of Child Protection Workers', *Social Work*, 40(6): 809–14.

Apple, A. and Holden, G. (1998), 'The Co-occurrence of Spouse and Physical Child Abuse: A Review and Appraisal', *Journal of Family Psychology*, 12(2): 578–99.

B.(R.) v. *Children's Aid Society of Metropolitan Toronto* (1995), 1 S.C.R. 315, 21, O.R. (3rd) 479 (note).

Bala, N. (2004), 'Child Welfare Law in Canada: An Introduction', in N. Bala, J. Hornick, R. Vogl, R.J. Williams, and M. Zapf (eds), *Canadian Child Welfare Law: Children, Families and the State* (Toronto: Thompson Educational Publishing).

Bennett, M., Blackstock, C., and De La Ronde, R. (2005), *A Literature Review and Annotated Bibliography on Aspects of Aboriginal Child Welfare in Canada* (Winnipeg: The First Nations Caring Society of Canada).

Bernstein, M. (2004), 'The Decision of the Supreme Court of Canada Upholding the Constitutionality of Section 43 of the *Criminal Code of Canada*: What This Decision Means to the Child Welfare Sector', *OACAS Journal*, 48(2): 2–14.

—— and Reitmeier, K. (2004), 'The Child Protection Hearing', in N. Bala et al., *Canadian Child Welfare Law*.

Bessner, R. (1999), 'The Duty to Report Child Abuse' (Ottawa: Department of Justice, Canada) (accessed at http://canada. justice. gc.ca/en/ps/yj/rp/doc/ Paper106.pdf).

Black, T., Trocmé, N., Fallon, B., and MacLaurin, B. (2006), 'The Canadian Child Welfare System Response to Exposure to Domestic Violence Investigations', CECW Information Sheet #39E (Toronto: University of Toronto, Faculty of Social Work) (accessed at www.cecw-cepb.ca/DocsEng/ Responsetodomviolence39E.pdf).

—— (2008), 'The Canadian Child Welfare System Response to Exposure to Domestic Violence Investigations', *Child Abuse and Neglect*, 32: 393–404.

Blackstock, C. (2003), 'First Nations Child and Family Services: Restoring Peace and Harmony in First Nations communities', in K. Kufeldt and B. McKenzie (eds), *Child Welfare: Connecting Research, Policy and Practice* (Waterloo, ON: Wilfrid Laurier University Press).

———, Brown, I. and Bennett, M. (2007), 'Reconciliation: Rebuilding the Canadian Child Welfare System to Better Serve Aboriginal Children and Youth,' in I. Brown, F. Chaze, D. Fuchs, J. Lafrance, S. McKay, and S. Thomas-Prokop (eds), *Putting a Human Face on Child Welfare: Voices from the Prairies* (Toronto: Centre of Excellence for Child Welfare).

Brown v. University of Alberta Hospital (1997), A.J. 289 (Q.B.).

Brunet, R. (1998), 'BC's Only Growth Industry: Complaints Quadruple Against Aggressive Children and Families Ministry', *British Columbia Report*, 9(33): 14–17.

Chief Coroner, Province of Ontario (1998), *Report on Inquests into the Deaths of Children Receiving Services from a Children's Aid Society* (Toronto: Province of Ontario).

Children's Aid Society of Belleville v. Linda T. and Gary K. (1987), 7 R.F.L. (3d) 191 (Ont. Prov. Ct.–Fam. Div.).

Children's Aid Society of Brant (2004), 'History of Child Welfare in Ontario' (accessed at www.casbrant.ca/history.html).

Children's Aid Society of the City of Kingston v. H. and G. (1979), 24 O.R. (2d) 146 (Ont. Prov. Ct.).

Children's Aid Society of Ottawa (2004), 'CAS History' (accessed at www.casott.on.ca/EN/inside_cas/ history.htm).

Children's Aid Society of Ottawa v. Mugford (1970), S.C.R. 261.

Christianweek (2001), 'Ontario Case Renews Spanking Debate' (accessed on 24 July 2001 at www.christianweek.org).

Cox, C., Kotch, J., and Everson, M. (2003), 'A Longitudinal Study of Modifying Influences in the Relationship Between Domestic Violence and Child Maltreatment', *Journal of Family Violence*, 18(1): 5–17.

Criminal Code of Canada, R.S.C. 1985, c. C-46, s. 43.

Department of Justice, Canada (2004), 'Child Abuse: A Fact Sheet from the Department of Justice Canada' (accessed at http://canada.justice.gc.ca/ en/ps/fm/childafs.html).

Dewart, D. (1985), 'Temporary Wardship', in D. Besharov (ed.), *Child Abuse and Neglect Law: A Canadian Perspective* (Washington, DC: Child Welfare League of America).

Dudding, P., executive director, Child Welfare League of Canada (2005), personal communication.

Durrant, J. and Ensom, R. (2004), 'Physical Punishment of Children', CECW Information Sheet #7E (Ottawa: Child Welfare League of Canada).

Durst, D., McDonald, J., and Rich, C. (1995), 'Aboriginal Government of Child Welfare Services: Hobson's Choice?' in J. Hudson and B. Galaway (eds), *Child Welfare in Canada: Research and Policy Implications* (Toronto: Thompson Educational Publishing).

First Nations Child and Family Caring Society of Canada (2005) *Wen: De—We Are Coming into the Light of Day* (Ottawa: First Nations Child and Family Caring Society of Canada).

——— (2008), Joint Declaration of Support for Jordan's Principle (accessed at http://www.fncaringsociety.com/more/jordansPrinciple.php).

Goldberg, D. (2004), 'Representing Children', in Bala et al., *Canadian Child Welfare Law*.

Gough, P., Blackstock, C., and Bala, N. (2005), 'Justidiction and Funding Models for Aboriginal Child and Family Service Agencies', CECW Information Sheet #30E (Toronto: University of Toronto).

Hatton, M., Bala, N., and Curtis, C. (2004), 'Representing Parents', in Bala et al., *Canadian Child Welfare Law*.

Hepton v. Maat (1957), S.C.R. 606.

Huth-Bocks, A. and Hughes, H. (2007), 'Parenting Stress, Parenting Behaviour and Children's Adjustment in Families Experiencing Intimate Partner Violence', *Journal of Family Violence*, 23: 243–51.

Jaffe, P., Wolfe, D., Wilson, S., and Zak, L. (1986), 'Family Violence and Child Adjustment: A Comparative Analysis of Girls' and Boys' Behavioural Symptoms', *American Journal of Psychiatry*, 143: 74–7.

Kanani, K., Regehr, C., and Bernstein, M. (2002), 'Liability in Child Welfare: Lessons from Canada', *Child Abuse and Neglect*, 26(10): 1029–43.

Kitzmann, K., Gaylord, N., Holt, A., and Kenny, E. (2003), 'Child Witnesses to Domestic Violence: A Meta-analytic Review', *Journal of Counselling and Clinical Psychology*, 71(2): 339–53.

Lavergne, C., Chamberland, C., Laporte, L., and Baraldi, R. (2003), 'Domestic Violence: Protecting Children by Involving Fathers and Helping Mothers', CECW Information Sheet #6E (Montreal: Institut de recherché pour le développement social des jeunes and Université de Montréal).

McKenzie, B. and Flette, E. (2003), 'Community Building Through Block Funding in Aboriginal Child and Family Services', in Kufeldt and McKenzie, *Child Welfare*.

———, Seidl, E., and Bone, N. (1995), 'Child Welfare Standards in First Nations: A Community-based Study', in Hudson and Galaway, *Child Welfare in Canada*.

Minister of Health and Community Services v. N.H. (1996), N.B.J. 660 (Q.B. Fam. Div.), per Young, J.

Morris, C. (1997, 26 November), 'NB to Review Suspicious Child Deaths', Canadian Press Newswire.

Munro, E. (1996), 'Avoidable and Unavoidable Mistakes in Child Protection Work', *British Journal of Social Work*, 26: 793–808.

Murray, M. (2004, 5 July), 'Native Child Agency Takes on New Powers', *Toronto Star* (accessed on 5 July 2004 at www.thestar.com).

New Brunswick (Minister of Health) v. G.(J.), [1999] 3 S.C.R. 46, 50 R.F.L. (4th) 63.

O'Donoghue, M. (1985), 'Permanent Wardship', in D. Besharov (ed.), *Child Abuse and Neglect Law: A Canadian Perspective* (Washington, DC: Child Welfare League of America).

Ontario Association of Children's Aid Societies (OACAS) (1998), *Ontario Child Mortality Task Force Recommendations: A Progress Report* (Toronto: OACAS).

Pike, R., manager divisional operations and support and director, migrant services, Provincial Services Division, Ministry of Children and Family Development, BC (2004), personal communication.

Regehr, C. and Antle, B. (1997), 'Coercive Influences: Informed Consent in Court Mandated Social Work Practice', *Social Work*, 42(3): 300–6.

———, Chau, S., Leslie, B., and Howe, P. (2002), 'Inquiries into the Deaths of Children: Impacts on Child Welfare Workers and Their Organizations', *Child and Youth Services Review*, 24(12): 885–902.

Repeal 43 Committee (2004), Section 43 of the Criminal Code (accessed at http://www. repeal 43.org).

Ross, S. (1996), 'Risk of Physical Abuse to Children of Spouse Abusing Parents', *Child Abuse and Neglect*, 20: 589–98.

R. v. Gyrgall, [1893] 2 Q.B. 232.

R. v. Stinchcombe, [1991] 3 S.C.R. 326.

S.D.K. v. Alberta, [2002] A.J. 70 (Alta. Q.B.).

Sinclair, M., Bala, N., Lilles, H., and Blackstock, C. (2004), 'Aboriginal Child Welfare', in Bala et al., *Canadian Child Welfare Law*.

Trocmé, N. (1991), 'Child Welfare Services', in R. Barnhorst and L. Johnson (eds), *The State of the Child in Ontario* (Toronto: Oxford University Press).

———, Durrant, J., Ensom, R., and Marwah, I. (2004), 'Physical Abuse of Children in the Context of Punishment', CECW Information Sheet #8E (Toronto: University of Toronto).

———, Fallon, B., MacLaurin, B., Daciuk, J., Felstiner, C., Black, T., Tonmyer, L., Blackstock, C., Barter, K., Turcotte, D., and Cloutier, R. (2005), *Canadian Incidence Study of Reported Child Abuse and Neglect—2003* (accessed at www. phac-aspc.gc.ca/cm-vee/csca-ecve/).

———, MacMillan, H., Fallon, B., and De Marco, R. (2003), 'Nature and Severity of Physical Harm Caused by Child Abuse and Neglect: Results from the Canadian Incidence Study', *Canadian Medical Association Journal*, 169(9): 911–15.

———, Siddiqi, J., Fallon, B., MacLaurin, B., and Sullivan, S. (2002), 'Ontario Incidence Study of Reported Child Abuse and Neglect 1993/1998: Maltreatment Cases', CECW Information Sheet #1E (Toronto: University of Toronto).

United Nations (1989), International Convention on the Rights of the Child.

Vayda, E. and Satterfield, M. (1997), *Law for Social Workers* (Toronto: Carswell).

Vickerman, K. and Margolin, G. (2007), 'Posttraumatic Stress in Children and Adolescents Exposed to Family Violence: Treatment', *Professional Psychology: Research and Practice*, 38(6): 620–8.

Vogl, R. and Bala, N. (2004), 'Initial Involvement: Reporting Abuse and Protecting Children', in Bala et al., *Canadian Child Welfare Law*.

Vulliamy, A. and Sullivan, R. (2000), 'Reporting Child Abuse: Pediatricians' Experiences with the Child Protection System', *Child Abuse and Neglect*, 20(11): 1461–70.

Waugh, F. and Bonner, M. (2002), 'Domestic Violence and Child Protection: Issues in Safety Planning', *Child Abuse Review*, 11: 282–95.

Winnipeg Child and Family Services v. G.(D.F.) (1997), 3 S.C.R. 925.

Winnipeg Child and Family Services v. K.L.W. (2000), 2 S.C.R. 519.

Zellman, G. (1990), 'Child Abuse Reporting and Failure to Report among Mandated Reporters', *Journal of Interpersonal Violence*, 5: 3–22.

Zolotor, A., Theodore, A., Coyne-Beasley, T., and Runyan, D. (2007), 'Intimate Partner Violence and Child Maltreatment: Overlapping Risk', *Brief Treatment and Crisis Intervention*, 7(4): 305–21.

CHAPTER FIVE

Adoption Law

OBJECTIVES

- To identify criteria for adoption in Canada including eligibility, child's best interest and consent
- To discuss adoptions by family members in Canada
- To discuss adoptions of Canadian children by third parties
- To discuss custom adoptions of Aboriginal children
- To discuss the adoption of international children by Canadians

CASE EXAMPLE 1

Cindy and Jason have been living together in a common-law relationship for six years. Living with them is Cindy's daughter, Shelby, who is now nine years of age, and their mutual child, Sarah, who is four years of age. Shelby was born when Cindy was married to Shelby's father, Danny. Cindy and Danny separated shortly after Shelby's first birthday. Danny was not in favour of the separation and remained extremely angry at Cindy for leaving him. He indicated that he was upset that his family had been torn apart and said that he would seek full custody of Shelby. The couple then entered into a messy legal dispute over custody and was referred to mediation. Through the process of mediation, they agreed to a shared custody arrangement, although this was not formalized through a court appearance. The agreement was that Shelby would share equal time at both homes. This was not a smooth arrangement because Cindy and Danny continued to have a great deal of conflict that often focused on access to Shelby and decisions regarding her life. These disagreements intensified when Cindy moved in with Jason, which Danny saw as a threat to his involvement in parenting. After three years of separation, Danny also became involved with a new partner who had two children of her own and then they had another child together. Danny's involvement with his new family lessened his focus on Shelby, and three years ago he suggested that he and Cindy file for divorce. The divorce included an arrangement for shared parenting. Danny and his new partner subsequently moved to another province for work and family reasons and Danny began to see Shelby less frequently. In the past year Danny and Shelby have had almost no contact. Shelby has suggested on a couple of occasions that she wished that Jason was her father, just like he is Sarah's. Cindy and Jason have recently been discussing whether he should adopt Shelby.

- Can Jason adopt Shelby?
- Who must consent to the adoption?
- What is the process of the adoption?

CASE EXAMPLE 2

Simon and Michael have been living in a committed relationship for five years. Last year, following changes to Canada's laws regarding same-sex marriage, they were married. Both Simon and Michael have successful careers. They both come from families who are supportive of each of them and their relationship. They have a circle of good friends with whom they spend time. In the past two years Simon and Michael have spent a great deal of time talking about their wish to have a child with whom to share their family and lives. They have approached the local child welfare agency to inquire about the possibility of adopting a child in need of a home.

- Can Simon and Michael adopt a Crown ward?
- What is the process of the adoption?
- What supports are available to them after the adoption?

CASE EXAMPLE 3

Paula is a stay-at-home mom and Mark is a professional who works in the community in which they live. Paula is active in the community and volunteers in their kids' school. Paula and Mark have one child aged six who is healthy and doing well in all aspects. Paula would like to have another child, but because of medical complications is unable to conceive again. Mark and Paula have decided that they wish to more fully utilize their skills, abilities, and resources by adopting a child. They have investigated a wide range of options with the assistance of the local child welfare agency, including adopting an older child. In the end, they have decided that an international adoption is the best option for them. They have engaged the services of a private adoption agency to assist them.

- Are Paula and Mark eligible to adopt an international child?
- What is the process that they will encounter?
- Can their child become a Canadian citizen?

What Is Adoption?

Adoption is the creation of a legal relationship between a parent and child by order of the court. This relationship severs the legal rights between the biological parents and the child. Thus, when an adoption order is made, a new parent–child relationship is created in law and the adopted child ceases to be the child of the biological parent. This severing of ties, however, does not apply when considering laws of incest or marriage. That is, marriage or sexual relationships between first-degree relatives continues to be prohibited under law, even though other responsibilities and rights no longer apply. Under law, the child is also assumed to be the natural child of the adopted parents and as such acquires all inheritance rights equal to that of biological children. As a result of adoption, the child's surname may be changed; however, it differs by jurisdiction as to whether or not this is assumed to be the norm. For instance, in Alberta and Saskatchewan the child is assumed to take on the surname of the adopting parent unless the court specifies otherwise. In Manitoba, the child can keep their former surname or assume a new one. In Ontario, the court can change the child's surname to that of the adopted parent if it is requested. If the surname is changed, parents can apply for a birth certificate that reflects the new name.

Adoption in Canada is provincially regulated and therefore each province and territory has somewhat different legislation regarding who can adopt, who can be adopted, and what processes should be in place. These varying pieces of legislation are outlined in Table 5.1.

History and Context

The principle of caring for an unrelated child as if that child were genetically related has existed since the beginning of humanity. For instance, in Exodus, Chapter 1, an Israelite baby is discovered hidden in the bulrushes by the daughter of the pharaoh. She names the child Moses meaning 'drawn up from the water' and raises him as her own. The Babylonian Code of Hammurabi, the oldest set of written laws, dealt extensively with issues of adoption. In ancient Rome, the adoption of male children was a relatively common occurrence among the ruling class in order to ensure that a proper heir was available to take on the responsibility of ruling. This often involved the adoption of an adult person who may in fact have had children of his own. The Roman term 'adoptio' referred to a ceremony in which a child was transferred from the power of his parent to the power of another. It was officiated by order of a magistrate with the consent of all parties involved. All property of an adopted son became the property of his adoptive father; however, a woman could not adopt because even her own children were not considered under her power (Long, 1875).

British common law did not recognize adoptions in order to protect inheritance in wealthy families. Therefore, children who were taken as 'wards' into wealthy families retained their previous inheritance rights, and the extended members of the wealthy family into which the child

was taken also retained their rights to inheritance. The first adoption laws in North America were enacted in Massachusetts in 1851, New Brunswick in 1873, and Nova Scotia in 1896. These laws reflected emerging values that children were in need of protection and nurturing.

This paralleled child-protection legislation described in Chapter 4 in which orphanages and training schools first became regulated in 1874 in Ontario and in 1893 the Children's Protection Act was enacted that allowed for the removal of children from their homes in situations of abuse. Further, adoption legislation significantly changed the long-standing common-law principle that parents could not be denied the rights over their children or divest themselves of legal responsibilities to their children.

The history of adoption legislation in British Columbia is extensively detailed by Strong-Boag (2005) and provides an excellent example of similar practices throughout Canada. In British Columbia, the Adoption Act of 1920 was amended to reflect modern principles of child welfare. That is, the superintendent of child welfare was charged to report on the child, the birth parents, and the adoptive parents, and a one-year probationary period was introduced before adoptions became finalized. In a 1953 amendment to the Act, adopted children were given equal inheritance rights to those of natural children. Subsequent revisions in 1956 and 1957 stated that adopted children were viewed under the law to be the same as those born to the parents in lawful wedlock. The permanency of adoptions was further affirmed in amendments to the Act in the 1960s. Resulting in a strong legislative sentiment that adopted children were legitimate children of the parents.

Best Interest of the Child

The overriding principle in consideration of adoptions is the 'best interest of the child'. For instance, the Manitoba Adoption Act states: 'The purpose of this Act is to provide for new and permanent family ties through adoption, giving paramount consideration in every respect to the child's

Table 5.1   Adoption Legislation by Jurisdiction

Province/ Territory	Adoption Legislation	Public Adoption	Name Change	International Adoption	Custom Adoption
British Columbia	Adoption Act, S.B.C. 1996, c. 5	Child, Family and Community Service Act, S.B.C. 1980, c. 11	Name Act, S.B.C. 1996, c. 328	Adoption Act, S.B.C. 1996, c. 5	Adoption Act, S.B.C. 1996, c. 5
Alberta	Adult Adoption Act, S.A. 1994, c. A-23 Child, Youth and Family Enhancement Act, S.A. 2000, c. C-12	Child, Youth and Family Enhancement Act, S.A. 2000, c. C-12	Change of Name Act, S.A. 2000, c. C-7	Child, Youth and Family Enhancement Act, S.A. 2000, c. C-12	Child, Youth and Family Enhancement Act, S.A. 2000, c. C-12
Saskatchewan	Adoption Act, S.S. 1998, c. A-5.2	Child and Family Services Act, S.S. 1989-90, c. C-7.2	Change of Name Act, 1995 S.S. 1995, c. C-6.1	International Adoption (Hague Convention) Implementation Act, S.S. 1995, c. I-D.10.01	None
Manitoba	Adoption Act, S.M. 1997, c. 47	Child and Family Services Act, 1985, c. C80	Change of Name Act, S.M. 1987, c. C50	Intercountry Adoption (Hague Convention) Act, S.M. 1995, c. 22	None
Ontario	Child and Family Services Act, S.O. 1990, c. C.11	Child and Family Services Act, S.O. 1990, c. C.11	Change of Name Act, S.O. 1990, c. C7	Intercountry Adoption (Hague Convention) Act, 1998, S.O. 1998, c. 29	None
Quebec	Adoption Act, S.Q. c. A-7	Youth Protection Act, R.S.Q. c. P-34.1	Civil Code of Québec C.C.Q.	Order respecting the certification of intercountry adoption bodies, R.Q. c. P-34.1, r.0.03	None
New Brunswick	Family Services Act, N.B. 1980, c. F-2.2	Family Services Act, N.B. 1980, c. F-2.2	Change of Name Act, N.B., 1987, c. C-2.001	Intercounty Adoption Act, N.B. 1996, c. I-12.01	None

Table 5.1   Adoption Legislation by Jurisdiction (Continued)

Province/Territory	Adoption Legislation	Public Adoption	Name Change	International Adoption	Custom Adoption
Nova Scotia	Adoption Information Act, S.N.S. 1996, c. 3 Child and Family Services Act, S.N.S. 1996 c. 10 Guardianship Act, S.N.S. 2002, c. 30	Child and Family Services Act, S.N.S. 1996 c. 10	Change of Name Act, S.N.S. 1989, c. 66	Intercountry Adoption Act, S.N.S. 1998, c. 29	None
Prince Edward Island	Adoption Act, S.P.E.I. 1992, c. 1 Child Status Act, S.P.E.I. 1988, c. C-6	Child Protection Act, S.P.E.I. 2003 c. C-51	Change of Name Act, S.P.E.I. 1988, c. C-3.1	Intercounty Adoption (Hague Convention) Act, S.P.E.I. 1994, c. 28	None
Newfoundland and Labrador	Adoption Act, S.N.L. 1999, c. A-2.1	Child, Youth and Family Services Act, S.N.L 1998, c. C-12.1	Change of Name Act, S.N.L. 1990, c. C-8	Adoption Act, S.N.L. 1999, c. A-2.1	None
Northwest Territories and Nunavut	Adoption Act, S.N.W.T. 1998, c. 9	Child and Family Services Act, S.N.W.T. 1997, c. 1	Change of Name Act, S.N.W.T. 2007, c. 12	Intercountry Adoption (Hague Convention) Act, S.N.W.T. 1998, c. 19	Aboriginal Custom Adoption Recognition Act, S.N.W.T. 1994, c. 26
Yukon Territory	Children's Act, R.S.Y. 2002, c. 31	Children's Act, R.S.Y. 2002, c. 31	Change of Name Act, R.S.Y. 1988, c. 51	Intercountry Adoption (Hague Convention) Act, R.S.Y. 2002, c. 121	None

best interests.' The Newfoundland and Labrador Act similarly states: 'This Act shall be construed so as to provide for new and permanent family ties through adoption while, in every respect, giving paramount consideration to the best interests of the child.'

In considering best interests of the child, most Canadian Acts provide a similar list of factors. The Manitoba Act specifies that considerations should include:

a) the safety of the child;
b) the child's opportunity to have a parent–child relationship as a wanted and needed member of a family;
c) the child's mental, emotional, physical, and educational needs and the appropriate care or treatment, or both, to meet such needs;
d) the child's mental, emotional, and physical stage of development;
e) the child's sense of continuity and need for permanency with the least possible disruption;
f) the child's cultural, linguistic, racial, and religious heritage;
g) the views and preferences of the child where they can reasonably be ascertained; and
h) the effect upon the child of any delay in the final disposition of the proceedings.

Although these principles seem straightforward, concerns continue to exist about how they are implemented. The Adoption Council of Canada, for instance, states: 'Although most adoption practitioners agree that the "best interests" of the child should prevail, "best interests" is a murky concept. "Best interests" from whose point of view? The birth family, adoptive family, child advocate, judge, Aboriginal community, social worker, foster family, or the child herself, if anyone has asked her?' (Scarth, 2003).

One important consideration in the best interest of the child is what the child believes is in his or her own best interest. Therefore, in every province the consent of a child over the age of 12 is required for an adoption order. In Ontario,

consent is required of children over the age of 7. On certain occasions, consent can be dispensed with if the court believes that acquiring consent would be detrimental to the child. For instance, in a case where the child believed the stepfather to be his biological father, the parents successfully petitioned that the child would be emotionally harmed to discover that he indeed had a different biological father (Giesbrecht, 2004).

Who Can Adopt a Child?

In most provinces it is required that in order to adopt, the individual must be of the age of majority and a resident of the province in which the adoption is petitioned. However, these requirements can be waived under certain conditions. For instance, in Ontario the minimum age to adopt is 18 unless the court is satisfied that there are circumstances that would make it advisable to waive this requirement. Similarly, in Nova Scotia a person who has not reached the age of majority (19) can adopt if he or she is married to a spouse that has reached the age of majority. People who adopt can be single or married (legally or by common-law).

In May 1995 an Ontario Court judge found that the Child and Family Services Act of Ontario infringed section 15 of the Charter of Rights and Freedoms because it did not allow same-sex couples to bring a joint application for adoption. Ontario then became the first province to make it legal for same-sex couples to adopt. British Columbia, Alberta, and Nova Scotia followed suit shortly thereafter and now adoptions by same-sex couples are permitted in most provinces and territories (CBC News, 2007). Interestingly, societal attitudes do not necessarily reflect what is held in law. Miall and March (2005b) surveyed 706 people across Canada regarding attitudes towards adoption. Of the respondents, 92 per cent said that adoption by married couples was very acceptable, 40 per cent felt that adoption by common-law couples was very acceptable, 25 per cent and 18 per cent thought that adoption by single women and single men was very acceptable, and 20 per cent thought that adoption by same sex-couples was very acceptable (although an additional 28 per cent felt that same-sex couple adoptions were somewhat acceptable).

International adoptions have criteria for adoption that is country-specific and thus people who wish to adopt a child from another country must carefully review the criteria of each country. These issues are briefly addressed in the section below on intercountry adoptions.

Categories of Adoption

There are three main options for people in Canada who wish to adopt a child. The first type of adoption is the statutory adoption of children within Canada. Statutory adoptions are governed by provincial regulations. Broadly speaking, statutory adoptions divide along two dimensions: 1) consent (that is, adoptions with parental consent versus adoptions without parental consent); and 2) relationship between the child and adoptive parent (that is, adoption by a kin or family member versus third-party adoptions).

The second type of adoption of children within Canada is custom or customary adoption and refers to the adoption of Aboriginal children following traditional customary processes. The final type of adoption is international adoption, which is governed by the Hague Convention on Protection of Children and Co-operation in Respect to Intercountry Adoption and is subject to both provincial regulations and federal citizenship and immigration regulations.

Statutory Adoptions of Children within Canada

Adoptions with Parental Consent

Adoption with parental consent is referred to as voluntary adoption. Where a parent voluntarily relinquishes a child, consent must clearly be free and informed. That is, the parent fully understands what she is consenting to and her consent is given without coercion. Anywhere in Canada, parental consent for adoption cannot be given before the child is born and some provinces further require that the child reach a minimum age before consent can be given. For instance, in Ontario consent cannot be given until the first week after a child's birth. See Chapter 6 for a more extensive discussion on issues of consent under Canadian law. Voluntary adoptions are facilitated through a government agency or private adoption firm. In the case of private adoptions, the birth parent(s) may be involved in the process of selecting adoptive parents. In this way, the birth parent can ensure that adoptive parents have similar values and share ideas about the child's future.

Adoption legislation across Canada requires every legal parent (biological or by previous adoption) to give written consent to the proposed adoption of a child by another person. Interestingly though, the term 'parent' is open to some interpretation. For instance, the Child and Family Services Act of Ontario is clear that the biological mother is a parent, but the father's role as parent is dependent on his relationship with the child and with the child's mother. Thus, in order to have the right to determine whether his child can be adopted, the father must meet at least one of several criteria: 1) he must establish paternity and have some degree of commitment to fatherhood as evidenced by the permanence of the relationship (for instance, by marriage); 2) he has lawful care, custody, and control over the child; 3) he has established himself as a 'parent of intention' by treating the child as his own, including providing support within the past 12 months; 4) he has a right of custody or access under a court order or agreement; 5) he has acknowledged parentage in a statutory declaration filed with the Registrar General (Fodden, 1999).

A frequently raised concern is in situations where a parent has consented to the adoption and then seeks to withdraw consent at a later time. All Acts provide for the withdrawal of consent within a specified period of time. For instance, the Adoption Act of British Columbia allows for withdrawal of consent within 30 days. Ontario and Manitoba legislation provides for a 21-day period within which consent can be withdrawn. Difficulties occur, however, when consent is revoked after this time period. Removing consent after this period raises a complex set of legal issues that pits the best interest of the child against parental rights (both of adoptive parents and biological parents). For the most part, however, the issue was settled in 1983 by the case of *Racine v. Woods*, which was heard in the Supreme Court of Canada. In this situation, a mother abandoned her child resulting in the child being taken into the care of the Children's Aid Society. The child was subsequently adopted with the mother's consent. Five years later, the mother returned, and wished to regain custody of the child. The court stated: 'The law no longer treats children as the property of those who gave them birth but focuses on what is in their best interest' (*Racine v. Woods*, 1983). In general, subsequent court decisions have also found that returning an adopted child to his or her birth parent as a result of withdrawn consent is not in the best interest of the child (Fodden, 1999).

Adoptions without Parental Consent

Adoptions without parental consent occur when a child has been found to be abused or neglected and has been taken into the care of a child welfare agency. The process for removing a child from his or her home and then obtaining a court order to make a child a permanent ward can be found in Chapter 4. As noted in that chapter, this outcome is only considered after all other avenues have been exhausted, because termination of parental rights is the most drastic of all state intrusions into the family. If parental rights to custody are terminated, the child can then be adopted. This requires, however, that all parental rights to contact the child cease.

Third-party Adoptions

Adoptions by people not related to the child can be arranged either through a public agency, such as a Children's Aid Society, or through private

agencies that are licensed by the relevant provincial government. Since there has been a decrease in the number of single mothers giving up their children for adoption, private adoptions, rather than adoptions through a public agency, have become increasingly more common. This change can be related both to changing attitudes related to single parenting and also to the availability of birth control and abortion in Canada (Strong-Boag, 2005). The result is that there are relatively few healthy infants who are available for adoption in Canada. A report in 1993 by the Royal Commission on New Reproductive Technologies reported that for every healthy infant placed by public agencies in Canada, eight other families continue to wait (Speirs et al., 2003). Speirs and colleagues reported in 2003 that 20,000 Canadian children were permanent wards of the state and fewer than 10 per cent of these were placed for adoption each year. At the same time, Citizenship and Immigration Canada (2003) reported that 1,925 international children were adopted by Canadians and brought to live in Canada. Speirs and colleagues suggest that the barriers to adopt Canadian children include child–parent match factors, agency factors, and legislative factors. Some examples of child–parent match factors are that children in the care of the state are often older (i.e., no longer infants), have experienced multiple placements that may result in emotional or behavioural challenges, and are more likely to have a disability. Although these factors in no way diminish the child, these characteristics are often not a match with the wishes and expectations of adoptive parents. Further, the policies, practices, and funding of child welfare agencies do not support and encourage adoption of children as a primary objective; consequently, fewer resources are directed to adoption services. Finally, legislation surrounding adoption in Canada that includes such issues as disclosure of information and continued access to the child by biological parents may dissuade potential parents from adopting. As a result, many Canadian families are turning to other options such as international adoptions and surrogacy.

Third-party adoptions can be facilitated by a government child welfare agency or by a licensed private adoption agency. Although processes vary to some degree, the general process is outlined in Figure 5.1. The process begins with an *intake interview* during which prospective parents can find out about the process of adoption and information that they will be required to share with the adoption agency. Prospective parents then proceed to a *formal application* in which they complete an adoption questionnaire, consent to a police record check, submit a medical examination report that has been completed by a physician, and provide names of references. Following this, a *homestudy* is

Figure 5.1   Third-party Adoptions

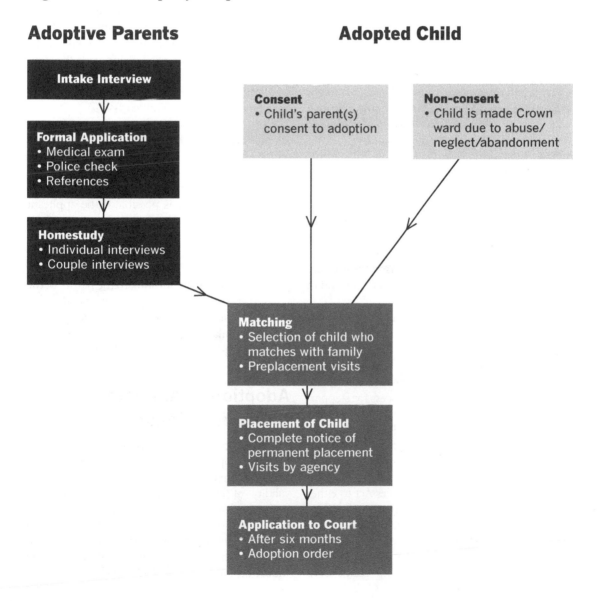

completed by a social worker in which various members of the family are interviewed together and separately to determine the strengths, challenges, and wishes of the family. Pending a successful application and homestudy, the agency works towards *matching* the family with a child that is eligible for adoption and currently in need of a family. Part of this process is a series of pre-placement visits in which the child and family can meet each other and see if they connect with one another. If the match seems right, the family and agency complete a notice of permanent *placement* and the child is placed with the family. During the initial six months, regular visits are scheduled with the social worker to ensure that the placement is suitable and to assist with any problems that might arise. After a period of time (six months in British Columbia, for instance) an *application is made to the court* for a permanent adoption order.

Adoptions by Relatives of the Child

Adoptions by family members are far less rigorous than those of third parties. The assumption is that adoption by a family member such as a grandparent or aunt allows the child a sense of continuity both in terms of links with extended family and in terms of their cultural heritage.

The most common form of family adoption is stepparent adoption. A stepparent is defined as the spouse of the child's parent. The definition of spouse includes married partners and partners living in common-law relationships whether of the same-sex or opposite sex. The process for stepparent adoption is relatively straightforward providing that all parties have consented to the adoption. In Ontario, an application is made for an order for adoption either individually by the spouse of the child's parent or jointly with the child's parent under the Child and Family Services Act to either the Ontario Court of Justice or the Family Court of the Superior Court of Justice. Both the applicant and the child must be residents of Ontario for the court to make an order. The stepparent must file an affidavit attesting to the relationship

with the child and the ability to care for the child. No homestudy or other investigation is required. The process of stepparent adoption becomes more complex if the parties are seeking to dispense with the consent of the other parent. The parent and stepparent must establish for the courts that consent of the absent parent is not possible and that it is clearly in the best interest of the child to grant an adoption order. Courts are reluctant to dispense with consent because this results in a permanent revocation of parental rights for the absent parent. Where dispensing with consent of the absent parent is permitted, it is generally based on the strength and length of relationship with the stepparent and the concomitant relationship with the biological parent being attenuated, non-existent, or potentially harmful (Fodden, 1999).

While most legislation pertaining to familial adoptions assumes that the person being adopted meets the legal criteria for being a child (see Chapter 4), familial adoptions are also possible for adults. In British Columbia, for instance, the adoption of an adult is possible if the applicant is able to show that he or she has maintained the adoptee as his or her own child. In Alberta and Saskatchewan, adult adoptions are similarly allowed if the court is satisfied with information provided in affidavits attesting to the nature of the relationship between the applicant and the perspective adoptee. Ontario allows for adult adoptions on similar grounds but adds that the person has not withdrawn from parental control.

Adoption of Aboriginal Children in Canada

Customary or custom adoption is a term used to describe adoption that takes place within Aboriginal communities following traditional law. The validity of custom adoptions is acknowledged under the Indian Act in a 1985 amendment, when it identified that the definition of child includes a child born in or out of wedlock, a legally adopted child, and a child adopted in accordance with Indian custom (McNeil, 1996). While customary adoption may have a wide range of meanings to different peoples, in general it can be seen as more closely related to guardianship in the Canadian legal system than it is to standard statutory adoption. Custom adoption arrangements may be fluid or more temporary in nature than other adoptions. Children often will have continuing contact with birth parents. Adoption agreements may have varying child-care plans that continue to involve the birth parent and may vary in the degree to which parental rights and responsibilities are distributed. Adopted children will generally have full knowledge of their birth parents. Quite commonly in custom adoptions, children are adopted by biologically related family members. For instance, one study of Inuit adoptions found that 75 per cent occurred between relatives, most frequently grandparents (Baldassi, 2006). In other cases, there may be specific rules about who bears the responsibility to care for children related by blood. For instance, the birth father's family is responsible for a child in the Gitksan tradition, and the birth mother's sister is responsible in the Carrier tradition.

As described in Chapter 4 on child welfare, the "60s scoop" represented a time when large numbers of Aboriginal children were identified by child welfare organizations as being at risk and were thus removed from their familial homes. By 1962, for instance, 85 per cent of children in foster care in British Columbia were Aboriginal children (Strong-Boag, 2005). Most of the children were placed in non-Aboriginal households and many were adopted by families who were non-Aboriginal, without band consultation. This situation was not merely by chance but represented a particular initiative to facilitate interracial adoptions, which were seen as in the best interest of Aboriginal children. Public and legal opinion on this matter shifted over the years with the realization that stripping children of their culture had highly negative consequences. Thus, in 1972, the adoption of an Aboriginal child by a white family was denied by the courts because of concern that the child would forfeit rights under the Indian Act. This resulted in a moratorium on such adoptions despite a subsequent BC Court of Appeal decision that a child

would continue to have status as a First Nation person even after adoption. The right to continued status was enshrined the following year in the BC Adoption Act.

In response to similar concerns related to the adoption of Aboriginal children, Alberta announced a moratorium on the adoption of Aboriginal children by non-Aboriginal families in 1996. The following year, adoption policies were revised and all adoptions of Aboriginal children needed consent of the band council. These adoptions are now overseen by agencies who have delegated authority from the province, the first of which was Yellowhead Tribal Services in Alberta, which was formed in 1987 (Adoption Council of Canada, 2003). In some ways, however, requirements of the legislation differ from traditional custom adoptions because background checks and homestudies are required. Other provinces also have provisions that address the unique nature of adoptions in Aboriginal communities. Nova Scotia, for instance, requires that children who speak Mi'kmaq must be placed in an environment where the language is spoken and/or understood, but the province does not recognize custom adoptions under its statutes. In Ontario there is an obligation to consult with a child's band in the adoption process and provide a written notice of an intention to place a child. Further, the child's Aboriginal heritage must be a factor in considering the child's best interest.

Three jurisdictions—Nunavut, the Northwest Territories, and British Columbia—recognize custom adoptions. The Northwest Territories have a specific Act, the Aboriginal Custom Adoption Recognition Act, that aims to set out a procedure to ensure that custom adoptions are respected and recognized. Under this Act a person can apply for a custom adoption to the Custom Adoption Commissioner. The commissioner can then prepare a certificate of custom adoption that is subsequently filed with the Supreme Court. These filed certificates are deemed to be orders of the Supreme Court. British Columbia has recognized custom adoptions within the Adoption Act. The goal is to allow for greater choice in permanency planning for Aboriginal children in continuing care and to allow families and communities the opportunities to share in both the care and planning for care. Under BC law, custom adoption is formalized by the courts and a declaration is made under the Adoption Act, which has the same effect as an adoption order. However, adoptive families work directly with the band and the First Nations or Aboriginal community in planning and caring for the child in order to meet the requirements of the court. Financial assistance may be available to families who have custody of a child under the Child, Family and Community Service Act (CFCSA) (British Columbia Ministry of Children and Family Development, 2008). BC legislation differentiates between adoption by the Ministry of Children and Family Development, temporary custody of Aboriginal children, and custom adoption as recognized by the courts. These policies are summarized in Table 5.2.

An important distinction between statutory adoptions and custom adoptions is the role of the courts. In *Re Tagornak Adoption petition*, the court confirmed that its role is declaratory (that is, confirming that a valid custom adoption has taken place). On the contrary, in statutory adoptions, the judge decides whether the adoption will

occur (Baldassi, 2006). Further, statutory adoption results in the termination of parental rights and obligations of the birth parent, whereas it is not clear that custom adoption has a similar effect. Case law in several provinces in which individuals are petitioning for support or survivor benefits in situations of custom adoptions appear to be moving custom adoption closer to statutory adoption in terms of rights and responsibilities. Custom adoption continues to be an area of developing legislation and case law precedents and increased activity in the development of governance models in Aboriginal communities will undoubtedly influence future directions (McNeil, 1996).

Supports for Families Following Adoption in Canada

Families who adopt children from child welfare agencies frequently assume the care of children who have special needs related either to emotional or physical health issues. The greatest challenges are experienced by parents adopting older children who have been victims of abuse and neglect and children who have experienced multiple

Table 5.2   British Columbia Custom Adoption Policies

	Adoption Placement through the Ministry of Children and Family Development	Transfer of Custody under the CFCSA	Custom Adoption Recognized by the Courts
Name change	Child's name may be changed during the adoption process	Child's name is not changed	Child's name may be changed
Homestudy	Homestudy required, including mandatory educational component	Formal educational component not required but is available; child's needs and the means by which caregivers will meet them are assessed	Homestudy and educational component not required but is available
Financial assistance for care of the child	Available	Available	Available
Support services	Obtained through community professionals and service providers	Obtained and developed within the community	Can be developed by Aboriginal agencies or other community agencies

Source: Adapted from data from the British Columbia Ministry of Children and Family Development, 2008 placements before being adopted. Postadoption services and supports are therefore viewed as vital to assist adoptive families in coping with challenges that they may encounter (Dhami, Mandel, and Sothmann, 2007). In a survey of 211 families who had adopted children in British Columbia, Dhami and colleagues found that 57 per cent of adoptive parents indicated that they needed postadoption services after a stressful event; 45 per cent indicated they needed services immediately after the adoption; 26 per cent said they needed services when their child began school; and 38 per cent needed services when the adopted child became a teenager. In general, three basic types of postadoption services are typically offered:

1. Education and information services—including information on child development, attachment issues, parenting, and available resources;
2. Clinical counselling services—including child, couple, and family counselling; and
3. Financial and other material services—including subsidies, medical care, and respite care.

Most provinces have financial-assistance plans in recognition of the need to support families who take on the care of children in the child welfare system. New Brunswick, for instance, states: 'The Department of Social Development recognizes that families who adopt children with special needs are often taking on extraordinary demands and may require financial or other support to meet the child's needs. The Subsidized Adoption Program is based on the services required to meet a specific child's needs. The program provides payment for specific services related to the child's special needs, which may include respite, counselling or therapy, equipment, corrective dental treatment or medical expenses not covered by the parents' extended medical plans' (New Brunswick Department of Social Development, 2008). Similarly, Manitoba provides assistance for families who adopt a child with special needs or for families who are adopting more than one child from the same family. This assistance may be available until the child reaches age 18 and may continue even if the family moves to another province. Manitoba Family Services

and Housing offers three types of assistance—families may be eligible for one or all three:

1. One-time start-up costs, such as for transportation, equipment, or necessary changes to the adoptive family's home.
2. Costs of special services for a child who has been diagnosed with special needs.
3. Ongoing maintenance payments to help with the daily care of a child with special needs or who is in a sibling group. The amount is based on the applicants' income and family size (Manitoba Family Services and Housing, 2008).

Other provinces also provide subsidies. For example, Alberta has a Post-Adoption Support Program that is funded by the province's Child and Family Services Authorities. In Nova Scotia the subsidized adoption program is funded under the Children and Family Services Act. Levels of funding in different provinces vary. Alberta will pay up to 90 per cent of foster care rates ($25 per day). Manitoba pays up to half the foster-care rate or $11 per day. Many provinces also offer other supports. For instance, Alberta provides medical and dental care, home renovations to meet a child's disability, therapy, daycare, respite care, remedial education, travel expenses, and rehabilitation (Adoption Council of Canada, 2008).

Ontario stands alone as the only province that does not have a provincially funded system of support for adoptive parents. Instead, some of the individual agencies provide postadoption financial support from their own budgets. This means that levels of support vary widely from one agency to another—with some offering no support at all (Adoption Council of Canada, 2008).

Adoption Disclosure

Early adoption law in Canada did not prohibit disclosure of the parties involved. In North America it was not until 1917 that the first legislation concealing identities was passed in Minnesota (Baldassi, 2006). Ontario in 1927 and British Columbia in 1935 passed legislation that limited access to information unless there was judicial authorization (Strong-Boag, 2005). It was then not until the 1970s that a few adoptees began to demand information about their birth parents. Provinces responded by creating registries where birth parents and adoptees who wished to meet each other could enter their names and if there was a match, could meet. For instance, Nova Scotia's Adoption Information Act provides for a 'passive' registry whereby people can receive information or be reunited if both parties register. In 1997, an active registry was created in which the Adoption Disclosure Services Program will conduct a search for birth relatives. If family is found, however, the registry will not release identifying information without the written consent of both parties to whom the information relates (Nova Scotia Community Services, 2008).

Ontario passed new legislation on 14 May 2008 that opened adoption records on 1 June 2009. This allows adopted adults to apply for copies of adoption orders and birth registrations and allows birth parents to apply for information from these documents. Any child or parent wishing to not have the information disclosed must have filed a veto with the Crown. This measure was retroactive only and allowed the information to remain confidential solely if the adoption was before 1 September 2008. Birth parents and adoptive parents can also file a 'No contact notice', indicating their preference to not be contacted (Ontario Ministry of Community and Social Services, 2008).

A particular issue exists around adoption disclosure and reunification of Aboriginal families related to the '60s scoop, when Aboriginal children were adopted by non-Aboriginal families. Several organizations in Canada are attempting to bring about reunification between Aboriginal adoptees and their birth families. For instance, the Southern Manitoba First Nations Repatriation Program (SMFNRP) is a coordinated effort of the First Nations Child and Family Services agencies and First Nations Bands of Manitoba to address the issues of treaty status adoptees (SMFNRP, 2009). Services offered by SMFNRP are: searches to locate birth parents; support groups for adoptees and birth parents; counselling and referral to legal, medical, financial, and spiritual resources; advocacy to obtain reinstatement of status under the Indian Act; and cultural resources.

Open versus Closed Adoptions

The degree to which an adoption is termed 'open' refers to the level of contact between adopted children and their biological families. In confidential or closed adoptions, identifying information is not shared and there is no contact between adopted children and their birth families. Mediated adoptions or semi-open adoptions refer to situations where information is shared through a mediator or third party. In fully disclosed or open adoptions, information is shared and contact is established, although the frequency and type of contact is highly variable (Korff, Grotevant, and McRoy, 2006). As indicated in the section above, changes to legislation will appear to make closed adoptions very rare in domestic adoptions of Canadian children. Thus the issue to be considered is not whether adoptions should be open or closed but what are the effects of contact after adoption and how can the contacts be put to the greatest advantage?

While open adoptions have been viewed with some skepticism at best by practitioners and society at large (Miall and March, 2005a), in general, research has shown positive effects of contact between adopted children and their birth families (Berge et al., 2003; Korff et al., 2006). Birth mothers have been found to benefit from being involved in choosing the adoptive parents, sharing medical and family history information, and seeing that their child is well cared for by the adoptive parent. This information-sharing is seen to facilitate grieving and reduce self-blame. Adoptive parents, while often fearful of contact between the child and birth parent, generally discover that the birth mother is not attempting to reclaim the child and thus they become less fearful for the future. They are also better able to answer questions that the child may have over time about his or her birth mother. Most importantly, however, there is evidence that the child benefits from contact with their birth parent, demonstrating more positive psychological adjustment and fewer externalizing behaviours. Adolescents who had been adopted indicated that contact with the birth mother increased the supports available in their lives, and helped them develop an increased sense of their own identity. Factors that facilitate positive relationships postadoption include empathy towards the birth parent, developing clear roles and boundaries, developing clear plans for contact, and ensuring that the purpose of contact is child-centred (Wolfgram, 2008). This is not to suggest however that contact is positive in all cases. For instance in the 1998 case of *New Brunswick v. L.(M.)*, the Supreme Court of Canada found that access to the child by the birth parents would jeopardize the adoption because of the unpredictable and emotionally distressed nature of the birth parents. Thus, access was not seen to be in the best interest or psychological well-being of the child.

International Adoptions

International adoptions have been characterized as occurring in two historical waves. The first wave occurred immediately after World War II and involved the placement of orphaned children from Europe. Children arriving in North America at that time came primarily from Poland, Czechoslovakia, Hungary, and Germany. However, the official process was somewhat ad hoc and barriers were in place regarding immigration policies due to concerns about unregulated migration. Further, the large numbers of children available for adoption domestically did not create a political will to modify policies to facilitate international adoptions (Lovelock, 2000). The second wave of international adoptions began in the mid-1970s and although there was a humanitarian element in terms of assisting children from war-torn countries, there was also a motivation related to decreased fertility rates in Canada and reduced numbers of domestic children available for adoption. This new wave was accompanied by political pressure to make the process of international adoption easier. It also resulted in concerns that the process was open to abuse.

On 29 May 1993, the Hague Convention on Protection of Children and Co-operation in Respect to Intercountry Adoption was established. Canada became a signatory in 1995. This convention was established to create safeguards for ensuring that intercountry adoptions are conducted in a manner that reflects the best interest of the child and the child's fundamental rights. The ultimate goal is to facilitate the opportunity for children and parents to develop permanent relationships while at the same time working to eliminate abuses. Specifically the convention seeks to ensure the rights of adopting parents and protect them from those who seek improper financial gain. It also seeks to protect birth parents from exploitation and undue pressure. More importantly, however, it seeks to protect children from abduction, sale, and trafficking. A process has been established whereby adoptions are conducted through signatory countries, following recognized practices by accredited individuals and organizations that are overseen by regulatory agencies. The Hague Convention ensures proper consent for the adoption, allows for the child's transfer from their country of origin, and allows the child to have status in the receiving country.

The availability of children for intercountry adoption reflects political upheavals, civil wars, natural disasters, and domestic family policies in the countries of origin (Lovelock, 2000). According to Citizenship and Immigration Canada, Canadians adopted 1,535 children from abroad in 2006, down 18 per cent from the year before. The largest number of international children adopted by Canadians originated from China (40 per cent), Haiti (8 per cent), Korea (7 per cent), the United States (6 per cent), Russia (6 per cent), Ethiopia (4 per cent), and the Philippines (3 per cent) (Adoption Council of Canada, 2007). Families in the major metropolitan areas account for most of the international adoptions: Montreal (17 per cent), Toronto (16 per cent), Vancouver (10 per cent), Ottawa (3.5 per cent), Calgary (3 per cent), and Quebec City (3 per cent) (Adoption Council of Canada, 2007). Each country that allows its children to be adopted internationally has individual criteria for eligibility. For instance, China requires that adoptive parents are married for at least two years if this is their first marriage and five years if they have been married

Figure 5.2 The Process of International Adoptions

Intake Information
- Acquire information from private adoption firm specializing in international adoption

Application Dossier
- Complete dossier information
- Send to agency for translation, notarizing, and authentification
- Send to child's country

Homestudy
- Contract for private homestudy

Canadian Immigration
- Complete sponsorship application

Offer of Child
- Receive offer and medical report from child's country
- Send written acceptance
- Receive notice to travel

Receive Child
- Travel to country to receive child
- Finalize adoption papers

Follow-up
- Postplacement supervision visits with adoption social worker
- Obtain birth certificate and adoption order from provincial court

before. Both parents must be older than 30 and under 50 years of age. They must both have a body mass index of less than 40. Pakistan requires that couples must be married for at least three years and at least one member of the couple must be East Indian. Ethiopia requires that couples are married for at least two years. Single women who are no older than 40 are also considered. The Philippines requires that couples have only been divorced a maximum of one time, are practising Christians, preferably Catholic (Alberta Children and Youth Services, 2008). Currently, there are no countries that will knowingly place a child with a same-sex couple. Thus, individuals in same-sex relationships wishing to adopt a child from another country must remain closeted during the process and arrange that only one parent adopt the child.

The process of international adoption is more complex than the processes for adoption of children within Canada because it involves laws and policies of the child's country of origin, international policies related to the Hague Convention, provincial regulations related to intercountry adoptions, and Canadian immigration policies. This process is summarized in Figure 5.2.

Children who are adopted from international countries often face challenges that are related to their early life experiences. These challenges can include delays in physical and mental development, motor delays, and delays in language development partly due to early nutritional deprivation and to the fact that often they spent their early years in institutions (Le Mare, Audet, and Kurytinic, 2007; Cohen et al., 2008). Such challenges create difficulties for adopting families given the scarcity of services available to them. Adoption agencies are mandated to provide some aftercare, but beyond private services, most services are generally limited to those available to any child in difficulty and not directed to the specific needs of these children and families.

CASE EXAMPLE 1 REVIEWED

We now return to the case of Cindy and Jason and consider how legislation discussed in this chapter relates to their wish to have Jason adopt Shelby.

Can Jason adopt Shelby?

As a stepparent, Jason can adopt Shelby provided proper consents are in place and the court is satisfied that he has a positive relationship with Shelby and is able to provide for her care.

Who must consent to the adoption?

All parties must consent in writing to the adoption: Cindy as Shelby's mother, Shelby herself if she resides in Ontario, and Shelby's father, Danny. It is possible in some circumstances that an absent parent's consent can be dispensed with. However, Danny has a court order for custody (through the divorce decree) and did have a continuing relationship until quite recently. He may also provide financial support. As a result, it is unlikely that a judge would agree to dispense with his consent.

What is the process of the adoption?

Jason, Cindy, and Shelby must all have independent legal advice. Jason must apply for the adoption and complete an affidavit attesting to his relationship with Shelby. Cindy and Shelby must provide written consent following legal advice as to the consequences of their consent. The application is filed with the court and a private court hearing is held, at which time the judge can make an order for adoption.

CASE EXAMPLE 2 REVIEWED

We now return to the case of Simon and Michael and consider how legislation discussed in this chapter relates to their wish to adopt a child.

Can Simon and Michael adopt a Crown ward?

According to the laws of most provinces and territories, as a same-sex couple, Simon and Michael would be eligible to adopt a child pending the outcome of the homestudy, police check, medical report, and reference check.

What is the process of the adoption?

As outlined in Figure 5.1, Simon and Michael would work with the adoption agency to select a child that matched their family. A series of preplacement visits would be arranged and if the visits were positive for both the prospective parents and the child, the child would be placed in their home. For the subsequent months, a worker from the agency would visit the family and assist with any difficulties. If the placement has been successful, a permanent adoption order can be made through application to the courts.

What supports are available to them after the adoption?

Depending on the province in which Simon and Michael reside and the specific needs of the child that they adopt, they will be eligible for varying levels of financial support. In addition, depending on where they live, they may also have counselling and educational services available.

CASE EXAMPLE 3 REVIEWED

We now return to the case of Paula and Mark and consider how legislation discussed in this chapter relates to their wish to adopt an international child.

Are Paula and Mark eligible to adopt an international child?

Paula and Mark may be eligible to adopt a child from an international country. This will depend on the outcome of the homestudy and the specific criteria of the country from which they wish to adopt. They meet the criteria of length of marriage for most countries; however, they may not meet criteria regarding race or religion.

What is the process that they will encounter?

A described in Figure 5.2, the process they will encounter involves many steps and therefore they will require the assistance of an agency specializing in international adoptions.

Can their child become a Canadian citizen?

Paula and Mark's child can become a citizen upon arriving in Canada provided they have completed all the necessary documentation with Citizenship and Immigration Canada. At that time they can also apply for a Canadian birth certificate for their child.

Key Terms

Adoption
A legal relationship between a parent and child created through a court order that severs the legal rights and responsibilities inherent in the relationship between the biological parents and the child if it is considered in the best interests of the child; the three categories of adoptions are: 1) domestic; 2) custom; and 3) international

**Adoption with Parental Consent/
Voluntary Adoption**
Domestic adoption governed by provincial statute where the birth parents plan for and consent in written form to the adoption and engage a government agency or private adoption firm to facilitate the adoption

**Adoption without Parental Consent/
Involuntary Adoption**
Domestic adoption governed by provincial statute that occurs when a child has been found to be abused or neglected and has been taken into the care of a child welfare agency through a court order terminating parental rights to the child, making the child a permanent ward

Adoption by a Third Party
Domestic adoption governed by provincial statute by people not related to the child that is arranged through a public or private agency; prospective parents must go through an intake interview, formal application, homestudy, and placement matching before an application is made to the court for a permanent adoption order

Confidential/Closed Adoption
Adoption where identifying information is not shared and there is no contact between the adopted child and the birth family

Customary/Custom Adoption
Adoption of Aboriginal children following traditional customary processes

Fully Disclosed/Open Adoption
Adoption where identifying information is shared and contact between the adopted child and the birth family is established

Homestudy
Process completed by a social worker where various family members are interviewed to determine the strengths, challenges, and wishes of the family to evaluate a family's adoption application

International Adoption
Intercountry adoption governed by the Hague Convention on Protection of Children and Cooperation in Respect to Intercountry Adoption, subject to provincial statutes, federal citizenship and immigration regulations, and laws and regulations from the child's country of origin

Matching
Process where an agency sets up preplacement visits between a child eligible for adoption and a family who has successfully completed an application and homestudy to determine if they connect with one another

Mediated/Semi-open Adoption
Adoption where identifying information is shared through a mediator or third party

Discussion Questions

1. Under what circumstances can a child be adopted without parental consent? What are the risks and benefits of dispensing with parental consent?
2. What is the rationale for not requiring home-studies in cases of familial adoption? Does this seem reasonable?
3. What are the strengths and limitations of open adoptions?
4. What might be the long- and short-term consequences of full adoption disclosure policies?
5. What opportunities and challenges are presented by custom adoptions?
6. Should additional publically funded services be offered for international adoptions and if so what types of services should be available?

Relevant Legislation

Federal

Citizenship Act, R.S. 1985, c. C-29
　http://laws.justice.gc.ca/en/C-29/
Immigration and Refugee Protection Act, 2001, c. 27
　http://www.irb-cisr.gc.ca/en/about/publications/irpa/index_e.htm
Indian Act, R.S. 1985, c. I-5
　http://laws.justice.gc.ca/en/I-5/

Alberta

Adult Adoption Act, S.A. 1994, c. A-23
　http://www.canlii.org/ab/laws/sta/a-4/20080715/whole.htm
Change of Name Act, S.A. 2000, c. C-7
　http://www.canlii.org/en/ab/laws/stat/rsa-2000-c-c-7/latest/rsa-2000-c-c-7.html
Child, Youth and Family Enhancement Act, S.A. 2000, c. C-12
　http://www.canlii.org/en/ab/laws/stat/rsa-2000-c-c-12/latest/rsa-2000-c-c-12.html

British Columbia

Adoption Act, S.B.C. 1996, c. 5
　http://www.qp.gov.bc.ca/statreg/stat/A/96005_01.htm
Child, Family and Community Service Act, S.B.C. 1980, c. 11
　http://www.qp.gov.bc.ca/statreg/stat/C/96046_01.htm

Name Act, S.B.C. 1996, c. 328
　http://www.qp.gov.bc.ca/statreg/stat/N/96328_01.htm
Vital Statistics Act, S.B.C. 1996, c. 479
　http://www.qp.gov.bc.ca/statreg/stat/V/96479_01.htm

Manitoba

Adoption Act, S.M. 1997, c. 47
　http://web2.gov.mb.ca/laws/statutes/ccsm/a002e.php?ccsm=a2
Change of Name Act, S.M. 1987, c. C50
　http://web2.gov.mb.ca/laws/statutes/ccsm/c050e.php
Child and Family Services Act, 1985, c. C80
　http://web2.gov.mb.ca/laws/statutes/ccsm/c080e.php
Intercountry Adoption (Hague Convention) Act, S.M. 1995, c. 22
　http://web2.gov.mb.ca/laws/statutes/ccsm/a003e.php

New Brunswick

Adoptive Applicant Regulation-Family Services Act, N.B. Reg. 85-14, ss. 1–10
　http://www.canlii.org/nb/laws/regu/1985r.14/20080715/whole.html
Change of Name Act, N.B. 1987, c. C-2.001
　http://www.gnb.ca/0062/acts/acts/c-02-001.htm
Family Services Act, N.B. 1980, c. F-2.2
　http://www.canlii.org/nb/laws/sta/f-2.2/20080715/whole.html

Intercounty Adoption Act, N.B. 1996, c. I-12.01
http://www.canlii.org/nb/laws/sta/i-12.01/
20080715/whole.html

Newfoundland

Adoption Act, S.N.L. 1999, c. A-2.1
http://www.canlii.org/nl/laws/sta/a-2.1/2008
0715/whole.html

Change of Name Act, S.N.L. 1990, c. C-8
http://www.assembly.nl.ca/legislation/sr/statutes/
c08.htm

Child, Youth and Family Services Act, S.N.L 1998,
c. C-12.1
http://www.assembly.nl.ca/legislation/sr/table
statutes/tableofpublicstatutes_c12-1.htm

Nova Scotia

Adoption Information Act, S.N.S. 1996, c. 3
http://www.canlii.org/ns/laws/sta/1996c.3/2008
0717/whole.html

Change of Name Act, N.S. 1989, c. 66
http://www.gov.ns.ca/legislature/legc/index.htm

Child and Family Services Act, N.S. 1996, c. 10
http://www.canlii.org/ns/laws/sta/1990c.5/2008
0717/whole.html

Guardianship Act, N.S. 2002, c. 30
http://www.gov.ns.ca/legislature/legc/index.htm

Intercountry Adoption Act. N. S. 1998, c. 29
http://www.e-laws.gov.on.ca/html/statutes/
english/elaws_statutes_98i29_e.htm

Ontario

Access to Adoption Records Act (Vital Statistics
Statute Law Amendment), S.O. 2008, C.5
http://www.ontla.on.ca/bills/bills-files/39_
Parliament/Session1/b012ra.pdf

Change of Name Act, S.O. 1990, c. C7
http://www.e-laws.gov.on.ca/html/statutes/
english/elaws_statutes_90c07_e.htm

Child and Family Services Act, S.O. 1990, c. C.11
http://www.e-laws.gov.on.ca/html/statutes/
english/elaws_statutes_90c11_e.htm

Intercounty Adoption (Hague Convention) Act,
1998, S.O. 1998, c. 29
http://www.e-laws.gov.on.ca/html/statutes/
english/elaws_statutes_98i29_e.htm

Prince Edward Island

Adoption Act, S.P.E.I. 1992, c. 1
http://www.canlii.org/pe/laws/sta/a-4.1/2008
0715/whole.html

Change of Name Act, S.P.E.I. 1988, c. C-3.1
http://www.gov.pe.ca/law/statutes/pdf/c-03_1.pdf

Child Status Act, S.P.E.I. 1988, c. C-6
http://www.gov.pe.ca/law/statutes/pdf/c-06.pdf

Child Protection Act, S.P.E.I. 2003 c. C-51
http://www.gov.pe.ca/law/statutes/pdf/c-05_1.pdf

Intercounty Adoption (Hague Convention) Act,
P.E.I. 1994, c. 28
http://www.canlii.org/pe/laws/sta/i-4.1/
20080715/whole.html

Quebec

Adoption Act, S.Q. c. A-7
http://www.canlii.com/qc/laws/sta/a-7/index.
html

Civil Code of Québec
http://www.canlii.org/qc/laws/sta/ccq/index.
html

Order respecting the certification of intercountry
adoption bodies, R.Q. c. P-34.1, r.0.03
http://www.canlii.org/qc/laws/regu/p-34.1r.0.03/
20080715/whole.html

Youth Protection Act, R.S.Q. c. P-34.1
http://www.canlii.org/qc/laws/sta/p-34.1/2008
0715/whole.html

Saskatchewan

Adoption Act, S.S. 1998, c. A-5.2
http://www.canlii.org/sk/laws/sta/a-5.2/2008
0715/whole.html

Change of Name Act, 1995 S.S. 1995, c. C-6.1
http://www.qp.gov.sk.ca/documents/English/
Statutes/Statutes/C6-1.pdf

Child and Family Services Act, S.S. 1989–90,
c. C-7.2
http://www.qp.gov.sk.ca/documents/english/
statutes/statutes/C7-2.PDF

International Adoption (Hague Convention) Implementation Act, S.S. 1995, c. I-D.10.01
http://www.canlii.org/sk/laws/sta/i-10.01/2008
0715/whole.html

Northwest Territories and Nunavut

Aboriginal Custom Adoption Recognition Act,
S.N.W.T. 1994, c.26
http://www.justice.gov.nt.ca/PDF/ACTS/
Aboriginal_Custom_Adopt_Recog.pdf

Adoption Act, S.N.W.T. 1998, c. 9
http://www.justice.gov.nt.ca/PDF/ACTS/
Adoption.pdf

Change of Name Act, S.N.W.T. 2007, c.12
http://www.justice.gov.nt.ca/pdf/ACTS/Change_
of_Name.pdf

Child and Family Services Act, S.N.W.T. 1997, c. 13
http://www.justice.gov.nt.ca/PDF/ACTS/Child_
&_Family_Services.pdf

Children's Law Act, S.N.W.T. 1997, c. 14
http://www.justice.gov.nt.ca/PDF/ACTS/
Childrens_Law.pdf

Intercountry Adoption (Hague Convention) Act,
S.N.W.T. 1998, c. 19
http://www.canlii.org/nt/laws/sta/1998c.19/
20080715/whole.html

Yukon

Children's Act, R.S.Y. 2002, c. 31
http://www.canlii.org/yk/laws/sta/31/20060728/
whole.html

Change of Name Act, R.S.Y. 1988, c. 51
http://www.gov.yk.ca/legislation/regs/oic1988_
051.pdf

Intercountry Adoption (Hague Convention) Act,
R.S.Y. 2002, c. 121
http://www.canlii.org/yk/laws/sta/121/2006
0728/whole.html

References

Adoption Council of Canada (2003), 'Yellowhead Tribal Services Pioneering Adoption Program Keeps Native Children on Reserve' (accessed at http://www.adoption.ca/news/031001ytsa.htm).

——— (2007), 'Downward Trend Continues: Citzenship and Immigration Canada Releases Statistics for 2006' (accessed at http://www.adoption.ca/ACCArticle_2006Stats.htm).

——— (2008), 'Subsidies for Domestic Adoption' (accessed at http://www.adoption.ca/news/050415subsidy.htm).

Alberta Child and Youth Services (2008), 'International Adoption', (accessed at http://www.child.gov.ab.ca/home/606.cfm).

Baldassi, C. (2006), 'The Legal Status of Aboriginal Customary Adoption across Canada: Comparisons, Contrasts and Convergences', UBC Law Review, 39(1): 63–100.

Berge, J., Mendenhall, T., Wrobel, G., Grotevant, H., and McRoy. R. (2006), 'Adolescents' Feelings about Openness in Adoption: Implications for Adoption Agencies', Child Welfare, 85(6): 1011–40.

British Columbia Ministry of Children and Family Development (2008), 'Custom Adoption Fact Sheet', (accessed at http://www.mcf.gov.bc.ca/adoption/custom_adoption.htm).

CBC News (2007), 'Same-sex Rights: Canada Timeline', CBC News (accessed at http://www.cbc.ca/news/background/samesexrights/timeline_canada.html).

Citizenship and Immigration Canada (2003), 'International Adoptions', The Monitor (accessed at http://www.cic.gc.ca/EnGLIsh/resources/statistics/monitor/issue03/06-feature.asp).

Cohen, N., Lojkasek, M., Zadeh, S., Pugiese, M., and Kiefer, H. (2008), 'Children Adopted from China: A Prospective Study of Their Growth and Development', Journal of Child Psychology and Psychiatry, 49(4): 458–68.

Dhami, M., Mandel, D., and Sothmann, K. (2007), 'An Evaluation of Post-adoption Services', Children and Youth Services Review, 29: 162–79.

Fodden, S. (1999), Family Law (Toronto: Irwin Law).

Giesbrecht, T. (2004), 'Adoption', in N. Bala, M. Zapf, J. Williams, R.Vogl, and J. Hornick (eds), Canadian Child Welfare Law, 2nd ed. (Toronto: Thompson Educational).

Korff, L., Grotevant, H., and McRoy, R. (2006), 'Openness Arrangements and Psychological Adjustment of Adolescent Adoptees', Journal of Family Psychology, 20(3): 531–4.

Le Mare, L., Audet, K., and Kruytnik, K. (2007), 'A Longitudinal Study of Service Use in Families Adopted from Romanian Orphanages', International Journal of Behavior Development, 31(3): 242–51.

Long, G. (1875), 'Adoptio', in W. Smith (ed.), A Dictionary of Greek and Roman Antiquities (London: John Murray (accessed at http://penelope.uchicago.edu/Thayer/E/Roman/Texts/secondary/SMIGRA*/Adoptio.html).

Lovelock, K. (2000), 'Intercountry Adoption as a Migratory Practice: A Comparative Analysis of Intercountry Adoption and Immigration Policy and Practice in the United States, Canada and New Zealand in the Post-WW II Period', International Migration Review, 34(3): 907–49.

Manitoba Family Services and Housing, (2008), 'Adoption of a Permanent Ward' (accessed at http://www.gov.mb.ca/fs/childfam/adopt_wards.html).

McNeil, K. (1996), 'Aboriginal Governments and the Canadian Charter of Rights and Freedoms', Osgoode Hall Law Journal, 34(1): 61–99.

Miall, C. and March, K. (2005a), 'Open Adoption as a Family Form: Community Assessments and Social Supports', *Journal of Family Issues*, 26(3): 380–410.

———— (2005b), 'Social Support for Changes in Adoption Practice: Gay Adoption, Open Adoption, Birth Reunions and Release of Confidential Identifying Information', *Families in Society*, 86(1): 83–113.

New Brunswick Department of Social Development (2008), 'Subsidized Adoption Program' (accessed at http://www.gnb.ca/0017/adoption/subsidized-e.asp).

New Brunswick (Ministry of Health and Community Services) v. L.(M.), [1998] 2 S.C.R. 534.

Nova Scotia Community Services (2008), 'Adoption Disclosure' (accessed at http://www.gov.ns.ca/coms/families/adoption/AdoptionDisclosure.html).

Ontario Ministry of Community and Social Services (2008), 'Frequently Asked Questions about Searching for Adoption Records in Ontario' (accessed at http://www.mcss.gov.on.ca/mcss/english/pillars/community/questions/adoption/about_adopt_disclose_sys.htm).

Racine v. Woods, [1983] 2 S.C.R. 173 at 174.

Re Tagornak Adoption Petition, [1984] 1 C.N.L.R. 185 (N.W.T.S.C.).

Scarth, S. (2003), 'Time for Straight Talk About Adoption': A Message from the President of the Adoption Council of Canada (accessed at http://www.adoption.ca/news/050101edad0308.htm).

Southern Manitoba First Nations Repatriation Program, (SMFNRP) (2009), 'Reuniting First Nations Adoptees and Birth Families' (accessed at http://www.wrcfs.org/repat/index.html).

Speirs, C., Duder, S., Grove, J., and Sullivan, R. (2003), 'Adoptable but Still in Limbo: The Forgotten Children in Canada', *Child and Youth Forum*, 32(2): 75–88.

Strong-Boag, V. (2005), 'Interrupted Relations: The Adoption of Children in Twentieth-Century British Columbia', *BC Studies*, 144: 5–30.

Wolfgram, S. (2008), 'Openness in Adoption: What We Know So Far – A Critical Review of the Literature', *Social Work*, 53(2): 133–42.

CHAPTER SIX

The Law of Consent and Capacity in Health Care

OBJECTIVES

- To outline how consent is obtained
- To discuss requirements for valid consent
- To highlight exceptions to the consent requirement
- To consider substitutes to individual consent
- To introduce common health care issues involving questions of consent
- To discuss mechanisms for dealing with disputes on capacity and consent

CASE EXAMPLE

Joseph Smith is a 20-year-old man who is a comatose patient in the intensive care unit of an urban general hospital. Two weeks ago Joe attempted suicide by overdosing on Tylenol. He sustained severe liver damage and physicians told his family that if he was to regain consciousness, he would require a liver transplant to survive. He has been surviving solely on life support for two weeks now and medical staff have determined that his brain activity indicates that he is clinically dead. They have approached his family for permission to remove the life-support apparatus and to request that they donate Joe's organs and tissue for transplant.

Joe was conceived when his parents were still in high school, after which they hastily married. The marriage, however, lasted only a few months and Joe's custody was awarded to his father because there were mental health concerns regarding his mother. Nevertheless, Joe's mother continued to have liberal access. Mr Smith raised his son with the help of his parents and was a devoted father. However, at 14 Joe felt displaced after Mr Smith remarried and had two more children; he began a course of truancy, drug use, and running away. This culminated in his overdose. Mr Smith remains Joe's primary support; however, his mother has also been involved in his life. The parents are unable to agree on a course of action.

- Who makes decisions regarding Joe's medical care if Joe is unable to consent or provide direction?
- Who has the right to decide whether Joe's life-prolonging treatment should be withdrawn?
- Who can make decisions about donating Joe's organs?
- How much information can be shared with Joe's family members about Joe's condition?
- If Joe continued to have financial resources and obligations, who would take responsibility for these matters?

Consent to Medical Treatment

It is enshrined in Canadian law and in the ethical guidelines of each health discipline that before a practitioner can provide health care for a person, she or he must receive the authorization of that person. Individuals generally have the right to consent to or refuse treatment. This principle has been enunciated by the Supreme Court of Canada as follows:

> every patient has a right to bodily integrity. This encompasses the right to determine what medical procedures will be accepted and the extent to which they will be accepted. Everyone has the right to decide what is to be done with one's own body. This includes the right to be free from medical treatment to which the individual does not consent. This concept of individual autonomy is fundamental to the common law (*Ciarlariello v. Schacter* (1993) 2 SCR 119 at 135).

Thus, the provision of health care requires consent. This begs the question, how is consent obtained?

How Is Consent Obtained?

There are two primary forms of consent: express and implied. Express consent is unequivocal and does not require any inference, for example, by the patient stating, 'I would like you to remove this wart from my finger.' It may be oral or in writing. In contrast, implied consent is derived when consent can be implied from the action or inaction of an individual. For example, consent for obtaining a blood sample is implied by the action of rolling up one's sleeve and presenting one's arm (Etchells et al., 1996).

When Will the Consent Obtained Be Valid?

For consent to be valid, the practitioner must ensure that the following elements have been satisfied.

The Person Must Have the Capacity to Consent

In order to have the capacity to consent, people must be able to understand information that is provided to them and be able to apply that information to their specific situation. The Ontario Health Care Consent Act (1996), for instance, states that a person is capable of consenting to treatment if 'the person is able to understand the information that is relevant to making a decision about the treatment . . . and able to appreciate the reasonably foreseeable consequences of a decision or lack of decision' (section 4(1)).

Capacity is not viewed as a blanket status—it is specific to a particular treatment and particular time frame. A person may be incapable of consenting to some treatments but able to consent to others. For example, a person may be able to consent to a procedure such as blood work but not to cardiac surgery (Nelson, 2002). In addition, consent is fluid. A person may be able to consent to a particular procedure at one time but not able to consent to the same procedure at another time.

There is considerable variation between provincial frameworks on minors' medical treatment decisions (Ferguson, 2004) (see Table 6.1). There are three legal doctrines applicable to minors' rights to participate in and make health care decisions and the nature of each of these doctrines varies according to provincial legislation and case law. First, when a minor is to receive a medical treatment, health care providers are guided by the provincial health care and consent legislation. There is considerable difference between provincial legislation with some provinces, such as British Columbia, using a 'best interests' model (for example, treatment is in the best interest of the minor), others, such as Ontario and Prince Edward Island, using capacity-based models (for example, whether the minor is capable of understanding and appreciating the nature and consequences of the specified treatment or procedure), and yet others, such as New Brunswick, adopting age based presumptions of entitlement to make medical treatment decisions (for example, minors who are 16 or older are entitled to consent to and refuse treatment as if they have reached the age of majority). Second, while early case law turned on the 'emancipated minor rule' (for example, a minor is taking care of his or her own needs as evidenced by such factors as having a job or being married), the dominant common-law framework has become the 'mature minor' doctrine. Maturity focuses on the intellectual and emotional development of the minor. When maturation sufficiently allows the young person to appreciate the risks and benefits of treatment, both immediate and long-term, the mature minor rule is applied (Downie, Caulfield, and Flood, 2002; Sneiderman, Irvine, and Osbourne, 2003). The applicability of the mature minor doctrine depends on the legislative framework of each province. For example, in Alberta the courts have held that the common-law rule has been superseded by child welfare legislation. In the case of *B.H. v. Alberta* (2002), a 16 year old refused to consent to blood transfusions to treat her leukemia. The court found that although she was a mature minor and her opinions must be considered, they did not necessarily need to be followed, and therefore a treatment order was issued. Lastly, child protection provisions may impact whether a minor receives medical treatment. The intersection of the child welfare legislation with consent legislation and the 'mature minor' doctrine has been unclear although there are strong arguments that when a minor is entitled to make decisions under consent legislation or found to be 'mature' at common law there is no legitimate role for child welfare provisions that are designed to protect minors from parental neglect. Recently, the Supreme Court of Canada looked at the interplay between a minor's right to autonomous decision-making and the responsibility of the state to protect children from harm. In *A.C. v. Manitoba (Director of Child and Family Services)* (2009), A.C. was almost 15 years old when she was admitted to the hospital for bleeding due to Crohn's disease. She was a Jehovah's Witness and refused a blood transfusion. As a result, the Manitoba Director of Child and Family Services apprehended her as a child in need of protection and the transfusion was administered

on the basis of the court's right under the child protection legislation to order medical treatment in the best interests of children under 16 years of age. A.C. argued that mature minors who have the capacity to make their own decisions should have a right to self-determination in health care. A.C. herself was not successful in demonstrating that her rights had been violated. However, the Supreme Court in its majority decision indicated that the best interests standard must operate on a sliding scale of scrutiny with the views of the child becoming more persuasive as the child achieves the intelligence and awareness needed to understand his or her interests fully. Justice Abella went on to say, '[I]n some cases, courts will inevitably be so convinced of a child's maturity that the principles of welfare and autonomy will collapse altogether and the child's wishes will become the controlling factor' (para. 87). The court outlined many factors to be considered, including the nature, purpose, and utility of the recommended medical treatment and its risks and benefits; the adolescent's intellectual capacity and the degree of sophistication to understand the information relevant to making the decision and appreciating the potential consequences; the stability of the adolescent's views and whether they are a true reflection of his or her core values and beliefs; the potential impact of the adolescent's lifestyle, family relationships, and broader social affiliations on his or her ability to exercise independent judgment; and the existence of any emotional or psychiatric vulnerabilities.

The determination of when a child has the capacity to consent is complex. Therefore, capacity evaluations should be conducted when minors are faced with treatment decisions. Despite the legal rules and precedent-setting cases regarding a minor's capacity to consent, there is considerable variability in practice, with some health care facilities placing emphasis on the rights of the mature minor and others insisting on parental involvement (Rozovsky, 2003). Even where minors have the capacity to consent, there are often concerns that children's wishes are not respected. A British study of a child and adolescent mental health unit,

Table 6.1   Health Care Legislation

Province/ Territory	Consent and Advance Directives Legislation	Power of Attorney for Property Legislation	Privacy Legislation	Organ Donation Legislation	Organ Donor Registration
British Columbia	The Health Care (Consent) and Care Facility (Admission) Act, R.S.B.C. 1996 Representation Agreement Act, R.S.B.C. 1996 Adult Guardianship Act, R.S.B.C. 1996	Power of Attorney Act, R.S.B.C. 1996 Patients Property Act, R.S.B.C. 1996 Public Guardian and Trustee Act, R.S.B.C. 1996	Personal Information Protection Act, R.S.B.C. 2003 Freedom of Information and Protection of Privacy Act, R.S.B.C. 1996	Human Tissue Gift Act, R.S.B.C. 1996	Register with Organ Donor Registry; registration available online or in many retail outlets or Driver Service Centres
Alberta	Personal Directives Act, R.S.A. 2000 Dependent Adults Act, R.S.A. 2000	Powers of Attorney Act, S.A. 1991	Health Information Act, R.S.A. 2000	Human Tissue Gift Act, R.S.A. 2000	Sign an organ donor card or the back of the Alberta Health Card; no official registry
Saskatchewan	Health Care Directives and Substitute Health Care Decision Makers Act, S.S. 1997	Powers of Attorney Act, S.S. 2002	Health Information Protection Act, S.S. 1999	Human Tissue Gift Act, R.S.S. 1978	Health cards are issued with an Organ and Tissue Donor sticker
Manitoba	Health Care Directives Act, C.C.S.M. 1998 Vulnerable Persons Living with a Mental Disability Act, S.M. 1993	The Powers of Attorney Act, C.C.S.M. 1996	Personal Health Information Act, C.C.S.M. 1997	Human Tissue Gift Act, C.C.S.M. 1987	Sign an organ donor card
Ontario	The Health Care Consent Act, S.O. 1996 Substitute Decisions Act, S.O. 1992	The Health Care Consent Act, S.O. 1996 Substitute Decisions Act, S.O. 1992	Personal Health Information Protection Act, S.O. 2004	Trillium Gift of Life Network Act, S.O. 1998	Fill in the Organ Donor Consent form, send it to your local Ministry of Health office, registered on health card, or sign and carry a donor card
Quebec	Civil Code of Québec S.Q. 1991 Public Curator Act, S.Q. 1989	Mandate Given in Anticipation of Incapacity	Act Respecting Access to Documents held by Public Bodies, S.Q. 1982 An Act Respecting the Protection of Personal Information In the Private Sector R.S.Q. 1993	Act Respecting Medical Laboratories, organ, tissue, gamete and embryo conservation, and the disposal of human bodies, R.S.Q. c. L-0.2	Sticker to indicate consent is distributed with all new Quebec Health Cards or can be obtained at hospitals, drug stores, or clinics; the sticker is placed on the Health Card

Table 6.1   Health Care Legislation (Continued)

Province/Territory	Consent and Advance Directives Legislation	Power of Attorney for Property Legislation	Privacy Legislation	Organ Donation Legislation	Organ Donor Registration
New Brunswick	Infirm Persons Act, R.S.N.B. 2000	Property Act, R.S.N.B. 1973	Protection of Personal Information Act, S.N.B. 1998	Human Tissue Gift Act, R.S.N.B. 1973	Indicate intention on Medicare renewal form; Medicare card will display wishes
Nova Scotia	Hospitals Act, R.S.N.S. 1989; Incompetent Persons Act, R.S.N.S. 1989; Medical Consent Act, R.S.N.S. 1989	Powers of Attorney Act, R.S.N.S. 1989	Freedom of Information and Protection of Privacy Act, S.N.S. 1993	Human Tissue Gift Act, R.S.N.S. 1989	Fill in the donor registration form with Nova Scotia Health Card renewal; Organ Donor Registry maintained by Dept. of Health
Prince Edward Island	Consent to Treatment and Health Care Directives Act, S.P.E.I. 1996	Powers of Attorney Act, R.S.P.E.I. 1988	Freedom of Information and Protection of Privacy Act, R.S.P.E.I. 1998	Human Tissues Donation Act, R.S.P., P.E.I. 1988	Affix a red sticker on PEI Health Card and by having a red heart engraved on driver's licence at renewal time
Newfoundland and Labrador	Advance Health Care Directives Act, R.S.N.L. 1995	Enduring Powers of Attorney Act, R.S.N.L. 1990	Access to Information and Protection of Privacy Act, S.N.L. 2002	Human Tissue Act, R.S.N.L. 1990	Sign an organ donor card or indicate consent on driver's licence
Northwest Territories and Nunavut		Powers of Attorney Act, S.N.W.T. 2001; Guardianship and Trustee Act, S.N.W.T. 1994	Access to Information and Protection of Privacy Regulations, S.N.W.T. 1994	Human Tissue Act, R.S.N.W.T. 1988	Residents of the Northwest Territories or Nunavut can register with H.O.P.E.; however, hospitals in Northwest Territories are unable to take organs
Yukon	Health Act, S.Y. 1989–90	Enduring Power of Attorney Act, S.Y. 1995	Access to Information and Protection of Privacy Act, S.Y. 2003	Human Tissue Gift Act, 2002	Donor registration cards are available at doctors' offices and health clinics; can also register with the Yukon Organ Donor Registry and the Yukon Health Care Insurance card will list you as a donor

for instance, revealed that in 4 of 42 consecutive cases children were unaware of their appointments and 14 of 42 came unwillingly (Paul, Foreman, and Kent, 2000).

Social workers are frequently in situations where they are working with both the child and the family and there is an obligation to ensure that children are informed about what is going to happen to them, that they have an opportunity to express their views, and that parents consider these views when making a decision regarding treatment and consent. The Canadian Association of Social Workers Guidelines on Informed Consent and Confidentiality (2007) states: 'Social workers who have children as clients must determine the child's capacity to consent and explain to the child (where appropriate), and to the child's parents/guardians (where appropriate), the nature of the social worker's relationship to the child and others involved in the child's care.' Where children do not have the legal capacity to provide consent, the practice of obtaining assent is becoming increasingly common, whereby children are asked to express their agreement with the treatment plan verbally or in writing. Although this is not legally binding, it does provide a formal way of ensuring that the child feels respected and that her or his views are clearly documented.

Whether an individual has the capacity to consent is to be evaluated by the practitioner who proposes the treatment. In some jurisdictions, persons may challenge capacity evaluations before consent and capacity boards (which will be discussed later in this chapter); in this case, formal capacity assessments may be completed by specially trained professionals who may include, depending on the circumstances, psychologists, psychiatrists, or social workers. Where an individual does not have the capacity to consent, substitutes to consent should be sought (discussed later in this chapter).

Consent Must Be Informed

Consent or refusal to consent must be offered by an individual based on information provided by the practitioner about the benefits and potential risks of the course of treatment. Clearly, in any treatment decision, there are a vast array of possible outcomes, some highly unlikely; disclosure of each and every one could result in information overload and impair the ability to make a decision. In *Reibl v. Hughes* (1980), the Supreme Court of Canada stated that practitioners have a duty to disclose 'all material risks'. In addition, the legislation in some jurisdictions defines specific information required to be disclosed, including the nature of the treatment, the expected benefits, the material risks, the material side effects, alternative courses of action, and the likely consequences of not having the treatment. Further, details of who will be participating in the procedure, including student interns, should also be provided (Dykeman, 2000).

However, in some situations an individual may be harmed by receiving the full scope and depth of disclosure as outlined above. In *Reibl v. Hughes* (1980) the Supreme Court stated: '[I]t may be the case that a particular patient may, because of emotional factors, be unable to cope with facts relevant to recommended surgery or treatment and the doctor may, in such a case, be justified in withholding or generalizing information as to which he would otherwise be required to be more specific' (p. 13). Therefore, if a health care provider believes the person's mental health would be compromised or emotional state would be significantly affected, the professional may limit the information provided to the patient. Dickens (2002) cautions, however, that this does not imply that the obligation to provide information is erased. Health care professionals may need to consider alternative means to ensure that information is conveyed to the patient in a manner that is less distressing.

Consent Must Be Voluntary

An individual's decision to consent or refuse consent must be free of coercion or undue influence. Such influence may include financial incentives, unnecessary fear, or influence created by the therapeutic alliance between the patient and the health care provider (Regehr and Antle, 1997). Information must not be presented in a manner that induces unnecessary fear in the patient—for instance, 'You must do this or die.' In addition, it is important that practitioners be keenly aware that the power of the therapeutic alliance itself can in some circumstances induce a person to suspend critical judgment in an effort to please the practitioner. For instance, if a surgeon is seeking consent for a procedure, the patient may feel that refusing consent will displease their doctor and indicate that he or she does not trust the doctor's skill. If a social worker is seeking consent, the person may feel that refusal may result in a withdrawal of social support.

The question of whether consent is voluntary often arises in cases involving minors. Even if a minor is found to have the capacity to consent, he or she must also be free to decide voluntarily; this may not be the case if the child is heavily influenced by his or her parents. For example, T.D. was a 13-year-old Saskatchewan boy with cancer whose parents had refused treatment on his behalf. The court determined that T.D. was a child in need of protection and granted authority to consent to the minister for social services. A petition was then made to the courts to declare T.D. a mature minor so that he could refuse treatment on his own accord. The courts, however, determined that he was highly influenced by his family and did not allow him to consent as a mature minor (*Re: T.T.D.*, 1999—also known as *Re: Dueck*, 1999).

When Must Consent Be Obtained?

Consent to treatment must be obtained before the treatment begins. Individuals cannot be treated without their consent. Further, once consent is provided it can be withdrawn. As stated by the Supreme Court of Canada: 'an individual's right to determine what medical procedures will be accepted must include the right to stop the procedure' (*Ciarlariello v. Schacter*, 1993). If consent has been withdrawn, medical staff are obligated to stop the procedure, although they must ensure that they do so at a stage where the patient's safety is not in jeopardy.

Any treatment provided without consent may result in criminal charges of assault or civil actions of negligence or battery (the unlawful application of force to another person) for which monetary damages can be awarded (Morris, Ferguson, and Dykeman, 1999; Rozovsky, 2003). No intent of harm is necessary for a finding of battery; the lack of consent to the named intervention will be sufficient to establish the liability of the practitioner.

Are There Any Exceptions to the Consent Requirement?

Emergency Situations

The first exception to consent is in emergency situations. Treatment can be provided without consent if a person for whom the treatment is proposed is incapable of consenting and the delay in consulting with a substitute decision-maker would result in prolonged suffering or put the patient at risk of sustaining serious bodily harm if treatment is not administered promptly. For example, in *Marshall v. Curry* (1933), a surgeon performed an unauthorized procedure during surgery and the court found 'where a emergency which could not have been anticipated arises . . . it is the surgeon's duty to act in order to save the life or preserve the health of the patient, and . . . in the honest execution of that duty he should not be exposed to legal liability.' However, it is critical that the procedure is indeed an emergency and that waiting until the patient is capable of consenting to a follow-up procedure is not an option. Courts have found in favour of the plaintiff when medical staff have extended the notion of emergency too broadly (*Murray v. McMurchy*, 1949).

If the individual has an advance directive (discussed later in this chapter), it cannot be ignored, even in an emergency. In *Malette v. Shulman* (1990), Ms Malette was severely injured in an automobile accident and was taken unconscious to the hospital where she was examined by a physician in the emergency department. The physician concluded that a blood transfusion was needed, but a nurse discovered a card in the plaintiff's purse identifying her as a Jehovah's Witness and requesting on the basis of her religious convictions that she not be given a blood transfusion under any circumstances. The physician believed that it was his professional responsibility to give his patient a transfusion and he was not satisfied that the card expressed her current view. The patient recovered and brought an action against the physician, the hospital, its executive director, and four nurses, alleging that the administration of blood constituted negligence, assault, and battery. In this case the Ontario Court of Appeal confirmed that the refusal of the blood transfusion made by the Jehovah's Witness who is capable of refusing consent should have been honoured by the treating physician in the patient's subsequent period of incapacity. It was stated that individuals have an interest in bodily security from unwanted physical interference and that the patient in this case had a right to control her own body.

Public Health Crises

Under public health legislation, medical officers of health can enter a place and conduct an examination to determine the existence of a communicable disease and can issue a certificate permitting apprehension, examination, detention, and treatment without consent (Nelson, 2002; Rozovsky, 2003). Ontario witnessed the exercise of such authority during the SARS outbreak in 2003 when hundreds of people were quarantined (Hawryluck et al., 2004).

Substitutes to Individual Consent

If valid consent cannot be obtained from an individual, it is appropriate for the practitioner to consider substitutes to individual consent.

Advance Directives

Increasingly, individuals who prepare a last will and testament are being encouraged to also complete an advance directive regarding their wishes

for care, should they at some point become incapable of consenting. Two types of directives exist. The first is an instructional directive, where a person indicates specific treatments that should or should not be administered (Sneiderman, 2002). People with serious mental illnesses may specify that they do not wish to be treated with certain types of medication. Individuals who want their care to be in accordance with their religious beliefs may specify such things as not agreeing to blood transfusions. In situations where alternative living arrangements may need to be made, specifications can be made regarding whether the person wishes to remain in the home with care or treated in a long-term-care facility (Carter, 2002).

Some jurisdictions allow for a second type of advance directive called a proxy directive, where someone designates a substitute decision-maker (in other provinces, like Ontario, substitute decision-makers may only be identified by the individual by way of power of attorney, which is discussed later). This designation supersedes the hierarchies of decision-makers prescribed in legislation. Advance directives only become operative when a person is deemed incapable of granting consent. The first province to enact legislation governing health care directives was Manitoba in 1992. Most provinces have now followed suit, although some restrict what an individual can direct. For example, Alberta's Personal Directives Act states in its recitals that directives cannot include instructions relating to aided suicide or euthanasia. Advance directives are viewed as binding by the courts.

Powers of Attorney

A power of attorney is the authority granted by one person to another to act on behalf of the grantor in making personal (or financial) decisions for the grantor. Note that a person may not act as a power of attorney for an individual if he or she is paid to provide health care, residential, social, training, or support services to that individual, unless the person is the individual's spouse, partner, or relative (Hill, 2000). The authority given may be comprehensive or may be restricted to specific acts or types of decisions. The appointed attorney acts as a fiduciary and must act in concert with the wishes and best interests of the grantor. A person who is capable of giving a power of attorney may revoke it so long as he or she is still mentally capable (Hiltz and Szigeti, 2004). Once the grantor has lost capacity, the power of attorney may be terminated if the attorney appointed resigns or by application to the court (Fowler, 2004).

The primary motivation for providing an advance directive or a power of attorney is to convey instructions about medical procedures or to give individuals, especially those who are not substitute decision-makers (see the section that follows), the authority to make decisions on behalf of the grantor when the grantor is no longer capable. These are useful tools for social workers to empower patients to make proactive decisions and maintain some sense of control in situations that often engender feelings of helplessness.

Substitute Decision-Makers

Where a patient is not capable of consenting to or refusing consent to treatment, a substitute decision-maker must be identified to make decisions on the incapable patient's behalf. The process for obtaining a substitute decision-maker and for deciding who is legally able to act as a substitute decision-maker is defined by legislation in most provinces. For instance, the Health Care (Consent) and Care Facility (Admission) Act of British Columbia sets out a list of substitute decision-makers, and health care providers must select the first one who qualifies. The Ontario Health Care Consent Act outlines a hierarchical list of those who may act as substitute decision-makers as follows: a statutory or court-ordered guardian, power of attorney for personal care, or representative appointed by the Consent and Capacity Board to make personal care decisions. If no legally appointed substitute decision-makers exist, the practitioner must look to the spouse or partner, child or parent, non-custodial parent with access rights, siblings, or any other relative. If none of these persons is available, the Office of the Public

Guardian and Trustee will make the decision to give or withhold consent for treatment.

The responsibility placed on those who are substitute decision-makers is to make consent decisions that are in accordance with the expressed wishes of a patient when he or she is capable, and if no such wishes have been expressed to make the decision that is in the patient's best interest (Rozovsky, 2003). Where decisions are not being made by the substitute decision-maker in accordance with the patient's best interest, applications may, depending on the jurisdiction, be made to a consent and capacity board, panel, or the courts to intervene. For example, when children do not have the capacity to consent, the role of providing consent passes to the parent (Gilmour, 2002). In most situations, parents act in the best interest of their children and the courts are reluctant to interfere with parental authority. But there are some instances where a parent's refusal of consent is not in the best interests of the child and the court must intervene. In B.(R.) v. the Children's Aid Society of Toronto (1995), a Jehovah's Witness couple refused care for their critically ill premature infant. The court decided that the refusal of care was not in the best interests of the child and the parents' right to freedom of religion did not supersede the court's responsibility to intervene when a child's welfare was in jeopardy. As a result, the responsibility to consent was awarded to the Children's Aid Society. Similarly, in New Brunswick v. R.B. and S.B. (1990), the court held that parents may not refuse treatment on the basis of the mental or physical disability of the child; so long as the treatment itself is not cruel, treatment refusal cannot be an excuse to end a life limited by such factors.

Common Health Care Issues Involving Questions of Consent

End-of-life Decision-making

No decisions in health care are as charged with emotion and controversy as those relating to ending a life. Despite policy shifts towards increased community care of individuals with health problems, most Canadians die in hospital. In a study reviewing 1997 registry data, Heyland and colleagues (2000) revealed that 73 per cent of all Canadians dying in that year died in hospital. This reflects a gradual increase from 45 per cent of deaths occurring in hospitals in 1950. These statistics parallel those in the United States (Sager et al., 1989; Lynn et al., 1997), England (Seals and Cartwright, 1994), and Australia (Hunt et al., 1991).

Deaths, particularly those in the intensive care unit (ICU) are often relatively sudden and are frequently the result of a decision to withdraw life support. A Halifax study (Hall and Rocker, 2000) reviewing deaths of 174 patients in an ICU over a one-year period revealed that 79.3 per cent were the result of the removal of life supports. This means that families today are increasingly faced with the decision to end life in highly technical and complex environments (Kjerulf et al., 2005).

Sneiderman (2002) suggests that end-of-life decision-making falls into three categories: 1) 'letting die' cases that involve either withdrawal of life supports such as respirators or withholding of life-prolonging measures such as antibiotic treatments for pneumonia; 2) cases that involve the provision of potentially life-shortening pain medication, for example, narcotics that may halt respiration; 3) euthanasia or 'mercy killings' and assisted suicide.

Withholding and Withdrawal of Life-Prolonging Treatment

The most straightforward end-of-life decision under the law is the refusal of treatment by a mentally competent person. Canadian law is clear that treatment cannot be administered without consent. Further, the Law Reform Commission of Canada (1982) stated that the Criminal Code should 'clearly and formally recognize the competent patient's absolute right to refuse medical treatment or demand its cessation' (p. 57). Thus, if a competent adult voluntarily makes the decision to refuse to have or to continue potentially life-sustaining treatment, this must be respected

by health care providers (Dalhousie Health Law Institute End of Life (EOL) Project, 2003). In respect of the decision to withdraw treatment that would prolong life, the landmark case is that of Nancy B. Nancy B. was a 25-year-old woman who suffered from Guillain-Barré Syndrome and required a respirator to sustain her life, with no hope of recovery. She wished to have the ventilator removed but was paralyzed and unable to do so herself. Under the Civil Code of Québec it was clear that Nancy B. could refuse treatment; however, there was a concern that if medical staff removed the ventilator, they could be charged under the Criminal Code. The courts upheld Ms B.'s right to refuse treatment and determined that the physician would not be assisting suicide if removal of treatment resulted in a natural death (*Nancy B. v. Hôtel-Dieu de Québec*, 1992).

If a patient is not capable of consenting but has left an advance directive, health care providers are similarly required to act according to the patient's wishes. This principle was upheld by the courts in Ontario in the previously discussed case of *Malette v. Shulman* (1990), where the doctor disregarded an advanced directive and administered a blood transfusion. From this case it is clear that health care providers cannot ignore advance directives to withhold treatment even in an emergency. The principle was similarly upheld in British Columbia when a 68-year-old woman who was incarcerated for arson went on a hunger strike and advised that she did not wish force-feeding should she become unconscious. The court acknowledged that Ms Astaforoff was attempting suicide. However, it stated that while it was a crime to counsel or assist with a suicide, and while there was a duty to use reasonable care in preventing suicide, it was not a crime to fail to prevent it. Thus the court determined that there was no obligation on the province to force-feed Ms Astaforoff to prevent her death (*British Columbia v. Astaforoff*, 1983).

One of the more common directives that practitioners encounter is the Do Not Resuscitate (DNR) order under which medical and health care staff are instructed not to perform cardiopulmonary resuscitation should the patient's heartbeat and breathing stop (Rozovsky, 2003). In situations where an adult is incapable of consenting and does not have an advance directive, substitute decision-makers and family members are consulted by medical staff about the withholding or withdrawal of life supports and their consent or refusal to consent must be followed. However, if the practitioner feels that the decision being made is not in the best interests of the patient, the practitioner may, depending on the jurisdiction, bring an appeal before a consent and capacity board, panel, or the courts.

Consent—whether from the individual or a substitute decision-maker—is the paramount consideration in end-of-life decisions for treatment to prolong life, if that has been offered to the individual or family. Whether to offer treatment is a decision made by the medical team at the outset and they have the prerogative not to suggest or to withhold treatment if it is inappropriate in the circumstances.

Provision of Potentially Life-shortening Treatment

Palliative care attempts to relieve the suffering and improve the quality of life of those dying from a terminal illness. Interventions can include pain medication, oxygen, feeding, blood products, and sedation. All palliative care measures aim to increase the patient's comfort level; however, some interventions carry the risk of hastening death (Dalhousie Health Law Institute End of Life (EOL) Project, 2003). The practice of administering palliative interventions that may shorten life is legal in Canada. Although the Supreme Court of Canada *Rodriguez* (1993) case dealt with assisted suicide, Judge Sopinka discussed palliative care, stating:

> The administration of drugs designed for pain control in dosages which the physician knows will hasten death constitutes active contribution to death by any standard. However, the distinction drawn here is one based upon intention—in the case of palliative care the intention is to ease pain, which has the

effect of hastening death, while in the case of assisted suicide, the intention is undeniably to cause death. . . . In my view, distinctions based upon intent are important, and in fact, form the basis of our criminal law. While factually the distinction may, at times, be difficult to draw, legally it is clear.

Thus, whether the administration of medication that shortens life constitutes palliative care or assisted suicide depends on whether the physician sought to relieve suffering at the risk of death or sought to cause death.

Assisted Suicide

Assisted suicide occurs when the patient is the agent of his or her death but death results from the assistance supplied by another person. In the United States, the highly publicized case of Jack Kevorkian, a retired pathologist who was convicted and sentenced in 1999 for the assisted suicide by injection of a man suffering from ALS, brought attention to the issue. Dr Kevorkian received a sentence of 10 to 25 years for the second-degree murder of Thomas Youk and for using a 'controlled substance' (lethal drug) he was sentenced to 3 to 7 years (Humphrey, 2003). In Canada, suicide and attempted suicide are not illegal, but assisting with a suicide is a criminal offence. Section 241 of the Criminal Code provides that everyone who: 1) counsels a person to commit suicide; or 2) aids or abets a person to commit suicide, whether suicide ensues or not, is guilty of an indictable offence and liable to imprisonment for a term not exceeding 14 years. Individuals with life-threatening illnesses and their doctors have gone before the courts attempting to establish a constitutional right to assisted suicide (Stein, 2004).

However, despite the efforts of Sue Rodriguez to change Canadian law on this point, in 1993 the law was upheld by the Supreme Court of Canada. Ms Rodriquez was a 42-year-old woman suffering from amyotrophic lateral sclerosis (ALS, also known as Lou Gehrig's Disease). The prognosis for her type of ALS was a steady loss of physical ability, followed by death. Near the end of her life, it was anticipated that she would be conscious and aware of her situation but completely dependent upon the care of others and the support of artificial respiration, hydration, and nutrition. She commenced a court action, asking that the Criminal Code provision prohibiting assisted suicide be declared contrary to the Canadian Charter of Rights and Freedoms. She requested that a qualified physician be allowed to set up technological means by which she might end her life when she was no longer able to enjoy it, by her own hand and at the time of her choosing. This request was denied. It is uncertain whether her death in 1994 involved assisted suicide or voluntary euthanasia; however, no charges have been laid (Special Senate Committee on Euthanasia and Assisted Suicide, 1995). Similarly, the US Supreme Court has also declined the right to assisted suicide (*Vacco v. Quill*, 1997).

Euthanasia

The Special Senate Committee on Euthanasia and Assisted Suicide (1995) describes euthanasia as a deliberate act undertaken with the intention of ending the life of another person to relieve suffering of that person. Euthanasia, like assisted suicide, is prohibited by the Criminal Code. Further, consent does not provide a defence to the charge of murder, even in the case of euthanasia. Section 14 of the Code states: 'No person is entitled to consent to have death inflicted upon him, and such consent does not affect the criminal responsibility of any person by whom death may be inflicted.' Similarly, the mercy motive of euthanasia does not provide a defence against a homicide charge.

The most highly publicized case of euthanasia in Canada was that involving Robert Latimer (*R. v. Latimer*, 2001). Mr Latimer was a father who had provided care to his 12-year-old daughter Tracey who was physically and mentally disabled because of cerebral palsy. In 1992, Mr Latimer placed his daughter in the cab of his truck into which he then vented the exhaust fumes, causing her to asphyxiate. Strong public opinions were voiced from opposing groups—those who supported the right and duty of individuals to relieve the pain

and suffering of others and those who feared for the safety of other disabled children whose parents may now have the permission to end their mutual torment. Nevertheless, in January 2001 the Supreme Court of Canada unanimously upheld Mr Latimer's conviction for second-degree murder, determining that his motive 'to put her out of her pain' was not relevant.

However, although the law is emphatic that mercy killing is murder, except for the Latimer case most Canadian mercy-killing cases are resolved by the Crown accepting a guilty plea to a lesser charge or acquittal (Downie, Caulfield, and Flood, 2002). Two Canadian cases of health care professionals where murder charges did not lead to convictions are those of Scott Mataya (*R. v. Mataya*, 1992) and Dr Alberto De la Rocha (*R. v. De la Rocha*, 1993). In each case the patient was an elderly cancer patient whose death was imminent and whose pain and suffering were unremitting but who continued to live despite the removal of life supports. In each case the patient was administered potassium chloride. In both cases the professional admitted to administering the substance and pleaded to a lesser crime. The families of the patients were openly supportive of the actions of the professionals in question and did not seek conviction or sentencing. Scott Mataya, a nurse in a Toronto hospital, pleaded guilty to the offence of administering a noxious substance and was placed on probation for three years and prohibited from practising nursing. Alberto de la Rocha, an Ontario doctor, pleaded guilty to the offence of administering a noxious substance and was given a three-year suspended sentence but was allowed to continue to practise medicine. Thus, while euthanasia is not permitted by Canadian law, there is evidence of compassion within the court system, though generally after a long and involved process.

Organ Donation

In the past two decades, significant medical advances, including the use of immunosuppressive agents, improved organ preservation, and improved surgical techniques have resulted in remarkable success and survival rates for organ recipients. For the year 2000, the Canadian Organ Replacement Register reported one-year survival rates of 95 to 98 per cent for kidney recipients, 84 per cent for liver recipients, 72 to 77 per cent for lung recipients, and 83 per cent for heart recipients. Despite this, the rates of donation have not kept pace with the demand, resulting in a critical shortage of available healthy organs. Waiting lists for organs have increased at a dramatic rate, leaving many excellent candidates without the option of accessing life-saving procedures (US Scientific Registry, 1999; United Network for Organ Sharing Scientific Registry Data, 2002).

Several studies in the United States, Canada, and England have documented that the problem is not a lack of suitable donors (Stark et al., 1984; Gore, Hinds, and Rutherford, 1989; Taylor, Young, and Kneteman, 1997). For example, Wight, Cohen, Roels, and Miranda (2000) reviewed 579 medical records in 11 ICUs in Spain, the Netherlands, the UK, and Canada and found that 69 per cent of potential donors were lost due to refusal to donate and failures to identify potential donors and manage viable organs. Despite several legislative attempts in the United States to increase organ donation by requiring health care professionals to make requests of families of suitable donors, it is estimated that only 15 to 20 per cent of the potential organ pool is being realized (Vrtis and Nicely, 1993). Thus, the procurement of organs for transplantation has emerged as a pressing health care issue. In Ontario alone, there were 100 cadaveric donations between January and October of 2005. At the same time, 1,828 people were on the waiting list for donations (Gift of Life, 2005). The need to improve procedures for identifying potential donors and approaching families of those at the end of life for the purposes of procurement of organs is frequently identified by commentators (Soukup, 1991; Siminoff, 1997; Sque, Payne, and Vlachonikolis, 2000).

There are many national and provincial statutes that apply to organ and tissue donation, including Human Tissue Gift acts; Fatalities Inquiry acts; and Personal Directives acts. Legislation covering donations has now been enacted by each province following the lead of the federal government. Further, each province has a mechanism for declaring an individual's intention to donate either through donor cards, or declarations on the health card and/or driver's licence (see Table 6.1 for the organ donation legislation in each jurisdiction). While these declarations serve as an advance directive, in most provinces doctors will not go ahead with organ procurement without the family's permission, even when a donor card has been signed. Therefore, individuals signing a card are advised to speak to their families about their wishes and intentions (Health Canada, 2004).

Once an individual has been declared brain dead by two doctors who are not involved in the transplantation process, he or she is maintained on a ventilator so that organs remain viable and suitable for transplantation. If the family has agreed to organ and tissue donation, ventilator support is continued while transplant personnel seek to find the most suitable recipients. Organs and tissue are generally removed at the hospital where the donor died and transported to the transplant facility. The anonymity of both the donor and the recipient are legally protected by human tissue gift legislation, although the recipient may write anonymous letters of gratitude that are forwarded to the donor's family through the transplant program (Health Canada, 2004).

Health Information

Confidentiality is central to the provision of health and mental health services. It has been described as 'the obligation upon an organization or person to protect information that has been entrusted in its care for a specific purpose, and to ensure that information is only accessible to those authorized to have access' (COACH, 2007) Confidentiality obligations are set out in common law, legislation, and professional standards and recognize that health care professionals and health care facilities, through the course of their duties, are entrusted with sensitive client information that is collected for a specific purpose: to provide care and treatment (Frelick, 2007). There is a corresponding duty to protect the confidentiality of that information and not to share such information with third parties unless the client provides informed consent or a legal obligation exists to share such information (CASW, 2007).

Privacy refers to the right of an individual to control who has access to his or her personal health information and under what circumstances. Confidentiality and the right to privacy are articulated in the Universal Declaration of Human Rights (United Nations, 1948) and the International Covenant on Civil and Political Rights (1966).

Public-sector Privacy Legislation

In Canada, the Privacy Act was enacted in 1985, which sought to protect the privacy of individuals with respect to personal information about themselves held by federally regulated government institutions and that provide individuals with a right of access to that information. In addition, most provincial jurisdictions have public-sector privacy legislation that applies to personal information held by public bodies. Of these, British Columbia, New Brunswick, Nova Scotia, Prince Edward Island, and the Northwest Territories have dealt with personal health information in their public-sector legislation, with privacy and access provisions being extended to hospitals, certain publicly funded clinics, and health services boards (Platt, 2006). For example, British Columbia's Freedom of Information and Protection of Privacy Act applies to the governmental health sector.

Over the past number of years, there has been increasing concern about the potential extraterritorial application of US laws to the personal information of Canadians. These concerns were triggered by an application by the British Columbia Government and Service Employees Union to stop the British Columbia Ministry of Health from contracting out the administration of its public health insurance program to a private, US-linked service provider. It was claimed that the outsourcing agreement contravened the Freedom of Information and Protection of Privacy Act by making personal health information accessible to US authorities when exercising powers under the USA Patriot Act. The USA Patriot Act authorizes the Foreign Intelligence Surveillance Court, which meets in secret, to issue orders permitting the seizure of 'any tangible thing' or document. This would allow the US Federal Bureau of Investigation to obtain any records for foreign intelligence purposes or to protect against international terrorism or clandestine intelligence activities. It can require any company under US jurisdiction to hand over information in its control, including information held in Canada, with stiff penalties for any company that reveals it has been ordered to do so. In response to concerns about the USA Patriot Act, a number of amendments were made to British Columbia's Freedom of Information and Protection of Privacy Act. For example, personal information in the custody or under the control of a public body is to be 'stored only in Canada and accessed only in Canada'. Further, there is an obligation to report foreign demands for disclosure to the minister responsible for the Act, which would presumably allow the minister to intervene with US authorities in situations where a foreign court has made an order requiring access to Canadian held information.

Private-sector Privacy Legislation

Historically, outside of specified organizations that were subject to privacy legislation for information held by government institutions, most health care facilities with custody or control of health information fell outside the scope of public-sector privacy legislation. Rather, access and disclosure of health and mental health information was governed by a patchwork of statutes, primarily through mental health legislation and legislation related to health care facilities.

In 2000, the Government of Canada passed the broad-reaching Personal Information Protection and Electronic Documents Act (PIPEDA). This Act was intended to establish: '[I]n an era in which technology increasingly facilitates the circulation and exchange of information, rules to govern the collection, use and disclosure of personal information in a manner that recognizes the right of privacy of individuals with respect to their personal information and the need of organizations to collect, use or disclose personal information for purposes that a reasonable person would consider appropriate in the circumstances.' As of 1 January 2004, the Personal Information Protection and Electronic Documents Act applied to every federal or provincial organization that collects, uses, or discloses personal information in the course of commercial activities, unless the province has enacted substantially similar legislation. Commercial activities are defined as 'any particular transaction, act or conduct, or any regular course of conduct that is of a commercial character, including the selling, bartering or leasing of donor, membership or other fundraising lists'.

Unfortunately, the Personal Information Protection and Electronic Documents Act does not specifically address the issues of personal information that are unique to the provision of health services. To address this issue, Industry Canada, in consultation with health care associations and the Office of the Privacy Commissioner, released its PIPEDA Awareness Raising Tools (PARTs) Initiative for the Health Sector to provide guidance about the scope and application of this legislation (Industry Canada, 2004). Although implied consent was not specifically addressed under PIPEDA, Industry Canada embraced its use in the health care sector relative to the exchange of personal health information for health care purposes within a construct of 'circle of care'. The term 'circle of care' does not exist within PIPEDA; however, Industry Canada defined this term as including the 'individuals and activities related to the care and treatment of a patient'. Thus, it covers the health care providers who deliver care and services for the primary therapeutic benefit of the patient and it covers related activities such as laboratory work and professional or case consultations with other health care providers (Frelick and Jovellano, 2009).

Currently, four provinces (i.e., Alberta, Saskatchewan, Manitoba, and Ontario) have legislation pertaining to the privacy of health information, such as Saskatchewan's Health Information Protection Act. Each of these acts regulates how information is collected, used, retained, transferred, disclosed, accessed by those with the right of access, and finally disposed of. Ontario's Personal Health Information Protection Act, 2004 is the only provincial health privacy legislation that has been found to be substantially similar to the Personal Information Protection and Electronic Documents Act. It applies to health information custodians that collect, use, and disclose personal health information in the course of their duties, and includes health care practitioners, hospitals, psychiatric facilities, pharmacies, laboratories, nursing homes, and ambulance services. Note that social workers are not included in the definition of 'health practitioners'; however, provisions pertaining to health practitioners under the Act generally reflect the principles under common law that continue to be applicable to social workers. Personal health information under the Act includes the individual's physical or mental condition and related family health history, health care received, the health card number, blood or body-part donations, payment or eligibility for health care, and the identity of a health care provider or a substitute decision-maker for the individual. Those who collect and maintain health records are required to: 1) collect only the information required; 2) take steps to safeguard information; 3) take reasonable steps to ensure that information is accurate; 4) provide a written description of practices to protect information; 5) disclose only with the consent of the individual or as provided under legislation. Patients under this legislation must consent to the collection, use, and disclosure of their information. The Act allows for either implied consent or express consent. In implied consent, it is assumed that the patient agrees to information-sharing for the purposes of providing care and/or assisting with the provision of health care, for instance, in the sharing of information between a general practitioner and a specialist to whom the patient has been referred. Express consent is required for sharing information with third parties, such as an employer.

In addition to the consent required to collect, use, and disclose personal health information, individuals also have the right to access their own health records. In 1992, a judgment of the Supreme Court of Canada (*McInerney v. MacDonald*) established the right of clients to have access to all mental health and medical records regarding their care. Access includes not only records compiled in the treatment facility to which the request for access is directed, but also all records obtained from other facilities following the signed consent of the client. This position of the Supreme Court is now reflected in health care privacy legislation under which patients may access their own health records by making a request in writing. For example, in Ontario, the custodian of the records must reply within 30 days and if all data is not shared, generally an explanation must be given. If the patient is unsatisfied with the reason, a complaint can be made to the information and privacy commissioner. A patient may request corrections to their records and may provide a written statement of disagreement to be placed on the health record if they believe it to be erroneous or inaccurate.

If a patient is incapable of providing consent, the substitute decision-maker acting on the patient's behalf for matters related to treatment can also consent to the collection, use, or disclosure of health information. If two or more equally ranking substitute decision-makers disagree, the public guardian and trustee breaks the deadlock (Ontario Hospital Association, 2004). The substitute decision-maker similarly has the right of access to all records. In the case of patients who are minors, consent for a child may be obtained from the child if capable, or from a parent or other lawful guardian. If a minor is capable of making decisions regarding their health care, he or she is also entitled to confidentiality and control of their health information (Gilmour, 2002).

Decisions Regarding Property

A person who is incapable of providing consent to medical treatment may be equally incapable to manage their financial affairs. A power of attorney for personal care does not encompass financial matters and is entirely distinct from a power of attorney for finances. Further, the substitute decision-maker for health care does not automatically become the decision-maker for financial issues.

Ideally, a person has, while they are competent, considered that there may be times when they are unable to manage their financial affairs because they are on vacation or ill and thus has assigned a financial power of attorney. As discussed earlier in this chapter, a power of attorney is the authority given by one person to another to act on his or her behalf. The authority can be comprehensive, or relate to certain specified acts or types of decisions (Fowler, 2004). If a power of attorney has not been signed while the person is competent, upon loss of capacity, an application can be made to the court designating someone known to the patient or the public trustee takes over the financial responsibilities of the individual. Note that when a family member or friend seeks authority to manage the finances for a person after the person is no longer capable of granting such authority on his or her own, the court process is lengthy and contains many steps that include: 1) a notice of application; 2) an affidavit of the applicant; 3) management plans that demonstrate the best interest of the incapable person; and 4) medical affidavits (Schnurr, 2004). The public trustee may or may not be involved in this process, depending on the jurisdiction. In Saskatchewan, for instance, the public trustee is charged with investigating all applications with respect to property decision-making. The public trustee may inform all other relatives about the application. In addition, the property decision-maker must provide the public trustee with an annual accounting and inventory of the person's property (Government of Saskatchewan, 2004).

The public guardian and trustee in each jurisdiction is an independent and impartial public official and is an officer of the court. The public guardian and trustee of British Columbia, for instance, 'operates under provincial law to protect the legal rights and financial interests of children, to provide assistance to adults who need support for financial and personal decision making, and to administer the estates of deceased and missing persons where there is no one else able to do so' (http://www. trustee.bc.ca). Application for the public guardian and trustee to assume responsibility requires documentation and a procedure specified by each province, verifying the incapability of the individual to manage his or her own affairs. At times, less formal options are available; for example, Alberta offers informal trusteeship to incapable parties who only require assistance with the handling of monthly government cheques, through which trusteeship arrangements are made with the government departments issuing the cheques.

Dealing with Disputes on Capacity and Consent

Some jurisdictions have mechanisms for appealing decisions dealing with capacity and consent of an individual through boards or panels, whereas in other jurisdictions recourse is only through the courts. One of the defining features of the consent and capacity legislation in Ontario, for instance, is the creation of the consent and capacity board (Rozovsky, 2003). This board is an administrative tribunal created to adjudicate disputes surrounding issues of capacity and consent in relation to treatment, admission to care facilities, personal assistance services, management of property, as well as involuntary admission and community treatment orders that are discussed in Chapter 7 (Hiltz and Szigeti, 2004).

Disputes may be brought before the board by filing an application. Disputes are heard before panels of the board, the composition and quorum for which are determined under legislation according to the matter being heard; but generally these panels include some combination of lawyers and psychiatrists. Because of the health of the patients involved, the board often travels to the hospital, psychiatric facility, or nursing home where the patient is located. A decision of the board may be appealed to the courts. Given the complex relationships among all parties, which extend beyond any matter brought before boards of this nature, professionals involved are well advised to cooperate to reduce the stressors for families in these already emotionally charged situations and to foster the therapeutic effects of the hearing process itself (Hiltz and Szigeti, 2004).

CASE EXAMPLE REVIEWED

We return now to the case of Joe and how the matters discussed in this chapter answer the questions directly related to his situation.

Who makes decisions regarding Joe's medical care if Joe is unable to consent or provide direction?

In an emergency situation, when a patient has not made an advance directive and sufficient time is not available to consult a substitute decision-maker, the health care provider may make a decision without consent. In non-emergency situations, a substitute decision-maker must be determined based either on the patient's pre-expressed wishes or by legislation. Usually, without an advance directive or a power of attorney, this is the next of kin. In Joe's case, his parents would be the substitute decision-makers and as his father had custody when he was younger, it would probably be his father in the case of a dispute. If one parent feels that the other parent is not making decisions in Joe's best interest, depending on the jurisdiction in which they reside, the dissatisfied parent may apply to a consent and capacity board for adjudication of the matter.

CASE EXAMPLE REVIEWED *(Continued)*

Who has the right to decide whether Joe's life-prolonging treatment should be withdrawn?

Since Joe is not able to engage in end-of-life decisions and he is living solely as the result of life support, his substitute decision-maker, in consultation with the rest of his family, has the right to make the decision whether the life-prolonging treatment should be withdrawn.

Who can make decisions about donating Joe's organs?

If Joe had discussed organ donation with his family or signed a donor card, his family members and medical staff would find this useful. Regardless of whether Joe signed a donor card, in practice, it is the family who ultimately consents to organ and tissue donation.

How much information can be shared with Joe's family members about Joe's condition?

Since Joe's parents are the substitute decision-makers, health information can be shared freely with them. Their consent will be required to share the health information with other family members.

If Joe continued to have financial resources and obligations, who would take responsibility for these matters?

If Joe has not signed a power of attorney for finances, his family will have to make application to the courts for decision-making authority.

Key Terms

Advance Directive
A written direction by a person of his or her wishes for care should he or she become incapable of consenting; directives may be instructional (specific treatments that should or should not be administered) and in some jurisdictions may be proxy directives (designates a substitute decision-maker who supersedes the traditional hierarchy of decision-makers as prescribed in legislation)

Assisted Suicide
Patient is the agent of his or her own death but death results from assistance supplied by another person; assisting with a suicide is a criminal offence under the Criminal Code

Capacity to Consent
One component of valid consent; people must be able to understand information that is provided to them, apply that information to their specific situation, and appreciate the reasonably foreseeable consequences of a decision or lack of decision

Confidentiality
Obligation to protect information entrusted to the care of an organization or professional for a specific purpose and ensure information is only accessible to those authorized to have access

Consent
Acknowledgment provided by a person to a practitioner that the person will accept treatment and

the extent of treatment that they will accept—consent may be expressed (oral or written) or implied (derived from action or inaction); for consent to be valid the person must have capacity to consent and consent must be voluntary and informed

Euthanasia

A deliberate act undertaken with the intention of ending the life of another person to relieve suffering of that person; the Criminal Code prohibits euthanasia and an individual cannot consent to have death inflicted upon him or her

Informed Consent

One component of valid consent; consent must be based on information provided by the practitioner about the benefits and potential risks of the course of treatment

Palliative Care

Measures taken to relieve the suffering and improve the quality of life of those dying from terminal illness (for example, pain medication, oxygen, sedation)

Power of Attorney

Authority granted by one person to another to act on behalf of the grantor in making his or her personal (or financial) decisions; the attorney must act in accordance with the wishes and best interests of the grantor

Privacy

Right of an individual to control who has access to his or her personal information and under what circumstances

Substitute Decision-Maker

Individual identified to make decisions on behalf of a patient who is no longer capable of consenting or refusing consent to treatment—this individual is responsible for making consent decisions according to the expressed wishes of a patient or, if no such wishes have been expressed, to make the decision that is in the patient's best interest; the process of obtaining a substitute decision-maker and who is legally able to act as one is usually defined by legislation

Voluntary Consent

One component of valid consent; an individual's decision to consent must be free of coercion or undue influence, such as financial incentives, unnecessary fear, or influence created by the therapeutic alliance between the patient and the health care provider

Discussion Questions

1. Identify the elements of valid consent.
2. When must consent be obtained?
3. Describe one exception to the consent requirement.
4. What are substitutes to individual consent and when may they be used?
5. Is the substitute decision-maker for health care also the decision-maker for financial issues? Explain.

Relevant Legislation

Federal

Canadian Charter of Rights and Freedoms: Part 1 of the Constitution Act, 1982, being Schedule B to the Canada Act (UK), c. 11
http://laws.justice.gc.ca/en/charter/

Criminal Code of Canada, R.S.C. 1985, c. C-46
http://laws.justice.gc.ca/en/C-46/
Personal Information Protection and Electronic Documents Act, 2000, c. 5
http://laws.justice.gc.ca/en/P-8.6/

Privacy Act, R.S. 1985, c. P-21
http://laws.justice.gc.ca/en/P-21/index.html

Alberta

Dependent Adults Act, R.S.A. 2000, c. D-11
http://www.canlii.org/ab/laws/sta/d-11/2005
1019/whole.html

Health Information Act, R.S.A. 2000, c. 5-H
http://www.qp.gov.ab.ca/documents/acts/H05.
cfm

Personal Directives Act, R.S.A. 2000, c. P-6
http://www.canlii.org/ab/laws/sta/p-6/2005
0110/whole.html

Powers of Attorney Act, S.A. 1991, c. P-13.5
http://www.canlii.org/ab/laws/sta/p-20/2005
1019/whole.html

British Columbia

Adult Guardianship Act, R.S.B.C. 1996, c. 6
http://www.qp.gov.bc.ca/statreg/stat/A/96006
_01.htm

Freedom of Information and Protection of Privacy
Act, R.S.B.C. 1996, c. 165
http://www.qp.gov.bc.ca/statreg/stat/f/96165_
01.htm

The Health Care (Consent) and Care Facility
(Admission) Act, R.S.B.C. 1996, c. 405 (enacted
in part only)
http://www.qp.gov.bc.ca/statreg/stat/H/96181_
01.htm

Human Tissue Gift Act, R.S.B.C. 1996, c. 211
http://www.qp.gov.bc.ca/statreg/stat/H/96211_
01.htm

Infants Act, R.S.B.C. 1996, c. 223
http://www.qp.gov.bc.ca/statreg/stat/I/96223_
01.htm

Patients Property Act, R.S.B.C. 1996, c. 349
http://www.qp.gov.bc.ca/statreg/stat/P/96349_
01.htm

Personal Information Protection Act, R.S.B.C. 2003,
c. 63
http://www.qp.gov.bc.ca/statreg/stat/P/03063_
01.htm

Power of Attorney Act, R.S.B.C. 1996, c. 370
http://www.qp.gov.bc.ca/statreg/stat/P/96370_
01.htm

Public Guardian and Trustee Act, R.S.B.C. 1996,
c. 383
http://www.qp.gov.bc.ca/statreg/stat/P/96383_
01.htm

Representation Agreement Act, R.S.B.C. 1996,
c. 405
http://www.qp.gov.bc.ca/statreg/stat/R/96405_
01.htm

Manitoba

Child and Family Services Amendment Act, S.M.
1995, c. 23
http://web2.gov.mb.ca/laws/statutes/1996/
c00496e.php

Health Care Directives Act, C.C.S.M. 1998, c. H-27
http://web2.gov.mb.ca/laws/statutes/ccsm/
h027e.php

Human Tissue Gift Act, 1987, C.C.S.M. c. H180
http://web2.gov.mb.ca/laws/statutes/ccsm/
h180e.php

Personal Health Information Act, C.C.S.M. 1997,
c. P33.5
http://web2.gov.mb.ca/laws/statutes/ccsm/
p033-5e.php

The Powers of Attorney Act, C.C.S.M. 1996,
c. P97
http://web2.gov.mb.ca/laws/statutes/ccsm/
p097e.php

Vulnerable Persons Living with a Mental Disability
Act, S.M. 1993, c. 29
http://www.gov.mb.ca/fs/pwd/vpact.html

New Brunswick

Hospital Act, R.S.N.B. 1992, c. H-6.1
http://www.canlii.org/nb/laws/sta/h-6.1/2005
0114/whole.html

Human Tissue Gift Act, R.S.N.B. 1973, c. H-12
http://www.canlii.org/nb/laws/sta/h-12.5/2008
0715/whole.html

Infirm Persons Act, R.S.N.B. 2000, c. I-8
http://www.canlii.org/nb/laws/sta/i-8/2005
0114/ whole.html

Medical Consent of Minors Act, R.S.N.B. 1976,
c. M-6.1
http://www.canlii.org/nb/laws/sta/m-6.1/2005
0114/whole.html

Property Act, R.S.N. B. 1973, c. P-19
http://www.canlii.org/nb/laws/sta/p-19/2005
0114/whole.html

Newfoundland and Labrador

Advance Health Care Directives Act, R.S.N.L. 1995, c. A-4.1
http://www.canlii.org/nl/laws/sta/a-4.1/2005
0112/whole.html

Human Tissue Act, R.S.N.L. 1990, c. H-15
http://www.canlii.org/nl/laws/sta/h-15/2005
0112/whole.html

Nova Scotia

Hospitals Act, R.S.N.S. 1989, c. 208
http://www.canlii.org/ns/laws/sta/r1989c.208/
20050110/whole.html

Human Tissue Gift Act, R.S.N.S. 1989, c. 215
http://www.canlii.org/ns/laws/sta/r1989c.215/
20041103/whole.html

Incompetent Persons Act, R.S.N.S. 1989, c. 218
http://www.canlii.org/ns/laws/sta/r1989c.218/
20080717/whole.html

Medical Consent Act, R.S.N.S. 1989, c. 279
http://www.canlii.org/ns/laws/sta/r1989c.279/
20041103/whole.html

Powers of Attorney Act, R.S.N.S. 1989, c. 352
http://www.canlii.org/ns/laws/sta/r1989c.352/
20041103/whole.html

Ontario

Health Care Consent Act, S.O. 1996, c. 2
http://www.e-laws.gov.on.ca/DBLaws/Statutes/
English/96h02_e.htm

Personal Health Information Protection Act, S.O. 2004, c. 3
http://www.e-laws.gov.on.ca/DBLaws/Statutes/
English/04p03_e.htm

Substitute Decisions Act, S.O. 1992, c. 30
http://www.e-laws.gov.on.ca/DBLaws/Statutes/
English/92s30_e.htm

Trillium Gift of Life Network Act, S.O. 1998, c. 18
http://www.e-laws.gov.on.ca/html/statutes/
English/elaws_statutes_90h20_e.htm

Prince Edward Island

Consent to Treatment and Health Care Directives Act, S.P.E.I. 1996, c. 10
http://www.canlii.org/pe/laws/sta/c-17.2/2004
1117/whole.html

Hospital Act, R.S.P.E.I 1988, c. H-10
http://www.canlii.org/pe/laws/sta/h-10/2004
1117/whole.html

Hospital Management Regulation, R.R.P.E.I. 1981, c. H-11
http://www.canlii.org/pe/laws/regu/1976r.574/
20050110/whole.html

Human Tissues Donation Act, R.S.P., P.E.I. 1988
http://www.canlii.org/pe/laws/sta/h-12.1/
20080715/whole.html

Powers of Attorney Act, R.S.P.E.I. 1988, c. P-26
http://www.canlii.org/pe/laws/sta/p-16/2004
1117/whole.html

Quebec

An Act Respecting Access to Documents held by Public Bodies, S.Q. 1982, c. A-2.1
http://www2.publicationsduquebec.gouv.qc.ca

An Act Respecting the Protection of Personal Information in the Private Sector, R.S.Q., 1993, c. 39
http://www2.publicationsduquebec.gouv.qc.ca

Mandate Given in Anticipation of Incapacity, Arts. 2130-2185 C.C.Q.

Civil Code of Québec, S.Q. 1991, c. 64, arts. 10–31
http://www.canlii.org/qc/laws/sta/ccq/2004
0901/ part1.html

Public Curator Act, S.Q. 1989, c. 54
http://www.canlii.org/qc/laws/sta/c-81/2005
0111/whole.html

Saskatchewan

Health Care Directives and Substitute Health Care Decision Makers Act, S.S. 1997, c. H-0.001
http://www.canlii.org/sk/laws/sta/h-0.001/2008
0715/whole.html

Hospitals Standards Act, R.S.S. 1978, c. H-10
http://www.canlii.org/sk/laws/sta/h-10/2004
1105/whole.html

Hospitals Standards Regulations, R.R.S. 1979, Reg. 3231
http://www.canlii.org/sk/laws/regu/1979r.331/20050113/whole.html

Health Information Protection Act, S.S. 1999, c. H-0.021
http://www.canlii.org/sk/laws/sta/h-0.021/2004 1105/whole.html

Human Tissue Gift Act, R.S.A. 2000, c. H-15
http://www.canlii.org/ab/laws/sta/h-15/2004 1104/whole.html

Powers of Attorney Act, 2002, S.S. 2002

Northwest Territories

Access to Information and Protection of Privacy Regulations, S.N.W.T. 1994, c. 20
http://www.canlii.org/nt/laws/sta/1994c.20/2004 0616/whole.html

Guardianship and Trustee Act, S.N.W.T. 1994, c. 29
http://www.canlii.org/nt/laws/regu/1997r.049/20040917/whole.html

Human Tissue Act, R.S.N.W.T. 1988, c. H-6
http://www.canlii.org/nt/laws/sta/h-6/2004 1110/whole.html

Powers of Attorney Act, S.N.W.T. 2001, c. 15
http://www.canlii.org/nt/laws/sta/2001c.15/20041110/whole.html

Yukon Territory

Enduring Power of Attorney Act, S.Y. 1995, c. 8
http://www.gov.yk.ca/legislation/acts/enpoat.pdf

Health Act, S.Y. 1989–90, c. 36, s. 45
http://www.canlii.org/yk/laws/sta/106/2006 0728/whole.html

Human Tissue Gift Act, 2002, c. 117
http://www.gov.yk.ca/legislation/acts/hutigi.pdf

References

A.C. v. Manitoba (Director of Child and Family Services) (2009), SCC 30.

B.(R.) v. Children's Aid Society of Metropolitan Toronto (1995), 1 S.C.R. 315 (S.C.C.) Canada.

B.H. v. Alberta (Director of Child Welfare) (2002), 329 A.R. 395 (Alta. Q.B.).

British Columbia (Attorney General) v. Astaforoff (1983), 6 W.W.R. 322 (B.C.S.C.).

Canadian Association of Social Workers (CASW) (2007), *Informed Consent and Confidentiality: CASW Guidelines*.

Canadian Organ Replacement Register (accessed at http://secure.cihi.ca).

Carter, T. (2002), *Your Personal Directive* (Vancouver: Self-Counsel Press).

Ciarlariello v. Schacter (1993), 2 SCR 119 at 135.

COACH: Canada's Health Informatics Association (2007), *Guidelines for the Protection of Health Information* (Toronto: COACH).

Dalhousie Health Law Institute End of Life (EOL) Project (2003), (accessed at http://as01.ucis.dal.ca/dhli).

Dickens, B. (2002), 'Informed Consent', in J. Downie, T. Caulfield, and C. Flood (eds), *Canadian Health Law and Policy* (Toronto: Butterworths).

Downie, J., Caulfield, T., and Flood, C. (eds) (2002), *Canadian Health Law and Policy* (Toronto: Butterworths).

Dykeman, M.J. (2000), *Canadian Health Law Practice Manual* (Toronto. Butterworths).

Etchells, E., Sharpe, G., Walsh, P., Williams, J., and Singer, P. (1996), 'BioEthics for Clinicians: 1. Consent', *Canadian Medical Association Journal*, 155: 177–80.

Ferguson, L. (2004), *The End of an Age: Beyond Age Restrictions for Minors' Medical Treatment Decisions* (Ottawa: Law Commission of Canada).

Fowler, L. (2004), *Powers of Attorney* (Toronto: Law Society of Upper Canada).

Frelick, K. (2007), 'Consent and the Personal Health Information Protection Act, 2004: Creating the Right Balance', Ontario Bar Association First Annual Privacy Summit.

———— and Jovellano, J. (2009), 'Legal Aspects of Health Information Management' in Canadian Healthcare Association Press, *Fundamentals of Health Information Management*.

Gift of Life (2005), *Statistics* (accessed 24 October 2005 at www.giftoflife.on.ca/english/statistics.html).

Gilmour, J. (2002), 'Children, Adolescents and Health Care', in J. Downie, T. Caulfield, and C. Flood (eds), *Canadian Health Law and Policy* (Toronto: Butterworths).

Gore, S., Hinds, C., and Rutherford, A. (1989), 'Organ Donation from Intensive Care Units in England', *British Medical Journal*, 299: 1193–7.

Government of Saskatchewan (2004), *Adult Guardianship Manual* (accessed at http://www.saskjustice.gov.sk.ca/Public Trustee/docs/Applicationpkg.pdf).

Hall, R. and Rocker, G. (2000), 'End-of-Life Care in the ICU: Treatments Provided When Life Support Was or Was Not

Withdrawn', *Clinical Investigations in Critical Care*, 118(5): 1424–30.

Hawryluck, L., Gold, W.L., Robinson, S., Pogorski, S., Galea, S., and Styra, R. (2004), 'SARS Control and Psychological Effects of Quarantine: Toronto, Canada', *Emergency and Infectious Disease*, 10(7): 1206–12.

Health Canada (2004), 'Canada's Official Organ and Tissue Information Site' (accessed at http://www.hc-sc.gc.ca/english/organandtissue/how_to/steps. htm).

Heyland, D., Lavery, J., Tranmer, J., Shortt, S., and Taylor, S. (2000), 'Dying in Canada: Is It an Institutionalized, Technology-supported Experience?' *Journal of Palliative Care*, 16 (Supp.): S10–S16.

Hill, I. (2000), *Power of Attorney Litigation* (Toronto: CCH Canadian Limited).

Hiltz, D. and Szigeti, A. (2004), *A Guide to Consent and Capacity Law in Ontario* (Toronto: LexisNexis Canada).

Humphrey, D. (2003), 'Prisoner of Conscience: Dr. Jack Kevorkian', *Euthanasia Research and Guidance Organization* (accessed at http://www.finalexit. org/dr.k.html).

Hunt, R., Bond, M., Groth, R., and King, P. (1991), 'Place of Death in South Australia: Patterns from 1910 to 1987', *Medical Journal of Australia*, 155(8): 549–53.

Industry Canada (2004), 'PIPEDA Awareness Raising Tools (PARTs) Initiative for the Health Sector' (accessed at http://www.ic.gc.ca/epic/site/ecic-ceac.nsf/en/h_gv00207e.html).

International Covenant on Civil and Political Rights (1966), International Covenant on Civil and Political Rights, G.A. res. 2200A (XXI), 21 UN GAOR Supp. (No. 16) at 52, UN Doc. A/6316 (accessed at http://www.umn.edu/humanrts/instree/b3ccpr.htm).

Kjerulf, M., Regehr, C., Popova, S., and Baker, A. (2005), 'Family Perceptions of End of Life Care in an Urban ICU', *Dynamics: Journal of the Canadian Association of Critical Care Nurses*, 16(3): 22–5.

Law Reform Commission of Canada, The Jury (Report 16, 1982).

Lynn, J., Teno, J., Phillips, R., Wu, A., Desbiens, N., Harrold, J., et al. (1997), 'Perceptions by Family Members of the Dying Experience Older and Seriously Ill Patients', *Annals of Internal Medicine*, 126(2): 97–102.

McInerney v. MacDonald (1992), 2 S.C.R. 138.

Malette v. Shulman (1990), 72 O.R. (2d) 417 (C.A.).

Marshall v. Curry (1933), 3 D.L.R. 260 (N.S.S.C.).

Morris, J., Ferguson, M., and Dykeman, M. (1999), *Canadian Nurses and the Law*, 2nd ed. (Toronto: LexisNexis Canada).

Murray v. McMurchy (1949), 2 D.L.R. 442 (B.C.S.C.).

Nancy B. v. Hôtel-Dieu de Québec et al. (1992), 86 D.L.R. (4th) 385 (Q.S.C.).

Nelson, E. (2002), 'The Fundamentals of Consent', in J. Downie, T. Caulfield, and C. Flood (eds), *Canadian Health Law and Policy* (Toronto: Butterworths).

New Brunswick (Minister of Health and Community Services) v. R.B. and S.B. (1990), 106 New Brunswick Reports (2d) 206 (N.B. Q.B.).

Ontario Hospital Association (2004), *Physician's Privacy Toolkit* (Toronto: Ontario Hospital Association, Ontario Medical Association).

Paul, M., Foreman, D. and Kent, L. (2000), 'Outpatient Clinical Attendance Consent from Children and Young People: Ethical and Practical Considerations', *Clinical Child Psychology and Psychiatry*, 5(2): 203–11.

Platt, P. (2006), 'The Individual's Right of Access to His or Her Own Personal Health Information', Insight Conference: Electronic Records, E-Discovery and Access to Information (Toronto, Canada).

Public Guardian and Trustee of British Columbia (2005), 'We're Here for You' (accessed at http://www.trustee.bc.ca).

R. v. De la Rocha (1993, 2 April), Timmins (Ont. Gen. Div).

R. v. Latimer (2001), 39 C.R. (5th) 1 (S.C.C.).

R.v. Mataya (1992) 24 August, Wren, J. (Ont. Gen. Div).

Re T.T.D. (1999), 171 Dominion Law Reports (4th) 761 (Sask. Q.B.).

Regehr, C. and Antle, B. (1997). 'Coercive Influences: Informed Consent in Court Mandated Social Work Practice', *Social Work*, 42(3): 300–6.

Reibl v. Hughes (1980), 114 D.L.R. (3d) 1 (S.C.C.).

Rodriguez v. British Columbia (Attorney General) , [1993] 3 S.C.R. 519.

Rozovsky, L. (2003), *The Canadian Law of Consent to Treatment* (Toronto: Butterworths).

Sager, M., Easterling, D., Kindig, D., and Anderson, D. (1989), 'Changes in Location of Death after Passage of Medicare's Prospective Payment System: A National Study', *New England Journal of Medicine*, 320: 433–9.

Seals, C. and Cartwright, A. (1994), *The Year before Death* (Avebury: Aldershot).

Schnurr, B. (2004), *Court Appointment of Guardians for Mentally Incapable Persons* (Toronto: Law Society of Upper Canada).

Siminoff, L. (1997), 'Withdrawal of Treatment and Organ Donation', *Critical Care Nursing Clinics of North America*, 9(1): 85–95.

Sneiderman, B. (2002), 'Decision-making at the End of Life', in J. Downie, T. Caulfield, and C. Flood (eds), *Canadian Health Law and Policy* (Toronto: Butterworths).

————, Irvine, J., and Osbourne, P. (2003), *Canadian Medical Law*, 3rd ed. (Toronto: Thompson).

Soukup, M. (1991), 'Organ Donation from the Family of a Totally Brain-Dead Donor: Professional Responsiveness', *Critical Care Nursing*, 13(4): 8–18.

Special Senate Committee on Euthanasia and Assisted Suicide (1995), 'On Life and Death' (accessed at http://www.parl. gc.ca).

Sque, M., Payne, S., and Vlachonikolis, I. (2000), 'Cadaveric Donotransplantation: Nurses' Attitudes, Knowledge and Behaviour', *Social Science and Medicine*, 50: 541–52.

Stark, J., Reiley, P., Osiecki, A., and Cook, L. (1984), 'Attitudes Affecting Organ Donation in the Intensive Care Unit', *Heart Lung*, 13: 400–4.

Stein, G. (2004), 'Improving Our Care at Life's End: Making a Difference', *Health and Social Work*, 29(1): 77–9.

Taylor, P., Young, K., and Kneteman, N. (1997), 'Intensive Care Nurses' Participation in Organ Procurement: Impact on Organ Donation Rates', *Transplant Proceedings*, 29: 3646–8.

United Nations (1948), Universal Declaration of Human Rights (accessed at http://www.un.org/Overview/rights.html).

United Network for Organ Sharing Scientific Registry Data. (accessed 17 October 2002 at http://www.unos.org [Newsroom, Critical Data link]).

U.S. Scientific Registry for Transplant Recipients and the Organ Procurement and Transplantation Network. Transplant Data: 1989–1998. Rockville, MD: U.S. Department of Health and Human Services, Health Resources and Services Administration, Office of Special Programs, Division of Transplantation; and Richmond, VA: United Network for Organ Sharing; 1999.

Vacco v. Quill (1997), 521 U.S. 793, 117 S. Ct. 2293.

Vrtis, M. and Nicely B. (1993), 'Nursing Knowledge and Attitudes Toward Organ Donation', *Journal of Transplant Coordination*, 3: 70–9.

Wight, C., Cohen, B., Roels, L., and Miranda, B. (2000), 'Donor Action: A Quality Assurance Program for Intensive Care Units That Increases Organ Donation', *Journal of Intensive Care Medicine*, 5: 104–14.

CHAPTER SEVEN

Serious Mental Illness and the Law

OBJECTIVES

- To present the historical context of mental health law in Canada
- To discuss circumstances leading to involuntary admission
- To discuss issues of consent to treatment and present alternative forms of consent
- To identify processes and procedures that occur when a person with a serious mental illness is charged with a criminal offence
- To identify the obligations of social workers to protect the safety of others if a person with a serious mental illness is at risk of inflicting harm

CASE EXAMPLE

As a community social worker, you are consulted by a woman who is seeking psychiatric treatment for her husband. The husband, Ron De Sousa, is a 38-year-old psychologist with a PhD who previously worked for a government ministry; he was fired because of bizarre behaviour. Two years ago, he had a psychotic episode in which he assaulted his wife. At that time, Dr De Sousa believed that he was 'the King' and wandered about the house with a crown, holding a fireplace poker as a scepter and destroying furnishings when he felt provoked. Isabel De Sousa left her husband temporarily and obtained a peace bond, which he ignored repeatedly. Eventually, he was hospitalized and diagnosed with bipolar affective disorder. Following treatment, he returned to live with his wife and children.

Although he has been relatively stable for more than a year, he discontinued his treatment several months ago and has become increasingly disorganized and bizarre. A few months ago, he cashed in the family's life savings without consulting his wife and lost most of the funds in a high-risk venture. He then spent the rest of the money on a Porsche and headed to the United States, where he crashed the car. He became argumentative with the police at the scene, but because he was clearly unwell the police decided not to charge him on the condition that he agreed to return to Canada for treatment. Once at the airport, however, he caught a plane to visit his mother in Atlanta instead—charging the flight to the couple's credit card. Mrs De Sousa senior arranged to have her son returned to a hospital in Canada, where he was admitted involuntarily.

CASE EXAMPLE *(Continued)*

While in the hospital, Dr De Sousa became enraged, saying that his wife and his previous government employer had conspired against him to keep him in the hospital—in part, because he believed that they were now lovers. He wrote many lengthy letters threatening them with litigation but not physical violence. He also threatened to leave the hospital ward and take a nurse hostage, although it was not believed that he had the means or capacity to do so. In hospital, Dr De Sousa refused all treatment and was unpredictable, irritable, aggressive, and verbally abusive. He was not physically violent. He then retained the services of an excellent lawyer to secure his release from hospital.

- Can Dr De Sousa be admitted and held in a psychiatric hospital against his will?
- Can Dr De Sousa be treated against his will while in the hospital?
- Can he be treated in the community instead of a psychiatric hospital?
- Are there mechanisms to protect the financial security of Dr De Sousa and his family?
- What could happen to Dr De Sousa if he were criminally charged?
- What are the obligations of the mental health system to protect the safety of Mrs De Sousa?

Individuals with serious mental health problems are not commonly predisposed to violence or threats (Glancy and Regehr, 1992). However, as mental health legislation focuses primarily on the issue of harm, this case example depicts a person who represented a possible threat.

The Context of Mental Health Legislation in Canada

Mental health legislation in Canada, as in other parts of the world, attempts to balance three things: the civil liberties of individuals to live as they choose; the responsibility of society to ensure the safety and well-being of individuals who can't understand the consequences of their choices because of diminished capacity; and the responsibility of a society to ensure that the choices and behaviour of one individual do not compromise the safety and security of others. Strong opinions are expressed on both sides of the issue. Psychiatric survivor groups have focused on abuses they endured as a result of involuntary admission and argue for its abolition (Capponi, 2003; PSAAO, 2004). Others, such as Hershel Hardin (2004), a member of the Vancouver Civil Liberties Association and a parent of a person with schizophrenia,

contend that civil liberties are not respected when people are denied involuntary treatment and left as prisoners of their illnesses. This is by no means a modern dilemma; rather, a brief history of mental health legislation in Ontario allows us to see how approaches to this issue have shifted with societal attitudes and treatment options.

Concern over the care and custody of someone with a mental health problem dates back to early civilization. Kaiser (2002) reports that this concern was recorded as early as 449 BC: 'If a person is a fool, let his person and his goods be under the protection of his family or his maternal relatives, if he is not under the care of anyone' (p. 258). Further, he reports that in the eighth or ninth century, hospitals specifically for those with mental illnesses were established in Arabic countries. In the 1700s, English law first took a role in regulating the conditions of mental hospitals, although these were known to exist far before then.

In Canada, as with all other aspects of law and culture, our history is considerably more recent. The first mental health legislation in Ontario was enacted in 1871 and was entitled An Act Respecting Asylums for the Insane. This Act was intended to address the rights of individuals residing in the 'Provincial Lunatic Asylum in Toronto, the Lunatic Asylum in London, and any other public asylums'. This Act indicated that no person could be confined in an asylum except under an order of the lieutenant-governor and a certificate of three medical professionals verified by the mayor or reeve. The medical professionals were required to certify that they had examined the patient and 'after due enquiry into all the necessary facts relating to his case, found him to be a lunatic. . . . Such certificate shall be a sufficient authority to any person to convey the lunatic to any of the said asylums, and to the authorities thereof to detain him so long as he continues to be insane.' These provisions were essential because detainment was tantamount to a life sentence. Asylums provided primarily custodial care. Staffing and financing were sparse and the etiology of mental health problems and avenues of treatment unknown.

More than 60 years later, the Mental Hospitals Act of 1935, while clearly specifying a process for involuntary admission of 'mentally ill and mentally defective persons', remained relatively vague regarding the criteria for admission under involuntary conditions. Nevertheless, this was the first Act to allow for the fact that a patient may recover and therefore to deal with the issue of release from hospital. In part this may have been due to the development of pharmacological treatments for mental illness. However, this Act coincided with an era of community psychiatry that continued to rise in the 1940s. Mental health institutions were viewed as causing, not relieving, mental health problems and the goal became deinstitutionalization (Martin and Cheung, 1985). Following this trend, the revisions of the 1967 Mental Health Act sought to limit the role of medicine and reduced the grounds for involuntary admission to any person who would not enter a hospital voluntarily and suffered 'from mental disorder of a nature or degree so as to require hospitalization in the interests of his own safety or the safety of others'. These revisions to mental health legislation occurred at a time of deep distrust in the medical profession (Goffman, 1961; Szasz, 1963) and during an era of legislative activism in the interests of social reform (Bagby, 1987). The concept of safety was further limited in the 1978 Act; it restricted the notion of safety to the likelihood of serious bodily harm to self or others or imminent and serious impairment due to lack of competence to care for self. In addition, the 1984 Act required that all certificates of involuntary admission be reviewed by the officer in charge of the facility and that the physician complete a form notifying the area director of legal aid that a certificate had been completed so a lawyer could instruct the patient about his or her rights to appeal.

There has been substantial legislative reform with regard to mental health, with each subsequent revision further defining the grounds for involuntary admission, the length of involuntary admission, and the scope of control over clients by those working in psychiatric institutions. This begs the question, Have the legislative reforms actually changed the procedures for involuntary admission in practice? Page (1980) examined involuntary admission certificates following changes in the Mental Health acts in 1967, 1970, and 1978 and reported no changes in the reasons provided in practice for involuntary admissions after each of the legislative revisions. Bagby (1987) and Martin and Cheung (1985) similarly concluded that changes in mental health legislation in Ontario did not have the effect of reducing involuntary admissions.

Nevertheless, experimental analyses indicate that dangerousness and the presence of psychiatric illness are the key factors in the decision to admit patients under involuntary conditions (Bagby et al., 1991). This would suggest that other factors are at play in maintaining the admission rate despite legislative reform. One such factor is that doctors and judges continue to use a 'common-sense' perspective to assess the risk that a person with an acute mental illness may present to themselves and their families (Gray, Shone, and Liddle, 2000). Further, families and others are thought to adapt to restrictive legislative criteria by exaggerating danger and violence elements in order to obtain treatment. This creates a tension between the letter of the law and what is perceived as morally right by the members of society (Appelbaum, 1994).

The 1960s can be heralded as the period of deinstitutionalization, and as early as 1959 proposals were drafted for community-based treatment and the establishment of psychiatric beds in general hospitals (Hartford et al., 2003). In part due to concerns about the cost of inpatient psychiatric treatment, in part due to the ability to relieve psychotic symptoms with new medications, and in part due to a belief in the benefits of community-based treatment as superior to institutional care, a revolution began in mental health care. The goal was to provide services outside the hospital so that hospital care would only occur when there were acute treatment needs. Between 1965 and 1981, the number of beds in provincial psychiatric hospitals across Canada dropped 70 per cent from 69,128 to 20,301 (Nelson, 2006). While the part of the deinstitutionalization plan was to have money flow to community-based programs, only a small proportion actually did. By the late 1970s there was a shortage of housing and support systems and a large number of these formerly hospitalized patients found themselves in poor-quality, unregulated boarding homes. Psychiatric ghettos developed in areas of all Canada's major cities. Meagre welfare payments received by patients were often taken and managed by boarding home operators, leaving those with serious mental illnesses impoverished. After-care programs were limited and often consisted only of medication. Community care became community neglect of those with major mental health problems.

In response to legislative restrictions on involuntary admission to hospital and the move to deinstitutionalize those with serious mental health problems, there has been a recent movement to community-based treatment. In 1995, Brian Smith, a popular sportscaster in Ottawa, was shot and killed by a man who was suffering from paranoid schizophrenia but had refused treatment. A coroner's inquest was conducted and recommended changes to mental health legislation in Ontario that, when introduced in the legislature in December 2000, received the support of all parties (*Burlington Post*, 2001). Known as 'Brian's Law', this legislation made two major changes to the Ontario Mental Health Act and the Health Care Consent Act. First, it deleted the word 'imminent' from the criteria of 'imminent and serious bodily harm', allowing for earlier intervention. Second, it created community treatment orders (CTOs) by which a person may choose to comply with treatment in the community instead of being involuntarily admitted to a hospital (Ministry of Health and Long-Term Care, 2000).

Similar histories across Canada and the rest of the Western World demonstrate the close connection between mental health legislation and prevailing societal values. Despite all the legislative changes, however, the application of legislation remains relatively stable since practitioners must always respond to the lived experiences of those with mental illnesses. We move now to the practical application of mental health law.

What Is a Mental Disorder?

Specific definitions of what constitutes a mental disorder vary. Nova Scotia, Ontario, and Newfoundland have relatively broad definitions that may include developmental disabilities or antisocial personality disorder. Nova Scotia specifically includes drug and alcohol addiction in the definition. Alberta, Saskatchewan, Manitoba, New Brunswick, PEI, and the territories limit the definition to substantial disorders that grossly or seriously impair functioning (Gray, Shone, and Liddle, 2000). That is, in those jurisdictions, the dangerous behaviour that the person is exhibiting must be due to factors such as psychosis or serious depression, not antisocial personality disorder.

When Can a Person Be Admitted Involuntarily for Psychiatric Treatment?

Initial Psychiatric Assessment

Throughout Canada, a person can only be admitted to a psychiatric facility against his or her will if he or she receives a psychiatric assessment and is found to meet the criteria for involuntary admission. In circumstances where a mentally ill individual will not voluntarily submit to a psychiatric assessment, other options exist as follows:

- A physician may complete an application for psychiatric assessment and the individual will then voluntarily or by the police be transported to the psychiatric facility for assessment.
- A judge can order a person with an apparent mental health disorder to be taken by the police to a mental health facility for psychiatric assessment.
- Family members or concerned community mental health workers can swear before the justice of the peace that a person with an apparent mental disorder is behaving in a manner that may meet the criteria for harm or danger. They are then issued an order that instructs the police to assist with transporting the individual to a psychiatric facility where a physician can complete an application for psychiatric assessment.
- A police officer may apprehend a person who is believed to meet the criteria under mental health legislation and transport them to a psychiatric facility for assessment. Police have specific guidelines for action depending on the circumstances (Hoffman and Putnam, 2004).

In these circumstances, some jurisdictions allow the individual to be detained in an approved psychiatric facility for a specified number of hours or days for the purpose of a psychiatric assessment to determine whether involuntary admission is warranted. It is important to recognize that while an individual is under detention for assessment he or she is not a patient of the psychiatric facility. Involuntary admission at law only occurs after the psychiatric assessment is completed and it has been determined that the individual meets the requisite criteria. Thus, in each of these cases, physicians must carry out independent assessments to determine whether the person indeed meets the criteria for involuntary admission. For practical purposes (specifically, the lack of physicians) the Northwest Territories also allows psychologists to complete certificates for involuntary admission and the Yukon Territories Act provides that nurses can perform this task. Table 7.1 summarizes mental health legislation and grounds for involuntary admission to psychiatric facilities across Canada.

Criteria for Involuntary Admission

There are several criteria considered when determining whether or not an individual may be involuntarily admitted to a hospital. The criteria for involuntary admission are similar throughout Canada, but some regional differences do exist. Generally, danger is the primary criterion for involuntary admission. For example, the 2006 Mental Health Care and Treatment Act of Newfoundland and Labrador requires that an individual has a mental disorder and as a result of the mental disorder: 'is likely to *cause harm to himself or herself or to others or to suffer substantial mental or physical deterioration or serious physical impairment* if he or she is not admitted to and detained in a psychiatric unit as an involuntary patient'.

The terminology used to define danger varies across Canada: Quebec uses the term 'grave and imminent danger to himself or others'; the term in New Brunswick is 'imminent physical or psychological harm'; and in other jurisdictions there are vague terms such as simply 'harm' or 'safety'. Regardless of the exact terminology, the courts have been attributing broad interpretations to the harm considered. For example, in Ontario

Table 7.1   Mental Health Legislation and Involuntary Admission

Province/ Territory	Governing Legislation	Involuntary Admission—Harm	Involuntary Admission—Impairment
British Columbia	Mental Health Act, R.S.B.C. 1996	Protection—broadly defined	Mental or physical deterioration
Alberta	Mental Health Act, R.S.A. 2000	Danger to self or others	None
Saskatchewan	Mental Health Services Act, S.S. 1984–85–86	Harm—undefined	Mental or physical deterioration
Manitoba	Mental Health Act, C.C.S.M.	Serious harm	Substantial mental or physical deterioration
Ontario	Mental Health Act, R.S.O. 1990	Serious physical harm	Imminent and serious physical impairment
Quebec	An act Respecting the Protection of persons whose mental state presents a danger to themselves or others, S.Q. 2002	Grave and imminent danger to himself or others	None
New Brunswick	Mental Health Act, R.S.N.B. 1973	Imminent physical or psychological harm	None
Nova Scotia	Hospitals Act, S.N.S. 1989	Danger interpreted as bodily harm	None
Prince Edward Island	Mental Health Act, S.P.E.I. 1994	Safety interpreted as including alleviation of distressing physical, mental, or psychiatric symptoms	None
Newfoundland and Labrador	Mental Health Care and Treatment Act, S.N.L. 2006	Harm—unspecified	Substantial mental or physical deterioration or serious physical impairment
Northwest Territories and Nunavut	Mental Health Act, R.S.N.W.T. 1988	Serious bodily harm	Imminent and serious physical impairment
Yukon Territory	Mental Health Act, R.S.Y. 2002	Serious bodily harm	Impending serious mental or physical impairment

the term 'serious bodily harm' is being increasingly interpreted to include both physical and emotional harm (Hiltz and Szigeti, 2004). Similarly, a PEI court included in the concepts of harm and safety the alleviation of distressing physical, mental, or psychiatric symptoms. As a relatively new addition, most jurisdictions have added the concept of substantial mental or physical deterioration as grounds for involuntary admission, acknowledging the risk that this deterioration presents to the client and others. Additional criteria for involuntary admissions are found in some jurisdictions: British Columbia, Saskatchewan, and Manitoba require that the patient needs treatment. Saskatchewan and Newfoundland and Labrador add that the person must be incapable of making independent treatment decisions. In other parts of Canada, the person can be competent to make treatment decisions, yet present a risk due to mental illness.

Involuntary Admission

In most jurisdictions, once it has been determined through the psychiatric assessment that the requisite criteria for involuntary admission are present, the physician files a certificate for involuntary admission with the director in charge of the facility, who as a check and balance reviews the same to ensure compliance with the legal requirements. In New Brunswick the final sign-off is provided by a tribunal, in Quebec by a judge, and in the Northwest Territories by a minister of the government. The time for which a person can be required to remain in hospital following involuntary admission is specified under each provincial and territorial Act.

Voluntary versus Involuntary Admission

If individuals are willing to be admitted voluntarily (that is, are capable of consent and do consent to admission) or can be admitted as informal patients (that is, are not capable of consent but consent is obtained from a substitute decision-maker) then involuntary admission will not be appropriate. In contrast to patients who have been admitted involuntarily, individuals who have been admitted voluntarily have the legal right to leave the psychiatric facility at any time. In practice, this right is often illusory. If at the time the patient wishes to leave, a psychiatric assessment reveals that the criteria for involuntary admission are met, the physician may simply detain the individual (Hiltz and Szigeti, 2004).

Challenges to Involuntary Admission

Under the Charter of Rights and Freedoms, involuntary patients must: 1) be informed promptly of the reasons for detention; 2) be given the opportunity to retain or instruct counsel without delay; 3) have the validity of the detention reviewed and determined. In some jurisdictions involuntary admissions may be challenged before review boards or panels, whereas in other jurisdictions recourse is only through the courts. In the mental health legislation in Ontario, for instance, patients are provided with information through a patient advocate or rights advisor and given a mechanism for appeal through the Consent and Capacity Board and secondarily through the courts. In addition to the involuntary patient, any other person on his or her behalf, the minister of health and the officer in charge of the psychiatric facility where the patient is detained may each bring applications to the Consent and Capacity Board to review whether the legislative criteria for involuntary admission have been met (Hiltz and Szigeti, 2004). Further, court actions for malicious prosecution and false imprisonment have also been brought against mental health facilities. For instance, in the BC case of *Ketchum v. Hislop* (1984), the patient was awarded damages for procedural irregularities and the fact that the statutory requirements for admission had not been met. This occurred despite the fact that the court found that the patient both needed and benefited from treatment (Schneider, 1988).

Can a Person Involuntarily Admitted to Hospital Be Treated Against His or Her Will?

Consent to Treatment

Prior to the 1960s the capacity to consent to treatment by the patient and the authority of hospital personnel to treat someone was not viewed as separate from the authority to hospitalize and detain against someone's will. That is, any person admitted to hospital against their will could be treated without consent. This was in large part because admission to a hospital was based on the presumption of need for treatment. The rise in consent legislation has distinguished involuntary admission from the right to consent to treatment once in the hospital (Gray, Shone, and Liddle, 2000). Each province now has consent legislation, the most comprehensive of which is Ontario's Health Care Consent Act (1996). This

Act and others make it clear that a health care professional cannot administer treatment to an individual without valid consent (Rozovsky, 2003). When valid consent cannot be obtained from an individual, alternative authority for consent must be sought. Newfoundland and Labrador and British Columbia legislation allows directors of psychiatric hospitals to authorize treatment for persons involuntarily committed to a facility without their consent. In Alberta, the hospital or attending physician can apply to a review panel for the right to administer treatment even if the patient is competent to consent, whereas in Ontario, the board can only authorize treatment if the person is incompetent to consent (Ambrosini and Crocker, 2007).

Advance Directives

An advance directive is written while a person is competent to specify what decision should be made about treatment if she or he becomes incapable of delivering consent. At times, people with severe mental disorders may be incapable of fully appreciating and weighing the relative risks and benefits of treatment options versus no treatment. At other times, these same people may clearly understand these issues and after careful consideration have a preferred course of action (Appelbaum, 1991). When patients remain in control of the content of advance directives, they can increase their sense of autonomy and decrease the sense of coercion that is associated with emergency mental health treatment (Ritchie, Sklar, and Steiner, 1998). A Ulysses Contract, named after the classical hero, is often included in a mental health advance directive. Ulysses, who knew he would be unable to resist the call of the sirens that would lead to the destruction of his ship, ordered that he be tied to the mast and be disregarded when he begged to respond. Under this contract, a person may request detainment or restraint and may waive the right of appeal of involuntary admission and treatment (Bay et al., 1996).

Manitoba was the first province to allow advance directives which the proxy decision-maker must follow unless pursuing the expressed wishes of the patient endangers the physical, mental health,

or safety of the patient or another person. Similarly, Quebec stipulates that the wishes expressed in an advance directive should be followed as far as possible, suggesting that others factors, such as safety, could be considered by the court (Ambrosini and Crocker, 2007).

Substitute Decision-makers

If the individual does not have an advance directive in respect of the treatment being considered, an alternative decision-maker will need to be identified for the individual. A person may designate a power of attorney (person granted authority to act on behalf of the grantor) for personal care prior to becoming incapable of consenting. If there is no power of attorney in place, then the decision-maker will be an individual or entity identified under the law. Substitute decision-makers are entitled to all information regarding the treatment of the person's care that may be relevant to the decision. In making decisions they must consider the patients' best interests as well as the wishes expressed by the patients when they were competent. For a more detailed discussion on the law of consent in health care, see Chapter 6.

Even if treatment is authorized for an incompetent patient, based on the necessary considerations and following the required procedures, certain treatments are still excluded; for instance, Saskatchewan and Ontario exclude psychosurgery. In addition, the Manitoba Vulnerable Persons Living with a Mental Disability Act of 1993 specifically excludes research and sterilization that is not medically necessary from the decision-making authority of a substitute decision-maker. Other interventions such as restraint and seclusion also remain controversial.

Can a Person Be Treated in the Community Instead of a Psychiatric Facility?

Orders for community mental health treatment (known as 'leash laws' by opponents) is one of the most controversial issues in mental health law. Under these laws, a person who suffers from a serious mental disorder may agree to a plan of community-based treatment. This is less restrictive than being detained in a psychiatric facility, but once the patient agrees to the order he or she will be required to comply with its terms and may be returned to the issuing physician for examination if there are reasonable grounds to suspect non-compliance (Hiltz and Szigeti, 2004). In the United States, which has a longer history of outpatient commitment, various measures are used as leverage to encourage compliance—access to welfare funds and housing; avoidance of hospitalization and jail (Monahan et al., 2001).

In Canada there are two types of compulsory community treatment provisions. The first type is conditional leave from hospital in which people who continue to meet the requirements of involuntary commitment are allowed to live in the community under certain specified conditions. This type of leave occurs in the mental health legislation of seven of the Canadian provinces. For instance, in PEI a psychiatrist of an involuntary patient can file a certificate of leave with the administrator if the care can be provided in a less restrictive environment (that is, the community) and the patient consents to the leave. Manitoba is the only province with this type of provision that does not allow the leave unless there have been three involuntary admissions or at least 60 days of inpatient stay. Some provinces (Ontario and PEI) do not allow for renewal without re-hospitalization and some have maximum lengths of leave, for instance, in New Brunswick the maximum is 11 days (Gray and O'Reilly, 2005).

The second type of community treatment provision are community treatment orders. Saskatchewan enacted CTOs in 1994, followed by Ontario in 2000 and Nova Scotia in 2005. Ontario enacted CTOs as 'part of the government's plan to create a comprehensive, balanced and effective system of mental health services that provides a continuum of community-based, outpatient and inpatient care' (Ministry of Health and Long-Term Care, 2000). The goal is to eliminate the revolving-door

syndrome, where individuals improve while in the hospital only to relapse after discharge because they don't take their medication. However, for the subjects of CTOs the prospect of 'being forcibly taken to a physician for examination, which may lead to an involuntary admission, simply for failing to take medication as prescribed, is often very troubling' (Hiltz and Szigeti, 2004, p. 273). Therefore, the topic of CTOs continues to be emotionally charged.

The Nova Scotia legislation provides that the physician may issue a CTO if his or her examination and other relevant facts communicated to the physician cause the physician to be of the opinion that:

- the person has a mental disorder for which the person is in need of treatment or care and supervision in the community and the treatment and care can be provided in the community;
- as a result of the mental disorder, the person is threatening or attempting to cause serious harm to himself or herself or has recently done so, has recently caused serious harm to himself or herself, is seriously harming or is threatening serious harm towards another person or has recently done so, or is likely to suffer serious physical impairment or serious mental deterioration, or both;
- as a result of the mental disorder, the person does not have the full capacity to make treatment decisions;
- during the immediately preceding two-year period, the person has been detained in a psychiatric facility for a total of 60 days or longer, or has been detained in a psychiatric facility on two or more separate occasions, or has previously been the subject of a community treatment order; and
- the services that the person requires in order to reside in the community exist in the community, are available to the person, and will be provided to the person.

In Ontario, a CTO can be issued for six months and renewed for another six months. In Nova

Scotia, a CTO is in effect for six months but can be renewed an unspecified number of times.

Studies evaluating CTOs report mixed results (Kisely and Campbell, 2006). A study conducted in Saskatchewan by O'Reilly and colleagues (2000) revealed findings similar to those in the US (Torrey and Kaplan, 1995): although psychiatrists view the orders positively, they rarely use them. For example, in the 21 months from April 1996 to December 1997, only 96 orders (each valid for 3 months after which they must be renewed) were issued in a population of approximately 1 million people. A Toronto study that compared clients on CTOs and a matched group not on CTOs found that patients on CTOs have fewer hospitalizations and reduced hospital days (Hunt et al., 2007). A qualitative study on views of CTOs by patients, family members, and professionals in Saskatchewan demonstrated that patients had contradictory feelings about CTOs. On one hand, they felt coerced into treatment but on the other hand many felt the order was necessary to improve their quality of life. Family members and clinicians believed that the orders were necessary to control chaotic life situations caused by the patients lack of insight into their treatment issues (O'Reilly et al., 2006).

Are There Mechanisms to Protect Financial Security?

Incapacity to manage finances is certainly not a ground for involuntary admission to a hospital, regardless of whether mental health problems impair judgment, but it is often a concern of family members seeking to have someone admitted against their will. Each jurisdiction has a mechanism to declare persons incapable of managing their own funds and have them managed by another authorized individual. In 1927, Ontario's Hospitals for the Insane Act provided a role for the public trustee to act as 'committee of the estate' for a person confined in a psychiatric hospital who had no other person to act as trustee. Interestingly, under this Act the power to appoint a trustee for persons in Saskatchewan

and Manitoba also resided with the lieutenant-governor-in-council of Ontario. Whereas a more recently enacted legislation, the Incompetent Persons' Act of Nova Scotia of 1989, continues to read: 'The relatives or friends of any insane person, or the social services committee of the social services district of which the insane person is an inhabitant, may apply to the court to have a guardian appointed for the insane person.'

The Ontario Substitute Decisions Act provides a mechanism by which someone can grant an individual power of attorney for property when they are capable, in anticipation of the possibility that they may become incapable of managing their finances. This form is often completed when preparing a last will and testament. Someone who is paid to provide health, social, or housing care cannot be designated as a power of attorney. For more discussion on decisions regarding property, see Chapter 6. However, if prior arrangements have not been made, in Ontario, under the Mental Health Act, a physician must assess financial competence upon admission to a psychiatric facility. However, the Act does not cover certificates of financial incompetence for those who are not inpatients (Lieff and Fish, 1996). According to the Ontario Court of Appeal, the test for financial competence includes:

- the ability to understand the nature of the financial decision and the choices available;
- the ability to understand his or her relationship to the parties to and potential beneficiaries of the transactions; and
- the ability to appreciate the consequences of making the decision.

What Might Happen If a Person with a Mental Disorder Is Criminally Charged?

According to US studies, psychotic symptoms are reported in 15 per cent of all prison inmates and 24 per cent of all jail inmates and 6.7 per cent of prisoners have histories of schizophrenia (Lamberti, 2007). In the United Kingdom the incidence of psychotic symptoms is 10 times higher in those in prisons than those in the general community. In Canada, statistics indicate that over the past decade the number of mentally disordered individuals charged with violations of the Criminal Code and entering the criminal justice system has escalated at a rate of 10 per cent annually, although overall arrest and prosecution rates have been declining (Schneider, 2004). Some observers suggest that this is the result of fewer inpatient beds available for treatment without increases in community-based programs and tougher criteria for involuntary admission: 'If the entry of persons exhibiting mentally disordered behaviour into the mental health system of social control is impeded, community pressure will force them into the criminal justice system of social control' (Abramson, 1972, quoted in Hartford et al., 2004).

This view has pushed the justice system to establish procedures to address the rights and needs of these individuals and to assure public safety. As a result, four main areas of difference may occur in some provincial justice systems for those with mental disorders: 1) the possibility of mental health diversion pretrial; 2) the possibility of trial in mental health court; 3) the consideration of whether the person is fit to stand trial; and 4) the possibility of a finding of not criminally responsible.

Mental Health Diversion from Court

Mental Health Diversion Programs are designed to give a more suitable response to low-risk mentally disordered offenders who find themselves in conflict with the criminal justice system because of their mental illness. These programs give offenders who suffer from a mental illness the opportunity to gain the necessary treatment and obtain supports to prevent future criminal activity rather than proceed with current charges through the criminal justice system (CMHA, 2004). Mental Health Diversion Programs have arisen as a result of concerns that people with serious mental illnesses are grossly overrepresented in the criminal justice system and in the detention centres

and jails across Canada. The possibility for court diversion is allowed for in the Criminal Code under the rubric of 'alternative' measures. Nevertheless, the initiation of mental health diversion programs is complex and requires interministerial agreements that deal with the interface between health and justice policies and services.

Currently these programs are available only in Ontario, Alberta, and Quebec. In Ontario, diversion was incorporated into the Crown attorneys' manual in 1994. In that province, when a person suffers from a mental disorder and the Crown believes it is the underlying cause for criminal behaviour, the candidate is seen as suitable for mental health diversion as long as the crime does not include serious violence (Hartford et al., 2004). A decision to proceed with diversion results in a stay of proceedings (that is, stopping of the legal process) with the understanding that the individual will undergo treatment in the community. Although it is still early days in terms of tackling the challenges of coordinating mental health services with legal processes, the program is viewed as a positive step by stakeholders in all constituencies (MacFarlane et al., 2004). Nevertheless, actual data on the effectiveness of these programs is almost non-existent (Hartford et al., 2006).

Fitness to Stand Trial

Under Canadian law, an individual must be both physically present and mentally capable of participating in and understanding a court proceeding against him or her. Mental status is determined at the time of trial (not at the time of offence) and the ability to participate in the court process is labelled 'fitness to stand trial'. Fitness to stand trial refers to the degree to which mental illness affects a person's ability to: 1) understand the nature or object of the proceedings that they face; 2) understand the possible consequences of the proceedings; and 3) communicate with counsel (Tollefson and Starkman, 1993). Fitness is determined via an assessment by a psychiatrist who makes a report to the court. The result of being found unfit to stand trial is that the accused will be subject to a court disposition that may include remaining in detention or treatment in an inpatient psychiatric facility until such time as they become fit (Schneider, 2004). The Criminal Code now contains a provision for treatment in the case of persons found unfit. That is: if there is specific medical evidence indicating that a person likely could become fit within 60 days and that the accused would likely remain unfit without treatment and the risk of treatment is not disproportionate to the benefit and treatment is the least restrictive and obtrusive option then the Court can (after application by the prosecution) order the accused to be treated for a period not exceeding 60 days (Simcoe County Mental Health and Addictions Education, 2005).

If the court declines to make a disposition, or orders either a conditional discharge or custodial disposition, the accused then becomes under the jurisdiction of the provincial review board. The review board can determine when the person is fit to stand trial and can be returned to court.

Mental Health Court

On 11 May 1998 a new courtroom (known as Court 102), designed specifically to deal with mentally disordered offenders, opened at Old City Hall Court in Toronto (Schneider, 1998). Following a 1989 US model introduced in Dade County, Florida, the court uses principles of therapeutic jurisprudence (Steadman, Davidson, and Brown, 2001). Therapeutic jurisprudence focuses on the therapeutic and antitherapeutic consequences of law, legal rules, and legal actions and seeks to apply principles of mental health to address the needs of individuals (particularly those with psychiatric illnesses) who find themselves before the courts (Madden and Wayne, 2003). The aim of Court 102 in Toronto is to enable the application of the rules, regulations, and punishments of the legal system in a manner that appreciates and is appropriate for the mental health system and the mental disorder in question. This is done through on-site assessments, special duty counsel, adjoining cells that are separate from other defendants, specially selected judges, and mental health

workers on-site. A second Mental Health Court opened in Saint John, New Brunswick, in November 2002. In its first seven years of operation, this court had 190 referrals; of these, 43 per cent of cases were for substance abuse disorders and 46 per cent were for schizophrenia, 22 per cent were for mood disorders (note, patients could have more than one diagnosis). People who are referred to this program must comply with treatment in order to be considered to have completed the program. Of those who did complete it, 83 per cent had not re-offended at the time of the 2007 annual review (Brien, 2007). Newfoundland and Labrador has a program in place that is a joint project of the provincial court, the Director of Public Prosecutions, legal aid, and the health service (Moulton, 2007). In 2007, Nova Scotia passed the Mental Health Court Act, which will establish a mental health court in that province as well.

Criminal Responsibility

Canada's first Criminal Code of 1892 made the 'insanity defence' available to an accused person who, because of a 'natural imbecility' or 'disease of the mind', was incapable of appreciating the nature and quality of the act or omission, and of knowing it was wrong. The defence rests on the principle that, in order to convict, the state must prove not only a wrongful act but also a guilty mind. It is based on a common-law defence formulated by the British House of Lords in 1843 (Raaflaub, 2004). In 1991, following a Supreme Court decision (*R. v. Swain*, 1991) that struck down the mental disorders section of the Criminal Code as an infringement of Charter rights, Parliament adopted Bill C-30, which contained provisions for individuals found not criminally responsible (NCR). This legislation was an attempt to balance the goals of fair and humane treatment of mentally disordered offenders with community and public safety (Schneider et al., 2000). It created the possibility for a jury or judge to render a verdict that the accused committed the act or made the omission, but was not criminally responsible on account of mental disorder. Further, it mandated the establishment of provincial review boards that were responsible for monitoring the treatment and confinement of individuals found NCR as a result of mental illness. These review boards are also responsible for individuals who are detained prior to trial and who are 'unfit to stand trial'.

When originally enacted, there was a presumption within Bill C-30 that someone found NCR was dangerous and the onus was on the offender to disprove dangerousness. The prejudice imbedded in this assumption was recognized by the Supreme Court of Canada when it reiterated the finding of the 1975 Law Reform Commission of Canada, that negative stereotypes of the mentally ill had found their way into the criminal justice system (*Winko v. British Columbia Forensic Psychiatric Institute*, 1999). According to the Supreme Court decision in *Winko*, if the board is unable to positively conclude that the NCR offender poses a significant threat (risk of serious physical harm) to the community, the person must be absolutely discharged (Schneider et al., 2000). In total, three discharge possibilities exist for the boards: 1) absolute discharge (no threat); 2) conditional discharge (threat exists, therefore conditions are imposed to manage the threat); and 3) custody order in which the client is in custody of a designated facility under the Criminal Code, usually a psychiatric hospital. The custody order can include community placement under supervision at the discretion of the review board. If a person is given a custody order or conditional discharge it must be reviewed annually by the review board.

Further revisions to section 672 of the Criminal Code were enacted on 30 June 2005 to expand the powers of provincial and territorial review boards by allowing them to order psychiatric assessments in certain restricted situations. They also recommend that the court conduct an inquiry for an unfit person who is not likely to ever become fit and who does not pose a risk to the public. This second provision is the direct result of the Supreme Court decision in *R. v. Demers* (2004), where it was noted that it was unconstitutional to have an individual who was unable to stand trial submit to the powers of the

review board indefinitely when they no longer represented a risk to society.

Recent evidence from the Canadian Centre for Justice Statistics (2003) indicated that in 2001 Canada had approximately 139 new 'unfit accused' before review boards and 581 new 'accused found not criminally responsible on account of mental disorder'. The total number of active cases was approximately 2,717. These numbers do not reflect the total cases before the courts involving a mentally disordered accused, because many accused will receive an absolute discharge by the courts that results in no follow-up by a review board (Raaflaub, 2004).

What Are Our Obligations to Protect the Safety of Family Members?

In 1997, a headline in the *Toronto Star* proclaimed: 'Doctors urged to turn in dangerous patients.' The story discussed the report of the Institute for Clinical Evaluative Studies (1996) that concluded: 'Protecting individuals or the public from likely risk of serious harm . . . should supersede the principle of confidentiality of doctor patient communication' (p. 5). This report was prompted after the killing of an Ottawa lawyer, Patricia Allen, by her estranged husband who six weeks earlier had told his physician that he planned to murder his wife. Colin McGregor was found guilty of first-degree murder in 1993. His physician, following codes of confidentiality prescribed by the Canadian Medical Association (1978), took no action to warn the intended victim. The Allen–McGregor case raised anew the issue of a positive or legal duty to warn innocent third parties (Glancy, Regehr, and Bryant, 1998).

The concept of duty to warn has a long tradition in the United States, where it was highlighted and clarified by the famous Tarasoff decision in California in 1976. In that case a patient told his treating psychologist that he intended to kill his former girlfriend, Ms Tarasoff. The therapist, concluding that the patient was dangerous, contacted the campus police but did not warn the intended victim. Ms Tarasoff was subsequently killed and her family sued the therapist. Despite defence arguments that the duty to warn violated the accepted ethical obligation to maintain confidentiality, the courts ruled in the plaintiff's favour. The court concluded that the confidentiality obligation to a patient ends when public peril begins. This was later codified by amendments to the California Civil Code (California Assembly Bill 1133, 1984) that, because of efforts of the California Psychiatric Association, limited the Tarasoff liability to a 'serious threat' against a 'reasonably identified victim'.

While the Tarasoff decision, requiring a duty to warn and protect third parties, did not apply in Canadian jurisdictions, it was generally assumed that Canadian courts would offer a similar decision should the issue arise (CASW, 2005). Twenty-five years after Tarasoff, the first Canadian precedent-setting case was decided. In *Wenden v. Trikha* (1991) action arose after a voluntarily admitted psychiatric patient left the hospital without the knowledge of hospital staff, drove his car in a dangerous and erratic manner at an excessive rate of speed, and collided with the plaintiff's vehicle. The accident resulted in severe injury to Ms Wenden and the eventual loss of custody of her children because she was unable to care for them. She commenced action against the hospital and the psychiatrist, claiming that they owed her a duty of care and were in breach of that duty by reason of the manner in which they had cared for the patient. Action against both the hospital and doctor was dismissed because it was determined that there was no indication that the patient presented a risk to others and there was no previous relationship between the injured party and the patient. However, the judge suggested that both hospitals and psychiatrists who become aware that a patient presents a serious danger to others owe a duty to warn and protect such a person or persons if a requisite proximity of relationship exists between them. Although this formed the basis of a common-law duty to warn, mental health practitioners continued to question their responsibilities because no provincial or federal statutes (except in Quebec) require or permit therapists to report

clients who threaten to seriously harm a member of the public (Carlisle, 1996).

The Supreme Court of Canada clarified this issue in the 1999 case of *Smith v. Jones* (Chaimowitz, Glancy, and Blackburn, 2000). In the course of a forensic psychiatric examination of Mr Jones, Dr Smith became concerned that Mr Jones would carry out his fantasies to kidnap, rape, and kill prostitutes. Dr Smith notified defence counsel of his concerns, who requested that Dr Smith keep this confidential under solicitor–client privilege. Dr Smith began civil action to allow for disclosure. After a series of appeal processes through the BC courts, the Supreme Court of Canada ruled that danger of serious harm to the public overrules solicitor–client privilege, the highest privilege recognized by the courts. As such, the duty to protect now exists when the following three elements are in place: 1) in the event that risk to a clearly identified person or group of persons is determined; 2) when risk of harm includes bodily injury, death, or serious psychological harm; and 3) when there is an element of imminence, creating a sense of urgency (Chaimowitz and Glancy, 2002).

From a practice perspective, what must a social worker do when caught between the duty to warn and protect and the duty of confidentiality? Appelbaum (1985) recommends a three-part approach: 1) assessing dangerousness; 2) selecting a course of action; and 3) implementing and monitoring. Figure 7.1 shows this process in action after the client makes a threat. First, during the clinical interview, the social worker assesses the risk that this person may present. This involves a thorough assessment, good note-taking, and possible consultation with other professionals, particularly if the social worker is not experienced or skilled in this area. Second, once a determination has been made that the person is dangerous, the social worker needs to determine if he or she suffers from a mental disorder that may qualify for certification under mental health legislation. If the social worker believes the person suffers from a mental disorder and has agreed to assessment, the social worker must ensure transport of the person to a hospital or physician for assessment regarding voluntary or involuntary hospitalization. If the social worker believes that the person does not suffer from a mental disorder or refuses assessment and there is an identifiable victim and a reasonable belief that imminent harm may be suffered by such victim, the social worker must warn the intended victim and law enforcement agencies. The third part of the approach requires monitoring the situation on an ongoing basis and ensuring that the intervention is effective. That is, the duty to protect does not end once someone has taken that person for assessment by a physician. There is no guarantee that the person will be admitted to hospital or will remain in hospital until the risk is eliminated. Therefore, ongoing monitoring is a duty. The process of assessment, intervention, and monitoring serves three important purposes: it ensures the protection of innocent third parties, it protects the client from legal and other consequences on inflicting injury upon others, and it safeguards the social worker against malpractice claims (Glancy et al., 1998).

Figure 7.1   Managing Threats by Clients

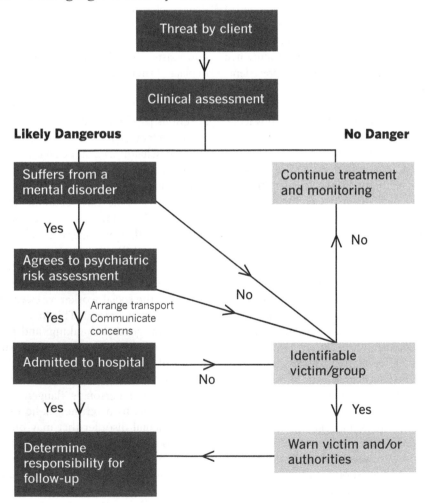

Source: Adapted from Chaimowitz, Glancy, and Blackburn, 2000.

CASE EXAMPLE REVIEWED

We return now to the case of Dr De Sousa and how the legislation discussed in this chapter answers questions directly related to his situation.

Can Dr De Sousa be admitted and held in a psychiatric hospital against his will?

Dr De Sousa clearly suffers from a mental disorder, bipolar affective disorder, which meets the criteria under all provincial and territorial mental health legislation in Canada. Further, his refusal of admission indicates that he cannot be a voluntary patient. There is no question that he meets broad definitions of harm as defined by provinces such as BC and PEI. In provinces that define harm more narrowly, it is questionable whether the previous history of violence and the non-specific threats would meet the criteria of risk of serious bodily harm. Dr De Sousa will need to submit to a psychiatric assessment to determine whether he meets the criteria for involuntary admission.

Can Dr De Sousa be treated against his will while in hospital?

If Dr De Sousa is admitted on an involuntary basis and is declared incapable of consenting to treatment, a treatment decision can be made by an individual holding power of attorney for personal care, a substitute decision-maker, or if necessary an entity authorized by the state. If he previously declared an aversion to particular types of treatments through an advance directive while competent, for instance, to antipsychotic medications, his wishes cannot be overruled.

Can he be treated in the community instead of a psychiatric hospital?

If Dr De Sousa resides in Ontario or Saskatchewan and meets the specified criteria, he may agree to a community treatment order that compels treatment.

Are there mechanisms to protect the financial security of Dr De Sousa and his family?

If Dr De Sousa is deemed incapable of managing his finances, his funds can be managed by a person designated with the power of attorney for property. Failing this, an application may be brought to the court designating someone known to him or the public guardian and trustee responsible for Dr De Sousa's finances.

What could happen to Dr De Sousa if he were criminally charged?

If Dr De Sousa were to commit a criminal offence and be charged, several issues would be considered: 1) the seriousness of the crime; 2) his fitness to stand trial; and 3) if he is found guilty of the offence, whether or not he is criminally responsible for his actions. If he was in Ontario, he may be seen by the Mental Health Diversion Program, at which time alternatives to court would be considered. However, if his offence was sufficiently grave (for example, murder) or he was charged in a province or territory without a diversion program, he would be assessed first for fitness. If unfit, he would be remanded to a psychiatric facility until he was fit to stand trial. Upon an NCR finding, he would go under the jurisdiction of the provincial or territorial review board, which would determine appropriate and safe placement, according to his needs weighed against the safety of the public.

What are the obligations of the mental health system to protect the safety of Mrs De Sousa?

If the treatment team believes that Dr De Sousa presents a risk to his wife, they are obligated to assess him for involuntary admission to hospital. If, for whatever reason, they are unable to keep him in hospital, they are obligated to inform Mrs De Sousa of the risk and perhaps inform the local police.

Key Terms

Community Treatment Orders (CTOs)
Issued by a certified physician to provide a person with community-based treatment or care and supervision that is less restrictive to the person than being detained in a hospital environment if the individual fulfills the requisite criteria

Duty to Protect/Warn
Overrides the solicitor–client confidentiality privilege in cases where there is a risk of harm to a clearly identified person or group of persons; the risk includes bodily injury, death, or serious psychological harm, and there is an element of imminence that creates a sense of urgency

Fitness to Stand Trial
Measurement of an individual's mental capability to participate in the court process determined by a psychiatric assessment at the time of the trial; this includes the degree to which mental illness affects the person's ability to understand the nature or object of the proceedings that they face, understand the possible consequences of the proceedings, and communicate with counsel

Involuntary Admission
The ability to admit an individual into a hospital without their consent; in general, the requirement is that an individual has a mental disorder of a nature or quality that will likely result in harm to self or another person—in some provinces this also includes the risk of substantial mental or physical deterioration

Mental Health Court
A courtroom designed specifically to deal with mentally disordered offenders that applies the principles of therapeutic jurisprudence to ensure that the rules, regulations, and punishments of the legal system are applied in a way that is appropriate for the mental health system and the mental disorder in question

Mental Health Diversion Program
Designed to give low-risk mentally disordered offenders who find themselves in conflict with the criminal justice system because of their mental illness the opportunity to gain necessary treatment and supports to prevent future criminal activity rather than proceed with the current charges in the criminal justice system

Not Criminally Responsible (NCR)
Legislation creating the opportunity for the jury or judge to render a verdict that the accused committed the act in question but was not criminally responsible due to their mental disorder; the legislation also creates provincial review boards to monitor the treatment and confinement of individuals found NCR because of mental illness

Therapeutic Jurisprudence
Focuses on the therapeutic and antitherapeutic consequences of law, legal rules, and legal actions and seeks to apply principles of mental health to address needs of individuals with psychiatric illnesses who have to go through the court process

Discussion Questions

1. How do politics and law intersect with respect to mental health legislation?
2. What are the general grounds by which individuals can be put into hospital against their will? How do these grounds balance the rights of the patient, the family, and society?
3. How do issues of consent to treatment intersect with social work values and ethics?
4. What are the positive and negative aspects of community treatment orders?
5. What alternatives could a social worker seek for a client with a mental disorder who commits a crime?

Relevant Legislation

Historical

An Act respecting Asylums for the Insane, Assented to 15th February 1871, Ontario

Hospitals for the Insane Act, Assented to 5th April 1927, Ontario

Mental Hospitals Act, Assented to 18th April 1935, Ontario

Mental Health Act, Assented to 15th June 1967, Ontario

Mental Health Act, 1978

Mental Health Act, RSO, 1984, c. 11, s. 194

Federal

Canadian Charter of Rights and Freedoms: Part 1 of the Constitution Act 1982, being Schedule B to the Canada Act (UK), c. 11
http://laws.justice.gc.ca/en/charter/

Criminal Code of Canada, R.S.C. 1985, c. C-46
http://laws.justice.gc.ca/en/C-46/

Alberta

Dependent Adults Act, R.S.A. 2000, c. D-11
http://www.canlii.org/ab/laws/sta/d-11/

Mental Health Act, R.S.A. 2000, c. M-13
http://www.canlii.org/ab/laws/sta/m-13/index.html

British Columbia

Mental Health Act, R.S.B.C. 1996, c. 288
http://www.qp.gov.bc.ca/statreg/stat/M/96288_01.htm

Manitoba

Mental Health Act, C.C.S.M., c. M110
http://www.canlii.org/mb/laws/sta/m-110/index.html

Vulnerable Persons Living with a Mental Disability Act, S.M. 1993, c. 29
http://www.gov.mb.ca/fs/pwd/vpact.html

New Brunswick

Mental Health Act, R.S.N.B. 1973, c. M-10
http://www.gnb.ca/0062/acts/BBR-2000/2000-52.pdf

Newfoundland and Labrador

Mental Health Care and Treatment Act, S.N.L. 2006, c. M-9.1
http://www.canlii.org/nl/laws/sta/m-9.1/index.html

Nova Scotia

Hospitals Act, S.N.S. 1989, c. 208
http://www.canlii.org/ns/laws/sta/r1989c.208/20080717/whole.html

Incompetent Persons Act, R.S.N.S. 1989, c. 218
http://www.canlii.org/ns/laws/sta/r1989c.218/20080717/whole.html

Involuntary Psychiatric Treatment Act, S.N.S. 2005, c. 42
http://www.canlii.org/ns/laws/sta/2005c.42/index.html

Mental Health Court Act, S.N.S., 2007
http://www.gov.ns.ca/legislature/legc/bills/60th_2nd/1st_read/b021.htm

Ontario

Health Care Consent Act, R.S.O. 1996, c. 2
http://192.75.156.68/DBLaws/Statutes/English/96h02_e.htm

Mental Health Act, R.S.O. 1990, c. M-7
http://www.e-laws.gov.on.ca/DBLaws/Statutes/English/90m07_e.htm

Substitute Decisions Act, S.O. 1992, c. 30
http://www.canlii.org/on/laws/sta/1992c.30/20080716/whole.html

Prince Edward Island

Mental Health Act, S.P.E.I. 1994, c. 39
http://www.gov.pe.ca/law/statutes/pdf/m-06_1.pdf

Quebec

An Act Respecting the Protection of persons whose mental state presents a danger to themselves or others, S.Q. 2002, c. P-38.001
http://www.canlii.org/qc/laws/sta/p-38.001/20040802/whole.html

Civil Code of Québec, S.Q. 1991, c. 64
http://www.canlii.org/qc/laws/sta/ccq/2004
0901/part1.html

Saskatchewan
Mental Health Services Act, S.S. 1984–85–86,
c. M-13.1
http://www.canlii.org/sk/laws/sta/m-13.1/

Northwest Territories
Mental Health Act, R.S.N.W.T. 1988, c. M-10
http://www.canlii.org/nt/laws/sta/m-10/

Nunavut
Mental Health Act (Nunavut), R.S.N.W.T. 1988,
c. M-10
http://www.nunavutcourtofjustice.ca/library/
consol-stat/CSNu_1999_126_Mental_Health.pdf

Yukon Territory
Mental Health Act, R.S.Y. 2002, c. 150
http://www.canlii.org/yk/laws/sta/150/index.
html

References

Ambrosini, D. and Crocker, A. (2007), 'Psychiatric Advance Directives and the Right to Refuse Treatment in Canada', *Canadian Journal of Psychiatry*, 52(6): 397–402.

Appelbaum, P. (1985), 'Tarasoff and the Clinician: Problems in Fulfilling the Duty to Protect', *American Journal of Psychiatry*, 142: 425–9.

——— (1991), 'Advance Directives for Psychiatric Treatment', *Hospital and Community Psychiatry*, 42: 983–4.

——— (1994), *Almost a Revolution* (New York: Oxford University Press).

Bagby, M. (1987), 'The Effects of Legislative Reform on Admission Rates to Psychiatric Units of General Hospitals', *International Journal of Law and Psychiatry*, 10: 383–94.

———, Thompson, J., Dickens, S., and Nohara, M. (1991), 'Decision-making in Psychiatric Commitment: An Experimental Analysis', *American Journal of Psychiatry*, 48: 28–33.

Bay, M., Fram, S., Silberfeld, M., Shushelski, C., and Bloom, H. (1996), 'Capacity and Substitute Decision Making for Personal Care', in H. Bloom and M. Bay (eds), *A Practical Guide to Mental Health, Capacity and Consent Law of Ontario* (Toronto: Carswell).

Brien, A. (2008), *Tackling Challenges: Mental Health Court Annual Report* (Saint John, NB: Provincial Court).

Burlington Post (2001, 17 October), 'Brian's Law Broadens Criteria for Treatment of Mentally Ill'.

California Assembly Bill 1133 (1984), McAllister, Sections 43–92.

Canadian Centre for Justice Statistics (2003), *Special Study on Mentally Disordered Accused and the Criminal Justice System* (Ottawa: Minister of Industry).

Canadian Charter of Rights and Freedoms, 1982.

Canadian Medical Association (1978), *Code of Ethics* (Ottawa: Canadian Medical Association).

Canadian Mental Health Association (CMHA) (2004), 'Mental Health Diversion' (accessed 11 November 2004 at http://www.cmha-tb.on.ca/ mhdiversion.htm).

Capponi, P. (2003), *Beyond the Crazy House* (Toronto: Penguin).

Carlisle, J. (1996, 21 July/August), 'Duty to Warn: Report from Council', *Members' Dialogue, Canadian Medical Association*.

CASW (2005), *Code of Ethics* (Ottawa: Canadian Association of Social Workers).

Chaimowitz, G. and Glancy G. (2002), 'The Duty to Protect', *Canadian Journal of Psychiatry*, 47: 1–4.

——— and Blackburn, J. (2000), 'The Duty to Warn and Protect: Impact on Practice', *Canadian Journal of Psychiatry*, 45: 899–904.

Fleming v. Reid (1991), 4 O.R. (3d) 74.

Glancy, G., Regehr, C., and Bryant, A. (1998), 'Confidentiality in Crisis: Part I, The Duty to Inform', *Canadian Journal of Psychiatry*, 43(12): 1001–5.

Goffman, I. (1961), *Asylums: Essays on the Social Situation of Mentally Ill and Other Inmates* (Chicago: Aldine).

Gray, J. and O'Reilly, R. (2005), 'Canadian Compulsory Community Treatment Laws: Recent Reforms', *International Journal of Law and Psychiatry*, 28: 13–22.

———, Shone, M., and Liddle, P. (2000), *Canadian Mental Health Law and Policy* (Toronto: Butterworths).

Hardin, H. (2004), 'Uncivil Liberties: Far from Respecting Civil Liberties, Legal Obstacles to Treating the Mentally Ill Limit or Destroy the Liberty of the Person', (accessed 5 November 2004 at http://www.psychlaws.org/JoinUs/CatalystArchive/CatWinter02.htm).

Hartford, K., Carey, R., and Mendonca, J. (2006), 'Pre-arrest Diversion of People with Mental Illness: Literature Review and International Survey', *Behavioural Sciences and the Law*, 24: 845–56.

———, Davies, S., Dobson, C., Dykeman, C., Furham, B., et al. (2004), *Evidence-based Practices in Diversion Programs for Persons with Serious Mental Illness Who Are in Conflict with the Law: Literature Review and Synthesis* (Toronto: Mental Health Foundation and Ontario Ministry of Long-Term Care).

————, Schrecker, T., Wiktorowicz, M., Hoch, J., and Sharp, C. (2003), 'Four Decades of Mental Health Policy in Ontario, Canada', *Administration and Policy in Mental Health*, 31(1): 65–73.

Hiltz, D. and Szigeti, A. (2004), *A Guide to Consent and Capacity in Ontario* (Markham, ON: LexisNexis Butterworths).

Hoffman, R. and Putnam, L. (2004), *Not Just Another Call: Police Response to People with Mental Illnesses in Ontario* (Toronto: Centre for Addiction and Mental Health).

Hunt, A., da Silva, A., Lurie, S., and Goldblum, D. (2007), 'Community Treatment Orders in Toronto: The Emerging Data', *Canadian Journal of Psychiatry*, 52(10): 647–56.

Institute for Clinical and Evaluative Studies (1996), *Final Recommendations of Ontario's Medical Expert Panel on the Duty to Inform* (Toronto: Institute for Clinical and Evaluative Studies).

Kaiser, H.A. (2002), 'Mental Disability Law', in J. Downie, T. Caulfield, and C. Flood (eds), *Canadian Health Law and Policy* (Toronto: Butterworths).

Ketchum v. Hislop (1984), 54 B.C.L.R. 327 (B.C.S.C.).

Kisely, S. and Campbell, L. (2006), 'Community Treatment Orders for Psychiatric Patients: The Emperor with No Clothes', *Canadian Journal of Psychiatry*, 51(11): 683–5.

Lamberti, S. (2007), 'Understanding and Preventing Criminal Recidivism among Adults with Psychotic Disorders', *Psychiatric Services*, 58(6): 773–81.

Lieff, S. and Fish, A. (1996), 'Financial Capacity, Contracts and Property', in H. Bloom and M. Bay (eds), *A Practical Guide to Mental Health, Capacity and Consent Law of Ontario* (Toronto: Carswell).

Macfarlane, D., Lurie, S., Bettridge, S., and Barbaree, H. (2004), 'Mental Health Services in the Courts: A Program Review', *Health Law in Canada* 25(2): 21–8.

Madden, R. and Wayne, R. (2003), 'Social Work and the Law: A Therapeutic Jurisprudence Perspective', *Social Work*, 48(3): 338–47.

Martin, B. and Cheung, K. (1985), 'Civil Commitment in Ontario: The Effect of Legislation on Clinical Practices', *Canadian Journal of Psychiatry*, 30(4): 259–64.

Ministry of Health and Long-Term Care (2000), 'Brian's Law, Mental Health Legislative Reform' (accessed 10 November 2004 at http://www. health.gov.on.ca/english/public/program/mentalhealth/mental_reform/brians_law.html).

Monahan, J., Bonnie, R., Appelbaum, P., Hyde, P., Steadman, H., and Swartz, M. (2001), 'Mandated Community Treatment: Beyond Outpatient Commitment', *Psychiatric Services*, 52(9): 1198–205.

Moulton, D. (2007), 'Mental Health Courts Gain Popularity across Canada', *The Lawyers Weekly*, 28(23), 17 October 2008.

Nelson, G. (2006), 'Mental Health Policy in Canada,' in A. Westhues (ed.), *Canadian Social Policy: Issues and Perspectives* (Waterloo, ON: Wilfrid Laurier University Press).

O'Reilly, R., Keegan, D., Corring, D., Shrikhande, S., and Natarajan, D. (2006), 'A Qualitative Analysis of the Use of Community Treatment Orders in Saskatchewan', *International Journal of Law and Psychiatry*, 29: 516–24.

O'Reilly, R., Keegan, D., and Elias, J. (2000), 'A Survey of the Use of Community Treatment Orders by Psychiatrists in Saskatchewan', *Canadian Journal of Psychiatry*, 45: 79–81.

Page, S. (1980), 'New Civil Commitment Legislation: The Relevance of Commitment Criteria', *Canadian Journal of Psychiatry*, 25: 646–50.

Psychiatric Survivor Action Association of Ontario (PSAAO) (2004), (accessed 5 November 2004 at http://www.icomm.ca/psaao/).

Raaflaub, W. (2004, 14 October), Bill C-10: An act to amend the Criminal Code (mental disorder) and to make consequential amendments to other acts, *Legislative Summaries* (accessed 12 November 2004 at http://www.parl.gc.ca).

Reference re Mental Health Act (1984), 5 D.R.L. (4th) 577 (P.E.I.C.A.).

R. v. Demers, [2004] 2 S.C.R. 489, 2004 SCC 46.

R. v. Swain (1991), 1 SCR 933.

Ritchie, J., Sklar, R., and Steiner, W. (1998), 'Advance Directives in Psychiatry: Resolving Issues of Autonomy and Competence', *International Journal of Law and Psychiatry*, 21(3): 245–60.

Rozovsky, L. (2003), *The Canadian Law of Consent to Treatment* (Toronto: Butterworths).

Schneider, R. (1988), *Ontario Mental Health Statutes* (Toronto: Carswell).

———— (1998, 4 December), 'Mental Disorder in the Courts', *Criminal Lawyers Association Newsletter*, 19.

———— (2004), 'The Mentally Disordered Offender', *Bar Admissions Course* (Toronto: Law Society of Upper Canada).

————, Glancy, G., Bradford, J., and Seibenmorgen, E. (2000), 'Canadian Landmark Case, *Winko v. British Columbia*: Revisiting the Conundrum of the Mentally Disordered Accused', *Journal of the American Academy of Psychiatry and the Law*, 28(2): 206–12.

Simcoe County Mental Health and Addictions Education (2005), 'Mental Health Processes in Ontario: Fitness to Stand Trial' (accessed at http://www.mhcva.on.ca/MHP/mhpfor3.htm).

Smith v. Jones (1999), 1 S.C.R. 455, 1999 CanLII 674 (S.C.C.).

Steadman, H., Davidson, S., and Brown, C. (2001), 'Mental Health Courts: Their Promise and Unanswered Questions', *Psychiatric Services*, 52(4): 457–8.

Szasz, T. (1963), *Law, Liberty and Psychiatry* (New York: Macmillan).

Tollefson, E. and Starkman, B. (1993), *Mental Disorder in Criminal Proceedings* (Toronto: Carswell).

Torrey, E. and Kaplan R. (1995), 'A National Survey of the Use of Outpatient Commitment', *Psychiatric Services*, 46: 778–84.

Wenden v. Trikha (1991), 116 A.R. 81 (Alta. Q.B.).

Winko v. British Columbia (Forensic Psychiatric Institute) (1999), 2 SCR 625.

CHAPTER EIGHT

Youth in the Criminal Justice System

OBJECTIVES

- To describe the history and context of youth criminal justice legislation in Canada
- To discuss the alternatives to charging of young offenders
- To describe the process for youth who are charged under youth criminal justice legislation
- To review alternatives in sentencing
- To discuss the role of parents in the youth criminal justice system

CASE EXAMPLE

Ray Larch is a 17-year-old man who has been charged under the Youth Criminal Justice Act in connection with a fire in his parents' home. Ray placed a gasoline bomb in a heating oven causing an explosion that resulted in $150,000 damage. The family dog and cat died in the fire. Ray's younger brother broke into the burning house in order to rescue the pets and suffered severe smoke inhalation and serious burns as a result; he had to be hospitalized in an intensive care unit.

Ray's mother is a salesclerk and his father is a manager in a manufacturing firm. Ray was adopted at 12 days of age. He was informed of the adoption at a very young age and did not appear to feel that it was an issue for him. His one younger brother is the biological child of his parents. Ray began to exhibit behavioural problems in grade 9. He stopped doing his homework, started skipping school, and then attempted to hide his report card from his parents. His parents began noticing items missing from the house, such as money, liquor, and jewellery. They believe that it was at this time he began using marijuana.

At the age of 14 he was charged with assault against another child under the Young Offenders Act, for which he received an absolute discharge. Over the next two years, he was charged with breaking and entering, grand theft, and assault. In replying to each charge, Ray denied that he was at fault and, according to his father, has never shown remorse. A year ago, Ray was remanded to a detention centre for one month because he drove stolen construction machinery down the middle of the road while he was stoned. Following the detention, he was placed on probation, with the stipulation that his parents monitor his behaviour. He refused to come home at night, however, and was destructive to property. As a result, his father reported him to the probation officer. Ray became enraged but still did not comply with the rules. The probation officer apparently commented to Mr Larch that he had never seen a youth with as much rage as Ray.

- Is Ray considered a youth offender?
- What are the alternatives to court and incarceration?
- Once charged, how do youth proceed through the justice system?
- What are the possible outcomes?
- How will Ray's parents be involved in the situation?

The Context of Young Offender Legislation in Canada

The history of legislation regarding youth offenders in many ways parallels that of child welfare legislation discussed in Chapter 4. During the 1700s and 1800s, as Canada developed into a country, children were at risk of delinquency because of social conditions. Large numbers of children were orphaned or abandoned for many reasons—the death of their parents on ships arriving from Europe, conditions within military garrisons, epidemics such as typhus, and a European practice of sending poor and unwanted children to the colonies. Nevertheless, most youth crime was petty in nature. For example, it is reported that most of the three hundred youth imprisoned in New Brunswick between 1846 and 1857 were charged with drunkenness, theft, and vagrancy (Department of Justice, 2004). Treatment of delinquent children paralleled practices in France and England at the time. Children were considered little adults and sentences meted out to them were cruel and harsh (Parkinson, 2003). These included such things as the death by hanging of a 16-year-old girl for theft in New France in 1649, placement in an iron collar or branding for servant girls breaking their contracts, the hanging of a 13-year-old boy for theft in Montreal in 1813, hard labour, starvation diets, and whipping (Department of Justice, 2004). Mercy was shown to children under the age of 7 who were deemed incapable of doing wrong. Children between the ages of 7 and 13 were also considered 'incapable', but this could be overturned if it was demonstrated that the child had the experience and intelligence to understand the nature and consequences of the crime.

By the late 1800s reformation of the laws dealing with young offenders began with the Industrial Schools Act of 1874, which directed the opening of special schools for children convicted of petty crimes. This was followed by amendments to the Criminal Code in 1875 to allow 16 year olds to be sent to reformatories instead of jail, An

Act respecting Arrest, Trial and Imprisonment of Youthful Offenders in 1894 that provided for the separation of youth and adult offenders (where possible), and further amendments to the Criminal Code in 1892. The major shift came with the passage of the Juvenile Delinquents Act (JDA) in 1908 that was grounded in the doctrine of *parens patriae* or the state as a kindly parent (Department of Justice, 2004). Under this Act youth were to be dealt with not as adult offenders, but as being in a condition of delinquency and requiring help and guidance and supervision. The Act provided for a separate justice system, a focus on rehabilitation, and increased parental involvement (Parkinson, 2003). Sentencing options varied, but included suspension of disposition, adjournment without penalty, fines, probation, placement with Children's Aid Society, and indeterminate committal to training school.

The JDA remained in effect for the next 73 years, despite rising concerns in the 1960s and 1970s about regional disparities in the application of the Act, the possibility for abuse of children in the reform school system, and the fact that children's treatment under the law did not reflect their rights as stated by the 1960 Canadian Bill of Rights. Therefore, in 1982, Parliament passed the Young Offenders Act (YOA). This Act reflected a shift in philosophy from previous legislation by incorporating such concepts as youth must take responsibility for their actions if they commit offences, society has a right to protection from youth crime, and sentencing of young offenders should reflect the seriousness of the crime. In addition it mandated consistency across the country, sought to ensure that children's rights under the Canadian Charter of Rights and Freedoms were protected, and raised the minimum age for criminal charges from 7 to 12 (Department of Justice, 2004; Parkinson, 2003). Nevertheless, criticisms of the Act suggested that it was too lenient and that sentences did not reflect the seriousness of some crimes. Subsequent amendments to the YOA in 1986, 1992, and 1995 extended the maximum penalties for murder and made provisions for transfer to adult court. Other critics suggested that the penalties for young people were too harsh and that youth were being incarcerated for relatively minor crimes; they cited high incarceration rates compared to other Western countries.

The Youth Criminal Justice Act (YCJA), which came into force on 1 April 2003, attempts to balance the legalistic framework of the YOA with the social justice approach of the JDA. This is clearly stated in the preamble to the Act:

> members of society share a responsibility to address the developmental challenges and the needs of young persons and to guide them into adulthood; . . . communities, families, parents and others concerned with the development of young persons should, through multi-disciplinary approaches, take reasonable steps to prevent youth crime by addressing its underlying causes, to respond to the needs of young persons, and to provide guidance and support to those at risk of committing crimes.

In addition, the Act seeks to rehabilitate young persons who commit offences and to reintegrate them into society while ensuring that they are subject to meaningful consequences. This Act increases the extrajudicial measures available (RGMP, 2005), reintroduces youth justice committees for community-based solutions, creates new models for trying youth who have committed serious crimes, and lowers the age for sentencing youth as adults if the youth has committed either aggravated sexual assault or murder (Parkinson, 2003). Despite these sentencing changes, critics remained concerned and headlines such as 'New law too soft on violent youth: Some walk out of court laughing' (Blackwell, 2005) appeared in national newspapers with regularity.

The criticisms of the Act rose to a crescendo in the federal election of the fall of 2008. Prime Minister Stephen Harper in his bid for re-election, presented the YCJA as a major election issue.

> Stephen Harper vowed that a re-elected Conservative government would reduce protections under the Youth Criminal Justice

Act for young people convicted of serious crimes. Under the Conservative leader's proposal, young people 14 and over found guilty of crimes such as manslaughter, murder or aggravated assault would face tougher sentences, and no longer have their identities protected. . . . 'In this new legislation, the main purpose will be not only to rehabilitate young offenders, but also to protect society, and the primary goal of sentencing will be to deter others from violating the law,' Harper said at an event (CBC, 2008).

The response to this position was immediate with some supporting stiffer sentences and others decrying the move as ignoring the complexities of youth crime and the plight of young people who are moved to commit crime (Clark, Alphonso, and Perreaux, 2008). The position stated by Mr Harper was not merely an election position and represented a part of a longer process that had been initiated by the federal government.

In 2007 Rob Nicholson, the Minister of Justice and Attorney General of Canada, presented a consultation paper on pretrial detentions under the Youth Criminal Justice Act (Department of Justice, 2007). One of the issues raised in that review was that jurisdictions had vast differences regarding the conditions of release of youth prior to their trial date. It was reported that the average number of bail conditions imposed on young people ranged from 2.9 in Edmonton to 4.4 in Scarborough and Vancouver. The use of specific types of conditions varied widely as well. For instance, prohibited possession of a firearm ranged from 1 to 48 per cent, and reporting to police or probation ranged from 0 per cent in Scarborough to 93 per cent in Vancouver. The report noted that the YCJA did not allow conditions of release to be either punitive or for the purposes of rehabilitation or treatment, yet in 13 per cent of cases the youth was ordered to seek treatment. As a result, questions were raised whether provisions of the Act were being differentially applied due to the inability of the Act to address some core issues. This particular consultation process is part a general trend to review the Act and consider whether provisions should be changed.

How Old Is a Youth Offender?

The YCJA applies to 'young persons' who were 12 to 17 years of age at the time of the offence (not the time of the charges or trial). Children under 12 are deemed too young to fully understand the nature and consequences of their behaviour and therefore are not criminally responsible under the Act. Even though they may seem 'street smart' and tough, it is believed that they cannot understand the complexities of the Canadian justice system and it would be unjust to allow the full weight of it to fall on them. This conceptualization of when a child is able to appreciate information affecting him- or herself and others parallels the guidelines for consent to medical treatment discussed in Chapter 6. The YCJA is premised on the notion that young people should be held responsible for their acts, but that they should be given the opportunity to mature, learn from their mistakes, accept the consequences of their actions, and make amends. Thus, they should be treated differently from adults who are expected to understand and be fully accountable for their actions (Alberta Law Foundation, 2005), except in cases of serious crimes where 14 to 16 year olds, depending on the jurisdiction, may be sentenced as adults. This is the provision that was mostly recently subject to debate, with the prime minister suggesting that the circumstances under which adult sentences are applied be expanded.

What Are Alternatives to Court and Incarceration?

One of the key aspects of the YCJA is the degree of discretion that is built in at various stages of the process. Extrajudicial measures occur at the police–youth contact level, at the time of contact by the Crown attorney, or later as extrajudicial sanctions. The goal is to deal with minor cases effectively outside of the court process, thereby reducing the expenditure of court time and allowing for early intervention and timely disposition. In large part, this was motivated by a House of Commons report that found that young offenders were being given custodial sentences at a rate four times higher than that of adults, twice as high as in the US, and 10 to 15 times higher than in Australia and many European countries (Bala and Anand, 2004). Some critics are skeptical about these findings and the methodologies used in the research, but it is generally acknowledged that minor cases, including theft under $5,000, possession of stolen property, failure to appear in court, and failure to comply with a court order or disposition such as probation, accounted for more than 40 per cent of the cases in youth court under the YOA (Department of Justice, 2002). The YCJA presumes that extrajudicial measures are an adequate means to hold a young person accountable if that person has committed a non-violent offence and has not previously been found guilty of an offence. Further, these measures may also be used for repeat offenders if they are adequate to hold a young person accountable. Other goals of extrajudicial measures are reparation of harm and encouragement of family, victim, and community involvement.

Thus, the YCJA reflects the growing international awareness of and commitment to restorative models of justice. The term 'restorative justice' is used to describe informal and non-adjudicative forms of dispute resolution, such as victim–offender mediation, family conferences, neighbourhood accountability boards, and peacemaking circles that promote joint decision-making power (Roach, 2000; Bazemore and Schiff, 2001). In general it involves three components: 1) restoring victims to their pre-offence state (both financially and psychologically (Zehr, 1995); 2) restoring offenders to a law-abiding lifestyle; and 3) repairing harms to the community (Gromet and Darley, 2006). During the process of restoration, victims of crime are provided with opportunities to discuss how the crime affected them, get information about the offender's motivation, and have input into sanctions and restoration (Bazemore, 2001).

Restoration to the victim or community involves two processes: 1) negotiation of a mutually agreeable restitution plan for compensating the victim (Umbreit, 1995); and 2) a process intended to allow healing, such as apologies to the victim, either by the offender or by an organization that allowed the abuse to occur through negligence. This model attempts to move from punishment to repairing the harms caused by the crime by balancing the needs of the victims, citizens, and offenders.

Restorative justice is a significant departure from the retributive model in which the needs of the victim are considered secondary to the needs of police, judges, and prosecutors and in which resources to assist victims are scarce. Early studies looking at the efficacy of restorative models suggested that victims felt satisfied, perceive themselves fairly treated by the justice system (Marshall, 1995; Umbreit, 1999; Umbreit, Coates, and Roberts, 2000), and feel less shame and fear (Helfgott et al., 2000). As a result, the Supreme Court of Canada has embraced restorative justice as a legitimate form of sentencing (Roach, 2000) and Canada is viewed by many as being at the forefront of advances in this type of justice (Braithwaite, 2000; Goren, 2001). Indeed, the first reported program of victim–offender mediation was initiated in Kitchener, Ontario, in 1974.

Critics are skeptical, however, of success claims for restorative justice in situations involving violence and, in particular, sexual violence. They argue that victims can feel pressured to engage in a process that serves to reproduce and reinforce the imbalance of power between the offender and the victim (Hudson, 1998; Griffiths, 1999; Shenk and Zehr, 2001; Cameron, 2006). In fact, the guilt, shame, and humiliation that the offender is intended to feel is often experienced by the victim (Koss, 2000). This has caused some critics to question whether the aims of restorative justice are indeed directed more towards the benefit of the offender than the victim (Roach, 2000) and whether restorative justice is simply another means of exercising social control (LaPraire, 1996). This leads some to continue to push for

longer sentences aimed at holding offenders responsible for their actions—acknowledging the degree of harm suffered by victims and protecting the public.

More recent writers suggest that the success or failure of restorative justice needs to be considered in a more nuanced manner (Balfour, 2008). The evidence suggests that relative to court processes, restorative justice programs tend to reduce re-offending, but with considerable variation between the type of offence and contexts. While some studies report overall better outcomes in terms of re-offence for youth referred to restorative justice programs (Bergseth and Bouffard, 2007), others find that restorative justice models may be more effective in some situations than others. For instance, one study of almost five thousand youth charged with offences in the United States discovered that girls (as opposed to boys) and those with minimal previous criminal history records exhibited the greatest success from participating in restorative justice programs (Rodriguez, 2007). Another study found improvement in youth charged with status offences (for instance, failing to appear in court or breaching a bail order) and youth with property crimes as a result of participating in restorative justice programs, but did not find as positive outcomes for youth with crimes of violence (de Beus and Rodriguez, 2007). Further, conclusions regarding success are often muddied by self-selection issues and the severity of cases referred to restorative justice when compared to those referred to the courts (Wenzel et al., 2008). That is, cases involving more serious crimes or involving repeat offenders tend to be referred to traditional criminal justice processes involving the courts and incarceration while more minor property violations by first offenders tend to be sent the restorative justice route. These findings of outcome and common practices for the most part parallel public attitudes. Research suggests that the public believes that as crimes increase in seriousness, restorative models should include a retributive component (such as jail sentences). In the absence of this, people believe that restorative models are not fair for victims (Gromet and Darley, 2006).

Police Discretion

The first stage at which discretion is exercised is at the point of contact between the police officer and the young person who is believed to have committed a crime. Section 6 of the YCJA requires that, in all cases where charges could be laid, police officers consider the following options:

1. *Taking no further action* may occur when the parents or the victim have taken sufficient steps to hold the young person accountable.
2. *Warning the young person* involves an informal warning or stern speaking to by the police officer. A study from England suggested that while parents felt that an informal warning was effective, juveniles expected and responded more favourably to a more formal approach (Tweedie, 1982).
3. *Giving the young person a formal caution* is generally done in the form of a letter to the young person and his or her parents or may involve the young person and the parents coming to the police station to speak to a senior officer. According to the Department of Justice (2002), studies reported in New Zealand and Australia suggest that 70 to 87 per cent of those cautioned do not come to the attention of police or are not convicted of an offence in the next two years. Other studies have found no differences between those dealt with by the courts and those issued warnings, leading to the conclusion that warnings are preferable for the purposes of freeing up the court system, reducing the stigma on the young person, and reducing the contact of the young person with others charged and convicted of crimes (Farrington and Bennett, 1981; Krause, 1981).
4. *With the consent of the young person, referring them to a community program* that may include recreational programs, counselling services, child welfare agencies, or mental health programs. Because a young person may feel coerced by the police officer to accept a referral, he or she is to be informed of the right to counsel (Department of Justice, 2002).

If these measures are not deemed sufficient or appropriate, the police officer can charge the young person or refer them to a Crown attorney who can issue a warning or consider an extrajudicial sanction.

In two jurisdictions, however, British Columbia and Quebec, the police do not lay charges against youth. In British Columbia, pre-charge screening is conducted by the Crown, which involves a review of police documentation and a Crown decision to charge or to take no further action, other than perhaps to send a Crown caution letter (Moyer and Basic, 2005).

Research suggests that the YCJA has had a significant impact on police-charging practices. In one study, data for 1986 to 2003 from the Uniform Crime Reporting Survey were analyzed in order to identify changes that occurred in 2003. The researchers found that in 2003 after the implementation of the Act, there was a substantial reduction at the national level and in most provinces and territories in the number of young people charged or recommended by police to be charged, and a corresponding increase in the use of extrajudicial measures with apprehended youth. Levels of charging for minor offences such as 'theft under' and drug-related offences were reduced by one-third, while levels of charging for serious property and violent offences (other than common assault) decreased only slightly. The researchers concluded that the impact of the YCJA on police-charging practices was remarkably strong, immediate, and consistent with the objectives and principles of the Act (Carrington and Schulenberg, 2005).

Extrajudicial Sanctions

Extrajudicial sanctions were referred to as alternative measures under the YOA and are not unlike diversion programs in adult mental health court (see Chapter 7). Essentially, these measures seek to hold youth accountable and provide opportunities for them to make amends outside of the court system. These programs are provincially operated and funded and, therefore, there is considerable variability across the country.

Community youth justice committees are one form of extrajudicial sanction. In Manitoba, justice committees began operating approximately 26 years ago. There are a total of 58 designated justice committees that are designated through an Order-in-Council. These are relatively small groups, however (4 to 15 members); generally, they do not require official training and receive little, if any, funding. The first youth justice committees in Ontario began in 1999 and now operate in 57 communities (Ministry of the Attorney General for Ontario, 2005). These youth justice committees bring together young people alleged to have committed non-violent offences, their parents, victims, and trained members of the community to negotiate an appropriate way for the young person to make amends for his or her actions (Youth Justice Committees of Ontario, 2008). In each case a youth offender must make an apology; in addition, however, they may be required to do community services, submit a written paper, attend counselling, provide financial restitution, or abide by curfews. Eligible offences for this program include: theft, possession under $5,000 (for example, shoplifting, possession of stolen property or goods); false pretences under $5,000 (for example, price switching); mischief under $5,000 (for example, breaking a shop window); causing a disturbance; fraud under $5,000; false statements under $5,000; and food, accommodation fraud. Ineligible offences are major property offences; weapons offences; serious assault, including sexual harassment (for example, stalking); and alcohol-related driving offences.

In July 2004, the Alberta government announced the funding of 109 youth justice committees across the province. The stated goals of the Alberta committees are to: 1) allow citizens to work out differences between young offenders, victims, and community members; 2) provide support for young offenders; 3) provide community-based resolutions to youth crime; and 4) provide young offenders with an alternative to the formal court process and the possibility of time in custody. The committee meets with the young person, ascertains his or her free consent to the program, and negotiates an extrajudicial sanctions agreement. The sanctions can include: personal or written apologies, essays, personal service to the victim, restitution or return of property, attendance for counselling, and/or supervision by a committee member (Solicitor General of Alberta, 2005).

Some provinces have instituted community accountability programs, which are local programs that accept referrals for relatively minor offences as extrajudicial options. In some provinces they have grown out of youth justice committees; in others they have emerged independently. For instance, in British Columbia 60 to 70 of these programs are funded by the Ministry of Public Safety and Solicitor General (Hillian, Reitsma-Street, and Hackler, 2004). These programs are eligible for one-time start-up grants of $5,000, with renewable grants of $2,500 in the years following, which clearly will not cover costs of staffing (Ministry of Public Safety and Solicitor General, 2008). Thus, they are heavily reliant on volunteer energy and time and it has yet to be seen how they might be maintained and continued.

Aboriginal communities are developing alternative methods for extrajudicial sanctions. For instance, the Community Council Project of the Aboriginal Legal Services of Toronto is a diversion program that employs a traditional Native restorative justice model. Most commonly, programs require an individual to participate in counselling, restitution, community services, treatment, or some combination of all these (see www.aboriginallegal.ca/council.php). Kochee Mena, a young offender group home in Edmonton, believes that a strong cultural identity is the foundation for the development of positive self-esteem in Aboriginal youth. The purpose of their program is to provide a safe and holistic residential environment for male Aboriginal youth offenders serving an open-custody disposition; advocate for residents within the justice system; and provide programs that address residents' needs for personal development (see www.ncsa.ca/RJust.asp).

The Prince George Urban Aboriginal Justice Society describes their program as follows:

The Prince George Urban Aboriginal Justice Society's Youth Diversion Program helps to resolve youth offending—outside of the traditional court system. Through the Society's resolution conferences the youth, victim, their families, the RCMP, an Aboriginal Elder advisor and any others involved, such as social workers or teachers, come together to determine appropriate actions to address a young person's offence and its underlying causes. The process provides youth the opportunity to change their behaviour without becoming involved in the formal court process, encourages the community to assume responsibility for what is happening to their youth and attempts to ensure balance between the needs of both the victim and the accused, ensuring balance in the community (Congress of Aboriginal Peoples, 2005).

If no extrajudicial measure is deemed appropriate or adequate or if the young person does not comply with an extrajudicial sanction, they will be formally charged with the offence they have committed.

Pretrial Detention

Detention of a youth at the pretrial stage under the YCJA is considered an exception because the goal of the Act is to reduce incarceration of youth. The negative consequences of incarceration for the youth are highlighted by the Act and the onus is on law enforcement and the judiciary to place the child with a responsible person whenever possible. This results in differential detention from adults in similar situations. For instance, in *R. v. H.E.* (2003) the judge in a Newfoundland and Labrador case struggled with the conflict that in certain cases the court simply cannot continue to release someone who commits offences when released and who has in the past demonstrated complete disdain for the undertakings during release. Nevertheless, as the crimes committed would not warrant custodial sentences under the YCJA (unlike for an adult), the judge determined

that the youth could not be detained. On the other hand, when the charges are numerous, serious, and/or involve violence, detention has been ordered (*R. v. J.G.*, 2004).

One aspect underlined by the Act is that detention is not to be used to deal with social problems. For instance, it is clearly stated that detention is not to be used as a substitute for child protection measures or to deal with mental health concerns. Judges have nevertheless interpreted that this does not mean at all costs. In a British Columbia case, for instance, a judge noted that a youth was uncontrollable in her foster and group homes. She stated that some intermediate level of care between the youth's current foster home and the detention facility was necessary in the province; however, because such a service did not exist, the detention facility was appropriate (*R. v. A.S.D.*, 2003).

The Judicial Process

After a young person is charged, he or she must appear before a judge or the justice of the peace. At this stage, the charge is read to the young person, who is informed of the right to counsel and is referred to legal aid if unable to pay for counsel. Further, she is informed if the Crown intends to apply for an adult sentence. The young person may plead guilty or not guilty to charges. If he or she pleads guilty and there are sufficient facts to support the plea, the case moves to sentencing. If the court is not satisfied with the facts or the young person pleads guilty, the case moves to trial. If the youth is found guilty at trial, the finding may be appealed.

The court may choose to order medical, psychiatric, psychological, or social work reports at several points: at the bail hearing, when deciding about the appropriateness of an adult sentence, at the time of sentencing, at the end of the custody portion of the sentence, or at the time when rehabilitation is being considered. The contents of this type of report are discussed in Chapter 11. These assessments can include a referral to child welfare services. Figure 8.1 outlines the youth criminal justice process.

Figure 8.1   The Process of Youth Criminal Justice

Under the YCJA, Parliament introduced the concept of conferences for youth in the justice system. The rationale is that inclusion of a broad range of perspectives and areas of expertise may lead to more creative options and better solutions (Barnhorst, 2004). The court, the Crown, or the police may choose to convene a conference at any decision-making stage under the YCJA. The

Department of Justice of the Northwest Territories (2003) identifies three stages at which conferencing can occur: 1) pre-charge, regarding the use of extrajudicial measures; 2) during the court process as advisory to the court; and 3) postsentence. Those in attendance at the conference can vary, but can include: any professional with information or expertise that may be useful in the decision-making process; the young person, his or her representative, and/or family; the victim, her support person, and/or lawyer. The young person may be excluded from the conference if his or her involvement undermines the safety or privacy of the victim or if the discussion may put the young person at mental health or emotional risk.

Definitions of conferencing under the YCJA are deliberately vague, and procedural rules are not defined. As a result, some provinces and territories, such as British Columbia and the Northwest Territories, have developed policies on the structure and implementation of these conferences and, not surprisingly, the process varies. In British Columbia there are a variety of conferences that occur (Hillian, Reitsma-Street, and Hackler, 2004):

- Multidisciplinary or integrated case management conferences are meetings of all parties working with the youth and their family to develop an integrated service plan. These are youth-focused, do not include the victim, and usually occur postsentence.
- Family group restorative conferences bring together the youth, the victim(s), and their families to find a mutually satisfying resolution to the harm caused by the offence. These occur at the sentencing for more serious crimes.
- Aboriginal sentencing circles are formal court proceedings chaired by a judge or elder. Again, held at the time of sentencing, they encourage community, victim, and offender representatives to come together to determine an appropriate sentence.

Sentencing

The goals of sentencing under the YCJA are significantly different from those under the Criminal Code. Specifically, the YCJA does not include denunciation, specific deterrence, general deterrence, or incapacitation as goals of sentencing. Rather, sentencing seeks to 'hold the young person accountable for the offence committed by imposing justice sentences . . . that have meaningful consequences and promote (not necessarily ensure) rehabilitation and reintegration of the young person into society' (Department of Justice, 2002). It is assumed that applying these principles will contribute to the long-term protection of the public, unlike adult sentencing that considers immediate public protection. Further, it is stated that all available sanctions other than imprisonment should be considered. Nevertheless, in an Ontario ruling the judge observed the YCJA did not address the serious issue of trafficking of heroin and thus determined that in this situation, deterrence should be considered in sentencing (*R. v. J.B.*, 2003). Following this, a British Columbia judge indicated that while general deterrence was not mentioned in the YOA, it had been applied to the sentence of young offenders under that Act. Similarly, therefore, he elected to consider general deterrence as one minor factor in determining an adult sentence for a youth (*R. v. B.N.*, *2004*; *R. v. B.V.N.*, 2004). The BC provincial court decision was eventually affirmed by the Supreme Court of Canada (SCC), but in its reasons the Supreme Court ruled that neither general nor specific deterrence can be a factor in sentencing under the YCJA. The decision was only upheld because the SCC found that the principle did not play a significant role in the determination of B's sentence (*R. v. N. (B.)*, 2006).

The sentence must be proportional to the seriousness of the offence and the degree of responsibility for the young person. Considerations regarding seriousness and responsibility include harm to victims, previous offences, and the degree of reparation made to society for previous offences, aggravating or mitigating circumstances, and the degree of participation in the criminal activity. For example, the leader of a group of youths that commits a series of offences would be considered more responsible than the group members. Further, the sentence must not exceed the sentence an adult would receive under the Criminal Code. The courts are expected to use several sources of information in determining a sentence such as: presentencing reports; conferences; victim impact statements; medical, psychological, or social work reports; and submissions or representations by interested parties such as the parents.

Non-custodial Options in Sentencing

As was stated earlier in the chapter, the YCJA focuses on alternatives to custody and therefore offers many non-custodial sentencing options. These include a reprimand by the courts, an absolute discharge, a conditional discharge, a fine, an order to pay compensation or restitution, personal service to the victim, community services, a prohibition order (such as prohibition from possessing a firearm), probation, an intensive support and supervision order, and an attendance order. An intensive supervision and support order refers to closer monitoring and support than traditional probation. An attendance order requires a young person to attend a program at specified times.

Custodial Options in Sentencing

Under the Act, custodial options can only be considered in four situations.

1. *The young person has committed a serious violent offence* (SVO). The YCJA defines a category of offences referred to as serious violent offences, which are offences where the youth caused or intended to cause serious bodily harm. Bodily harm as defined by the Criminal Code is 'any hurt or injury to a person that interferes with the health or comfort of the person and that is more than merely transient or trifling in nature' (Department of Justice, 2002). Judges

are defining SVOs somewhat more broadly than assault, attempted murder, or sexual assault. For instance, in sentencing a young person who was convicted of criminal negligence causing death and impaired driving, a British Columbia Youth Court judge determined that this constituted a serious violent offence due to the youth's disregard for public safety (*R. v. S.S.*, 2004). This was similarly determined in Alberta (*R. v. C.D.K.*, 2004).

2. *The young person has failed to comply with previous non-custodial sentences.* In this case the young person must be a repeat offender with two or more previous sentences.

3. *The young person has committed a crime for which an adult would be liable to imprisonment for more than two years and has a history of previous findings of guilt.* The previous findings of guilt must represent a pattern of criminal behaviour.

4. *In exceptional cases or when there are aggravating circumstances.* These are not well defined by the Act.

The first custodial option is *deferred custody and supervision* for youth found guilty of offences not determined to be SVOs. This sentence is served in the community for a maximum of six months under conditions specified by the judge. The second option is a *custody and supervision order*. Under the YCJA, all custody orders must include a period of supervision in the community. These periods of supervision carry a series of conditions, which if breached may result in return to custody. Finally, *intensive rehabilitative custody and supervision orders* are for situations where the young person has been found guilty of murder, attempted murder, manslaughter, or sexual assault; the young person suffers from a mental disorder and an individualized treatment plan has been established. Any custodial sentences exceeding one year are subject to annual reviews where the young person's behaviour and progress are considered. Parents are notified of these reviews and may attend, as may the young person's lawyer. More frequent reviews are optional.

One principle of sentencing under the YCJA is that custodial sentences cannot be used to address social or mental health problems that would not otherwise require a custodial sentence. In this regard, the BC Court of Appeal overturned a youth court judge's decision to place a youth in custody, in part because it would allow the youth to address his substance abuse problems (*R. v. S.L.*, 2003). Similarly, a Newfoundland court decided that it could not sentence a youth to custody despite the fact that his home environment included neglect, physical and sexual abuse, and criminal behaviour, as it would constitute a resort to using a custodial sentence as a substitute for appropriate child protection (*R. v. C.P.*, 2004).

Although the sentences under the YCJA are directed to be short, judges have recently decided that because rehabilitation is a central goal of the Act, they must be long enough to allow complete treatment. Therefore, so long as the sentence is less than would be served by an adult, if it is long enough to allow for treatment it is considered appropriate (*R. v. B.V.N.*, 2004). A number of other rulings under the YCJA suggest that short custodial sentences may be used less frequently than anticipated because they do not support rehabilitation or reintegration (Bala and Anand, 2004).

Central to the custody provisions under the YCJA is reintegrative custody and supervision. This requires that a youth worker be assigned to the young person as soon as he or she enters custody and that planning begin immediately for reintegration into the community. Over the course of custody, reintegration leaves can be ordered to allow the young person to attend school or training, get a job, or attend a program or treatment. These leaves can be up to 30 days long and can also be issued on compassionate grounds or for medical reasons. During the community portion of the custody, the youth worker is responsible for case management, support, and supervision to ensure that the youth is following the provisions of the community supervision outlined by the court. Again, provisions may involve compensation, restitution, community service, or treatment. There are also six mandatory conditions to be followed during community supervision: 1) keep the peace and be of good behaviour; 2) report to the provincial director immediately upon release; 3) inform the provincial director upon being arrested or questioned by the police; 4) report to the police or any named individual as directed; 5) advise of any changes in address, employment, family situation, financial situation, or education; and 6) not own or possess a firearm. When a young person breaches these conditions, the provincial director can issue a warrant for apprehension.

Adult Sentencing

Practitioners familiar with the YOA will remember the concept of 'transfer to adult court' for charges deemed to be of a sufficient serious nature. Under the YCJA, the Crown can pursue an adult sentence but all trials remain in youth court. This new procedure is in large part because the transfer occurred before a finding of guilt and thus a youth presumed innocent under the law did not receive the procedural protections of youth court. In order to be considered for an adult sentence, a youth must have been at least 14 years of age when the offence was committed and she or he must be found guilty of an offence for which an adult could receive a sentence of more than two years. Three categories of offences may receive an adult sentence.

1. *Presumptive 'a' offences* involve murder, attempted murder, manslaughter, or aggravated assault. In these situations, the Crown is not required to make an application for an adult sentence nor give notice to seek an adult sentence. It is presumed that a longer sentence is required to hold the youth accountable for his or her behaviour. The young person may apply to the court for an order that a youth sentence be applied rather than an adult sentence.

2. *Presumptive 'b' offences* are repeated serious violent offences. This applies when the youth has a history of violent activity and is presently charged with an offence involving

serious violence. In such cases, the onus is on the Crown to make an application to have the court designate the current offence as an SVO after a finding of guilt has been made. The Crown must make notice that it intends to seek an adult sentence prior to the youth entering a plea on the charges.

3. *Non-presumptive offences* for which an adult would receive a sentence of more than two years may result in a Crown application for an adult sentence. Again, the Crown must make notice of its intention prior to the youth entering a plea of guilty or not guilty.

Parental Involvement

The YCJA is founded on the assumption that young people are not fully able to meaningfully participate in criminal proceedings due to lack of understanding regarding their legal rights and the legal processes and due to other factors such as compliance with pressures from peers, perspectives of risk, and views of authority. As a result, research has suggested that young offenders may make judgments that are detrimental to their case such as waiving their rights to silence or legal counsel prior to police interrogation (Badali and Broeking, 2005). Thus, the YCJA strongly supports parental involvement and specifically states, 'measures taken against young persons who commit offences should . . . where appropriate, involve parents, [and] the extended family' (YCJA, 2002, s. 3(1)(c)(iii)). Under the Act, parents must be notified: 1) at the time of arrest or detention; 2) when the young person receives a summons or appearance notice; 3) when the youth is released with an order to appear in court; and 4) when a youth is issued a ticket. If a parent is unavailable, the notification can be given to another responsible adult. If the parent does not attend court with their child, the court may order his or her attendance. Despite this, however, a study conducted by Badali and Broeking (2005) on parental involvement found that involvement is often quite limited. Many young people had no parental support while they were at the police station, did not see or talk to their parents during their stay in detention facilities, and had no parent with them when they were at court. At times this lack of involvement was due to the fact that young people did not believe that their parents had the capacity to provide assistance or meaningful advice. Other youth were in conflict with parents and did not want them involved. Still others did not understand that they had a right to contact parents. Parents who were interviewed often felt that they had little influence over the proceedings at the police station phase of the investigation. In reality, however, parental presence at the police station was associated with increased rates of release. Interestingly, one-third of parents actually felt that they should be assisting the police in the investigation. Both parents and youth often (but not always) felt that parental presence at court helped to influence the outcome of the process. However, parental involvement was not in fact related to court outcome, in large part due to the weight placed on the youth's record and current charges in the sentencing decisions.

CASE EXAMPLE REVIEWED

We now return to the case of Ray and how the legislation in this chapter answers questions directly related to his situation.

Is Ray considered a youth offender?

At the time of the offence, Ray was 17 years of age and therefore considered to be a young person under the YCJA. However, he is older than the minimum age for the presumption of adult sentencing; depending on the nature of the crime, a 17 year old can be considered for adult sentencing.

What are alternatives to court and incarceration?

If this were a less serious crime and Ray did not have a record of previous offences, he may have received a warning, a caution, or a referral to a community program by the police. Further, he may have received a caution from the Crown attorney or he may have had his situation turned over to a community youth justice committee in his area for consideration of such reparations as restoration or community service.

Once charged, how do youth proceed through the justice system?

Now that Ray has been charged, a hearing that reviews pretrial detention will be held. At this time it will be determined whether he is a risk to the community and whether his parents are willing to undertake that they will monitor his behaviour. Because the family is the victim of his crime, they may not make such an undertaking or the court may determine that they should not be expected to or are unable to monitor his behaviour. He will need to undertake that he will return for his court appearances and adhere to the conditions of release. The Crown will declare whether or not they will seek an adult sentence because he has not committed a crime for which adult sentencing is mandatory. If he pleads guilty to his charges, he will move on to sentencing. If he pleads not guilty, a trial will ensue after which, if he is found guilty, there will be a sentencing hearing.

What are the possible outcomes?

Considering the severity of the current charges and the pattern of repeated offences and noncompliance with non-custodial care, a custodial sentence may be imposed. In part, this will be determined by the jurisdiction in which Ray is tried because some areas, such as Alberta and Ontario, have higher rates of incarceration than others, such as British Columbia (O'Shaunghnessy, 2005). Because Ray has a previous conviction regarding violence, the Crown may elect to petition the court to declare the current charges to be serious violent offences. If they are so determined, adult sentencing can be imposed.

How will Ray's parents be involved in the situation?

Ray's parents will be formally notified at all stages of the hearing. They may or may not undertake to monitor his behaviour during the pretrial period.

Key Terms

Community Accountability Programs
One form of extrajudicial sanction—local programs that accept referrals for minor offences that commonly require the young offender to participate in counselling, community service, and/or treatment

Community Youth Justice Committees
One form of extrajudicial sanction that allows citizens to work out differences among young offenders, victims, and community members, provide support for young offenders, provide community-based resolutions to youth crime, and provide young offenders with an alternative to the formal court process

Conference for Youth
Meeting that can be convened at various stages (pre-charge, during the court process, or post-sentencing) and involve various parties (offender, family, victim, professionals, lawyers, etc.) to include a broad range of perspectives and areas of expertise that may lead to more creative options and better solutions for the young person

Custody and Supervision Order
All custody orders must include a period of community supervision which carries a series of conditions that if breached, may result in a return to custody for the young offender

Deferred Custody and Supervision
Custody option involving a sentence served in the community for a maximum of six months for youth found guilty of offences not determined to be serious violence offences

Extrajudicial Sanctions
Alternative measures that seek to hold youth accountable and provide opportunities for them to make amends outside of the court system

Intensive Rehabilitative Custody
Custody option for a young offender found guilty of murder, attempted murder, manslaughter, or sexual assault

Non-custodial Sentencing Option
An alternative to putting the young offender in custody that can include absolute or conditional discharge, fines, community services, intensive support and supervision order, or attendance order to attend a program

Non-presumptive Offence
For offences where an adult would receive a sentence of more than two years, the Crown may apply for the adult sentence to be applied to the young person and must give notice that it intends to seek an adult sentence prior to the youth entering a plea on the charges

Police Discretion
Options held by police authorities when dealing with young offenders: these include taking no further action, warning the young person, issuing a formal caution to the young person, or referring the young person to a community program

Presumptive 'A' Offence
For murder, attempted murder, manslaughter, or aggravated assault, the Crown does not have to make an application for an adult sentence; for these offences, the young person may apply to the court for an order that a youth sentence be applied rather than an adult sentence

Presumptive 'B' Offence
For repeated serious violence offences, the Crown must give notice that it intends to seek an adult sentence prior to the youth entering a plea on the charges

Pretrial Detention

Incarcerating a young offender after being charged but before trial

Reintegration Leave

The young person can leave custody for up to 30 days to attend school or training, to obtain employment, or to attend a program or treatment

Reintegrative Custody and Supervision

When a young person is put into custody, a youth worker is assigned to the young person as soon as he or she enters custody and begins planning for reintegration into the community; when the young person begins the community portion of the custody, the youth worker is responsible for case management, support, and supervision to ensure that t[...] the communi[...]

Restorative Justice

Informal and non-adjudicative forms of dispute resolution where the goal is to move away from punishment and instead to repair the harms of crime and restore what has been lost by balancing the needs of the victims, citizens, and offenders (for example, victim–offender mediation, a mutually agreed upon restitution plan to compensate the victim)

Youth Offender

A young person aged 12 to 17 years at the time of the offence

Discussion Questions

1. What could be possible motivators for changes proposed to the Youth Criminal Justice Act during the 2008 federal election?
2. Do the age guidelines under the YCJA make sense in consideration of child and adolescent development?
3. How can the effectiveness of community youth justice committees be examined?
4. How can parental involvement be used to greater effect in the youth criminal justice system?

Relevant Legislation

Historical

An Act respecting Arrest, Trial and Imprisonment of Youthful Offenders, Statutes of Canada, 1894, 1, c. 58

An Act respecting Industrial Schools, Statutes of the Province of Ontario, 1874, c. 29

An Act to amend the Act respecting Procedure in Criminal Cases and other matters relating to Criminal Law, Statutes of Canada, 1875, 1, c. 43

Canadian Bill of Rights, 1960, c. 44

Criminal Code, 1892, Statutes of Canada, 1892, 1 and 2, c. 29

Juvenile Delinquents Act, Statutes of Canada, 1908, c. 40

Young Offenders Act, 1982, c. Y-1

Federal

Youth Criminal Justice Act, 2002, c. 1
http://laws.justice.gc.ca/en/showtdm/cs/Y-1.5

References

Alberta Law Foundation (2005), *Youth Criminal Justice Act FAQs* (accessed at http://www.law-faqs.org/ nat/ycja04.htm).

Badali, M. and Broeking, J. (2005), *Parents' Involvement in Youth Justice Proceedings: Perspectives of Youth and Parents* (Ottawa: Department of Justice) (accessed at http://www.justice.gc.ca/eng/pi/yj-jj/res-rech/parents/index.html).

Bala, N. and Anand, S. (2004), 'The First Months under the Youth Criminal Justice Act: A Survey and Analysis of Case Law', *Canadian Journal of Criminology and Criminal Justice*, 46(3): 251–71.

Balfour, G. (2008), 'Falling Between the Cracks of Retributive and Restorative Justice: The Victimization and Punishment of Aboriginal Women', *Feminist Criminology*, 3(2): 101–20.

Barnhorst, R. (2004), 'Youth Criminal Justice Act: New Directions and Implementation Issues', *Canadian Journal of Criminology and Criminal Justice*, 46(3): 231–50.

Bazemore, G. (2001), 'Young People, Trouble and Crime: Restorative Justice as a Normative Theory of Informal Social Control and Social Support', *Youth & Society*, 33(2): 199–226.

—— and Schiff, M. (2001), *Restorative Justice: Repairing Harm and Transforming Communities* (Cincinnati: Anderson Press).

Bergseth, K. and Bouffard, J. (2007), 'The Long-term Impact of Restorative Justice Programming for Juvenile Offenders', *Journal of Criminal Justice*, 35: 433–51.

Blackwell, T. (2005, 10 January), 'New Law Too Soft on Violent Youth', *National Post*, p. A1.

Braithwaite, J. (2000), 'Shame and Criminal Justice', *Canadian Journal of Criminology*, 42(3): 281–98.

Cameron, A. (2006), 'Stopping the Violence: Canadian Feminist Debates on Restorative Justice and Intimate Violence', *Theoretical Criminology*, 10(1): 49–66.

Carrington, P. and Schulenberg, J. (2005), *The Impact of the Youth Criminal Justice Act on Police Charging Practices with Young Persons: A Preliminary Statistical Assessment* (Ottawa: Department of Justice) (accessed at http://www.justice.gc.ca/eng/pi/yj-jj/res-rech/prelimin/index.html).

CBC (2008, 22 September), 'Conservatives Vow to Toughen Youth Criminal Justice Act', *CBCnews.ca* (accessed at http://www.cbc.ca/news/canadavotes/story/2008/09/22/harper-elxn.html).

Clark, C., Alphonso, C., and Perreaux, L. (2008), 'Harper Pitches Two-Tier Youth Justice Plan', *Globe and Mail*, 22 September 2008 (accessed at http://www.theglobeandmail.com/servlet/story/RTGAM.20080922.welxntory0922/BNStory/politics).

Congress of Aboriginal Peoples (2005), *Youth Justice Renewal Initiative* (accessed at http://www.abo-peoples.org/Youth Pages/PLEI/PLEIthree.htm).

de Beus, K. and Rodriguez, N. (2007), 'Restorative Justice Practice: An Examination of Program Completion and Recidivism', *Journal of Criminal Justice*, 35: 337–47.

Department of Justice, Canada (2002), *Youth Criminal Justice Act Explained* (accessed at http://www.justice.gc.ca/en/ps/yj/repository/index.html).

—— (2004), *The Evolution of Juvenile Justice in Canada* (accessed at http://canada.justice.gc.ca/ en/ps/inter/juv_jus_min/sec01.html).

—— (2007), *Pretrial Detention under the Youth Criminal Justice Act: A Consultation Paper* (accessed at http://www.justice.gc.ca/eng/pi/yj-jj/ycja-lsjpa/consultation/consultation.html).

Department of Justice, Northwest Territories (2003), *Justice Conferencing Guidelines* (accessed at http://www.justice.gov.nt.ca/pdf/YouthJustice/NWT_Justice_Conferencing_Guidelines.pdf).

Farrington, D. and Bennett, T. (1981), 'Police Cautioning on Juveniles in London', *British Journal of Criminology*, 21(2): 123–35.

Goren, S. (2001), 'Healing the Victim, the Young Offender, and the Community via Restorative Justice: An International Perspective', *Issues in Mental Health Nursing*, 22: 137–49.

Griffiths, C. (1999), 'The Victims of Crime and Restorative Justice: The Canadian Experience', *International Review of Victimology*, 6(4): 279–94.

Gromet, D. and Darley, J. (2006), 'Restoration and Retribution: How Including Retributive Components Affects the Acceptability of Restorative Justice Procedures', *Social Justice Research*, 19(4): 395–432.

Helfgott, J., Lovell, M., Lawrence, C., and Parsonage, W. (2000), 'Results from the Pilot Study of the Citizens, Victims and Offenders Restoring Justice Program at the Washington State Reformatory', *Journal of Contemporary Criminal Justice*, 16(1): 5–31.

Hillian, D., Reitsma-Street, M., and Hackler, J. (2004), 'Conferencing in the Youth Criminal Justice Act of Canada: Policy Developments in British Columbia', *Canadian Journal of Criminology and Criminal Justice*, 46(3): 343–66.

Hudson, B. (1998), 'Restorative Justice: The Challenge of Sexual and Racial Violence', *Journal of Law and Society*, 25(2): 237–56.

Koss, M. (2000), 'Blame, Shame and the Community: Justice Responses to Violence against Women', *American Psychologist*, 55(1): 1332–43.

Krause, J. (1981), 'Police Caution of Juvenile Offenders: A Research Note', *Australian and New Zealand Journal of Criminology*, 14(2): 91–4.

LaPraire, C. (1996), *Examining Aboriginal Corrections in Canada* (Ottawa: Ministry of the Solicitor General).

Marshall, T. (1995), 'Restorative Justice on Trial in Britain', *Mediation Quarterly*, 12(3): 217–31.

Ministry of Public Safety and Solicitor General, British Columbia (2008), *Community Accountability Program Grants* (accessed at http://www.pssg.gov.bc.ca/community_programs/justice/pdf/CAPInformationPackage.pdf).

Ministry of the Attorney General for Ontario (2005), *Youth Justice Program* (accessed at http://www.attorneygeneral.jus.gov.on.ca/english/news/2004/20040614-youthjustice-fs.asp).

Moyer, S. and Basic, M. (2005), *Crown Decision Making Under the Youth Criminal Justice Act* (Ottawa: Department of Justice) (accessed at http://www.justice.gc.ca/eng/pi/yj-jj/res-rech/moyer_basic/decision/index.html).

O'Shaughnessy, R., clinical director, Youth Forensic Psychiatric Services of British Columbia (2005), personal communication.

Parkinson, L. (2003), *The Youth Criminal Justice Act: A New Strategy for Youth Justice* (accessed at http:// www.mapleleafweb.com/features/crime/youth-act/ index.html).

R. v. A.S.D. (2003), B.C.J. No. 1831 (B.C.Y.C.).

R. v. B.N. (2004)/R. v. B.V.N. (2004), B.C.J. No. 974.

R. v. B.V.N. (2004), B.C.J. No. 974 (B.C.C.A.).

R. v. C.D.K. (2004), A.J. No. 237 (Alta. C.A.).

R. v. C.P. (2004), N.J. No. 41 (N.L. Prov. Ct.).

R. v. H.E. (2003), N.J. No.299 (N.L. Prov. Ct.).

R. v. J.B. (2003), O.J. No. 2339 (Ont. C.J.).

R. v. J.G. (2004), N.S.J. No. 160 (N.S.Y.J. Ct.).

R. v. N. (B.) (2006) 1 S.C.R. 941.

R. v. S.L. (2003), B.C.J. No. 2397 (B.C.C.A.).

R. v. S.S., 2004 BCCA 79 (B.C.C.A.).

RCMP (2005), *Youth Criminal Justice Act* (accessed at http://www.rcmp.gc.ca/ycja/background_e.htm).

Roach, K. (2000), 'Changing Punishment at the Turn of the Century: Restorative Justice on the Rise', *Canadian Journal of Criminology*, 42(3): 249–80.

Rodriguez, N. (2007), 'Restoring Justice at Work: Examining the Impact of Restorative Justice Resolutions on Juvenile Recidivism', *Crime and Delinquency*, 53(3): 355–79.

Shenk, B. and Zehr, H. (2001), 'Restorative Justice and Substance Abuse: The Path Ahead', *Youth & Society*, 33(2): 314–28.

Solicitor General of Alberta (2005), *Youth Justice Committees* (accessed at http://www.solgen.gov.ab.ca/yjc/default.aspx).

Tweedie, I. (1982), 'Police Cautioning of Juveniles: Two Styles Compared', *Criminal Law Review* (March): 168–74.

Umbreit, M. (1995), 'The Development and Impact of Victim-Offender Mediation in the United States', *Mediation Quarterly*, 12(3): 263–76.

——— (1999), 'Victim-Offender Mediation in Canada: The Impact of an Emerging Social Work Intervention', *International Social Work*, 42(2): 215–27.

———, Coates, R., and Roberts, A. (2000), 'The Impact of Victim-Offender Mediation: A Cross-national Perspective', *Mediation Quarterly*, 17(3): 215–29.

Wenzel, M., Okimoto, T., Feather, N., and Platow, M. (2008), 'Retributive and Restorative Justice', *Law and Human Behavior*, 32: 375–89.

Youth Criminal Justice Act (YCJA), 2002 (accessed at http://laws.justice.gc.ca/en/showtdm/cs/Y-1.5)

Youth Justice Committees of Ontario (2008), *Overview* (accessed at http://www.yjcontario.ca/overview.php).

Zehr, H. (1995), 'Justice Paradigm Shift? Values and Visions in the Reform Process', *Mediation Quarterly*, 12(3): 207–16.

CHAPTER NINE

Criminal and Civil Law for Victims of Violence

OBJECTIVES

- To outline victim rights in Canada
- To present legal protections for victims in the community
- To describe the criminal justice process that victims encounter
- To describe civil litigation as a process for receiving compensation for harms
- To inform readers about the potential for access to treatment records of victims
- To introduce restorative justice models for victims of violence

CASE EXAMPLE 1

Dolly and Surjit began dating after they were introduced by their parents, who were business colleagues. Several months later, they were married and Dolly moved into the home of Surjit and his family. While initially this went well, family problems in Surjit's home resulted in increased distress in all members. During this time, Dolly and Surjit also began to have fights, and on more than one occasion Surjit's mother asked Dolly to leave their home to end the arguments. Fights between Dolly and Surjit intensified, at times including physical assaults against Dolly, and after nine months of marriage, Dolly elected to leave in July. Surjit responded by suddenly leaving his parents' home, without indicating where he had gone, and not returning for one week. Upon his return, he told his mother that his brain no longer worked, and that he had to quit university and leave the country. His mother dissuaded him from this. Surjit began contacting Dolly with increasing intensity, hanging around outside her university classes, parking in front of her home for hours on end, and calling her incessantly. In each encounter he insisted that she was mistaken in breaking up with him and was not telling him the truth about the reason for the break up, which he believed to be another man. Surjit became increasingly tearful, sleepless, angry, and withdrawn.

In October of that year, Dolly's father attempted to intervene by confronting Surjit's father. Shortly thereafter, Surjit physically assaulted Dolly as she was leaving a university class, resulting in severe bruising. He was arrested and charged with assault. After he was released from jail, Surjit continued to experience emotional and physical decline and continued to contact and follow Dolly. One month later he approached her at the hospital where she worked part-time and stabbed her. Fortunately Dolly survived the attack.

- What are the legal avenues by which someone like Dolly can protect herself from harassment, abuse, and assault?
- What is the criminal justice process that is likely to occur?
- Is Dolly eligible for compensation?

CASE EXAMPLE 2

Jason is a 43-year-old man who was sexually assaulted in 1972 by the director of a boys' choir of which he was a member. The choir was highly prestigious in the community and Jason's parents experienced great pride in his accomplishments within the choir. The choir also demanded a great deal of time and dedication and this was supported by the parents of all participating boys. The director, Mel, was seen as an intense, involved person who was constantly driving for perfection. In the choir, he treated the boys as musicians, not children, and as a result he was described as demanding, and, at times, harsh. It was not uncommon for children to begin crying during choir practice. In contrast to his harshness during practice, Mel used what he described as a friendlier, softer approach in private lessons. He contended that at these times he would pat a boy on the head or knee to encourage them. Jason, however, recounts experiences of sexual abuse involving genital contact. He felt unable to resist these advances for fear that he would lose his place in the choir. Jason now identifies issues with self-esteem, guilt, shame, embarrassment, difficulties in peer relationships, substance abuse, and depression. He has recently discovered that other boys suffered similar abuse from Mel.

- Can Mel be charged with offences committed against children 35 years ago?
- Can Jason and the other men commence a civil suit against Mel and the choir?
- What process is likely to occur in the civil proceeding?
- Can Jason's counselling records for the abuse be called into court?

Legislative Protection of Victims

The 2004 General Social Survey on criminal victimization suggests that young people aged 15 to 24 are at highest risk of being victims of violent crime, and the risk steadily declines as age increases. Rates in this age group are 1.5 times higher than those for people aged 25 to 34, and 19 times higher than for seniors aged 65 and older (Statistics Canada, 2005a). This is not to suggest that assaults against older people are not also a serious social issue in Canada. Approximately 7 per cent of 4,000 adults aged 65 and older who responded to the 1999 General Social Survey on Victimization (GSS) reported that they had experienced some form of emotional abuse by an adult child, spouse, or caregiver in the past five years, 1 per cent reported physical abuse, and 1 per cent reported financial abuse (Statistics Canada, 2002). One-quarter of older adults who are

victims of homicide are killed by family members, most commonly a spouse (39 per cent), adult child (37 per cent), or an extended family member (24 per cent). Although overall rates of violent victimization do not differ between men and women, men are at greater risk of physical assault and women are at higher risk of sexual assault. The Violence Against Women survey found that over one-half (51 per cent) of Canadian women have experienced at least one incident of sexual or physical violence in their lifetime. Of these women, almost 60 per cent were the targets of more than one such incident (Statistics Canada, 1993). In 2002, there were more than 205,000 victims of violent crime reported to a subset of 94 police departments across Canada (103,001 female and 102,447 male victims). Females were much more likely than their male counterparts to report intimate partner violence (85 per cent versus 15 per cent). Female victims of intimate partner violence were more than twice as likely to be injured as male victims. Women were also three times more likely to fear for their life, and twice as likely to be the targets of more than 10 violent episodes (Canadian Centre for Justice Statistics, 2005). The 2004 General Social Survey revealed that rates of intimate partner violence were twice as high among same-sex partners than in heterosexual couples (Statistics Canada, 2005b). In US samples, women in lesbian relationships are reported to have higher levels of violence than men in gay relationships and they are also more likely to come from heterosexual relationships where violence was an issue (Pattavina et al., 2007). Further, research suggests that victims of same-sex intimate partner violence are less likely to disclose the abuse and are less likely to receive police protection if they do disclose (Stanley et al., 2006). Clearly, legislative protection for victims of violence continues to be a pressing issue in Canada.

The history of the treatment of victims in the justice system is both shocking and saddening. For example, the right of women who were wives to be free of sexual assault committed by their husbands was not acknowledged until the offence of marital rape was formally recognized as a crime in Canada in 1983 (MacKinnon, 1987). According to a long-standing common-law standard, finally overruled by the House of Lords in England in 1991, 'the husband cannot be guilty of a rape committed by himself upon his lawful wife, for by their mutual matrimonial consent and contract the wife hath given up herself in this kind unto her husband, which she cannot retract' (Hale, 1739, p. 629). 'The ideology of the family, as constructed by the middle- to late-nineteenth century in England, defined the "good wife" as a woman devoted to and responsible for the maintenance of family members, sexually monogamous (if not asexual), subordinate to her husband, and responsive to his sexual, material, and emotional needs and desires at the expense of her own' (Wiegers, 1994, p. 18). As such, until relatively recently in historical terms, women have been unable to sue their husbands, divorce their husbands, or obtain legal protection from assault. A similar theme emerges when we consider the history of sexual

assault. In most ancient cultures, the law treated rape primarily as a crime against property, a man's property, and linked the act to the theft of a woman's value (Brownmiller, 1975). While notions of sexual assault changed throughout the twentieth century, victims, both male and female, continued to be treated with skepticism, disrespect, and disregard. The historically low conviction rates for sexual violence have reinforced the observation that, traditionally, the law has been more likely to be merciful to those who dishonour, than to those who were dishonoured (Strange, 1992).

In Canada, attention to the plight of victims rose during the 1980s and beyond. MacLeod made the first attempt to estimate the incidence of wife assault in Canada in 1980 and suggested that 1 in 10 Canadian women were victims of intimate violence. As public awareness and outrage of the issue grew, commitment to services for victims, public education, and legislative reform increased. By 1989 MacLeod documented significant gains being made 'applauding our progress' in bringing the problem of woman abuse from the private sphere into the public domain. Organizations such as LEAF challenged the laws on a case-by-case basis and began a movement to change the way in which the courts dealt with victims (Razack, 1991). The government of Canada became interested in victims and victimization and enacted legislation addressing issues of wife assault and sexual assault. Crime victims in these initiatives were defined as the new consumers of criminal justice and the personal and emotional experiences of crime victims became politically salient (Roach, 1999).

Victims' Bill of Rights

The United Nations (1985) Declaration of the Basic Principles of Justice for Victims of Crime and Abuse of Power identified the need for state action in protecting the rights of victims. In recognition of this, various provincial governments agreed to the basic principles of justice for victims of crime by enacting victims' rights legislation (see Table 9.1), beginning with Manitoba's Justice for Victims of Crime Act (1986). The Manitoba legislation included provisions such as crime prevention, mediation, conciliation, and reconciliation procedures as means of assisting victims. By contrast, 10 years later in 1995 Ontario enacted the Victims' Bill of Rights that focused entirely on crime control. While such differences and others exist, victims' bills of rights throughout Canada generally contain the following rights:

- to be informed of the final disposition of the case;
- to be notified if any court proceeding for which they have received a subpoena will not occur as scheduled;
- to receive protection from intimidation;
- to be informed of the procedure for receiving witness fees;
- to be provided with a secure waiting area (when practical);
- to have personal property in the possession of law enforcement agencies returned as soon as possible; and
- to be provided with appropriate employer intercessions to minimize loss of pay due to court appearances (Young, 2001).

Nevertheless, critics have expressed concern that despite the best intentions, these bills of rights fail to meet the needs of victims for several reasons. First, there exists no remedy for lack of compliance by law enforcement and the courts with notification requirements. For instance, the Ontario Victims' Bill of Rights states: 'No new cause of action, right of appeal, claim or other remedy exists in law because of this section or anything done or omitted to be done under this section.' This was upheld in an Ontario case in which the judge stated, 'I conclude that the legislature did not intend for section 2(1) of the Victims' Bill of Rights to provide rights to the victims of crime … they have no claim before the courts because of it' (*Vanscoy and Even v. Her Majesty the Queen in Right of Ontario*, 1999). Bill of rights' legislation does not afford victims the right to override the discretion of the Crown prosecutor and therefore

victims do not have control over whether charges proceed to court or not. Further, they do not have the right to participate in proceedings. This is discussed in more detail later in the chapter. Finally, victims are not provided the right to have legal representation paid for by the state. Nevertheless, victims do have legal recourses available to them and, increasingly, protections for victims are in place in our society.

Child Protection and Intimate Partner Violence

As noted in Chapter 4 on child protection legislation, recent legislative changes in Canada resulted in the recognition that the exposure of children to violence between their parents constitutes a form of child abuse. As a result, child protection agencies in Canada experienced a dramatic rise in reports of emotional abuse, the largest proportion of which were children exposed to intimate partner violence (IPV) (Black et al., 2008). The 2003 Canadian Incidence Study of Reported Child Abuse and Neglect revealed that 34 per cent of all substantiated cases of child abuse in Canada involved some form of children witnessing IPV (Black et al., 2008). In response to legislative changes and in an attempt to better protect children, child welfare services have developed policies and practices to assess and intervene (Shlonsky and Friend, 2007). However, if child exposure is equated with child abuse, the abused parent is placed in the position of culpability for 'failure to protect'. That is, an abused parent who chooses not to, or cannot, leave the abusive relationship may be held responsible for exposing their child to violence. Ultimately, this may result in the removal of the child—a double jeopardy, in effect, for the abused parent. If the abused person discloses abuse to a health care or social service professional in an effort to obtain assistance, he or she may be penalized with the loss of the child. In a study conducted by Alaggia and colleagues (2007), this was particularly true for women who were marginalized due to race, sexual orientation, or immigration status. These women found that

Table 9.1 Legislation for Victims of Violence

Province/ Territory	Victims' Rights Legislation	Court Support Services*	Criminal Injuries Compensation Legislation	Family Violence Acts	Limitations Legislation	Limitation Period for Making Claim
British Columbia	Victims of Crime Act, R.S.B.C. 1996, c. 478	There are 150 programs for victims of crime in 180 cities/towns. Services range from police-based victim services to specialized victim-assistance programs.	Criminal Injuries Compensation Act, R.S.B.C. 1979, c. 83 amended by S.B.C. 1995, c. 36	Family Relations Act, R.S.B.C. 1996, c. 128, ss. 9 and 37	Limitation Act, R.S.B.C. 1996, c. 266	No limitation for sexual assault or abuse claims
Alberta	Victims of Crime Act, R.S.A. 2000, c. V-3	There are 73 police-based Victim Service Programs operating 117 victim-service units, plus community-based services.	Victims Restitution and Compensation Payment Act, S.A. 2001, c. V-3.5	Protection Against Family Violence Act, R.S.A. 2000, c. P-27	Limitations Act, R.S.A. 1996, c. L-15.1	2 years after awareness of act or consequences, or 10 years after claim commenced
Saskatchewan	Saskatchewan Victims of Crime Act, S.S. 1995, c. 4-6.011	A Saskatchewan Justice program for child victims is available, as well as police-based programs, and court-based victim/witness programs in Prince Albert, Regina, and Saskatoon.	Saskatchewan Victims of Crime Act, S.S. 1995 c. 4-6.011	Victims of Domestic Violence Act, S.S. 1994, c. V-6.02	Limitations Act, S.S. 2004	2 years after awareness of act or consequences; 15-year maximum
Manitoba	Victims' Bill of Rights, C.C.S.M., c. V55	Court support services for children/ youth are provided by the Child Witness Support Program. Several victim-service units that operate out of local police and RCMP detachments.	Domestic Violence and Stalking Act, S.M. 1998, c. 41		Limitation of Actions Act, C.C.S.M., c. L150	No limitation for sexual assault or abuse claims
Ontario	Victims' Bill of Rights, 1995, S.O. 1995, c. 6	Associated with the Crown Attorney's Office, victim-assistance workers support victims/witnesses from the time a court file is opened to disposition. Specialized services for child and youth victims/witnesses are available at seven sites.	Compensation for Victims of Crime Act, S.O. 1990, c. 24	Domestic Violence Protection Act, S.O. 2000, c. 3	Limitations Act, 2002, S.O. 2002, c. 24, Sch. B	2 years unless at the time of the assault one of the parties to it had charge of the person assaulted, was in a position of trust or authority in relation to the person, or was someone on whom he or she was dependent, whether financially or otherwise or the person is incapable of commencing the proceeding because of his or her physical, mental, or psychological condition

Table 9.1   Legislation for Victims of Violence (Continued)

Province/ Territory	Victims' Rights Legislation	Court Support Services*	Criminal Injuries Compensation Legislation	Family Violence Acts	Limitations Legislation	Limitation Period for Making Claim
Quebec	Assistance for victims of crime, An Act respecting, R.S.Q., c. A-13.2	Centre d'Aide Aux Victimes d'Actes Criminels—Québec provides court preparation and support at 12 different community-based organizations.	Crime Victims Compensation Act 1994, S.Q. c. 1-6		Civil Code of Québec, C.C.Q.	
New Brunswick	Victims Services Act, R.S.N.B. 1987, c. V-2.1	Victim Services assists victims of crime through the provision of a range of services. The Court Support and Preparation Program provides information concerning procedures, and victim/witness rights.	Victims Services Act, R.S.N.B. 1987, c. V-2.1	Family Services Act, R.S.N.B. Reg. 97-71, s. 128	Limitation of Actions Act, R.S.N.B. 1973, c. L-8	2 years
Nova Scotia	Victims' Rights and Services Act, S.N.S. 1989, c. 14	Court support services are provided by the Victim Service Division of the Department of Justice. Police-based services also are available in many rural areas.	Victims' Rights and Services Act, S.N.S. 1989, c. 14	Domestic Violence Intervention Act, S.N.S. 2001, c. 29	Limitation of Actions Act, R.S.N.S. 1989, c. 258	2 years
Prince Edward Island	Victims of Crime Act, R.S.P.E.I. 1988, c. V-3.1	Court support services are available throughout the province. Community and Correctional Services of the Office of the Attorney General have two Victim Service regional offices located in Charlottetown and Summerside.	Victims of Crime Act, R.S. P.E.I. 1988, c. V-3.1	Victims of Family Violence Act. R.S.P.E.I. 1996, c. V-3.2.	Statute of Limitations, R.S.P.E.I. 1988, c. S-7	2 years
Newfoundland and Labrador	Victims of Crime Services Act, R.S.N.L. 1990, c. V-5	Victims services funded through the Department of Justice are delivered through a network of 10 offices located throughout Newfoundland and Labrador.	No program for compensation	Family Law Act, R.S.N.L. 1990 c. F-2, s. 81	Limitations Act, S.N.L. 1995, c. L-16.1	No limitation for sexual assault or abuse claims
Northwest Territories and Nunavut	Victims of Crime Act, R.S.N.W.T. 1988, c. 9 (Supp.)	Victim Services are coordinated out of the Community Justice Division, which makes funding available to community-based agencies to provide services to victims.	No program for compensation	Family Law Act, S.N.W.T. 1997, c. 18	Limitation of Actions Act, R.S.N.W.T. 1988, c.L-8	No limitation for sexual assault or abuse claims
Yukon	Crime Prevention and Victim Services Trust Act, R.S.Y 2002, c.49	Two Crown-based programs operate in Dawson City and Whitehorse; workers travel to remote areas.	Crime Prevention and Victim Services Trust Act, R.S.Y 2002, c. 49	Family Violence Prevention Act, R.S.Y. 2002, c. 84	Limitation of Actions Act, R.S.Y. 2002, c. 139	No limitation for sexual assault or abuse claims

*See the reference for Department of Justice, Canada (2008).

the risks associated with seeking help were simply too high. Thus, the unintended consequence of legislation to protect child victims may in fact increase both their risk and the risk to their abused parent.

What Protections Exist for Victims of Violence in the Community?

While victimization may be a one-time occurrence, in some situations such as IPV and stalking, an ongoing risk exists for victims and community safety measures are essential. According to the 2004 General Social Survey, more than 1.4 million females 15 years of age and older (11 per cent of the population) and just under one million males (7 per cent of the population) were stalked in the preceding five years in a way that caused them to fear for their life or the life of someone known to them. Obscene phone calls (47 per cent), being spied on (28 per cent), and being threatened or intimidated (43 per cent) were the most frequently reported forms of stalking experienced by female victims. The majority of victims (80 per cent) were stalked by males regardless of the sex of the victim. Results of the survey indicate that Aboriginal people are twice as likely as non-Aboriginal people to have reported experiencing some form of stalking in the previous five years which caused them to fear for their life (17 per cent versus 9 per cent) (Statistics Canada, 2005a). These results in many ways parallel studies from the United States. The National Crime Victimization Survey in the United States (US Department of Justice, 1997) found a lifetime prevalence of 8.1 per cent for women and 2.2 per cent of men which by extrapolation translates to 2.04 million women and 820,000 men in the United States who at some time in their lives have been victims of stalking behavior (Douglas and Dutton, 2001). The US National Violence Against Women Survey revealed that 87 per cent of victims of stalking were women and 87 per cent of stalkers were men. Of all groups in the survey, Native American

women were significantly more likely to report being stalked than members of other ethnic and racial groups (Tjaden and Thoennes, 1998).

There is no question that victims of spousal violence who attempt to separate from their abusive partner require protection from further abuse. According to Statistics Canada, 21 per cent of women and 16 per cent of men in 2004 reported some type of violence (including physical, sexual, and psychological abuse) perpetrated by a former partner, either while living together or after separation. In most cases (63 per cent) violence ended at separation; however, 39 per cent of women and 32 per cent of men indicated that they were assaulted after the relationship ended. Of these, 24 per cent indicated that the violence became worse and 39 per cent indicated that the violence only began after separation. Further, marital separation is a factor that elevates the rate of spousal homicide. Ex-marital partners are responsible for 26 per cent of all homicides against women and 11 per cent of all homicides against men (Statistics Canada, 2005b).

Peace Bonds

A peace bond is a court order that requires another person to keep the peace and follow certain conditions. The purpose is to prevent anticipated future harm by a feared individual. This can be initiated by a victim who fears they or their family will be harmed by the offender, through the Crown's office or the police. If the person named agrees to the peace bond, it will be granted immediately by a judge. If the person named does not agree, a hearing will be ordered that must be attended by the victim. The judge must be satisfied that: 1) the informant subjectively fears that an offence will be committed; 2) there are objectively provable reasonable grounds for these fears; and 3) the fear is of a serious and imminent danger (*R. v. Budre*, 2000). The standard of proof for the victim's fears is the balance of probabilities, that is, it is more likely to be true than not. A peace bond can be issued for a maximum of 12 months. If the complainant chooses to renew the order, a new hearing must be conducted. Conditions can include weapons prohibition, restricted access to particular areas (for example, the home of the victim, or playgrounds, if the person is a sexual offender), and restrictions on communicating with a particular person (Barrett, 2004). If the conditions of a peace bond are broken, the person named can be charged with a criminal offence. A Ministry of Justice study, however, suggests that many people believe that obtaining a peace bond is time-consuming, fraught with delays, and in the end results in weak charges and sentences. Therefore, it is viewed by many as a last resort (Rigakos, 2002).

Restraining Order

A restraining order is an order made under provincial civil law in family court. It forbids a spouse or partner from molesting, annoying, harassing, or communicating with any person except as set out in the order. To obtain a restraining order, a person must make an application to the court, often done with the assistance of a lawyer. A restraining order is not dependent on fear of personal safety. It serves basically the same function as a peace bond but does not necessarily carry the same penalties if the person disobeys it. Further, the police do not enforce civil orders such as a restraining order, and breach of the civil order does not result in criminal charges. If the designated person ignores the order, a civil contempt proceeding must be initiated. At the contempt hearing, the judge can order that the person be fined or go to jail until such time as he or she obeys the court order. Unlike a peace bond, the restraining order carries no time limit; however, although peace bonds are enforceable throughout Canada, restraining orders may not be enforced in other provinces.

Protection Order

Protection orders are civil court orders issued under provincial family violence legislation. Not all provinces have such legislation. Where it exists, it provides various emergency and long-term orders to protect victims of family violence.

Short-term orders normally last from 30 to 120 days. They can be obtained 24 hours a day, by telephone or by appointment, from a Justice of the Peace. Usually, the police or Victim Services workers are the ones who seek these orders on behalf of the victim. In the case of Saskatchewan, the First Nations' community case workers, can apply for protection orders by calling the police on behalf of a survivor. Long-term orders require legal representation; thus, if legal aid is not available, only women who can afford a lawyer are able to obtain one. A protection order may give temporary custody of children and the home to the victim, while ordering the abusive person out of the home. It can include conditions such as not allowing any contact. Consequences of breaching a protection order vary between jurisdictions. In Manitoba, breach can lead to a maximum $5,000 fine and/or up to two years' imprisonment (Ontario Women's Justice Network, 2006).

What Happens If a Victim Enters the Criminal Justice System?

It is important that victims entering the criminal justice process are aware of the aims and structure of the criminal court system. The Criminal Code of Canada, for instance, identifies the goals of the justice system to include: deterrence for both the individual offender and others witnessing the punishment; promotion of a sense of responsibility in offenders and acknowledgment of harm done to victims; reparation of harm done to victims; and rehabilitation for offenders. This would appear to make the courts a victim-friendly environment. However, concerns are frequently raised that this is not the case (Hudson, 1998; McElrea, 1999; Goren, 2001). A study conducted by Regehr and Alaggia (2005) sought to understand the perceptions of professionals involved in the criminal justice system regarding the purpose and processes of the system and to determine the impact of the system on victims. Key legal informants were lawyers and judges who described the focus of attention of the justice system to be strictly on the illegal act, which is described precisely in Criminal Codes. From their points of view, the goal of the criminal justice system is to determine whether a crime has been committed. The outcome of a finding of guilt will result in the loss of liberty of the accused individual; therefore, the focus of protection is on the rights of the accused to a fair trial. Rules are applied to protect the presumption of innocence. Thus, the controversial issue of accessing victim treatment or medical records is viewed as necessary, if producing them will ensure that the accused can make a full answer and defence (Regehr, Glancy, and Bradford, 2000). Sentencing is proportional to the definition of the act, not to the degree to which the victim was hurt. That is, the punishment is retributive—it is matched to the crime, not to the effects of the crime.

In contrast to the key legal informants' perspectives, the goals of justice were seen by therapists and advocates who participated in the 2005 study to be restorative, reaching beyond deterrence, rehabilitation, and community safety to the victim. Thus, the two primary groups most likely to deal with victims of sexual violence—legal and therapeutic professionals—reported more divergent than convergent views around significant and pivotal aspects of the legal process. The researchers express concern that these divergent views may shape the expectations of victims, potentially contributing to disappointment and a sense of revictimization (Regehr and Alaggia, 2005).

The Initial Report

Although victimization is not uncommon in Canada, reporting to the police is. According to the 2004 Criminal Victimization Survey, only 8 per cent of sexual assaults were reported to police, compared with 54 per cent of break-ins, 49 per cent of thefts of motor vehicle/parts, 39 per cent of physical assaults, and 46 per cent of robberies (Statistics Canada, 2005a). Nevertheless, a criminal court matter involving victimization generally begins with a report to the police by the victim of

the crime (see Figure 9.1). The police take a statement from the victim regarding the events that have occurred, and seek to determine whether there is sufficient evidence to support the contention that a crime has been committed. If so and if the offender is unknown to the victim, the investigation will focus on locating the offender. When the probable offender is identified, known or unknown to the victim, the police will decide whether there are reasonable grounds to charge the person with an offence.

A common misconception of victims at this point is that they have the power to lay charges against an alleged offender (Regehr and Alaggia, 2005). In fact, this decision is initiated by the police and the decision whether to proceed with the charges is made by the Crown attorney based on the belief that there is a reasonable prospect of conviction. According to Statistics Canada, in 2002, approximately one in six sexual offences reported to police were declared unfounded, meaning that the police concluded that no violation of law took place or was attempted. In addition, sexual assaults are cleared by police at a lower rate than other types of violent offences. In 2002, 44 per cent were cleared by laying charges and in 19 per cent of cases the offender was identified but not charged (Kong et al., 2002).

An exception to police discretion in charging a person suspected of committing a crime occurs in domestic violence cases. In May 1981 the first policy that instructed police to lay charges of assault against perpetrators of domestic violence, regardless of the wishes of the parties, was instituted in London, Ontario (Jaffe et al., 1993). Following this, in 1982, Parliament passed a resolution encouraging all police forces across the country to establish mandatory charging policies, and in 1983 a directive to this effect was issued to the RCMP and federal and territorial Crown prosecution offices (Brown, 2000). Mandatory charging in London, Ontario, resulted in a dramatic increase in the laying of charges in domestic violence cases in that city from charges being laid in 2.7 per cent of occurrences in 1979 to 67.3 per cent of occurrences in 1983 and 89.3 per cent of

Figure 9.1   The Process of a Criminal Case

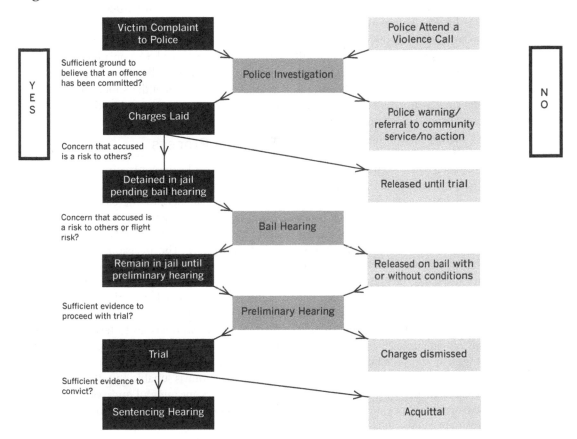

occurrences in 1990. Research on the effects of this policy suggested that in the majority of cases, there was a statistically significant reduction in the level of violence after the police intervention. Further, according to researchers, the majority of victims reported satisfaction with this approach.

Not all findings have been this positive. Although the majority of women in a British Columbia study on the effects of mandatory charging expressed support for the policy, 40 per cent indicated that they did not wish to proceed with prosecution of the offender, in 72 per cent of these cases because the woman wished reconciliation (Brown, 2000). Further, despite positive reviews by some researchers, concerns have been raised that mandatory charging policies

undermine the power and control of victims, treating victims of domestic violence like children who need others to determine what is in their best interest (Valverde, MacLeod, and Johnson, 1995). The Alberta Court of Appeal, for instance, resisted women's pleas that their partners not be imprisoned suggesting that their requests were the product of Battered Women Syndrome and a sense of powerlessness (Roach, 1999). Nevertheless, there is a high attrition rate of domestic abuse cases. One study in Manitoba suggested that charges are only laid in 21 per cent of cases; only 12 per cent of cases result in convictions and 4 per cent in incarceration. Almost 30 per cent of the cases were stayed, in half of these cases because the victim refused to testify (Landau, 1998).

The police officer laying charges against an accused person may elect to arrest them or alternatively may give them an appearance notice or a summons to appear in court. If there is a concern either that the person is a danger to others or will not appear in court, he or she may be held in jail awaiting trial. If this is the case, a bail hearing is arranged at which time a judicial decision is made whether or not to release the person. Information presented at that time includes previous criminal convictions, the seriousness of charges pending, the degree of risk posed to the victim or witnesses, and the degree to which the person poses a flight risk (for example, ties to the community that may keep him or her here or contacts in other countries). If the accused is released on bail, the judge may impose conditions such as not communicating with the victim, not using alcohol, and not possessing weapons. If the person breaches the conditions of the bail, he or she will be returned to jail. Victims are entitled to copies of the bail order and information regarding the conditions of bail (Department of Justice, 2005).

At various stages in the judicial process, the Crown and defence may engage in plea bargaining. In fact, in Canada, the United States, and Australia, approximately 90 per cent of all cases are resolved through guilty pleas that are the result of plea bargaining. Although plea bargaining is not officially regulated, it is sanctioned by the Supreme Court of Canada. Supreme Court Justice Iacobucci in *R. v. Burlingham* (1995) explicitly referred to plea bargaining as an integral element of the Canadian justice process. In general, a plea bargain addresses one or more of three issues, the nature of the charges to be laid, the ultimate sentence sought, and the facts that the Crown will bring to the attention of the courts. With the exceptions of Manitoba and Ontario, Canadian jurisdictions have not enacted legislation that affords victims the right to be informed of, or consulted about, plea agreements. Consequently, it has been suggested that victims are passive consumers rather than active participants in the decision-making process (Roach, 1999). In addition, there is no formal process by which plea

bargains are scrutinized in order to ensure that the rights and interests of all parties, the Crown, the accused, the victims, and members of society are adequately protected (Verdun-Jones and Tijerino, 2004). This may lead to considerable concern among victims who believe that the case should go to court and the offender should not be able to plead to a lesser charge or reduced sentence.

The Trial Process

The trial process begins with a preliminary inquiry at which time the judge determines whether there is sufficient evidence for the case to proceed to trial. The Crown attorney presents evidence against the accused that may or may not include victim testimony. The decision to testify either at the preliminary hearing or the trial does not reside with the victim. Rather, it is up to the prosecutor to determine whether the victim's input is relevant and supportive of the case being put forward. A victim who wishes to testify may not be permitted to do so. The reasoning for this is best depicted by a quote from an attorney who stated that if the victim is 'unable to tell the story in a manner that is meaningful and coherent [within a legal system], the case may be lost' (Regehr and Alaggia, 2005). At the conclusion of the preliminary hearing, the case may be dismissed by the judge, the accused may plead guilty, or the case may be committed to trial.

The trial often occurs a considerable time after the preliminary hearing, not uncommonly one to three years later. In the intervening period, the victim may or may not be contacted by prosecuting attorneys who are preparing the case. At trial, the Crown presents its evidence, which may include the testimony of the victim. If the victim does testify, he or she will generally be cross-examined by the defence attorney who often will test the credibility of the testimony of the victim. Victim accounts of the event tend to vary dramatically from that of the accused and as time elapses since the event, the divide between the two accounts widens. This is in part because the accounts of both victims and alleged offenders become shaped by police, lawyers, and other professionals who wittingly or unwittingly encourage facts to be presented in a way that will serve the interests of their clients and the system itself (Regehr and Glancy, 1993). Cross-examination is often viewed to be a difficult and sometimes devastating experience.

However, if the victim chooses not to testify, he or she may be subpoenaed and in rare cases arrested and forced to testify (Regehr and Alaggia, 2005). Once all the information has been presented, closing arguments are made by the lawyers on both sides. If the Crown prosecutor has proved the case against the accused beyond a reasonable doubt, a guilty finding will be rendered (Department of Justice, 2005) and the case will proceed to a sentencing hearing.

Trial decisions can be appealed by either the Crown or the defence. Offenders have the right to appeal the conviction, or appeal for a reduced sentence. Prosecutors can only appeal on the grounds of a question of law, such as the admissibility of evidence or the interpretation of the Criminal Code. Appeals are considered by the next level of court and generally are limited to reviews of the transcripts, not a rehearing of evidence.

Sentencing

Sentences are specified by the Criminal Code, although within this specification judges have discretion. The principles of sentencing were first codified in the Criminal Code in 1995.

Both the Crown and the defence attorneys make recommendations to the court about sentencing. The judge may request a presentence report from probation or from a mental health professional that addresses issues of safety, mitigating circumstances in the commission of the offence, and the potential for rehabilitation (see Chapter 11 for court reports). Other considerations may include previous criminal records and the impact of the crime on the victim. Sentences may include:

- *Absolute discharge*—no criminal record is retained in a discharge;

- *Conditional discharge*—discharge is dependent on complying with conditions, for example, probation;
- *Suspended sentence and probation*—sentencing is put off pending compliance with a probation order;
- *Fine*—may be combined with another penalty;
- *Conditional sentence*—sentences are served in the community under certain conditions, for example, house arrest;
- *Imprisonment*—sentences of less than two years are served in provincial institutions and longer than two years are served in federal penitentiaries;
- *Intermittent sentence*—if the sentence is 90 days or less, it may, for instance, be served on weekends;
- *Indeterminate sentence*—if the person has committed a series of violent acts demonstrating an inability or failure to restrain dangerous behaviour or has committed an offence of such a brutal nature that one is compelled to conclude that the offender is unlikely to be inhibited by normal standards in the future, the person may be found to be a dangerous offender (Glancy, Regehr, and Bradford, 2001); such a finding results in an indeterminate sentence;
- *Restitution order*—payment of the victim's losses due to the crime.

Principles of Sentencing
- punishment of the offender
- denunciation of the crime
- general (the public) and specific (the offender) deterrence from committing crimes of this nature
- separation of offenders from vulnerable members of society
- rehabilitation of the offender
- reparations made to the victim and/or society
- promotion of a sense of responsibility in the offender

Victim Impact Statements

Courts have traditionally not allowed victims to participate in the sentencing process. In 1982, for instance, Justice McLachlin, in denying a victim's request to have input into the sentencing of an offender, concluded that crime victims have no standing under the Criminal Code. Subsequently, in 1988, the government of Canada introduced victim impact statements as part of the revisions to the Code. Six demonstration projects were funded by departments of justice in Victoria, North Battleford, Winnipeg, Calgary, Toronto, and Montreal. Nevertheless, victim impact statements have not been extensively used in Canada. Evaluations of five of the projects in 1988 found considerable disparity regarding the use of victim impact statements, with a high of 83 per cent in Toronto to a low of 14 per cent in Calgary.

A British Columbia study published in 1992 suggested that victim impact statements were obtained in only 2 to 6 per cent of cases and filed into court in only 1 to 2 per cent of cases. It has been suggested that this, in part, is due to the reluctance of victims to expose their suffering to adversarial challenge (Roach, 1999). Another study found that between 14 and 18 per cent of victims expressed concerns about participating in preparing impact statements, fearing retribution from the offender and/or his friends (Giliberti, 1991). Similarly, in a US study it was found that only 15 per cent of victims prepared written statements and only 9 per cent were permitted oral submissions despite their right to do so (Finn-DeLuca, 1994). Thus, while victim impact statements may be enshrined in law, in the end, it may be that very few of the statements are used in court. Reasons given by prosecutors for not using them included the belief that they contained no new information, that they were too vague or irrelevant, and that they were of doubtful accuracy.

One of the cited reasons for using victim impact statements is that victims therefore have the opportunity to have their voices heard. Research conducted by Regehr and colleagues (2008), for instance, found that those victims who were able to present their victim impact statement in court felt empowered and positive about the experience. However, those who were not able to read their statement, for reasons such as the offender pled guilty or there was a plea bargain, felt cheated by the process. Researchers have concluded that completing a victim impact statement does not necessarily lead to victim satisfaction, nor does it increase a victim's willingness to cooperate with systems in the future (Young, 2001). Rather, satisfaction is dependent on whether the statement is considered and acknowledged by the judge and the degree to which the victims continued to be informed of the process.

Supports and Protection of Victims in the Criminal Justice Process

While court proceedings are generally open to the public, the Criminal Code empowers judges to exclude any or all members of the public from all or part of the proceedings. One such area of discretion is when it is felt that exclusion of the public is necessary to protect the privacy of the victim. Further, the court may issue a publication ban that prohibits the public and media from disclosing the identities of victims and witnesses. Publication bans must be ordered to protect the identity of a victim or witness who is under the age of 18. An older victim must request a publication ban in writing with arguments as to why the ban is necessary (Department of Justice, 2005). Further protections are awarded to child witnesses or those who may have difficulty testifying in court due to mental disorders or physical impairment. In such cases, the witness may be allowed to testify from outside the courtroom or behind a screen separating the witness from the accused.

The 1983 reforms to the Criminal Code, which replaced 'rape' with the more inclusive term 'sexual assault', contained a provision called 'rape-shield' that restricted the ability of the defence to introduce evidence of the victim's past sexual behaviour. Thus, the victim's sexual reputation and sexual history became inadmissible except under certain restricted conditions. However, the rape-shield was vulnerable to Charter challenge because it limited the ability of the accused to make full answer and defence, and in *R. v. Seaboyer* (1991) the rape-shield law was declared unconstitutional. As a consequence of *Seaboyer*, the parliamentary subcommittee on the status of women recommended that the rape-shield law be reinstated using the notwithstanding clause of the Charter. However, these efforts were not successful. Instead, Bill C-49 was enacted, which focused on the issue of consent or the right of women to express lack of consent through words or conduct. Further, consent was considered invalid if induced by trust, power, or authority (Roach, 1999). Therefore, victims no longer have the rape-shield law to protect them, but consent and not the previous sexual history of the victim is the basis for conviction.

All provinces and territories have programs designed to support victims who are going through the criminal justice system. A summary of these programs can be found in Table 9.1. In general, four types of programs are available: 1) police-based services; 2) Crown/court-based victim witness services that emphasize court preparation; 3) community-based victim services; and 4) system-based services (offered in PEI and Nova Scotia). Victim support programs are in part paid for by a victim surcharge that is added to the sentence of any offender—amended to the Criminal Code in 1989. This amount is defined as 15 per cent of any fine imposed on an offender or, if no fine is imposed, $50 for a summary conviction (or minor offence) and $100 for an indictable (or serious) offence. Nevertheless, in 1992 it was discovered that the surcharge was only being applied to 10 per cent of eligible cases in British Columbia. This was consistent throughout Canada where only 15 per cent of the expected fines have been imposed and of those, only 2.7 per cent was collected. The lack of compliance seems to be due to judicial resistance to the surcharge and the failure of provinces, such as Ontario, to establish the fund towards which the surcharges were to be applied (Young, 2001).

Release from Jail

Parole is considered for offenders that have served one-third of their sentence. The goal is to provide a period of state monitoring when offenders are reintegrating into the community. If parole is granted, the offender must report to a parole officer and comply with any conditions. Parole can be revoked if these conditions are not met. Statutory or mandatory release occurs when two-thirds of the sentence has been served and is not determined by a parole board. Statutory release can also be revoked if the offender is not complying with release orders. However, if Correctional Services Canada believes that an offender will likely commit a serious offence, such as that involving death or serious harm, they can refer the case to the parole board for review, who can overrule statutory release (Department of Justice, 2005). At the end of a sentence, an application can also be made under the long-term offender legislation, which adds a 10-year federal parole to the sentence of those not released on statutory release (Glancy, Regehr, and Bradford, 2001). Those serving an indeterminate sentence are not eligible for statutory release but may obtain parole.

Victims have a right, upon written request, to information about the sentence of offenders serving federal time (longer than two years) including the date of incarceration, place of incarceration, dates of parole reviews, and date of release. Victims can present impact statements to parole boards considering early release of the offender. Victims can also attend parole board hearings as observers. It is important to note that the National Parole Board and Correctional Services of Canada are required to disclose to the offender any information that will be considered during the decision-making process (Solicitor General of Canada, 2002). As a result, victims must provide a text of their statement 30 days before the hearing or 45 days before if it requires translation.

An additional measure aimed at controlling the behaviours of dangerous individuals, for the safety of others in society, is the preventative peace bond to be issued at the time of release. The legislation governing preventative peace bonds (section 810.1 of the Criminal Code) states that any person who fears, on reasonable grounds, that another person will commit a sexual offence as specified in the Code, against someone who is under the age of 14, may lay the information before a provincial court judge who has a duty to have the parties appear before him. If the judge finds that there are reasonable grounds for fear, she can order the defendant to enter into a recognizance and comply with certain conditions. The Code specifically states that provisions may involve: 1) prohibiting any contact with persons under the age of 14 years; 2) prohibiting the defendant from attending a public park or public swimming area where persons under the age of 14 are present or can reasonably be expected to be present; or 3) attending a daycare centre, playground, school ground, or community centre, for any period up to 12 months. If the defendant fails or refuses to enter into the recognizance, he or she may be sent to prison for up to 12 months. In practice, however, this provision has rarely been used (Glancy, Regehr, and Bradford, 2001).

The Criminal Code only notes two cases of relevance to this legislation. The first case was the 1996 case of *R. v. Budreo* in which the constitutionality of this section was challenged unsuccessfully. The higher court judge noted that this legislation is intended to keep individuals at risk away from their child targets, but he went on to note that the word 'fear' must be objectively provable. The judge cautioned his colleagues to take care when using this legislation. He believed that the appropriate threshold would be quite high, demonstrating on a balance of probabilities that there is a risk of serious and imminent danger. In the related case of *R. v. Harding* (1998) the information was laid by a police officer regarding Otis Harding who had pleaded guilty to forcing a 12-year-old girl to have sex with him, although he later denied this admission at a hearing regarding his application. He also pleaded guilty to performing activities as a pimp for a 14- and a 16-year-old girl, and to sexually assaulting one of these girls. At the hearing, evidence was presented regarding the risk of recidivism of Mr Harding; however, the judge found that the evidence fell short of establishing, on a balance of probabilities, that there were grounds for believing that Mr Harding would commit a sexual offence on a child under the age of 14. The judge noted that the police officer believed that Mr Harding would become involved in pimping again but found that section 810.1 is not specifically concerned with pimping activities and that it would be an abuse of the court's authority to use it as such. The application was therefore dismissed.

Faint Hope Hearings

Faint hope hearings were established in 1976 when Parliament abolished capital punishment and instituted sentences for first-degree murder of 25 years without parole. Under this provision, murderers could apply to a jury to be declared eligible for parole after serving 15 years of their sentence. Public outcry, the advocacy of victim groups such as CAVEAT and the use of victim impact statements to express the anguish of the families of those murdered (Roach, 1999) led to reluctance on the part of juries to allow the applications. In addition, in 1996 Parliament placed further restrictions on faint hope hearings, including denying them for multiple murders and therefore, although they have not been abolished, they are rarely used.

Victim Compensation

In 1969, Alberta developed the first legislation in Canada that led to the development of a victim compensation program (Young, 2001). Victim compensation plans allow victims of violent crimes to recover some of the costs associated with the crimes that were perpetrated against them. Studies of victims receiving this compensation suggest that they view the compensation not as financial assistance or compensation, but rather as a public acknowledgment of the harms committed against them. Further, given that civil litigation is expensive, lengthy, and possibly emotionally arduous, receiving compensation from a criminal injuries board is an attractive option for many victims. However, in 1992, the federal government discontinued transfer payments for victim compensation and as a result Newfoundland, the Yukon, and the Northwest Territories abandoned their compensation programs (Roach, 1999). Subsequently, the Yukon under the Crime Prevention and Victim Services Trust Act (2002) established a fund for victims accrued from lottery proceeds, money received from the Klondike Visitors Association, and fines paid into the courts by offenders.

An award for compensation is not dependent on a criminal conviction; however, in some jurisdictions (Alberta, Ontario, PEI, and Nova Scotia) a claim may be denied or reduced if the victim failed to report the offence within a reasonable time or refused reasonable cooperation with a law enforcement agency. Where eligibility is determined, entitlement is not automatic and falls within the discretionary power of the board. For instance, in determining whether to make an order for compensation, all provinces except Saskatchewan allow the board to consider the behaviour of the victim that may have contributed to his or her injury. In some circumstances, consideration may also be given to the character of the applicant. Awards can include compensation for expenses actually and reasonably incurred, loss due to disability and inability to work, maintenance of a child born due to sexual assault, and pain and suffering (Barrett, 2004). It is important to note that awards made under victim compensation programs are generally perceived to be quite low.

Civil Litigation

Civil litigation has seen a rise since the 1990s as a means for victims of childhood sexual abuse and sexual assault to receive compensation for their harms and acknowledgment of the crimes committed against them. Victims often turn to civil courts because they have more control over the court process than in criminal justice forums.

They can choose to initiate proceedings and withdraw or settle as they wish. Further, the burden of proof in civil cases is based on the balance of probabilities, rather than beyond a reasonable doubt as is found in criminal proceedings. Feminist authors have seen civil action as a means for social action, educating judges, the woman's family and friends, and the general public about the incidence and consequences of sexual assault (Sheehy, 1994).

Nevertheless, justice through civil courts remains an arduous process and some of the protections for victims found in the criminal courts, such as reduced access to victim records, are not found in the civil courts. Other barriers include short limitations periods that continue to exist in some provinces and territories (see Table 9.1), legal costs for pursuing legal action, or if the complainant is eligible for legal aid, difficulties in finding a lawyer willing to accept legal aid rates, and in the end the chances of collecting an award, especially if the offender is in jail (Sheehy, 1994). Initial statements of claim frequently assert damages and costs at well over $1 million, and as a result, plaintiffs develop unrealistic expectations about the amount of settlement that they are likely to receive.

In reality, financial awards for victims of violence in Canada remain relatively modest. In general, the largest settlements are against institutions in which abuse occurred or government agencies that placed the individual in the institution; however, even these settlements can be very small. For instance, in *R.A.R.B. v. British Columbia* (2001) the plaintiff sought damages for sexual abuse against staff and residents at a residential school he was placed in by children's services. It was determined by the courts that several events had a significant impact on the plaintiff, including the physical and sexual abuse inflicted by his father. The Crown was found to be liable for one assault inflicted on the plaintiff but it could not be said that the assault significantly aggravated or worsened his pre-existing condition. Therefore, the plaintiff was awarded non-pecuniary damages in the amount of $20,000. Because there was no evidence confirming any past wage loss or loss of earning capacity, no damages were awarded for these claims. Other cases involving residential schools and institutions, such as the Church, have fallen in the $100,000 to $200,000 range (for example, *T.W.N.A. v. Clarke*, 2003; *G.B.R. v. Hollett*, 2003; *C.H. v. British Columbia*, 2003). Some of the awards against family members who have sexually abused a plaintiff have fallen into a similar range (for example, *M.K. v. S.K.*, 1999; *J.G. v. S.A.G.*, 1998); others have been between $10,000 and $50,000 (*A.D.C. v. J.H.P*, 1996; *K.E.G. v. G.R.*, 1992; *R.L.L. v. R.L.*, 1999). Many of these awards occurred after appeals, making the case take months to years longer to settle. Out of these awards, 30 to 40 per cent can go to legal fees; court costs may be subtracted from the awards as well. Thus, civil action should not be viewed as an easy alternative to the criminal process for recognition of harms caused to victims.

Causes of Action

Against an individual
- *Assault*—the tort of assault protects one's right to be free from threat of imminent physical harm. It occurs when someone has disturbed the victim's sense of security and unlike the criminal context does not require physical contact or the carrying out of a threat.
- *Battery*—protects a person's right to be free of offensive physical contacts. The contact can be intentional or unintentional and does not have to be physically harmful.
- *Intentional infliction of mental suffering*—requires that an act or statement has been made that was calculated to produce harm and did produce harm.
- *Breach of fiduciary duty*—requires the assailant to have been in a position of special trust or confidence in relation to the victim and to have breached an obligation to act in his or her best interest.

Third-party liability
- *Vicarious liability*—is not a discrete tort but rather is the responsibility that someone may have for the actions of another; most commonly this involves the responsibility of an employer for the abusive actions of an employee.
- *Crown or governmental liability*—can be either direct or vicarious liability; all jurisdictions in Canada now have legislation permitting actions against the Crown.
- *Occupiers' liability*—is the care that is owed by persons who control land to visitors who enter that land; for example, this may apply when someone is assaulted in a parking lot that is not adequately lit.
- *Breach of fiduciary duty*—requires the third party to have been in a position of special trust or confidence in relation to the victim and to have breached an obligation to act in his or her best interest.

Grounds for Commencing a Civil Action

Civil litigation is based on 'tort law' or wrongful acts or injuries for which a person can be compensated. In cases where a victim of violence wishes to sue their abuser, three main torts of intentional interference apply: assault, battery (both intentional and unintentional), and intentional infliction of mental suffering (Klar, 2003). In addition, victims of violence can initiate claims against third parties based on negligence under three categories: vicarious liability, Crown or governmental liability, and occupiers' liability (Grace and Vella, 2000; Osborne, 2003). Third-party liability is frequently sought as the third party frequently has more financial resources to draw upon. The most famous examples of this would be situations where someone assaulted by a member of the clergy sues the Church, or someone abused in a residential facility sues the government. Crown liability can also arise from negligence in providing services or protections to injured individuals.

Further, both the abuser and third parties may face civil actions due to breach of fiduciary duty where the abuser and/or third party are in positions of special trust or confidence in relation to the victim and have breached their obligation to act in his or her best interest.

Once it is established that there are grounds to commence an action, it is necessary to ensure that the action was commenced within the specified period of limitations. Each province and territory has legislation governing the time frame in which civil actions can occur (see Table 9.1). In some provinces (British Columbia, Newfoundland, and Manitoba) and in the territories, there are no limitations in situations of sexual violence. In others, such as Saskatchewan and Alberta, it is necessary to demonstrate why it would not be possible to have commenced action earlier, generally because the individual was unaware that the harms they suffered were caused by the sexual violence; whereas in Ontario there is no limitation in respect of proceedings arising from sexual assault if at the time of the assault the assailant had charge of the person assaulted, was in a position of trust or authority in relation to the person, or was someone on whom he or she was dependent, whether financially or otherwise or if the person was incapable of commencing an action due to their physical or mental condition. In all other jurisdictions, special provisions have not been made for victims of sexual violence and the common limitation of two years applies.

The ability of sexual abuse victims to sue on the basis of historical abuse was facilitated by a Supreme Court finding (*M.(K.) v. M.(H.)*, 1992) that created a presumption that in recognition of postincest syndrome, the statute of limitations should not begin until the victim has received treatment. In this case the court stated:

> Incest is both a tortious assault and a breach of fiduciary duty. The tort claim, although subject to limitations legislation, does not accrue until the plaintiff is reasonably capable of discovering the wrongful nature of the defendant's acts and the nexus between those acts and the plaintiff's injuries. In this case, that discovery occurred only when the appellant entered therapy, and the lawsuit was commenced promptly thereafter. The time for bringing a claim for breach of a fiduciary duty is not limited by statute in Ontario, and this breach therefore stands along with the tort claim as a basis for recovery by the appellant (*M.(K.) v. M.(H.)*, p. 7).

Thus, because in the case of incest, two torts have been committed, both battery and that of breach of fiduciary duty, the limitation on battery did not apply.

The Process of a Civil Action

Once it is determined that there is a good cause of action and it is within the limitations period, actions are commenced by a statement of claim issued by the court clerk. The defendant must then be located, and a copy of this statement served to him or her. This statement of claim explains the action and notifies the defendant that if he or she does not take steps to defend, a judgment may be made against him or her by default. The initial statement of claim is a summary of the facts of the case, but not the evidence that will be used to support the claim. Often the plaintiff will employ the services of the sheriff's office or hire a private process server for the purpose of notification. If the defendant appears to be avoiding notification, the court can allow an alternative to personal service, such as an ad to be placed in the newspaper (Watson et al., 1999).

Once the statement of claim is received, the defendant may ask the court to dismiss the action if it is believed that there is no cause of action. Alternatively, the defendant will file a statement of defence containing the facts that will be relied upon in defence. The defendant can also make a counterclaim, stating that he or she has suffered injuries as a result of the plaintiff's conduct or they can make a third-party claim, stating the damages are in fact the fault of someone else. The plaintiff can then respond to any claims made.

The next stage of the case is the discovery process, during which time each party can obtain information about the other's case. This can include examination of documents and affidavits, oral examination under oath, orders to inspect property, examination of medical or counselling records, medical or psychiatric examinations by an expert selected by the defendant, and medical or other expert evidence that the plaintiff will use at the trial. At this point, the case may settle because either side realizes the strength of the other side and wishes to make a financial settlement (Grace and Vella, 2000).

Following the discovery process, cases may be referred either for case management or alternative dispute resolution (ADR). In case management, the court controls the pace of litigation, such as the time each party takes to respond. ADR includes such mechanisms as mediation, arbitration, and conciliation. The aim is to reduce court and legal costs, speed up the process, and afford the parties greater control (Watson et al., 1999). If not settled, the case may proceed to trial, which is usually before a judge alone and not a jury. The plaintiff carries the burden of persuading the court that the actions of the defendant were negligent or that they violated a legal standard. In the trial, the plaintiff's lawyer makes an opening statement outlining the facts to be presented. The plaintiff witnesses are presented and examined, after which the defence can cross-examine and the plaintiff can re-examine. The defendant then presents his or her case. Both lawyers summarize their cases and the judge makes a judgment. These judgments can be appealed.

Possible Outcomes of a Civil Action

If a civil case is found in favour of the complainant, damages for personal injuries can be awarded. Damages are restitutionary in nature, designed to place the victim in the position he or she would have been in if the tort had not occurred. The means for calculating these awards was established in 1978 following three Supreme Court decisions (*Andrews v. Grand and Toy*, 1978;

Thornton v. Prince George School District, 1978; *Arnold v. Teno*, 1978). As a result, full compensation of all probable future losses can be awarded based on mathematical calculation of actuarial and economic predictions. Lump sum awards are ordered based on itemization of expenses and needs and an explanation of the means of calculation (Osborne, 2003). Awards can cover:

- all pretrial losses, such as loss of income, medical expenses, and out-of-pocket expenses;
- future care costs;
- loss of earning capacity;
- pain and suffering; and
- loss of expectation of life.

Access to Treatment Records

Access to victim records in criminal matters has been a hotly contested issue in Canada over the past 15 years (Regehr, Glancy, and Bradford, 2000). This controversy began with a highly publicized 1991 case in Canada, where a Roman Catholic bishop was charged with the sexual assault of four Native children at a residential school during the 1960s. Defence counsel representing Bishop O'Connor obtained a court order requiring disclosure of the complainants' entire medical, counselling, and school records. The defence successfully argued that that the records would assist in determining the credibility of the witnesses and determining whether the allegations were corroborated by the complainants' statements to others. In a unanimous decision on this issue, the Supreme Court of Canada ruled the request could be made and stated that if specified conditions were met, third parties may be required to produce therapeutic records relevant to a criminal court matter. They concluded that concerns for fairness in the trial proceedings supersede the individual patient's privacy rights.

While the deliberations of the Supreme Court of Canada in *R. v. O'Connor* (1995) and that of a companion judgment in 1995, *A.(L.L.) v. B.(A.)*, attempted to establish strict guidelines under which confidentiality of patient records could be violated in the context of criminal cases, they fuelled the debate on the rights of victims in criminal proceedings. These cases resulted in courts across Canada granting access to such records at an unprecedented rate (Denike, 2002) leading therapists and women's advocacy groups to become highly vocal in their concerns that victimized women no longer had access to safe and confidential treatment.

In response, the government amended the Criminal Code with Bill C-46 (Statutes of Canada, 1997). Parliament stated that it wished to encourage the reporting of incidents of sexual violence and abuse and support the prosecution of offences within a framework of laws that are consistent with the principles of fundamental justice and are fair to both complainants and accused persons. It was recognized that the compelled production of personal information could deter victims of sexual violence from reporting offences to the police and seeking necessary treatment. In addition it was acknowledged that compelled production of records and the process entailed would detrimentally affect those providing services for victims of sexual violence. Bill C-46 set a higher threshold for access to complainant records by the accused.

Bill C-46 was immediately challenged and within four months of its passage, it was overturned by three superior court judges—one in Alberta (*Regina v. Mills*, 1997) and two in Ontario (*R. v. Lee*, 1997; *R. v. G.J.A.*, 1997). In considering the case of Mills, the Supreme Court of Canada overturned the ruling of the Supreme Court of Alberta and upheld Bill C-46 (*L.C. and the Attorney General of Alberta v. Mills*, 1999). In doing so, the ruling discussed at length the relationship between the courts and the legislature. It was noted that the court must maintain a 'posture of respect' to Parliament and that the relationship between the two bodies must be based on dialogue and a balance of power. In particular, the ruling noted that courts do not hold a monopoly on the protection and promotion of rights and freedoms. Parliament, in its role as an elected governing body, is often able to act as an ally to vulnerable groups, in this case, victims of sexual violence. The court acknowledged that the history

of treatment of sexual assault complainants by our society and our legal system has been an unfortunate one and that despite changes to the system, treatment of sexual assault complainants remains an ongoing problem.

While this limits the access to records for victims of sexual violence in criminal matters, it is important to note that civil cases do not follow the standards for access to records. In Canada, individuals who initiate civil legal proceedings that put their treatment, medical condition, or health at issue are viewed as waiving the right to confidentiality and implicitly consenting to the disclosure of all confidential information that may be relevant to the action. The Supreme Court noted that in criminal matters, subsequent damage to the complainant is not in question and thus the requirement for disclosure in civil cases does not apply.

The Restorative Justice Model for Victims of Violence

The restorative justice model has arisen as an alternative approach to the criminal and civil justice system for two main reasons. First, in response to concerns that the criminal justice and civil justice models have at best been inadequate in addressing issues of victimization and at worse revictimized people. Second, in response to legitimate concerns about the overrepresentation of Aboriginal peoples in the correctional institutions in Canada. Aboriginal people comprise 3.3 per cent of the nation's population (Statistics Canada, 2001), yet they account for approximately 12 per cent of Canada's federal offender population (CCJA, 1997). For example, in Manitoba, Aboriginal people constitute approximately 12 per cent of the population, yet Aboriginal people account for over one-half of the 1,600 people incarcerated on any given day of the year in correctional institutions (Aboriginal Justice Implementation Commission, 2004). Consequently, in 1996, the federal government passed Bill C-46: An Act to amend the Criminal Code. This amendment introduced restorative principles into sentencing and attempted to balance the objectives of denunciation of the crime with reparation to victims and communities (Balfour, 2008). It also created a legitimate role for Aboriginal justice models. Under the Act, alternatives to incarceration were to be used whenever possible.

The term 'restorative justice' refers to informal and non-adjudicative forms of dispute resolution. This concept also includes offender mediation, family conferences, neighbourhood accountability boards, and Aboriginal peacemaking or sentencing circles that promote joint decision-making power (Bazemore and Schiff, 2001). Originally developed as a means for addressing more minor crimes such as property crimes committed by youth, the model has more recently been applied to violent crime. This has been controversial and has raised concerns regarding victim safety and the attribution of responsibility for crimes of violence (Curtis-Fawley and Daly, 2005; Cheon and Regehr, 2006; Balfour, 2008).

A central concept of restorative justice is that it can repair the harms of crime and restore what has been lost (Zehr, 1995). In this model it is believed that victims and offenders when put together in the right circumstances will be able to negotiate a mutually agreeable plan for easing the burden on the victim both psychologically and materially (Umbreit, 1995). Restorative justice is not about determining guilt or innocence, it is rather a means for negotiating ways to mediate the effects of crime. This model attempts to move from punishment to repairing the harms caused by the crime by balancing the needs of the victims, citizens, and offenders. From the perspective of Aboriginal communities, restorative justice brings together the cultural and political intentions of self-determination of Aboriginal peoples (Balfour, 2008).

Restorative justice models generally have a number of elements. First, restorative justice involves not only the victim and the offender, but also the members of the community because the community is viewed to have a stake in the outcome. Community members are expected to have an ongoing role in supporting victims in the healing process, enforcing agreements, and

influencing the offender's behaviour to prevent further offending (Presser and Gaarder, 2000; Dodd, 2002). The involvement of community members has another purpose, however; that is, to bring the crime out of the closet and into the open light. This exposure has been described as shaming by people important to the offender, including family and community members (Braithwaite, 2000). This shaming is then followed by gestures of reintegration and support, which are seen to deter antisocial behaviour and enable more prosocial behaviour in the future.

A second key element is the role of the victim. The model generally involves a meeting or series of meetings that community members, the offender, and the victim each attend. The victim describes the impact of the offence and what might be needed to assist him or her in healing. During the process of restoration, victims of crime are provided with opportunities to discuss how the crime affected them, get information about the offender's motivation, and have input into sanctions and restitution (Bazemore and Schiff, 2001). This is a significant departure from the criminal justice model in which the needs of the victim are considered secondary to the needs of police, judges, and prosecutors and in which resources to assist victims are scarce. In the end, victims are expected to benefit from reparative words, such as an apology by the offender or statements of support by others, and actions offered by the offender and/or community. This can be augmented by the provision of financial compensation by the offender or material assistance by the community.

Finally the role of the offender is key to the success of the model. The offender is expected to accept responsibility for his or her harmful actions and to make amends (Dodd, 2002). As stated above, an important part of this process often includes apologies to the victim and some type of restoration. For instance, if the offender is a juvenile who has committed a property crime against a member of the community, he or she may be expected to pay for the repair of the damage or to offer their own physical labour to restore the damage. The aim is to return offenders to a law-abiding life and reintegration into the community (Presser and Gaarder, 2000).

Early literature on restorative justice models suggested they were highly successful in meeting their goals. Statements can be found in the literature such as: 'The evidence of victim satisfaction as a result of face-to-face confrontation with the offender and mediation of a restitutionary response is overwhelming' (Haley, 1998). Indeed, several studies looking at the efficacy of restorative models have suggested that as a result of them victims feel satisfied and perceive themselves to have been fairly treated by the justice system and feel less shame and fear (Marshall, 1995; Umbreit, 1999; Umbreit, Coates, and Roberts, 2000). Program evaluations of restorative justice programs in the case of property and other minor crimes generally report high rates of victim satisfaction with procedures and outcomes, and lower rates of recidivism among participants compared to non-participants (Umbreit and Coates, 1999; Masters, 2002; Latimer, Dowden, and Muise, 2005).

To date, however, restorative justice has been primarily used to deal with minor property crimes and youth offending. Yet, encouraged by these findings, some have begun to apply restorative approaches to more serious offences, including sexual violence and domestic assaults (Carbonatto, 1995; Strang and Braithwaite, 2002). Concerns have been raised, however, whether studies conducted on the use of restorative justice in minor crimes can be applied to more serious situations (Hudson, 2002). Some critics have suggested that restorative justice models applied to IPV or sexual assault can result in unintended negative consequences (Stubbs, 2004; Cheon and Regehr, 2006). For instance, victims may feel pressured to engage in a process that serves to reproduce and reinforce the imbalance of power between the offender and the victim (Hudson, 1998; Griffiths, 1999; Shenk and Zehr, 2001) and the guilt, shame, and humiliation that the offender is intended to feel may in fact be experienced by the victim (Koss, 2000). This has caused some critics to question whether the aims of restorative justice are indeed directed more towards the benefit of the offender than

the victim (Shenk and Zehr, 2001) and whether restorative justice is simply another means of exercising social control (LaPraire, 1996). This leads some to continue to push for longer sentences aimed at holding offenders responsible for their actions—acknowledging the degree of harm suffered by victims and protecting the public.

Research findings have been contradictory on the use of restorative justice in cases of violence (Cheon and Regehr, 2006). In a study of the impact of restorative justice models on Aboriginal women in British Columbia, Stewart, Huntley, and Blaney (2001) found that women perceived themselves to have less power in their communities than men and believed that restorative justice models were designed to benefit men. 'Focus group participants expressed tremendous concern with diversion of cases of violence against women and children because they felt that the majority of support goes to offenders and that there was a prevalence of victim-blaming mentality' (p. 39). In general, these women felt there was a lack of accountability in existing alternative justice models. Stubbs (2004) reports on several other studies with indigenous women with similar findings. As stated earlier, one of the motivations for using restorative models in Aboriginal communities is to address the overrepresentation of Aboriginal peoples in the correctional institutions. Balfour (2008), however, identifies that restorative models have been ineffective in this aim. Conversely, Umbreit and colleagues (2002) report the findings of a multisite qualitative study of programs involving victim–offender dialogue in the United States; they conclude that: 'Victim offender dialogue in crimes of severe violence has been found to be highly effective as reported by individual victims or family survivors and offenders/inmates' (p. 3).

There are many possible reasons for the contradictory research with respect to whether restorative justice does or does not work in cases of IPV. Bazemore and Green (2007) suggest that there are definitional and theoretical problems with restorative justice models and research emanating from them. For instance, there is a lack of clear standards about what practices qualify for inclusion in the model, and outcomes are not well tied to interventions. Alternatively, disparate findings regarding the efficacy of restorative justice with all populations and specifically with victims of intimate violence can be largely attributed to the ideologies of the program developers and researchers (Cheon and Regehr, 2006). Their ideological stance is often clearly stated at the outset of the report and, not surprisingly, the results are consistent with the stated views. Other studies indicate that the outcomes of restorative justice interventions vary on the dimension of severity. That is, property-crime offenders are less likely to recidivate after restorative justice interventions than violent offenders (de Beus and Rodriguez, 2007). The public further expects that in the cases of more serious crimes, the restorative model should include some retributive measures, such as incarceration (Gromet and Darley, 2006). A recent case of a Saskatchewan father, Christopher Pauchey, who allowed his two young daughters to freeze to death in a blizzard while he was drunk, underscored this issue. While a sentencing circle recommended drug and alcohol treatment as well as cultural and spiritual work with Aboriginal elders, a provincial court judge overruled this and imposed a jail sentence (CBC, 2009).

There is clearly a need for controlled studies with measurable outcomes to support claims of efficacy of restorative models when considering crimes of violence (Wenzel et al., 2008). In the meantime, it is important to use caution when applying these models to situations of violence and abuse.

CASE EXAMPLE 1 REVIEWED

We now return to the case of Dolly and how the legislation in this chapter answers questions directly related to her case.

What are the legal avenues by which someone like Dolly can protect herself from harassment, abuse, and assault?

While Surjit is free in the community, Dolly can obtain a peace bond or restraining order so that he does not have access to her. If Surjit ignores the order, Dolly can contact the police. Once Surjit has committed an offence, Dolly can report it to the police and charges may be laid.

What is the criminal justice process that is likely to occur?

Dolly has reported the offence to the police and charges have been formally laid against Surjit, so the case will now commence through the criminal courts. Because Surjit was out on bail for a previous assault against Dolly when he attacked her, it is likely that a request will be made to have bail denied and have him remain in detention until the pretrial or preliminary hearing. If the judge determines that there is sufficient evidence that a crime has been committed, a trial will be scheduled and if at trial Surjit is found guilty, he will be sentenced. Dolly may or may not be required to testify at the preliminary hearing or trial. At any stage of the process, a plea-bargain deal may be reached, resulting in a range of outcomes. If questions are raised about Surjit's mental state, a psychiatric assessment may be requested by the Crown prosecutor, the defence attorney, or the courts and the process defined in Chapter 7, for mentally disordered offenders may be followed.

Is Dolly eligible for compensation?

Dolly can apply for victim compensation through the process defined by her province or territory, unless she lives in Newfoundland or the Northwest Territories, where compensation programs have been disbanded due to the discontinuation of transfer payments from the federal government for this purpose. Dolly can also commence civil action against her attacker under the tort of battery.

CASE EXAMPLE 2 REVIEWED

We now return to the case of Mel and how the legislation in this chapter answers questions directly related to his case.

Can Mel be charged with offences committed against children 35 years ago?

Although there are time limitations on whether or not someone can commence a civil action, the Canadian Criminal Code has no limitations specified on criminal prosecutions. Therefore, Mel can be charged with his previous offences. However, many factors make these cases more difficult to both prosecute and defend because evidence is lost or damaged over time, and witnesses have scattered, died, or their memories have faded (Greenspan, 1999).

Can Jason and the other men commence a civil suit against Mel and the choir?

Whether or not Jason can commence a civil action against the abuser and the choir that employed him is subject to the statute of limitations in the province or territory in which he lives. As indicated in Table 9.1, if he lives in British Columbia, Newfoundland, Manitoba, or the territories, there is no question that he can commence action. If he lives in Alberta, Saskatchewan, or Ontario, he will have to meet certain criteria to be permitted to commence action. If he lives elsewhere, the period for commencing action has expired.

What process is likely to occur in the civil proceeding?

If Jason makes a statement of claim, this will be served on the defendants. Assuming they reply with a statement of defence, the case will proceed to discoveries, possibly mediation or arbitration, and if not resolved at this stage, to trial. If the judge finds that the balance of probabilities is in favour of Jason's claim, a judgment for damages can be ordered. Jason and his counsel must then collect this award from the defendants.

Can Jason's counselling records for the abuse be called into court?

Because this is a civil action commenced by Jason and he is seeking compensation for damages occurring as a result of the abuse, his counselling records will be compellable (that is, required to be produced in court) and the defendant and his counsel will have full access to the records. The manner in which his counsellors can best protect his confidentiality and interests is outlined in Chapter 11.

Key Terms

Absolute Discharge
Sentence where no criminal record is retained in a discharge

Assault
Threat or imminent physical harm—it does not require physical contact

Battery
Intentional or unintentional offensive physical contact—it does not have to be physically harmful

Breach of Fiduciary Duty
Where someone in a position of special trust or confidence in relation to the victim has breached an obligation to act in his or her best interest

Civil Contempt
Failure to follow a court order that benefits someone else

Civil Litigation
Court proceeding that provides a means for victims to receive compensation for the harms and acknowledgment for the crimes committed against them from the assailant

Conditional Discharge
A sentence where discharge is dependent on complying with conditions

Conditional Sentence
A sentence served in the community under certain conditions (for example, house arrest)

Damages
An award to the victim if he or she is successful in a civil court claim

Dangerous Offender
Designation for a person who has committed a series of violent acts, which demonstrates an inability or failure to restrain dangerous behaviour, or for a person who has committed an offence of such a brutal nature that it is unlikely that the offender will be inhibited by normal standards in the future

Discovery Process
Stage during a civil action when each party can obtain information about the other's case, which can include examination of documents and affidavits, oral examination under oath, orders to inspect property, and examination of medical or counselling records, etc.

Faint Hope Hearing
Provision where an offender convicted of first-degree murder (and 25 years in prison without parole) can apply to a jury to be declared eligible for parole after serving 15 years of his or her sentence

Indeterminate Sentence
Undetermined sentence for those found to be dangerous offenders

Intermittent Sentence
Sentence that can be served on weekends only (if 90 days or less)

Limitation Period
Time frame that a victim has to bring forth a civil court action, as defined by law

Parole
Release of an offender from jail after serving one-third of his or her sentence to provide a period of state monitoring during reintegration into society

Peace Bond
Court order initiated by a victim requiring another person to keep the peace and follow certain conditions to prevent anticipated future harm by a feared individual

Plea Bargaining
An agreement in a criminal case where the Crown attorney offers the defendant the opportunity to plead guilty in exchange for a lesser charge or lighter sentence

Preliminary Inquiry
Beginning of the trial process where the judge determines whether there is enough evidence to proceed to trial

Protection Order
Civil court order issued under provincial family violence legislation that provides various emergency and long-term orders to protect victims of family violence

Restraining Order
An order under family court that forbids a spouse or partner from molesting, annoying, harassing, or communicating with any person as set out in the order

Statutory/Mandatory Release
Release of the offender from jail when two-thirds of the sentence has been served; this can be revoked if the offender does not comply with the release orders and can be overruled by the parole board if they believe the offender will likely commit a serious offence

Subpoena
A written order to a person to appear in court or face punishment

Suspended Sentence and Probation
Sentence that is put off, pending compliance with a probation order

Third-party Liability
Law that allows a victim to bring an action against someone else other than the perpetrator in some instances

Vicarious Liability
Third-party liability encompassing the responsibility an individual may have for the actions of another; this most commonly involves the responsibility of an employer for abusive actions of an employee

Victim Compensation Plan
Plan that allows victims of violent crime to recover some of the costs associated with the crimes perpetrated against them

Victim Impact Statement
Written or oral presentations by the victim for use in the court proceedings

Discussion Questions

1. What rights do victims' bills of rights afford and what protections should be expanded?
2. What protections exist for a person who believes that someone will threaten or assault them in the future? Do these seem adequate?
3. What should a victim consider before reporting a crime to the police?
4. In what ways can a victim be compensated for crimes against them?

Relevant Legislation

Federal
Criminal Code of Canada, R.S.C. 1985, c. 22, s. 6
  http://laws.justice.gc.ca/en/C-46/

Alberta
Limitations Act, S.A. 1996, c. L-15.1
  http://ql.quicklaw.com
Protection Against Family Violence Act, R.S.A. 2000, c. P-27
  http://www.canlii.org/ab/laws/sta/p-27/2008 0715/whole.html
Victims of Crime Act, R.S.A. 2000, c. V-3
  http://www.canlii.org/ab/laws/sta/v-3/2008 0715/whole.html

Victims Restitution and Compensation Payment Act, S.A. 2001, c. V-3.5
  http://www.canlii.org/ab/laws/sta/v-3.5/2008 0715/whole.html

British Columbia
Criminal Injuries Compensation Act, R.S.B.C. 1996, c. 85
  http://www.qp.gov.bc.ca/statreg/stat/C/96085_ 01.htm
Family Relations Act, R.S.B.C. 1996, c. 128
  http://www.qp.gov.bc.ca/statregstat/F/96128_ 01.htm

Limitation Act, R.S.B.C. 1996, c. 266
    http://ql.quicklaw.com
Victims of Crime Act, R.S.B.C. 1996, c. 478
    http://www.qp.gov.bc.ca/statreg/stat/V/96478_
    01.htm

Manitoba

Domestic Violence and Stalking Act, S.M. 1998,
    c. 41
    http://web2.gov.mb.ca/laws/statutes/ccsm/
    d093e.php
Limitation of Actions Act, C.C.S.M., c. L150
    http://www.canlii.org/mb/laws/sta/l-150/
Victims' Bill of Rights, C.C.S.M., c. V55
    http://www.canlii.org/mb/laws/sta/v-55/2005
    0110/ whole.html

New Brunswick

Family Services Act, N.B. Reg. 97-71
    http://www.canlii.org/nb/laws/regu/1997r.71/
    20080715/whole.html
Limitation of Actions Act, R.S.N.B. 1973, c. L-8
    http://www.canlii.org/nb/laws/sta/l-8/2008
    0715/whole.html
Victims Services Act, S.N.B. 1987, c. V-2.1
    http://www.gnb.ca/acts/acts/v-02-1.htm

Newfoundland and Labrador

Family Law Act, R.S.N.L. 1990, c. F-2
    http://www.canlii.org/nl/laws/sta/f-2/2008
    0715/whole.html
Limitations Act, S.N.L. 1995, c. L-16.1
    http://www.canlii.org/nl/laws/sta/l-16.1/2008
    0715/whole.html
Victims of Crime Services Act, R.S.N.L. 1990,
    c. V-5
    http://www.canlii.org/nl/laws/sta/v-5/2008
    0715/whole.html

Nova Scotia

Domestic Violence Intervention Act, S.N.S. 2001,
    c. 29
    http://www.canlii.org/ns/laws/sta/2001c.29/
    20080717/whole.html

Limitation of Actions Act, R.S.N.S. 1989, c. 258
    http://www.canlii.org/ns/laws/sta/r1989c.258/
Victims' Rights and Services Act, S.N.S. 1989,
    c. 14
    http://www.gov.ns.ca/legislature/legc/statutes/
    victims.htm

Ontario

Compensation for Victims of Crime Act, S.O. 1990,
    c. 24
    http://www.e-laws.gov.on.ca/html/statutes/
    english/elaws_statutes_90c24_e.htm
Domestic Violence Protection Act, S.O. 2000, c. 3
    (not yet in force)
    http://www.e-laws.gov.on.ca/html/statutes/
    english/elaws_statutes_00d33_e.htm
Limitations Act, 2002, S.O. 2002, c. 24, Sch. B
    http://www.canlii.org/on/laws/sta/2002c.
    24sch.b/20080716/whole.html
Victims' Bill of Rights, 1995, S.O. 1995, c. 6
    http://www.e-laws.gov.on.ca/html/statutes/
    english/elaws_statutes_95v06_e.htm

Prince Edward Island

Statute of Limitations, R.S.P.E.I. 1988, c. S-7
    http://www.gov.pe.ca/law/statutes/
Victims of Crime Act, R.S.P.E.I. 1988, c. V-3.1
    http://www.canlii.org/pe/laws/sta/v-3.1/2004
    1117/ whole.html
Victims of Family Violence Act, S.P.E.I. 1996,
    c. V-3.2
    http://www.canlii.org/pe/laws/sta/v-3.2/

Quebec

Assistance for victims of crime, An Act respecting,
    R.S.Q. c. A-13.2
    http://www.canlii.org/qc/laws/sta/a-13.2/2008
    0715/whole.html
Civil Code of Québec, C.C.Q.
    http://www.canlii.org/qc/laws/sta/ccq/2008
    0715/whole.html
Crime Victims Compensation Act, 1994 S.Q.,
    c. 1-6
    http://www.canlii.org/qc/laws/sta/i-6/

Saskatchewan

Limitations Act, S.S. 2004
http://www.qp.gov.sk.ca/documents/English/
Statutes/Statutes/L16-1.pdf

Saskatchewan Victims of Crime Act, S.S. 1995,
c. 4-6.011
http://www.qp.gov.sk.ca/documents/English/
Statutes/Statutes/V6-011.pdf

Victims of Domestic Violence Act, S.S. 1994,
c. V-6.02
http://www.canlii.org/sk/laws/sta/v-6.02/2008
0715/whole.html

Northwest Territories

Family Law Act, S.N.W.T. 1997, c. 18
http://www.canlii.org/nt/laws/sta/1997c.18/
20080715/whole.html

Limitation of Actions Act, R.S.N.W.T. 1988, c. L-8
http://www.canlii.org///nt/laws/sta/l-8/2008
0715/whole.html

Victims of Crime Act, R.S.N.W.T. 1988, c. 9 (Supp.)
http://www.canlii.org/nt/laws/sta/supp.9/2008
0715/whole.html

Yukon Territory

Family Violence Prevention Act, R.S.Y. 2002,
c. 84
http://www.gov.yk.ca/legislation/acts/favipr.pdf

Limitation of Actions Act, R.S.Y. 2002, c. 139
http://www.canlii.org/yk/laws/sta/139/2006
0728/whole.html

Crime Prevention and Victims Services Trust Act,
R.S.Y. 2002, c. 49
http://www.gov.yk.ca/legislation/acts/cpvst.pdf

References

Aboriginal Justice Implementation Commission (2004), *The Justice System and Aboriginal People* (accessed 8 April 2004 at www.ajic.mb.ca/volume1).

A.D.C. v. J.H.P. (1996), B.C.J. No. 741.

Alaggia, R., Jenney, A., Mazzuca, J., and Redmond, M. (2007), 'In Whose Best Interest? A Canadian Case Study of the Impact of Child Welfare Policies in Cases of Domestic Violence', *Brief Treatment and Crisis Intervention*, 7(4): 275–90.

A.(L.L.) v. B.(A.) (1995), 4 S.C.R. 536 (Can.).

Andrews v. Grand and Toy Alberta Ltd. (1978), 2 S.C.R. 229.

Arnold v. Teno (1978), 2 S.C.R. 287.

Balfour, G. (2008), 'Falling between the Cracks of Retributive and Restorative Justice: The Victimization and Punishment of Aboriginal Women', *Feminist Criminology*, 3(2): 101–20.

Barrett, J. (2004), *Balancing Charter Rights: Victims Rights and 3rd Party Remedies* (Toronto: Thompson-Carswell).

Bazemore, G. and Green, D. (2007), 'Yardsticks for Victim Sensitive Process: Principle-based Standards for Gauging the Integrity of Restorative Justice Process', *Victims and Offenders*, 2(3): 289–301.

——— and Schiff, M. (2001), *Restorative Justice: Repairing Harm and Transforming Communities* (Cincinnati: Anderson Press).

Black, T., Trocmé, N., Fallon, B., and MacLaurin, B. (2008), 'The Canadian Child Welfare System Response to Exposure to Domestic Violence Investigations', *Child Abuse and Neglect*, 32: 393–404.

Braithwaite, J. (2000), 'Shame and Criminal Justice', *Canadian Journal of Criminology*, 42(3): 281–98.

Brown, T. (2000), *Charging and Prosecution Policies in Cases of Spousal Assault: A Synthesis of Research, Academic and Judicial Responses* (Ottawa: Department of Justice, Canada) (accessed at http://canada. justice.ca).

Brownmiller, S. (1975), *Against Our Will: Men Women and Rape* (London: Secker and Warburg).

Canadian Centre for Justice Statistics (2005), *Family Violence in Canada: A Statistical Profile* (accessed at http://www. phac-aspc.gc.ca).

Canadian Criminal Justice Association (1997), *Aboriginal Peoples and the Criminal Justice System* (accessed at http://www.ccja-acjp.ca/en/abori2.html).

Carbonatto, H. (1995), 'Expanding Intervention Options for Spousal Abuse: The Use of Restorative Justice', *Occasional Papers in Criminology, New Series No. 4* (Wellington, AU: Institute of Criminology, University of Victoria).

CBC (2009), 'Father of Girls Who Froze to Death Gets 3 Years in Prison', CBC News, 6 March 2009 (accessed at http://www.cbc.ca).

Cheon, A. and Regehr, C. (2006), 'Restorative Justice in Cases of Intimate Partner Violence: Reviewing the Evidence', *Victims and Offenders* 1(4): 369–94.

C.H. v. British Columbia (2003), B.C.J. 1706.

Curtis-Fawley, S. and Daly, K. (2005), 'Gendered Violence and Restorative Justice: The Views of Victim Advocates', *Violence Against Women* 11(5): 603–38.

de Beus, K. and Rodriguez, N. (2007), 'Restorative Justice in Practice: An Examination of Program Completion and Recidivism', *Journal of Criminal Justice*, 35: 337–47.

Denike, M.A. (2002), 'Myths of Women and the Rights of Man: The Politics of Credibility in Canadian Rape Law', in J.F. Hodgson and D.S. Kelley (eds), *Sexual Violence: Policies, Practices and Challenges in the United States and Canada* (Westport, CT: Praeger).

Department of Justice, Canada (2005), *Criminal Harassment* (accessed at http://canada.justice.gc.ca).

——— (2008), *A Canadian Directory of Court Support Services for Child and Youth Victims and Witnesses* (accessed at http://www.justice.gc.ca).

Dodd, J.D. (2002), 'Dialogue on Restorative Justice and Women Who Are Victims of Violence: A Discussion Paper in Preparation for the Restorative Justice and Violence against Women Workshop', *Justice Options for Women Project* (accessed on 20 February 2005 at http://www.mshta.org/Resources).

Douglas, K. and Dutton, D. (2001), 'Assessing the Link between Stalking and Domestic Violence', *Aggression and Violent Behavior*, 6: 529–46.

Finn-DeLuca, V. (1994), 'Victim Participation at Sentencing', *Criminal Law Bulletin*, 403–28.

G.B.R. v. Hollet (1996), N.S.J. No. 345.

Giliberti, C. (1991), 'Evaluation of Victim Impact Statement Projects in Canada: A Summary of Findings', in G. Kaiser, H. Kury, and J. Albrecht (eds), *Victims and Criminal Justice* (Freiburg: Max-Planch Institute).

Glancy, G., Regehr, C., and Bradford, J. (2001), 'Sexual Predator Laws in Canada', *Journal of the American Academy of Psychiatry and the Law*, 29(2): 232–7.

Goren, S. (2001), 'Healing the Victim, the Young Offender, and the Community via Restorative Justice: An International Perspective', *Issues in Mental Health Nursing*, 22: 137–49.

Grace, E. and Vella, S. (2000), *Civil Liability for Sexual Abuse and Violence in Canada* (Toronto: Butterworths).

Greenspan, E. (1999, 29 June), 'Set the Clock on Criminal Charges', *National Post* (accessed at http://www.efc.ca/pages/media/national-post.29 jun99.html).

Griffiths, C. (1999), 'The Victims of Crime and Restorative Justice: The Canadian Experience', *International Review of Victimology*, 6(4): 279–94.

Gromet, D. and Darley, J. (2006), 'Restoration and Retribution: How Including Retributive Components Affects the Acceptability of Restorative Justice Procedures', *Social Justice Research*, 19(4): 395–432.

Hale, M. (1739), *History of Pleas of the Crown*, vol. 1 (London).

Haley, J. (1998), 'Apology and Pardon: Learning from Japan', *The American Behavioral Scientist*, 41(6): 842–67.

Hudson, B. (1998), 'Restorative Justice: The Challenge of Sexual and Racial Violence', *Journal of Law and Society*, 25(2): 237–56.

——— (2002), 'Restorative Justice and Gendered Violence: Diversion or Effective Justice?' *British Journal of Criminology*, 42: 616–34.

Jaffe, P., Hastings, E., Reitzel, D., and Austin, G. (1993), 'The Impact of Police Laying Charges', in Z. Hilton (ed), *Legal Responses to Wife Assault* (Newbury Park: Sage).

J.G. v. S.A.G. (1998), N.S.J. No. 234.

Justice for Victims of Crime Act, S.M. 1986–87, c. 28.

K.E.G. v. G.R. (1992), B.C.J. 256.

Klar, L.N. (2003), *Tort Law*, 3rd ed. (Toronto: Thompson).

Kong, R., Johnson, H., Beattie, S., and Cardiool, A. (2002), 'Sexual Offences in Canada', Statistics Canada Cat. no. 85-002-XPE, vol. 23, no. 6.

Koss, M.P. (2000, November), 'Blame, Shame, and Community: Justice Responses to Violence against Women', *American Psychologist*, 1332–43.

Landau, T. (1998), 'Synthesis of Department of Justice Canada Research Findings on Spousal Assault', Department of Justice—Research and Statistics Division (accessed at http://canada.justice.gc.ca).

LaPraire, C. (1996), *Examining Aboriginal Corrections in Canada* (Ottawa: Ministry of the Solicitor General).

Latimer, J., Dowden, C., and Muise, D. (2005), 'The Effectiveness of Restorative Justice Practices: A Meta-analysis', *The Prison Journal*, 85(2): 127–44.

L.C. (The complainant) and the Attorney General of Alberta v. Brian Joseph Mills (1999), S.C.C. Judgment, 25 November 1999 (Can.).

Marshall, T. (1995), 'Restorative Justice on Trial in Britain', *Mediation Quarterly*, 12(3): 217–31.

Masters, G. (2002), 'Family Group Conferencing: A Victim's Perspective', in B. Williams (ed.), *Reparation and Victim-focused Social Work* (Philadelphia: Jessica Kingsley Publishers).

M.(K.) v. M.(H.) (1992), 3 S.C.R.

M.K. v. S.K. (1999), O.J. No. 3378.

McElrea, F. (1999), 'Taking Responsibility in Being Accountable', in H. Bowen and J. Considine (eds), *Restorative Justice: Contemporary Themes and Practices* (Lyttelton, NZ: Ploughshares Publications).

MacKinnon, C. (1987), *Feminism Unmodified: Discourses on Life and Law* (Cambridge: Harvard University Press).

MacLeod, L. (1980), *Wife Battering in Canada: The Vicious Cycle* (Hull, QC: Canadian Government Publishing Centre).

——— (1989), *Battered but Not Beaten: Wife Battering in Canada* (Hull, QC: Canadian Government Publishing Centre).

Ontario Women's Justice Network (2006), *A Comparative Look at Protection Orders Across Canada* (accessed at http://www.owjn.org/info/protection.htm).

Osborne, P. (2003), *The Law of Torts*, 2nd ed. (Toronto: Irwin Law).

Pattavina, A., Hirshel, D., Buzawa, E., Faggiani, D., and Bentley, H. (2007), 'A Comparison of the Police Response to Heterosexual versus Same-sex Intimate Partner Violence', *Violence Against Women*, 13(4): 374–94.

Presser, L. and Gaarder, E. (2000), 'Can Restorative Justice Reduce Battering? Some Preliminary Considerations', *Social Justice*, 27(1): 175–95.

R.A.R.B. v. British Columbia [2001] C.C.S. No. 16175.

Razack, S. (1991), *Canadian Feminism and the Law: The Women's Legal Education and Action Fund and the Pursuit of Equity* (Toronto: Second Story Press).

Regehr, C. and Alaggia, R. (2005), 'Perspectives on Justice for Victims of Sexual Violence', *Crime Victims and Offenders: An International Journal of Evidence-Based Practice*, 1(1).

———, Lambert, L., and Saini, M. (2008), 'Victims of Sexual Violence in the Canada Criminal Courts', *Victims and Offenders*, 3(1): 1–15.

Regehr, C. and Glancy, G. (1993), 'Rape or Romance? Perspectives on Sexual Assault', *Annals of Sex Research*, 6(4): 305–18.

———, and Bradford, J. (2000), 'Canadian Landmark Cases: LC (The complainant) and Alberta Crt v. Mills', *Journal of the American Academy of Psychiatry and the Law*, 28(4): 460–4.

Rigakos, G. (2002), *Peace Bonds and Violence Against Women: A Three-Site Study of the Effect of Bill C-42 on Process, Application and Enforcement* (Government of Canada: Department of Justice).

R.L.L. v. R.L. (1999), B.C.J. No. 1764.

Roach, K. (1999), *Due Process and Victim's Rights: The New Law and Politics of Criminal Justice* (Toronto: University of Toronto Press).

R. v. Burlingham (1995), 2 S.C.R. 206.

R. v. Budreo (1996), 104 CCC (3d) 245 (Ont. Gen. Div.) (Can.).

R. v. Budreo (2000), 46 O.R. (3d) 481 (Ont. C.A.).

R. v. G.J.A. (1997), O.J. 5354 (Ont. Gen. Div.) (Can.).

R. v. Harding (1998), OJ 2499 (Can.).

R. v. Lee (1997), O.J. No.3795 (Ont. Gen. Div.) (Can.).

R. v. O'Connor (1995), 4 S.C.R. 411 (Can.).

Regina v. Mills (1997), A.J. 891 (Alta. Ct. Q.B.) (Can.).

R. v. Seaboyer (1991), 66 C.C.C. (3d) 321 (S.C.C.).

Sheehy, E.A. (1994), 'Compensation for Women Who Have Been Raped', in J.V. Roberts and R.M. Mohr (eds), *Confronting Sexual Assault: A Decade of Legal and Social Change* (Toronto: University of Toronto Press).

Shenk, B. and Zehr, H. (2001), 'Restorative Justice and Substance Abuse: The Path Ahead', *Youth & Society*, 33(2): 314–28.

Shlonsky, A. and Friend, C. (2007), 'Double Jeopardy: Risk Assessment in the Context of Child Maltreatment and Domestic Violence', *Brief Treatment and Crisis Intervention*, 7(4): 253–74.

Solicitor General of Canada (2002), *An Information Guide to Assist Victims: Federal Corrections and Conditional Release* (accessed at http://www. psepc-gc.ca/publications/corrections/infor victims_e.asp).

Stanley, J., Bartholomew, K., Taylor, T., Oram, D., and Landolt, M. (2006), 'Intimate Violence in Male Same-sex Relationships', *Journal of Family Violence*, 21(1): 31–41.

Statistics Canada (1993), *The Violence Against Women Survey* (Ottawa: Statistics Canada).

——— (2001), *Aboriginal People of Canada* (accessed 1 June 2006 at http://www12.statcan.ca).

——— (2002), *Family Violence in Canada: A Statistical Profile* (Ottawa: Statistics Canada).

——— (2005a), 'General Social Survey: Crime Victimization', *The Daily* (accessed at http://www.statcan.ca/Daily/English/051124/d051124b.htm).

——— (2005b), 'Family Violence in Canada: A Statistical Profile', *The Daily* (accessed at http://www.statcan.ca/Daily/English/050714/d050714a.htm).

Statutes of Canada (1997), c. 30 (Bill C-46, 1996) An Act to Amend the Criminal Code.

Stewart, W., Huntley, A., and Blaney, F. (2001), *The Implications of Restorative Justice for Aboriginal Women and Children Survivors of Violence: A Comparative Overview of Five Communities in British Columbia* (Ottawa: Law Commission of Canada).

Strang, H. and Braithwaite, J. (2002), *Restorative Justice and Family Violence* (New York: Cambridge University Press).

Strange, C. (1992), 'Wounded Womanhood and Dead Men: Chivalry and the Trials of Clara Ford and Carrie Davies', in F. Iacovetta and M. Valverde (eds), *Gender Conflicts: New Essays in Women's History* (Toronto: University of Toronto Press).

Stubbs, J. (2004), 'Restorative Justice, Domestic Violence and Family Violence', *Australian Domestic and Family Violence Clearinghouse*, Issues Paper 9.

Thornton v. Prince George School District No.5 (1978), 2 S.C.R. 267.

Tjaden, P. and Thoennes, N. (1998), *Stalking in America: Findings From the National Violence Against Women Survey* (Washington, DC: US Department of Justice, National Institute of Justice, NCJ 169592.U.S).

T.W.N.A. v. Clark (2003), B.C.J. No. 2747 [2004] C.C.S. No. 3542.

Umbreit, M. (1995), 'The Development and Impact of Victim–Offender Mediation in the United States', *Mediation Quarterly*, 12(3): 263–76.

——— (1999), 'Victim–Offender Mediation in Canada: The Impact of an Emerging Social Work Intervention', *International Social Work*, 42(2): 215–27.

——— and Coates, R.B. (1999), *Research and Resources Review*, 1(1) (Minneapolis, MN: Center for Restorative Justice and Peacemaking).

———, and Roberts, A.W. (2000), 'The Impact of Victim–Offender Mediation: A Cross-national Perspective', *Mediation Quarterly*, 17(3): 215–29.

United Nations (1985), Declaration of Basic Principles of Justice for Victims of Crime and Abuse of Power (accessed at http://www.unhchr.ch/html/ menu3/b/h_comp49.html).

United States Department of Justice (1997), *Domestic Violence and Stalking: The Second Annual Report to Congress Under the Violence Against Women Act* (Washington, DC: US Department of Justice Office of Justice Programs).

Valverde, M., MacLeod, L., and Johnson, K. (1995), *Wife Assault and the Canadian Criminal Justice System* (Toronto: University of Toronto Press).

Vanscoy and Even v. Her Majesty the Queen in Right of Ontario, (1999) O.J. No.1661 (Ont. Sup. Ct. Jus.).

Verdun-Jones, S. and Tijerino, A. (2004), 'Four Models of Victim Involvement During Plea Negotiations: Bridging the Gap Between Legal Reforms and Current Legal Process', *Canadian Journal of Criminology*, 46(4): 471–500.

Watson, D., Bogart, W.A., Hutchinson, A.C., Mosher, J.E., Pinos, T., and Walker, J. (eds) (1999), *Civil Litigation Process: Cases and Materials*, 5th ed. (Toronto: Emond Montgomery).

Wenzel, M., Okimoto, T., Feather, N., and Platow, M. (2008), 'Retributive and Restorative Justice', *Law and Human Behavior*, 32: 375–89.

Wiegers, W. (1994), 'Compensation for Wife Abuse: Empowering Victims?' *UBC Law Review*, 28: 247–307.

Young, A. (2001), *The Role of the Victim in the Criminal Justice Process: A Literature Review 1989–1999* (Ottawa: Policy Centre for Victims' Issues, Department of Justice, Research and Statistics Division).

Zehr, H. (1995), 'Justice Paradigm Shift? Values and Visions in the Reform Process', *Mediation Quarterly*, 12(3): 207–16.

CHAPTER TEN

Immigration and Refugee Law

OBJECTIVES

- To review the general categories of admission and process for admission into Canada as an immigrant
- To introduce contemporary immigration issues
- To review the criteria and process for obtaining refugee status in Canada
- To highlight the rights and obligations of permanent residents
- To outline the process for becoming a Canadian citizen

CASE EXAMPLE

Nela was born in the Philippines. Nela's family had meagre economic means and desperately wanted their daughter to have a better life. When Nela was 19 a family friend gave her the email address of a man in Canada who was looking for a wife. He was 36 and a taxi driver in Vancouver. Nela agreed to write to him and they corresponded by email for three months. Eventually, he asked Nela to marry him and to come to Canada. Nela and her family were overjoyed. She married him and he sponsored her to come to Canada.

Shortly after Nela joined him in Canada, the relationship began to turn sour. He was very controlling—limiting Nela's phone calls, making her follow a regimented schedule throughout the day, and getting very upset when anything wasn't done the way he liked. He yelled at her constantly and this eventually escalated into physical beatings. He warned her repeatedly that if she did not do as he said, he would send her back to the Philippines. One day he beat her very badly before he left the house to go to work. A neighbour heard loud screaming from the house and thought that they were having an argument. She was concerned and came by after he left to check on Nela. She found Nela bruised and bleeding. Nela refused to go to the hospital but she was so upset that in broken English she told her neighbour the whole story. Nela does not want to be with her husband but she does not want to go back to the Philippines either.

Nela's neighbour frantically called a friend who works at a women's shelter for advice.

- Is Nela an immigrant or a refugee?
- Which immigrant class does Nela fit into?
- Can Nela's husband send her back to the Philippines?
- If Nela leaves her husband, can Canada send her back to the Philippines?
- Once she leaves her husband, can Nela apply for social assistance if she has no money of her own?

Every year, millions of people enter Canada—some planning to stay in Canada for a short time, others wanting to make Canada their home, and yet others simply returning from trips abroad. All these individuals are affected by Canada's laws with respect to immigration and refugees. This chapter provides an overview of the legal rules, rights, and processes applicable to immigrants and refugees in Canada.

Immigration

Canada is home to immigrants from almost every nation around the world, and there are a myriad of service agencies across the country focused on the settlement and integration of immigrants and refugees, examples of which are listed in Table 10.1. The federal Immigration and Refugee Protection Act addresses the entry and departure of all persons from Canada. In addition to the Immigration and Refugee Protection Act, immigration is governed by regulations made by the governor in council and policies published by the Department of Citizenship and Immigration.

The federal government has entered into agreements or letters of understanding with various provinces and territories on immigration law and policy covering a range of issues including settlement, integration, and labour market access. The most comprehensive of these agreements is with Quebec, which has its own immigration system and policies but shares the Immigration and Refugee Board with the rest of Canada (Wong and Munn, 2000) (for more detail on the Quebec immigration system, see an Act Respecting Immigration to Quebec, R.S.Q., c. I-0.2). An individual may apply to the Department of Citizenship and Immigration for admission into Canada as a permanent resident under three categories: Family Class Immigrants, Economic Class Immigrants, and Refugees. Social workers will very likely work with individuals and families who are newcomers to Canada so they need to be familiar with the various immigration classes under Canadian law and the implications for individuals of being included

in these categories. Social workers assisting this client population should also advise individuals who accept assistance of immigration consultants to ensure they are appropriately qualified. The Canadian courts have affirmed the authority of the Canadian Society of Immigration Consultants (CSIC) to regulate immigration consultants—more information can be found on the CSIC website at www.csic-scci.ca.

Family Class

What Are the Sponsorship Requirements under the Family Class?

The Family Class applies to people who live outside Canada, and in some cases spouses or common-law partners who are already living in Canada, who can be sponsored by an eligible Canadian citizen or permanent resident who is 18 years or older (CIC, 2003). There are several determinants of sponsor eligibility. First, individuals will not be eligible to act as sponsors if they are in jail, facing criminal charges or removal from Canada, are an undischarged bankrupt, owe money to Citizenship and Immigration Canada, are in default of court-ordered support payments, have not repaid social assistance benefits of past individuals they have sponsored, have been convicted of a sexual or other criminal offence against a family member, or are on social assistance for reasons other than disability (CLEO, 2007a). Second, individuals may have to meet certain income requirements before they may sponsor an immigrant under the Family Class. Third, the Family Class applicant must be related to the sponsor in one of the following ways:

- spouse, common-law or conjugal partner;
- dependent child, including a child adopted abroad;
- child under 18 to be adopted in Canada;
- parents or grandparents;
- an orphaned child under 18 who is a brother, sister, niece, nephew, or grandchild and is not a spouse or common-law partner; and

Table 10.1   Resources For Immigrants and Refugees by Region

Jurisdiction	Immigrant-serving Organizations			
British Columbia	SUCCESS 28 West Pender Street Vancouver, BC V6B 1R6 (604) 684-1628 SUCCESS 5834 Fraser Street Vancouver, BC V5W 2Z5 (604) 324-1900 www.success.bc.ca	Surrey Delta Immigrant Services Society 1107-7330 137th Street Surrey, BC V3W 1A3 (604) 597-0205 www.dcrs.ca	Kamloops Immigrant Services 109 Victoria Street Kamloops, BC V2C 1Z4 (250) 372-0855 www.immigrantservices.ca	Immigrant and Multicultural Services Society of Prince George 1633 Victoria Street Prince George, BC V2L 2J7 (250) 562-2900 www.mag-net.com/~imss/ www.imss.ca	Victoria Immigrant and Refugee Centre 305-535 Yates Street Victoria, BC V8W 2Z6 (250) 361-9433 www.vircs.bc.ca
Alberta	Calgary Immigrant Aid Society 12th fl, 910-7th Avenue South West Calgary, AB T2P 3N8 (403) 265-1120 www.calgaryimmigrant aid.ca	Central Alberta Refugee Effort (C.A.R.E.) Committee 202-5000 Gaetz Avenue Red Deer, AB T4N 6C2 (403) 346-8818 www.intentr.com/immigrantctr/care.htm	Edmonton Immigrant Services Association Ste 201, 10720-113 Street Edmonton, AB T5H 3H8 (780) 474-8445 www.eisa-edmonton.org	Lethbridge Family Services Immigrant Services 1107 2nd Avenue 'A' North Lethbridge, AB T1J 2E2 (403) 327-5724 Fax: (403) 329-4924 www.lethbridge-family-services.com/immigrant.cfm	SAAMIS Immigration Services 177-12th Street North East Medicine Hat, AB T1A 5T6 (403) 504-1188 Fax: (403) 504-1211 sisa@telusplanet.net
Saskatchewan	Moose Jaw Multicultural Council 60 Athabasca Street East Moose Jaw, SK S6H 0L2 (306) 693-4677 www.mumcinc.ca	Prince Albert Multicultural Council 1410 Central Avenue Prince Albert, SK S6V 4W5 (306) 922-0400	Saskatoon Open Door Society Inc.—Services to Immigrants & Refugees 247 First Avenue North Saskatoon, SK S7K 1X2 (306) 653-4464 Fax: (306) 653-4460 skopendoor@sasktel.net http://www.sods.sk.ca/	Immigrant, Refugee, and Visible Minority Women of Saskatchewan 2nd fl, 2248 Lorne Street Regina, SK S4P 2M7 (306) 359-6523 Fax: (306) 522-9952	
Manitoba	Manitoba Interfaith Immigration Council Inc. Welcom Place, 397 Carlton Street Winnipeg, MB R3B 2K9 (204) 977-1000 http://www.miic.ca	Winnipeg Refugee Education Network 935 Warsaw Avenue Winnipeg, MB R3M 1B9 (204) 261-1026	International Centre of Winnipeg 406 Edmonton Street, 2nd fl Winnipeg, MB R3B 2M2 (204) 943-9158 www.international-centre.ca	Westman ESL & Settlement Services (WESLS) 729 Princess Avenue Brandon MB R7A 0P5 (204) 727-6031 Fax: (204) 725-4786 Email: weslss@mts.net www.wesls.com	Immigrant Women Association of Manitoba 200-323 Portage Avenue Winnipeg, MB R3B 2C1 (204) 989-5800

Table 10.1   Resources For Immigrants and Refugees by Region (Continued)

Jurisdiction	Immigrant-serving Organizations			
Ontario	Newcomer Information Centre YMCA of Greater Toronto, 42 Charles Street East, 3rd fl Toronto, ON M4Y 1T4 (416) 928-6690 www.ymcatoronto.org/en/newcomers/index.html	Ottawa Community Immigrant Services Organization 959 Wellington Street Ottawa, ON K1Y 4W1 (613) 725-0202 www.ociso.org	Jewish Immigrant Aid Services of Canada 4580 Dufferin Street, Ste 306 Toronto, ON M3H 5Y2 (416) 630-9051 www.jias.org	Settlement and Integration Services Organization of Hamilton 360 James Street North Hamilton, ON L8L 1H5 (905) 667-7476 www.siso-ham.org	Intercede for the Rights of Domestic Workers, Caregivers and Newcomers 234 Eglinton Avenue East, Ste 404 Toll-free: 1-877-483-4554 Greater Toronto Area: 416-483-4554 http://www.settlement.org/sys/faqs_detail.asp?faq_id=4000620
Quebec	Ministère des relations avec les citoyens et de l'immigration (MRCI) (various locations) South Island 800, boulevard de Maisonneuve Est Place Dupuis, bureau 200 Montréal, QC H2L 4L8 (514) 864-9191 All locations: http://www.micc.gouv.qc.ca/english/index.asp	Centre social d'aide aux immigrants 4285 boul. de Maisonneuve Ouest Montréal, QC H3Z 1K7 (514) 932-2953 Fax: (514) 932-4544 csai@generation.net	Service d'aide aux Néo-Canadiens 535, rue Short SHERBROOKE J1H 2E6 (819) 566-5373 Fax: (819) 566-1331 sanc@aide-internet.org http://www.aide-internet.org/sanc/	TCRI 518, rue Beaubien Est Montréal QC H2S 1S5 (514) 272-6060 Fax: (514) 272-3748 tcri@cam.org http://www.tcri.qc.ca/	Amnistie internationale Section canadienne francophone 6250 boul Monk Montréal, QC H4E 3H7 (514) 766-9766 Toll-free: 1-800-565-9766 Fax: (514) 766-2088 info@amnistie.qc.ca http://www.amnistie.qc.ca
Maritimes	Newfoundland and Labrador Association for New Canadians 144 Military Road St. John's, NF A1C 5R6 (709) 722-9680 www.anc-nf.cc	Nova Scotia Metropolitan Immigrant Settlement Association Chebucto Place 7105 Chebucto Road, Ste 201 Halifax, NS B3L 4W8 (902) 443-2937 www.misa.ns.ca	Prince Edward Island PEI Association for Newcomers to Canada 25 University Avenue, Ste 400, Holman Building, 4th fl Confederation Court Mall Charlottetown, PEI C1A 8C4 (902) 628-6009 Mailing address: P.O. Box 2846 Charlottetown, PEI C1A 8C4 www.peianc.com	New Brunswick Multicultural Association of Fredericton 123 York Street, Ste 201 Fredericton, NB E3B 3N6 (506) 454-8292 www.mcaf.nb.ca	

- another relative if there is no one else in Canada or anywhere else in the world who qualifies as a sponsor for the applicant under the Family Class (CIC, 2008e).

The relationship between the sponsor and the applicant must be proven through birth or marriage certificates and must be shown to be genuine (that is, not entered into for immigration purposes) (CLEO, 2007a). Family Class does not include couples who are engaged.

An applicant may include his or her dependent children in the application where dependent children are under the age of 22 and are not married or in a common-law relationship; have been full-time students before age 22, are attending a postsecondary institution, and are dependent for financial support; or are over the age of 22 and have been dependent on financial support because of a physical or mental condition (CIC, 2008e). While the term 'applicant' is used in this section to refer to the individual seeking immigration status, most Family Class applications are actually commenced by the sponsors. Potential sponsors may obtain information on Family Class sponsorship by calling Citizenship and Immigration Canada toll-free at 1-888-242-2100 or by visiting the Citizenship and Immigration Canada website at www.cic.gc.ca. Family Class immigration applications may take months to be processed (CLEO, 2007a).

What Are the Rights of Successful Applicants?

If an individual is recognized as an immigrant through the Family Class then he or she will become a permanent resident of Canada and accordingly will receive the right to live, study, and work in Canada for as long as he or she remains a permanent resident. However, the sponsored individual may not receive any social assistance while under sponsorship and if the sponsored person collects social assistance during this time the sponsor will be obligated to repay it (CIC, 2008e).

What Are the Obligations of the Sponsor?

Once an applicant under the Family Class is granted permanent residence, the sponsor is asked to sign an Undertaking with the Minister of Citizenship and Immigration under which he or she promises to be responsible for supporting: 1) his or her spouse, common-law or conjugal partner for three years; 2) his or her dependent children under the age of 22 for 10 years or until they turn 25, whichever is earliest; 3) his or her dependent children 22 years of age or over for three years; and 4) all other family members, including their dependent children, for 10 years (CIC, 2008e). Support includes housing, clothes, food, and financial resources (CLEO, 2007a). The sponsor may also be required to sign a Sponsorship Agreement with the individual he or she is sponsoring, for example, a spouse or common-law partner, which outlines the mutual commitments of both individuals (that is, the sponsor's promise to support and the immigrant's promise to make best efforts to become self-supporting) (CIC, 2007c).

Economic Class

Economic Class immigrants are selected because of their skills or other assets that will contribute to the Canadian economy. There are several different subclasses within the Economic Class, including skilled workers, investors, entrepreneurs, and self-employed persons as well as the new Canadian experience class. Each subclass has its own criteria for determining admission to Canada as an immigrant.

Skilled Workers

Skilled workers are assessed based on a points system provided in the regulations under the Immigration and Refugee Protection Act. The points system assigns certain points to several categories of consideration, including education, knowledge of official languages, work experience, age, arranged employment in Canada, and adaptability (CIC, 2007d). Canada has a large backlog in the skilled worker category and wait times have been as long as six years for admission into Canada (CIC, 2008c). In June 2008 the Canadian Parliament approved changes to the Immigration and Refugee Protection Act designed to modernize the system and shorten the time it takes to immigrate to Canada. The result of the changes is that for new applications made on or after 27 February 2008, Citizenship and Immigration Canada will not be required to process all applications that it receives, and the minister has the authority to issue instructions to immigration officers for categories of applicants with certain skills and experience to have their applications processed more quickly. Citizenship and Immigration Canada consulted with the provinces and territories and business, labour, and other stakeholders to develop instructions. In November 2008 the Minister of Citizenship, Immigration and Multiculturalism issued instructions for processing skilled worker applications; under the instructions, applications are eligible for processing if they:

- include an offer of arranged employment; or
- if the applicant is a foreign national living legally in Canada for one year as a temporary foreign worker or international student; or
- if the applicant has at least one year of experience in one or more of 38 identified occupations (these are in high demand areas such as health, skilled trades, finance, and resource extraction).

Skilled worker applications will now be assessed for eligibility based on these instructions and those that do not meet the criteria will not be processed. Citizenship and Immigration Canada has indicated that with the instructions in place they anticipate that new skilled worker applicants could receive a decision in six months to a year (CIC, 2008c). The instructions may be adjusted over time in accordance with labour market changes. The instructions do not apply to family and refugee applicants.

Investors

Immigration applicants who seek to be granted immigration status as investors under the Economic Class must demonstrate that they have:

- business experience as defined in the regulations (that is, have either managed and controlled a percentage of equity of a qualifying business or managed at least the equivalent of five full-time employees per year in a business for at least two years in the last five years before the application);
- a legally obtained net worth of at least $800,000 (Cdn); and
- invested $400,000 (Cdn) before receiving a visa.

The Canadian government allocates the investment to provinces and territories that guarantee the investment and use it to develop their economies. The investments are interest-free and are to be repaid after five years (CIC, 2005a).

Entrepreneurs

Individuals who are applying for immigration status under the Economic Class as entrepreneurs must prove that they have managed and controlled a percentage of equity of a qualifying business (as determined by criteria in the regulations related to sales, net income, assets, and jobs) for at least two years in the period beginning five years before they apply, have a legally obtained net worth of at least $300,000 (Cdn), and intend to manage and control 33 1/3 per cent or more of the equity of a qualifying business and create a full-time job for a Canadian citizen or permanent resident within three years (CIC, 2005a).

Self-employed Persons

Immigration applicants who are self-employed must show that they can, and intend to, create their own employment in Canada and that they can contribute significantly to the Canadian economy by purchasing or managing a farm, by contributing to cultural activities or athletics in Canada, or for those selected by a province (as discussed later in this chapter) by contributing to economic activities specified by that province (CIC, 2005a).

Canadian Experience Class

As of September 2008, a new 'Canadian Experience Class' for immigration was created for certain temporary foreign workers and foreign student graduates to make Canada more globally competitive in attracting and retaining individuals with skills needed in our country (CIC, 2008d). The Canadian Experience Class allows an applicant's experience in Canada to be considered as a key selection factor. More particularly, an individual may apply in this category if he or she:

*   is a temporary foreign worker with at least two years of full-time skilled work experience in Canada; or
*   is a foreign graduate student from a Canadian postsecondary institution with at least one year of full-time skilled work experience in Canada;
*   has gained experience in Canada with proper work or study authorization;
*   is able to apply while working in Canada or within one year of leaving a job in Canada.

A Note on Provincial/Territorial Nomination

Most provinces and territories are involved with identifying nominees among foreign workers who can meet their specific labour-market needs. Provincial and territorial requirements for consideration as nominees can be found in the federal–provincial agreements discussed earlier in this chapter. These nominees are not required to pass the federal skilled worker points assessment (CIC, 2005a).

Background Checks and Medical Testing

All applicants who wish to enter Canada with permanent resident status or to work in occupations where the protection of public health is essential will be subject to criminal and background checks as well as medical examinations (CIC, 2007a).

Permanent residents may be denied entry into Canada if they have engaged in criminal activity or if there are reasonable grounds to believe they will engage in criminal activity. The Immigration and Refugee Protection Act categorizes offences by their seriousness such that the more serious the offence, the more difficult it is for an individual to be admitted as a permanent resident (Waldman, 2004). Background checks are used to determine whether individuals should be denied entry into Canada because of security concerns or past human rights violations. The Immigration and Refugee Protection Act provides that individuals will not be admissible if they fall under any one of the following:

*   engaging in an act of espionage or an act of subversion against a democratic government, institution, or process as they are understood in Canada;
*   engaging in or instigating subversion by force of any government;
*   engaging in terrorism;
*   being a member of an organization that there are reasonable grounds to believe engages, has engaged, or will engage in acts referred to above;
*   being a danger to the security of Canada;
*   engaging in acts of violence that would or might endanger the lives or safety of persons in Canada;
*   committing an act outside Canada that constitutes an offence referred to in sections 4 to 7 of the Crimes Against Humanity and War Crimes Act;
*   being a prescribed senior official in the service of a government that, in the opinion of the minister, engages or has engaged in terrorism, systematic or gross human rights violations, or genocide, a war crime, or a crime against humanity within the meaning of subsections 6(3) to (5) of the Crimes Against Humanity and War Crimes Act; or

- being a person, other than a permanent resident, whose entry into or stay in Canada is restricted pursuant to a decision, resolution, or measure of an international organization of states or association of states, of which Canada is a member, that imposes sanctions on a country against which Canada has imposed or has agreed to impose sanctions in concert with that organization or association.

Medical examinations are to be carried out by doctors designated by Citizenship and Immigration Canada and may include physical examinations, mental examinations, reviews of past medical history and records, and routine tests, including urinalysis, chest x-rays, syphilis, blood tests, and HIV tests (CIC, 2007a). If applicants are found to be a danger to public health or safety or if they could be demanding on Canada's health and social services due to their health condition, entry into Canada may be denied. Of those individuals who are admitted, some will be placed under medical surveillance if, for example, their tests revealed inactive tuberculosis or evidence of a previous syphilis infection, the purpose of which is to encourage appropriate treatment and follow-up. The Immigration and Refugee Protection Act contains an 'excessive demand' exemption under which Family Class–sponsored spouses, common-law partners, conjugal partners, and their dependent children, as well as refugees and persons in need of protection (discussed later in this chapter), will not be refused entry just because they have a health condition that may place excessive demand on health or social services.

Who Decides Who May Enter Canada as an Immigrant?

The immigration officers at Citizenship and Immigration Canada are the first line of individuals determining admissibility of persons into Canada as immigrants. In addition, the Immigration Division of the Immigration and Refugee Board (IRB), an independent, quasi-judicial administrative tribunal, conducts admissibility hearings for certain categories of people believed to be inadmissible to

or removable from Canada, and it also conducts detention reviews. If someone is not satisfied with the Immigration Division's decision regarding admissibility, they may be able to appeal to the Immigrant Appeal Division of the IRB, which is an independent tribunal that has the powers of a court. If still unsatisfied, the applicant or the minister may obtain leave from a federal court judge to initiate an application for judicial review by the Federal Court of Canada (CIC, 2006b). Judicial review is the power of the courts to determine whether the appeal division of the IRB has acted within the powers that have been statutorily delegated by the Immigration and Refugee Protection Act. Unlike the appeal, the scope of intervention by the courts during judicial review is restricted to errors of law and egregious errors of fact and the case will not be reopened to consider the merits of the application for immigration (Jones and de Villars, 2004).

Contemporary Issues
International Adoption

Approximately two thousand foreign children are adopted by Canadians every year. There are several different sources of law that must be complied with when attempting an international adoption—social welfare laws, international laws, and immigration laws. The social welfare laws that govern adoptions depend on the province or territory in which the adoptive parents reside and applications for adoption must be filed with the central authority in the adoptive parents' province or territory. As discussed earlier in this chapter, adopted children may be granted immigration to Canada through sponsorship under the Family Class. It is an offence in some Canadian provinces and territories to bring an adopted or soon to be adopted child into the province or territory in Canada without prior authorization. Thus, sponsors should not plan to go abroad and bring the child back to Canada before the immigration process is complete because Canadian immigration requirements will not necessarily be waived just because the adoption has been completed.

The Child, Family, and Community Division of Human Resources Development Canada coordinates intercountry adoptions including the sharing of information among Canadian jurisdictions and with foreign authorities and non-governmental organizations. For a more detailed discussion of international adoptions, see Chapter 5.

Live-in Caregivers

The Live-in Caregiver Program allows for qualified individuals from foreign countries to come to Canada and work without supervision in a private household providing care for children, the elderly, or people with disabilities if there are no Canadian citizens or permanent residents available to fill the positions. To qualify as a live-in caregiver under this program, a candidate must have:

- successfully completed a course of study that is equivalent to a Canadian secondary school diploma;
- completed within the last three years, 6 months of full-time training in a classroom setting or 12 months of full-time paid employment (including at least 6 months of continuous employment with one employer) in a field or occupation related to the job of a live-in caregiver;
- the ability to speak, read, and understand either English or French at a level sufficient to communicate independently; and
- a written contract with their future employer.

The prospective employer must obtain a positive labour-market opinion from Human Resources and Skills Development Canada. Once such an opinion has been obtained, a candidate who meets the requirements above must apply for a work permit to come into Canada. Live-in caregivers do not qualify for entry into Canada under the Economic Class of immigrants. Instead, they are issued work visas and may apply for permanent resident status only after completing a minimum of two years employed as a live-in caregiver within the three years following their entry into Canada (CIC, 2008a).

The live-in caregiver is only authorized to work for the employer named in the work permit but may change employers by obtaining a signed contract with the new employer and a new work permit in the new employer's name. The ease with which caregivers may now change employers marks an improvement from the previous laws on foreign domestic workers that required workers to obtain 'release letters' from their employers prior to switching employment (Macklin, 1992). Gaps of time between employers are acceptable and will not result in deportation provided that these gaps do not interfere with permanent residence eligibility as described later in the chapter (CIC, 2008a). However, while a caregiver is employed, the Live-in Caregiver Program requires that he or she live in the employer's home.

Some commentators have suggested that because the women who are caregivers are segregated to domestic work and required to live with their employers for two years, they are often isolated and vulnerable and look where possible to marry their employers (Philippine Women Centre of BC, 2000). The Live-in Caregiver Program is viewed by some as a form of trafficking in women, where trafficking is defined as the movement of women between countries differentiated by economic inequality resulting in the exploitation of women for their services with or without their consent by persons in an unequal power relationship. To this end, it has been recommended that the Live-in Caregiver Program be discontinued or at a minimum be revised to grant these women permanent residence upon arrival, remove the obligation that they must reside with their employer, regulate agencies recruiting such caregivers, and grant those who do work as live-in caregivers in Canada full protection under Canadian labour laws (Langevin and Belleau, 2000).

Mail-order Brides

A second form of trafficking of women from foreign countries is mail-order brides. It has been suggested that the demand for domestic workers in Canada is on the rise and there will therefore be an increase in the entry of mail-order brides into

Canada because they provide a package deal as wife, nanny, and housekeeper (Philippine Women Centre of BC, 2000). One activist poignantly stated, '[T]he thin line between servant and prostitute is bridged by the mail-order bride' (Rosca, 1999). Why then do women become mail-order brides? For women who cannot meet the education and experience requirements for entering Canada as live-in caregivers, finding a husband in Canada may be one of the few options to enable entry into Canada. Mail-order bride agencies operate primarily through catalogues or over the Internet to assist consumer husbands in industrialized nations find women from developing countries to bring to Canada as their wives. Consumer husbands may pay between $10,000 to $15,000 for a bride. One expert has described the mail-order bride phenomenon as a multimillion-dollar industry (Langevin and Belleau, 2000).

Most women who are mail-order brides come to Canada as immigrants sponsored by their husbands under the Family Class. As such, the power imbalance between consumer husbands and their mail-order brides is established early because the sponsorship process is largely under the control of the husband; subordination is systematically drawn out over the required 10-year sponsorship period (Philippine Women Centre of BC, 2000). These marital relations, marked by bonds of subordination, may engender situations of abuse; but one notable difference between live-in caregivers and mail-order brides is that the latter do have significant legal protections under immigration law (Langevin and Belleau, 2000). This will be discussed in more detail in the section on 'Intimate Partner Violence' later in this chapter.

Sex-trade Workers

The degeneration in working conditions for exotic dancers in Canada, including the advent of lap dancing and the introduction of other contact forms of sexual performance into the exotic dance repertoire, has resulted in a decline in the number of Canadian citizens and permanent residents entering into the exotic dancing industry.

Today the demand for strippers exceeds the supply, which has resulted in the entry of Asian and Latin women into the field—women who are from poorer countries and who have fewer options and less information. Owners of clubs in Canada negotiate with smugglers, traffickers, and brokers who guarantee the delivery of dancers to meet the Canadian demand. Canadian immigration law allows for temporary work visas to be issued to exotic dancers. Based on the job offers issued by Canadian clubs, the women from foreign countries looking to enter Canada as sex-trade workers can obtain temporary work permits at ports of entry into Canada (Macklin, 2003). However, foreign women coming to Canada as exotic dancers often do not have advance knowledge of the full nature of the work expected from them. As stated by one Hungarian woman:

> I heard that they keep the rules very strictly so I shouldn't worry about the dance. They knew I'd never danced before that's why they said it. That nobody can ever touch me . . . always security everywhere. And so I won't have any problems with any customers, nobody can come close to me. . . . The difference was that of course people tried to touch me, of course they were closer to me than I expected. There was no security where we danced. So the customers could do whatever they wanted (McDonald, Moore, and Timoshkina, 2000, pp. 44–45).

In addition, club owners often seize the women's passports, confine their movements and interactions, intimidate them through physical and sexual violence, and threaten them with deportation. Furthermore, once the women are in Canada, regardless of their expectations on arrival, they must tolerate the wages and working conditions imposed on them because their permission to remain in Canada is linked to the service they are to provide under their exotic-dancer work permits (Macklin, 2003).

Controversy over and exposure of the trafficking of women in Canada has resulted in various immigration policy developments. Under the current immigration regime, the exotic-dancer work permit has been retained in name but applicants have been turned away in large numbers on the basis that they are unqualified or have more than a 'temporary intent' to remain in Canada. However, the *de facto* prohibition of lawful entry of exotic dancers does not actually prevent entry but rather pushes the trafficking of women into the underground, unregulated market. As stated by one author, the result is that 'women are no longer victims but now are doubly criminalized as illegal immigrants and as prostitutes . . . the spectre of imprisonment as a criminal or deportation as an illegal worker simply constitute further reasons to endure abuse rather than seek assistance' (Macklin, 2003).

There have been movements to ensure that these women and other non-status immigrants are not isolated from social services because of the fear of deportation. For example, in Toronto a number of social service agencies and organizations, and even the Toronto police, have endorsed a 'Don't Ask Don't Tell' campaign under which access to city services, such as housing, social services, health care, emergency services, police services and education are to be offered without discrimination on the basis of immigration status. Workers providing such services are not to inquire about immigration status or to report those who do not hold status to Citizenship and Immigration Canada (University of Toronto, 2005). However, while such movements are beneficial in ensuring that non-status immigrants, such as underground sex-trade workers, have access to medical services and social supports, the fact remains that the current immigration policies in Canada do not prevent or protect against the human rights abuses associated with this form of human trafficking (Macklin, 2003).

Intimate Partner Violence

We often think of sponsors as giving new lives of hope and promise to their relatives who come to Canada as Family Class immigrants.

Unfortunately, this is not always the case. Some sponsors believe that the relatives whom they have sponsored are in Canada at their pleasure and that if they decide they do not want to sponsor them anymore they can simply have them sent back home. Where such an attitude prevails, isolation, subjugation, and abuse often fester. As stated by one journalist:

> I have seen immigrants endure all kinds of abuse because they were unaware of their legal rights. Sometimes this ignorance is compounded by cultural factors. Some complain that they are denied telephone calls and access to friends and family. Some are treated like indentured servants by their sponsors. Some are forced to work full-time jobs during the day and then forced to cook and clean all night as repayment for their new so-called 'life' in Canada. . . . No doubt, some suffer worse (Mamann, 2005).

Immigrant women in abusive relationships often believe that if they report abuse or leave an abusive relationship they may be deported. Where a woman has permanent resident status this is not the case. A woman who is sponsored from outside Canada will arrive on a permanent resident visa and will become a permanent resident upon entering Canada (CLEO, 2007b). Permanent residents cannot be forced out of Canada unless they gained the permanent resident status through a material misrepresentation, failed to maintain their Canadian residency obligations, or commit a serious crime. If a woman who is a permanent resident or Canadian citizen is being abused by her sponsor she may flee the abusive situation without fear of deportation. The sponsorship 'Undertaking' also remains effective for its duration even if the sponsor and immigrant are not living under the same roof anymore . In addition, if abusive sponsors refuse to honour their support obligations and if immigrants cannot support themselves, the latter may apply for social assistance (Mamann, 2005).

In contrast, women who have been sponsored from within Canada and have not yet obtained permanent resident status may be at risk of being removed from Canada if they leave an abusive situation (CLEO, 2007b). In such cases, the woman may still pursue her application to remain in Canada but will need to make a new application on humanitarian and compassionate grounds; such an application should set out the history of abuse and include copies of reports from shelters, medical professionals, and police, where available. Note that an application on humanitarian and compassionate grounds will require the woman to show how established she is in Canada, so it will be important for her to try to improve her skills and find work, housing, and child care. Social workers who assist immigrant women should be attuned to their permanent resident status and aware of its implications. Abused women looking to make applications on humanitarian and compassionate grounds should be counselled to seek legal advice before contacting Citizenship and Immigration Canada so that legal issues affecting their situation can be appropriately addressed in their best interest.

Family Class immigrants do not have to remain imprisoned in destructive environments with their sponsors in order to remain in Canada. However, the reality is that many of these women are so isolated that they do not have access to the information and support needed to leave the abusive situations and even those who do leave may face numerous barriers in accessing housing and services, including inaccessibility of shelters and drop-in centres, lack of culturally appropriate services, and discriminatory practices (Access Alliance Multicultural Community Health Centre, 2003).

Refugees

A woman subjected to repeated physical abuse by her husband in a country where conjugal violence is condoned, a union leader threatened by businesses who enjoy the support of the government, a member of an ethnic group persecuted by the state—what do all these people have in common? Their circumstances may make them refugees. Generally, refugees are people who are forced to leave their home countries because of serious human rights abuses (CCR, 2008). Historically, refugees were unwelcome in Canada. Many countries, Canada included, refused asylum to Jewish refugees during the Holocaust. Canadian anti-Semitism was openly evident. When asked how many Jewish refugees Canada would accept, an official responded: 'None is too many.' In the 1950s Canadian refugee policy took a turn with the 1951 establishment of the United Nations Convention Relating to the Status of Refugees, which was among the first human rights treaties signed after the Second World War. Over the next decades groups of refugees from specific regions were admitted into Canada following local turmoil or conflict: Estonians in 1948; Hungarians in 1956; Czechs in 1968; Tibetans in 1970; Ugandan Asians in 1973; and 'boat people' from Vietnam, Cambodia, and Laos from 1978 to 1981.

In 1986 the United Nations High Commissioner for Refugees awarded Canada the Nansen Medal in recognition of Canada's major and sustained contribution to the cause of refugees (Amnesty International Canada, 2008a). As a party to the United Nations Convention Relating to the Status of Refugees, Canada is obliged to protect refugees from persecution; indeed, one of the objectives of the current Canadian Immigration and Refugee Protection Act is that 'the refugee program is in the first instance about saving lives and offering protection to the displaced and persecuted' (CCR, 2004b). There are two ways for refugees to receive protection in Canada: the refugee claim process and the resettlement program.

Refugee Claim Process

Individuals may make claims for refugee status in Canada at a port of entry or immigration office. However, under the Canadian refugee protection system, claims made under the following circumstances will not be eligible for consideration:

- if the claimant has ever before made a refugee claim in Canada;
- if the claimant has been recognized as a refugee in another country and can be returned to that country;
- if the claimant came to Canada through a designated 'safe third country' (as discussed later in this chapter); or
- if the claimant has been determined to be inadmissible on the basis of security, serious criminality, organized criminality, or violating human or international rights.

Eligibility determinations are made by Citizenship and Immigration Canada. If a claim is eligible for consideration, under the Immigration and Refugee Protection Act an individual may be granted refugee status if he or she is found to be a Convention refugee or a person in need of protection. Those who make a claim in Canada and are granted refugee status must make a separate application for permanent residence (often referred to as 'landing') and this process generally takes six months to a year (CCR, 2008).

Who Is a Convention Refugee?

A Convention refugee is defined as a person outside his or her home country who has a well-founded fear of being persecuted for reasons of race, religion, nationality, political opinion, or membership in a particular social group. This definition comes from the United Nations Convention Relating to the Status of Refugees. To provide guidance on definition interpretation, the United Nations has developed its *United Nations Handbook on Procedures and Criteria for Determining Refugee Status under the 1951 Convention and the 1967 Protocol Relating to the Status of Refugees* (1992). Although this handbook is not legally binding, it is considered to be highly persuasive by tribunals and courts (Wong and Munn, 2000). The Canadian IRB also publishes papers and guidelines on elements of the definition. The definition is broken down into a number of elements, all of which must be proven by a claimant in order to be found to be a Convention refugee. Required elements are: 1) a well-founded fear; 2) persecution that is targeted at the person; 3) the persecution is on one of the specified grounds; and 4) the state in the country from which the person originates is unable to provide protection.

Well-founded Fear

A refugee claimant must show on a balance of probabilities that there is a reasonable chance that if returned to his or her country of nationality or residence, he or she would be persecuted. It does not matter what happened in the past, the claimant only has to establish that he or she has a well-founded fear of persecution. This is assessed both subjectively (Does the claimant fear persecution?) and objectively (Is the claimant's fear reasonable? Is there a valid basis for the fear?) (Wong and Munn, 2000).

Targeted Persecution

Persecution has been defined as 'a particular course or period of systematic infliction of punishment, persistent injury or annoyance from any source directed against those holding a particular belief' (Wong and Munn, 2000, p. 118). Examples of persecution include arrest, detention, torture, harassment, extortion, economic sanction, obligatory military service, or threat of death. The claimant must fear that such acts will be committed against him or her because he or she is a member of a specific group. In other words, the claimant must be specifically targeted and not just a general victim. Persons who are victims of natural disasters, war, domestic unrest, or common crime will not meet the definition of refugee. For example in *Abdulle v. Canada (Minister of Employment and Immigration)* (1993), the claimant was held not to have a well-founded fear of persecution for the purposes of refugee status because she did stand a reasonable chance of persecution if she returned to Somalia, but she was unable to demonstrate that this was any different from the fear facing all Somalis.

Persecution on a Specified Ground

The refugee claimant must establish that the persecution is on one of the grounds enumerated in the definition which include race, religion, nationality, political opinion, or membership in a particular social group. Race is broadly defined and includes all kinds of ethnic groups as well as perceived race. Religion is also interpreted liberally and includes religious beliefs and the right to practise one's religion. Nationality does not just refer to citizenship but also includes membership in ethnic or linguistic groups and political opinions rooted in national aspirations. Political opinions include opinions on any matter in which the state or government may be engaged. Membership in a particular social group includes women who are subjected to domestic violence when there is no state response, women forced to be sterilized by the state, and women forced into marriages against their will (Wong and Munn, 2000).

Notably, gender is not specifically listed in the Convention definition as an enumerated ground and as a result protection from gender persecution is one area that has evolved over time. While the Convention definition has not itself been amended to explicitly include gender, in 1991 the United Nations issued guidelines calling for a liberal interpretation of 'social group' to include gender-related persecution as a consideration for refugee status (these guidelines were updated in 2002). In 1993 Canada became the first country in the world to issue guidelines recognizing that the enumerated grounds can and should be interpreted to include the persecution of women based on their gender (CCR, 2008). The Canadian guidelines, entitled *Women Refugee Claimants Fearing Gender-Related Persecution*, were last updated in 1996. Many other countries have followed suit and formally implemented guidelines for gender-related refugee claims, including the United States, Australia, the United Kingdom, and Sweden (Erdman and Sanche, 2004).

State Unable to Provide Protection

A refugee claimant must be unable to seek protection from his or her own country. There is no need to prove state complicity or condonation of the persecution. The question is only whether the state is unable to provide protection or the claimant is unwilling to seek out state protection in cases where the state condones the abuse. In addition, prosecution by the state for violations of laws of general application does not generally constitute persecution. However, if the law is applied by the state in a discriminatory way or if the punishment is out of proportion with the offence, then prosecution by the state may constitute persecution for the purpose of refugee status. If a claimant has more than one country of nationality, then refugee status will only be granted if the claimant can establish that he or she is unable to pursue alternative national status available to him or her (Wong and Munn, 2000).

Who Is a Person in Need of Protection?

The Canadian Council for Refugees defines a person in need of protection as 'a person who may not meet the Convention definition but is in a refugee-like situation defined in Canadian law as deserving of protection' (CCR, 2004a). The standard under Canadian law for those deserving of protection are derived from Canada's international obligations as a party to the Convention Against Torture (1984) and to the International Covenant on Civil and Political Rights (1966) that include persons who face a substantial danger of torture, a risk to their life, or a risk of cruel and unusual treatment or punishment (CCR, 2008).

Who Decides Refugee Claims?

The IRB, discussed earlier in the chapter, decides claims for refugee protection made by persons in Canada. Citizenship and Immigration Canada decides refugee protection claims made outside Canada, in Canadian embassies and consulates. Claimants considered by the Refugee Protection Division of the IRB must fill out a detailed Personal Information Form and generally appear for a hearing before a member of the IRB. It is advisable for claimants before the IRB to be represented by legal counsel but it is important for social workers to know that not all Canadian jurisdictions provide legal aid coverage for refugees (Amnesty International Canada, 2008b). If the applicant or the minister is unsatisfied with the decision of the Refugee Protection Division of the IRB then they may obtain leave from a federal court judge to initiate an application for judicial review by the Federal Court of Canada (CIC, 2006b). If leave to initiate an application is not granted, then claimants face removal from Canada and may need to pursue a pre-removal risk assessment or application on humanitarian and compassionate grounds. Social workers working with individuals who have been persecuted and tortured in their countries of origin need to be aware that not only can the outcome of a hearing be highly distressing, but the hearing process itself can also be traumatizing for some refugee claimants who must tell their stories of abuse and degradation. Support during this process is essential.

Pre-removal Risk Assessment

Claimants in Canada who have been found ineligible or who have been refused refugee status by the IRB may make a pre-removal risk assessment (PRRA) application to an official of Citizenship and Immigration Canada. Essentially, Citizenship and Immigration Canada will provide an individual with a PRRA application form when an individual is considered to be 'removal ready', meaning that an order for removal of the individual from Canada could be enforced. PRRA applications must be submitted within 15 days of the notification date (that is, the date the PRRA application is received or seven days after it is mailed by Citizenship and Immigration Canada). The PRRA also assesses whether the claimant is a Convention refugee or a person in need of protection, but in the case of a claimant who was initially found ineligible, the PRRA can only result in a temporary stay of removal and in the case of a claimant previously refused refugee status the PRRA only considers changes in circumstances since the IRB hearing (CCR, 2008). If the PRRA is rejected then

the individual can apply for leave to the Federal Court to have the PRRA decision reviewed but this will not stop the removal unless the individual is successful in having the court issue an order that the removal be stayed (that is, put on hold) pending its decision. Very few PRRA applications are successful (CLEO, 2008a).

The Resettlement Program

Under the resettlement program refugees are brought to Canada through a formal referral from the United Nations High Commission for Refugees or other organizations with which the government has an agreement. Those persons who have fled persecution often have no imminent prospects for a safe return to their home country nor can they build stable lives in the countries to which they have fled where they may be living in refugee camps, have no status, and few if any rights. Approximately a dozen countries have established resettlement programs for refugees. Canada's resettlement program provides for two categories of refugees—those who will receive support from the government for their first year in Canada or until they are able to support themselves and those who will receive support from private groups for one to three years. Private sponsorship groups include faith communities, ethnic communities, and unions. To qualify for resettlement the refugee must:

- be at risk for meeting the definition of a Convention refugee (discussed earlier in this chapter);
- qualify for Country of Asylum Class (a person outside their country of origin who is seriously and personally affected by civil war, armed conflict, or massive violations of human rights) or Source Country Class (meeting one of the other two categories but still within the country of origin, which country must be designated under Canadian law);
- not have committed a crime, represent a security risk, or pose a danger to public health and safety;

- show a capacity to become successfully established in Canada;
- have no prospect of another durable solution; and
- be sponsored by the government, by a private group, or have enough money themselves.

The resettlement approval process may take longer than two years. For those refugees who cannot afford to wait, the law recognizes refugees in need of protection and those who are vulnerable and gives such refugees priority in processing and exemption from the successful establishment requirement (CCR, 2003a). Refugees who are resettled from overseas typically become permanent residents in Canada upon their arrival.

National Security and Refugee Claimants

Since the terrorist attacks on the United States on September 11th, 2001, there has been increased concern about national security in general and about the admission of refugees in particular. There are a range of tools used by Canada to protect national security including visa requirements, document examination before boarding aircrafts, fines for airlines bringing refugee claimants into Canada, and immigration control officers posted overseas (Dolin and Young, 2002). Among the security measures instituted in the wake of September 11th is what is called the 'Safe Third Country' agreement between Canada and the United States which declares the United States a safe third country for refugees and accordingly closes the Canadian door to refugees who have passed through the United States. The Canadian Council for Refugees has expressed concern about the Safe Third Country agreement, arguing that the United States is not safe for refugees because of the risk of being held in detention, the risk of being denied status as a refugee in the United States, and the possibility that a greater number of refugee claimants will attempt to enter Canada in other irregular ways, perhaps at risk to their lives (CCR, 2004a). The Canadian Council for Refugees,

Amnesty International, and the Canadian Council of Churches, along with a Colombian asylum seeker in the United States, filed a legal challenge of the designation of the United States as a safe third country for refugees. In 2007, the Federal Court held that the Safe Third Country agreement violates refugees' rights to life, liberty, and security of the person and to non-discrimination under the Canadian Charter of Rights and Freedoms. In January 2008 the Federal Court issued an order for the Safe Third Country agreement to be quashed but the Government appealed this decision to the Federal Court of Appeal and was successful. At this time, the Safe Third Country agreement remains in effect.

Permanent Residents

Persons who have been granted permanent resident status receive a Permanent Residence Card and enjoy all of the rights guaranteed under the Canadian Charter of Rights and Freedoms. Permanent residents have the right to enter and remain in Canada provided they have not lost their status by failing to meet residency requirements or by engaging in criminal acts (CIC, 2007e).

Residency Obligations

In order to maintain permanent residency, immigrants are obliged to accumulate two years of physical presence in Canada within a five-year period (CIC, 2007b). Time spent outside Canada will count in the residency calculation if the permanent resident is a child accompanying a parent or an adult accompanying a spouse or common-law partner, employed on a full-time basis by a Canadian business or the Public Service of Canada, or accompanying a spouse or common-law partner so employed. In addition, when making residency determinations, Citizenship and Immigration Canada officers may take into account humanitarian and compassionate concerns (for example, best interests of the child, absence because of family illness, hardships to others) (CLEO, 2008b). If a permanent resident fails to meet the residency requirements, he or she may be issued a Departure Order but may appeal such a Departure Order to the Immigration Appeal Division within 30 days for those in Canada at the time and within 60 days for those outside of Canada at the time. If the Departure Order is not appealed, the permanent residency status is lost and the individual is required to leave Canada (CIC, 2005b).

Criminal Acts

A permanent resident may also be subject to a deportation order if convicted of an offence in Canada that is punishable under any act of Parliament by 10 years of imprisonment (regardless of the actual sentence imposed on the individual) or if sentenced to more than six months of imprisonment for any federal offence. However, permanent residents who are convicted are not automatically removed from Canada. A delegate of the Minister of Public Safety and Emergency Preparedness will review each case and determine whether a removal order should be issued by the IRB. If the permanent resident received a sentence of less than two years then he or she may appeal the IRB decision, failing which he or she may request leave for judicial review. However, if the permanent resident received a sentence of two years or more there is no right of appeal, and he or she may only seek judicial review (CIC, 2004).

Citizenship

The Citizenship Act addresses who may become citizens of Canada, procedures for obtaining citizenship, and conditions under which citizenship will be revoked.

Who Can Be a Canadian Citizen?

Generally, an individual born in Canada is automatically a Canadian citizen. An individual born outside of Canada may, depending on the citizenship of his or her parents, be automatically entitled to Canadian citizenship or be required to proceed through the general citizenship application process.

To become Canadian citizens, applicants must be permanent residents in Canada (see discussion on permanent residents in the foregoing section on immigration), 18 years of age or older, and have lived in Canada for at least three out of the four years preceding the application for citizenship. As with permanent resident status, time calculations are more complex than a simple count; for instance, in calculating the three years, the time the applicant lived in Canada after becoming a permanent resident will be counted as full-time whereas the time before becoming a permanent resident will only be counted as half-time (CIC, 2006a). There are, however, certain individuals who are prohibited from becoming citizens even if they meet the criteria discussed above, for example, anyone who:

- is under a deportation order;
- is on probation or parole;
- is in prison;
- has been charged or within the past three years been convicted of an offence;
- is under investigation for a war crime or a crime against humanity;
- is considered a security risk; or
- has had his or her Canadian citizenship revoked within the past five years.

The minister of citizenship and immigration has the power to waive certain citizenship requirements and to grant citizenship on compassionate grounds. In the case of a minor, the minister may waive age requirements, residence requirements, and the requirement to take an oath. In the case of any person, the minister may waive requirements for knowledge of one of the official languages of Canada and/or the privileges of citizenship, or the requirement to take the oath where the person is prevented from understanding the oath by reason of mental disability. Furthermore, the governor in council has the power to direct the minister to grant citizenship to any person to alleviate cases of special or unusual hardship or to reward services of an exceptional value to Canada.

What Is the Process for Becoming a Canadian Citizen?

The citizenship process involves three stages that can take several months to complete:

*   *Application.* Every individual applying for citizenship must complete an application form. Both natural and adoptive parents, who themselves are Canadian citizens or are applying to be citizens at the same time, or legal guardians may apply for citizenship on behalf of children under the age of 18 (CIC, 2006a). There are different application forms for adults and children.
*   *Citizenship test.* Applicants between the ages of 18 and 54 are required to take a citizenship test. This is usually in writing but may also be in the form of an interview. The purpose of the test is to determine the applicant's ability to understand English and French and his or her knowledge of Canada. The test includes questions on Canadian history and geography and on the rights and responsibilities of citizens (CIC, 2008b).
*   *Citizenship oath.* If the applicant passes the test they will receive a 'Notice to Appear to Take the Oath of Citizenship' which will indicate the time and place of the citizenship ceremony. During the citizenship ceremony, the applicant will take the oath of citizenship and receive a citizenship certificate (CIC, 2006a). Through the oath, the applicant swears allegiance to the Queen of Canada and her successors, and confirms that he or she will observe the laws of Canada and fulfill the duties of Canadian citizens.

Individuals interested in becoming Canadian citizens may obtain a Citizenship Application Kit by calling Citizenship and Immigration Canada toll-free at 1-888-242-2100 or by visiting the Citizenship and Immigration Canada website at www.cic.gc.ca.

What If the Application for Canadian Citizenship Is Denied?

If an application for citizenship is denied by Citizenship and Immigration Canada then the applicant has a right to appeal that decision to the Trial Division of the Federal Court of Canada. In addition, applicants who have been refused have the right to re-apply for citizenship. An appeal of the denial does not need to be made before an applicant can re-apply.

What Rights Do Canadian Citizens Have?

After an individual receives a Canadian Citizenship Certificate he or she will have all the rights enjoyed by Canadian citizens. Under the Canadian Charter of Rights and Freedoms, Canadian citizens have the right to be candidates in federal, provincial, and territorial elections, to be educated in either official language, to apply for a Canadian passport, to vote in federal and provincial elections, and to freely enter and leave Canada.

Can You Be a Citizen of More Than One Country?

Under Canadian law you may hold citizenship in more than one country. However, dual citizenship may not be allowed under the laws of other countries. Thus, it is possible that an individual may lose his or her citizenship in another country by becoming a Canadian citizen. To determine the laws in other countries with respect to citizenship, individuals in Canada may make inquiries to the consulate or embassy of the country in question. Those who maintain citizenship in other countries should be aware that if they visit the country in which they hold citizenship they may be subject to its laws (CIC, 2006a).

Can Canadian Citizenship Be Revoked?

Citizenship may be revoked if the minister is satisfied that the person obtained, retained, or resumed Canadian citizenship by false representation or fraud or by knowingly concealing material circumstances. However, the minister cannot recommend to the governor in council that an individual's citizenship be revoked unless the person is given notice of the revocation and does not within 30 days of such notice request that a court determine whether citizenship should be revoked.

New Citizenship Rules

In April 2008, Bill C-37 (An Act to Amend the Citizenship Act) received royal assent. The new law came into force on 17 April 2009. The purpose of the new law is to address issues of loss of citizenship due to outdated provisions in existing and previous legislation. The new law restores Canadian citizenship for certain individuals who lost their citizenship and gives citizenship to others who are being recognized for the first time (CIC, 2008f). For updates on the status of the new law and its implementation, consult the Citizenship and Immigration Canada website at www.cic.gc.ca.

CASE EXAMPLE REVIEWED

We return now to the case of Nela and use the legislation discussed in this chapter to answer questions directly related to her situation.

Is Nela an immigrant or a refugee?

Nela is an immigrant. Refugees are persons who are forced to leave their home countries because of serious human rights abuses. Nela did not flee persecution in the Philippines. Rather, she came to Canada as a 'mail-order bride'.

Which immigrant class does Nela fit into to?

Nela is a Family Class immigrant because she was sponsored by her husband to come to Canada.

Can Nela's husband send her back to the Philippines?

No. As a landed Family Class immigrant, Nela is a permanent resident in Canada. Permanent residents have the right to remain in Canada. A sponsor cannot, at pleasure, send the immigrant for whom he or she is responsible back to his or her country of origin.

If Nela leaves her husband, can Canada send her back to the Philippines?

No. As discussed above, Nela is a permanent resident and has the right to remain in Canada. Permanent residents cannot be forced out of Canada unless they gained permanent resident status through a material misrepresentation, failed to maintain the residency obligations, or committed a serious crime.

Once she leaves her husband, can Nela apply for social assistance if she has no money of her own?

Yes. Typically, sponsored individuals such as Nela are not to receive social assistance while under sponsorship. However, if a sponsor refuses to honour his support obligations, social assistance may be granted to the immigrant.

Key Terms

Canadian Citizenship
Status granted to an individual by being born in Canada or by application after a required period of residency and the completion of a citizenship test and oath

Convention Refugee
Under the United Nations Convention Relating to the Status of Refugees, a person outside his or her home country who has a well-founded fear of being persecuted for reasons of race, religion, nationality, political opinion, or membership in a particular social group and the country from which the person originates is unable to provide protection

Economic Class
Category of immigrants selected because of their skills or other assets that will contribute to the Canadian economy; includes several subclasses such as skilled workers, investors, entrepreneurs, self-employed persons, and the Canadian experience class

Family Class
Category of immigration where an individual living outside of Canada (or in some cases spouses or common-law partners who are already living in Canada) can be sponsored by an eligible Canadian citizen or permanent resident 18 years or older

Immigration and Refugee Board (IRB)
An independent, quasi-judicial administrative tribunal that makes certain decisions on who may enter and/or remain in Canada as an immigrant or refugee

Live-in Caregiver
A qualified individual from a foreign country who is issued a work visa to come to Canada and work without supervision in a private household to provide care for children, elderly persons, or people with disabilities; these individuals do not qualify

for entry into Canada under the Economic Class of immigrants and instead may apply for permanent resident status after completing a minimum of two years as a live-in caregiver within the three years following their entry into Canada

Mail-order Bride
A woman from a developing country who is selected by a consumer husband in an industrialized nation to come to Canada as his wife, sponsored by him as an immigrant under the Family Class

Permanent Resident
An individual granted permanent resident status, who has the right to live, study, and work in Canada and enjoys all the rights guaranteed under the Charter of Rights and Freedoms; status may be lost by failing to meet residency requirements or by engaging in criminal acts

Person in Need of Protection
A person who may not meet the Convention Refugee definition but is in a refugee-like situation that is defined in Canadian law as deserving of protection. This includes a person who faces a substantial danger of torture, a risk to their life or a risk of cruel and unusual treatment or punishment

Pre-removal Risk Assessment
An application made by a claimant in Canada who has been found ineligible or been refused refugee status when the individual is considered by Citizenship and Immigration Canada as ready for removal from Canada

Refugee
A person who is forced to leave his or her home country because of serious human rights abuses; a person may be granted refugee status in Canada if he or she is found to be a Convention Refugee or a person in need of protection

Resettlement Program

A program where refugees are brought into Canada through a formal referral from the United Nations High Commission for Refugees or other organizations with which the government has an agreement; this program provides support to refugees through the Canadian government or private groups

Sex-trade Worker

A woman from a foreign country entering Canada on an exotic dancer work permit

Sponsor

A person who meets certain eligibility criteria to sponsor an applicant for immigration under the Family Class, who has signed an Undertaking to provide housing, care, and financial support to the immigrant, and who may be required to sign a Sponsorship Agreement with the individual he or she is sponsoring, outlining the mutual commitments of both individuals

Discussion Questions

1. Who decides who may enter and/or remain in Canada as an immigrant or refugee?
2. Who can sponsor an immigrant under the Family Class and what will be his or her obligations as a sponsor?
3. Give two examples of contemporary immigration issues. Discuss.
4. What is the difference between a Convention refugee and a person in need of protection? Explain.
5. Under what circumstances may permanent resident status be lost?
6. What is the process for becoming a Canadian citizen?

Relevant Legislation

International

Convention against Torture and Other Cruel, Inhuman or Degrading Treatment or Punishment, December 10, 1984, G.A. Res. 39/46, UN GAOR, 39th Sess., Supp. No. 51, UN Doc. A/39/51 (entered into force 26 June 1987)
http://www.ohchr.org/english/law/cat.htm

Convention Relating to the Status of Refugees, 28 July 1951, 189 U.N.T.S.
http://www.ohchr.org/english/law/refugees.htm

Hague Convention on Protection of Children and Co-Operation in Respect of Intercountry Adoption, 29 May 1993 (entered into force 1 May 1995)
http://hcch.e-vision.nl

International Covenant on Civil and Political Rights, 19 December 1966, 999 U.N.T.S. 171, Can. T.S. 1976 No. 47, 6 I.L.M. 368 (entered into force 23 March 1976, accession by Canada 19 May 1976)
http://www.ohchr.org/english/law/ccpr.htm

Protocol Relating to the Status of Refugees, 31 January 1967, 606 U.N.T.S. 267 (entered into force 4 October 1967)
http://www.ohchr.org/english/law/protocol refugees.htm

Federal and Constitutional

Canadian Charter of Rights and Freedoms: Part 1 of the Constitution Act, 1982, being Schedule B to the Canada Act (UK), c. C-12
http://laws.justice.gc.ca/en/charter/

Citizenship Act, R.S. 1985, c. C-29
http://laws.justice.gc.ca/en/index.html

Crimes Against Humanity and War Crimes Act, 2000, c. 24
http://laws.justice.gc.ca/en/C-45.9/text.html

Criminal Code, R.S.C. 1985, c. C-46
http://laws.justice.gc.ca/en/C-46/

Immigration and Refugee Protection Act, 2001, c. 27
http://laws.justice.gc.ca/en/I-2.5/text.html

Federal–Provincial Agreements

Alberta

Agreement for Canada–Alberta Co-operation on Immigration, May 2007, Annex A: Provincial Nominees

Amendment to the Memorandum of Understanding between Citizenship and Immigration Canada and Alberta Human Resources and Employment on Sponsorship, December 2004
www.cic.gc.ca/English/department/laws-policy/agreements/Alberta/index-alberta.asp

Canada–Alberta Memorandum of Understanding on Information Sharing, September 2003
http://www.cic.gc.ca/EnGLIsh/department/laws-policy/agreements/alberta/can-alberta-mou.asp

British Columbia

Agreement for Canada–British Columbia Co-Operation on Immigration, April 2004
http://www.cic.gc.ca/english/department/laws-policy/agreements/bc/bc-2004-agree.asp

Amendment to the Agreement for Canada–British Columbia Co-operation on Immigration, June 2005
http://www.cic.gc.ca/english/department/laws-policy/agreements/bc/index-bc.asp

Canada–British Columbia Memorandum of Understanding on the Off-campus Work Permit Program for International Students, April 2006
http://www.cic.gc.ca/ENGLISH/department/laws-policy/agreements/bc/can-bc-mou-students.asp

Manitoba

Canada–Manitoba Immigration Agreement, June 2003
http://www.cic.gc.ca/EnGLIsh/department/laws-policy/agreements/manitoba/can-man-2003.asp

Canada–Manitoba Memorandum of Understanding on the Off-Campus Work Permit Program for International Students, November 2005
http://www.cic.gc.ca/english/department/laws-policy/agreements/manitoba/can-man-mou-students.asp

Canada–Manitoba Memorandum of Understanding on a Pilot Project to Issue Work Permits for International Students, October 2003
http://www.cic.gc.ca/english/department/laws-policy/agreements/manitoba/can-man-mou-students.asp

MOU on the Private Refugee Sponsorship Assistance Program, November 2002
http://www.cic.gc.ca/english/department/laws-policy/agreements/manitoba/index-man.asp

New Brunswick

Canada–New Brunswick Agreement on Provincial Nominees, January 2005
http://www.cic.gc.ca/ENGLISH/department/laws-policy/agreements/nb/nb-agree.asp

Canada–New Brunswick Memorandum of Understanding on the Off-Campus Work Permit Program for International Students, June 2006
http://www.cic.gc.ca/english/DEPARTMENT/laws-policy/agreements/nb/can-nb-mou-students.asp

Canada–New Brunswick Memorandum of Understanding on a Pilot Project to Issue Work Permits for International Students, March 2004
http://www.cic.gc.ca/english/department/laws-policy/agreements/nb/index-nb.asp

Newfoundland and Labrador

Canada–Newfoundland and Labrador Agreement on Provincial Nominees, December 2006
http://www.cic.gc.ca/EnGLIsh/department/laws-policy/agreements/nfld/can-nfld-2006.asp

Nova Scotia

Canada–Nova Scotia Co-operation on Immigration, September 2007, Annex A: Provincial Nominees
http://www.cic.gc.ca/english/department/laws-policy/agreements/ns/ns-2007-agree.asp

Canada–Nova Scotia Memorandum of Understanding on the Off-Campus Work Permit Program for International Students, October 2005
http://www.cic.gc.ca/EnGLIsh/department/laws-policy/agreements/ns/can-ns-mou-students.asp

Canada–Nova Scotia Memorandum of Understanding on Post-Graduation Employment for Foreign Students, April 2004
http://www.cic.gc.ca/english/department/laws-policy/agreements/ns/index-ns.asp

Ontario

Canada–Ontario–Toronto Memorandum of Understanding on Immigration and Settlement, September 2006
http://www.cic.gc.ca/EnGLIsh/department/laws-policy/agreements/ontario/can-ont-toronto-mou.asp

Canada–Ontario Memorandum of Understanding on the Off-Campus Work Permit Program for International Students, November 2005
http://www.cic.gc.ca/ENGLISH/department/laws-policy/agreements/ontario/can-ont-mou-students.asp

The Canada–Ontario Immigration Agreement, December 2005
http://www.cic.gc.ca/EnGLIsh/department/laws-policy/agreements/ontario/can-ont-index.asp

Letter of Intent with Respect to a Canada–Ontario Immigration Agreement, April 2004
http://www.cic.gc.ca/english/department/laws-policy/agreements/Ontario/index-ont.asp

Prince Edward Island

Agreement for Canada–Prince Edward Island Co-operation on Immigration, June 2008
http://www.cic.gc.ca/English/department/laws-policy/agreements/pei/index-pei.asp

Quebec

Canada–Quebec Memorandum of Understanding on the Off-Campus Work Permit Program for International Students, November 2005
http://www.cic.gc.ca/english/DEPARTMENT/LAWS-POLICY/agreements/quebec/can-que-mou-students.asp

Canada–Quebec Memorandum of Understanding on a Pilot Project to Issue Work Permits for International Students, May 2004
http://www.cic.gc.ca/english/DEPARTMENT/LAWS-POLICY/agreements/quebec/can-que-agree-2004.asp

Canada–Quebec Accord Relating to Immigration and Temporary Admission of Aliens, February 1991
http://www.cic.gc.ca/English/department/laws-policy/agreements/quebec/index-que.asp

Saskatchewan

Canada–Saskatchewan Memorandum of Understanding on the Off-campus Work Permit Program for International Students, April 2006
http://www.cic.gc.ca/ENGLISH/department/laws-policy/agreements/sask/can-sask-mou-students.asp

Canada–Saskatchewan Immigration Agreement, May 2005
http://www.cic.gc.ca/english/DEPARTMENT/MEDIA/backgrounders/2005/2005-06-01.asp

Canada–Saskatchewan Memorandum of Understanding on Post-Graduation Employment for Foreign Students, May 2004
http://www.cic.gc.ca/English/department/laws-policy/agreements/sask/index-sask.asp

Yukon Territory

Agreements/Yukon/index-yukon.asp

References

Abdulle v. Canada (Minister of Employment and Immigration) (1993), 67 F.T.R. 229 (Fed T.D.).

Access Alliance Multicultural Community Health Centre (2003), *Best Practices for Working with Homeless Immigrants and Refugees: A Community-Based Action-Research Project* (Toronto: Access Alliance Multicultural Community Health Centre) (accessed at http://www.settlement.org).

Amnesty International Canada (2008a), *Refugees in Canada* (accessed at http://www.amnesty.ca/Refugee/history.php).

——— (2008b), *Refugee Protection in Canada* (accessed at http://www.amnesty.ca/Refugee/Canada.php).

Canada v. Canadian Council for Refugees et al. (2008) FCA 229.

Canadian Council for Refugees (CCR) (2004a, 22 April), *Talking About Refugees and Immigrants: A Glossary of Terms* (accessed at http://www.web.net/~ccr/glossary.htm).

——— (2004b, 14 July), *Refugee Determination System: CCR Essential Principles* (accessed at http://www.web. net/~ccr/essprinc.html).

——— (2008), *State of Refugees in Canada* (accessed at http://ccrweb.ca/en/content/state-refugees-canada).

Canadian Council for Refugees et al. v. Canada (2007) FC 1262.

Canadian Immigration and Refugee Board (1996), *Guidelines on Women Refugee Claimants Fearing Gender-Related Persecution* (Ottawa: Immigration and Refugee Board, 1996).

Citizenship and Immigration Canada (CIC) (2003), *Family Class Immigration* (accessed at http://www.cic.gc.ca/english/sponsor/index.html).

——— (2004), *Criminal Justice and the Immigration and Refugee Protection Act* (accessed at http://www.cic.gc.ca/english/resources/publications/justice.asp).

——— (2005a), *You Asked About . . . Immigration and Citizenship* (accessed at http://www.cic.gc.ca/english/pdf/pub/you-asked.pdf).

——— (2005b), *ENF 23 - Loss of Permanent Resident Status* (accessed at: http://www.cic.gc.ca/english/resources/manuals/enf/enf23e.pdf).

——— (2006a), *How to Become a Canadian Citizen* (accessed at http://www.cic.gc.ca/english/resources/publications/howto-e.asp).

——— (2006b), *ENF 09 - Judicial Review* (accessed at http://www.cic.gc.ca/english/resources/manuals/enf/enf09e.pdf).

——— (2007a), *Medical Testing and Criminal Checks* (accessed at http://www.cic.gc.ca/english/information/medical-criminal.asp).

——— (2007b), *Residency Obligations for Permanent Residents* (accessed at http://www.cic.gc.ca/english/resources/publications/welcome/wel -16e.asp#52).

——— (2007c), *Sponsoring Your Family* (accessed at http://www.cic.gc.ca/english/immigrate/sponsor/index.asp).

——— (2007d), *Skilled Workers and Professionals: Who Can Apply* (accessed at http://www.cic.gc.ca/english/immigrate/skilled/apply-who.asp).

——— (2007e), *About Being a Permanent Resident of Canada* (accessed at http://www.cic.gc.ca/english/newcomers/about-pr.asp).

——— (2008a), *The Live-in Caregiver Program, Extending Your Stay* (accessed at http://www.cic.gc.ca/english/ work/caregiver/extend-stay.asp).

——— (2008b), *A Look at Canada* (accessed at http://www.cic.gc.ca/english/resources/publications/look/look-21.asp).

——— (2008c), *Backgrounder: Action Plan for Faster Immigration: Ministerial Instructions* (accessed at http://www.cic.gc.ca/English/department/media/backgrounders/2008/2008-11-28.asp).

——— (2008d), *Canadian Experience Class Now Open for Business* (accessed at http://www.cic.gc.ca/English/department/media/releases/2008/2008-09-05c.asp).

——— (2008e), *Sponsorship of Spouse, Common-law Partner, Conjugal Partner or Dependent Child Living outside Canada. Part 1: The Sponsor's Guide* (accessed at http://www.cic.gc.ca/english/information/applications/guides/3900ETOC.asp).

——— (2008f) *New Citizenship Rules* (accessed at http://www.cic.gc.ca/ENGLISH/citizenship/rules-citizenship.asp).

Community Legal Education Ontario (CLEO) (2007a), *Immigration and Refugee Fact Sheet, Sponsoring a Member of the Family Class* (accessed at http://www.cleo.on.ca/english/pub/onpub/subject/refugee.htm).

——— (2007b), *Immigration and Refugee Fact Sheet, Immigrant Women and Domestic Violence* (accessed at http://www.cleo.on.ca/english/pub/onpub/subject/refugee.htm).

——— (2008a), *Immigration and Refugee Fact Sheet, Pre-Removal Risk Assessment* (accessed at http:// www.cleo.on.ca/english/pub/onpub/subject/refugee.htm).

——— (2008b), *Immigration and Refugee Fact Sheet, Your Status as a Permanent Resident* (accessed at http://www.cleo.on.ca/english/pub/onpub/subject/refugee.htm).

Dolin, B. and Young, M. (Law and Government Division, Parliamentary Research Branch) (2002), *Canada's Refugee Protection System* (accessed at http://www.parl.gc.ca/information/library/PRBpubs/bp185-e.htm).

Erdman, J. and Sanche, A. (2004), 'Talking About Women: The Iterative and Dialogic Process of Creating Guidelines for Gender-Based Refugee Claims', *Journal of Law and Equality*, 3(1).

Jones, D.P. and de Villars, A.S. (2004), *Principles of Administrative Law*, 4th ed. (Toronto: Thomson Canada).

Langevin, L. and M. Belleau (2000), *Trafficking in Women in Canada: A Critical Analysis of the Legal Framework Governing Immigrant Live-in Caregivers and Mail-Order Bride*

(Ottawa: Status of Women Canada) (accessed at http://www.swc-cfc.gc.ca).

McDonald, L., Moore, B., and Timoshkina, N. (2000), *Migrant Sex Workers from Eastern Europe and the Former Soviet Union: The Canadian Case* (Toronto: Centre for Applied Social Research, University of Toronto) (accessed at http://www. swc-cfc.gc.ca).

Macklin, A. (1992), 'Foreign Domestic Worker: Surrogate Housewife or Mail Order Servant?' *McGill Law Journal*, 37: 681.

——— (2003), 'Dancing Across Borders: Exotic Dancers, Trafficking, and Canadian Immigration Policy', *The International Migration Review*, 37(2).

Mamann, G. (2005), 'Sponsors Don't Rule', Metro newspaper, 14 February 2005.

Philippine Women Centre of BC (2000), *The New Frontier for Filipino Mail Order Brides* (accessed at http://www.swc-cfc.gc.ca).

Rosca, N. (1999), *Creating the Modern-Day Slave* (Vancouver: 7 December 1999) (accessed at http://www.swc.cfc.gc.ca).

United Nations High Commissioner for Refugees (UNHCR) (1991), *Guidelines on the Protection of Refugee Women*, UN Doc. EC/SCP/67.

——— (1992), *Handbook on Procedures and Criteria for Determining Refugee Status under the 1951 Convention and the 1967 Protocol Relating to the Status of Refugees* (accessed at http://www.unhcr.ch).

——— (2002), *Guidelines on International Protection: Gender-Related Persecution within the context of Article 1A(2) of the 1951 Convention and/or its 1967 Protocol relating to the Status of Refugees*, UN Doc. HCR/GIP/02/01 (2002) (accessed at http:// www.unhcr.ch).

University of Toronto (2005), *Don't Ask Don't Tell: Faculty of Social Work Endorsement Resolution* (Toronto: University of Toronto, Faculty of Social Work).

Waldman, L. (2004), *Canadian Immigration and Refugee Law Practice* (Markham, ON: LexisNexis Butterworths).

Wong, P. and Munn, J. (2000), 'Immigration and Refugees', in *Canadian Encyclopedic Digest*, 3rd ed., vol. 15 (Toronto: Carswell).

CHAPTER ELEVEN

The Social Work Record and the Courts

OBJECTIVES

- To describe the elements of a complete clinical record
- To outline who has access to clinical records
- To outline obligations to ensure confidentiality of records
- To describe elements of a forensic report
- To explain the process and content of expert testimony

CASE EXAMPLE 1

Janine, a woman who was brutally assaulted and raped by an acquaintance, attends a sexual assault centre for treatment. A social worker assists Janine to manage her symptoms of posttraumatic stress, including nightmares of the event, heightened anxiety, fear of being alone at night, and self-enforced social isolation. During the treatment, Janine has discussed at length issues related to her personal and sexual history and the manner in which this event has resurrected previous life traumas. She reported the assault to police and now, 18 months later, a criminal trial is ensuing. She has also decided to launch a civil suit, seeking damages for her emotional distress and the loss of earnings due to her difficulty concentrating at work and interacting with co-workers and customers. The social worker receives a subpoena in the mail demanding her records regarding Janine's treatment. The subpoena has been initiated by the lawyer defending Janine's attacker.

- What should be recorded or not recorded in a good clinical record?
- Who can get access to social work records?
- What are the implications of the confidentiality and privacy obligations on record-keeping?

CASE EXAMPLE 2

A defence lawyer retains a social worker to write a report for the courts expressing an expert opinion. The client in question has been charged with assaulting his employer. While the lawyer and his client are not contesting the charges, they assert that there are several factors that should be considered in mitigation at the time of sentencing. These factors include torture and trauma in the client's country of origin, racism and discrimination in Canada resulting in demeaning work despite his professional credentials in his own country, a recent marital separation that he perceived as due to his occupational failures, subsequent financial hardship, and finally a threatened demotion at work. Since the charges, the client has been attending educational upgrading for Canadian certification and social work treatment in another agency. The social worker is asked to assess the client and provide a report for the purposes of sentencing.

- What should be included in a court report?
- What are the ethical concerns about providing a court report?
- What makes someone an 'expert' witness?
- What happens if a social worker is called to court?

What Is a Good Clinical Record?

It is widely suggested that good record-keeping is an essential component of clinical social work practice. Thorough documents allow social workers to maintain a record of their clinical assessment and clinical interventions—to assist with ongoing work and to clearly communicate their opinions, findings, and interventions to other members of the treatment team. In addition, in the case of legal action, careful records can demonstrate that decisions were well considered and that adequate measures were taken to guarantee the safety and well-being of clients and others. Good records also provide a basis upon which to write social work reports to assist the courts in the administration of justice.

Record-keeping consumes a substantial portion of social work time. Indeed, estimates from research in the 1950s indicated that social workers spent up to 25 per cent of their time recording information in client files (Streat, 1987). More recent research shows that 10 to 60 per cent of social workers' time is spent in the practice of

documenting their work with clients (Edwards and Reid, 1989; Ames, 1999). Nevertheless, record-keeping is rarely a task that is approached with enthusiasm by social workers (Tebb, 1991). As a result, when faced with time constraints, recording is often placed low on the priority list (Gelman, 1992; Kagle, 1984; 1993).

History of the Social Work Record

The history of record-keeping in social work begins in the 1800s with the 'friendly visitor movement' initiated by Mary Richmond (Coady, 1993), when documentation consisted primarily of register-type records. As this movement led into the 1900s, and accompanying the work of Jane Adams in the Settlement Houses, records were expanded to include the verified facts of the case, the resources provided, and the subjective opinion of the worker regarding the impact of these resources on the client (Tebb, 1991). Psychoanalytic theory, pioneered by Sigmund Freud in the 1920s, and the functional school developed by Otto Rank in the 1930s led to the development of process recordings. In these documents the therapist would describe the process of treatment and particularly the interaction between the worker and the client for the purposes of reviewing techniques and supervision. The extensive procedure of process-recording gave way to summary recordings during the 1940s and 1950s, when casework, as conceptualized by Helen Pearlman, was practised. Throughout this history, records were highly subjective and worker opinion played a central role in the documents.

The contemporary social work record differs markedly from that of the past. The record now serves primarily to facilitate service delivery rather than to provide a basis for supervision. That is, a shift has occurred from analysis to action and from process to product. Because time constraints increasingly affect the ability of workers to keep records, agencies are moving towards brief recording strategies such as outlines, checklists, or brief forms to replace long narratives (Kagle, 1983). Further, recording has become an important form of accountability for the practices of workers (Gelman, 1992; Ames, 1999). As workers are being held more responsible for the results of their decisions in both the criminal and civil courts (Alexander, 1995), recording practices have become increasingly focused on fact and less on opinion or conjecture. Thus, recordings now should also be considered from the perspective of managing risk (Reamer, 2005). Further, current legislation in Canada permits client access to records and has resulted in the need to be concise and accurate and to ensure that opinions are well substantiated by facts.

Current Expectations for Recording

The *Canadian Association of Social Workers Code of Ethics, Guidelines for Professional Practice* (2005b) makes the following statements regarding record-keeping:

> 1.7—Social workers maintain one written record of professional interventions and opinions. . . . Social workers document information impartially and accurately and

with the appreciation that the record may be revealed to clients or disclosed during court proceedings. Social workers are encouraged to: report only essential and relevant details; refrain from using emotive or derogatory language; acknowledge the basis of professional opinions; protect clients' privacy and that of other people involved (p. 9).

Provincial guidelines, such as those of the Ontario College of Social Workers and Social Service Workers (2000), may provide more explicit guidelines; for example: records should be legible and systematic; recordings should be made when the event occurs or as soon as possible thereafter; record-keeping guidelines apply to social workers employed in agencies and those in independent practice; records must be kept for a period of seven years; and confidentiality of records must be ensured.

There is little ambiguity that records must be kept, but what is less clear is what constitutes a good clinical record. In a 1979 US study of 147 social agencies and social work departments, Kagle (1983) identified that the typical social work record contained: 1) a social history; 2) the worker's assessment of the client's situation; 3) a goal statement; 4) a service plan; 5) progress notes; and 6) a closing summary. Guidelines for the content of clinical records offered by other sources (Kagle, 1984; OCSWSSW, 2000) are incorporated into the suggested framework in Table 11.1.

Record-keeping must be adapted to meet the idiosyncratic purposes and constraints of a variety of practice settings. For instance, shorter interventions may require more concise and structured forms of reporting (Kagle, 1984; Streat, 1987). Regardless of the setting—whether a worker is in a large institution, small agency, or independent practice—guidelines for recording should be established and followed in every case. At bare minimum the record should contain identifying data of the client, a brief assessment, and dated notations of each contact (OCSWSSW, 2000). The record should describe the treatment or intervention employed and the rationale for selecting it

Table 11.1 Aspects of a Clinical Record

Assessment Phase

Initial information
- name and contact information for the client
- reason for referral and referral source
- other agency involvement or outstanding legal issues
- client's perception of the problem
- any collateral information included in the assessment

Description of the client
- brief personal history
- relevant relationships
- social/cultural factors
- current situation (stressors, supports, strengths, and limitations)

Formulation
- summary of predisposing, precipitating, perpetuating, and protective factors
- worker's opinion

Plan
- client's wishes
- goals for treatment
- tentative agreement

Intervention Phase

Progress notes
- relevant events in client's life
- summary of intervention

Additional data
- record of any additional contacts with client or collaterals
- inclusion of any additional data obtained
- consents for release of information

Termination Phase

Closing notes
- evaluation of service
- referral, if any
- plans for follow-up, if any

(Ames, 1999). It should contain enough detail and be organized so that a reader can understand why a particular approach was used and to allow another person to continue the care should the social worker be unable to (Solomon and Visser, 2005). On the other hand, it should not contain too much irrelevant detail which could be used against the person. For instance, as noted below, when the client is a victim of a crime that is currently or will be considered by the courts. In addition, any significant clinical issues, such as a risk of harm to self or others and the relevant assessment and measures taken to ensure safety, must be documented. The reasons for any decision to breach confidentiality should be clearly noted (Glancy, Regehr, and Bryant, 1998a). Recordings should be goal-directed and should relate directly to the problem identified;

interesting but irrelevant information should be excluded. Finally, it is critical to differentiate between factual information and worker opinion (Gelman, 1992; CASW, 2005b).

Who Can Get Access to Social Work Records?

Although the *Canadian Association of Social Workers Code of Ethics* requires that 'social workers respect the importance of the trust and confidence placed in the professional relationship by clients and members of the public' (CASW, 2005a, p. 7), the code does identify several exceptions to the rule of confidentiality. These include written authorization by the client, information required by a statute or order of a court of competent jurisdiction, or a threat of harm to self or others (Duty to protect issues are discussed in greater detail in Chapters 7 and 12). Although these standards for practice appear clear, the actual application of them creates a number of dilemmas for social workers. Recent legislative enactments and court decisions have muddied the waters further regarding what information is confidential and what information the social work practitioner ought to reveal (Regehr, Bryant, and Glancy, 1997; Glancy, Regehr, and Bryant, 1998b).

In addition to the ethical confidentiality obligations, social workers will be subject to legislation specific to confidentiality and privacy that govern the collection, maintenance, use, and disclosure of information. Federal and provincial public-sector privacy legislation applies to government-related entities that hold personal information. Canada's Personal Information Protection and Electronic Documents Act sets out ground rules for how private-sector organizations may collect, use, or disclose personal information in the course of commercial activities. This legislation incorporates the Canada Standards Association Model Code for the Protection of Personal Information, which constitutes a central part of the Act. The 10 privacy or 'fair information' principles that make up the code appear in Schedule 1 of the Personal Information Protection and Electronic Documents Act and form the basis of any substantially similar provincial privacy legislation.

Many of the provinces and territories have also enacted legislation governing the collection, use, and disclosure of personal information (see 'Relevant Legislation' at the end of the chapter). These Acts prescribe the circumstances under which practitioners may grant access to the individual from whom it was collected and disclose personal information to third parties. Further, social workers should be aware that they may also be subject to various provincial statutes governing confidentiality, access, use, and disclosure in their specific areas of practice, including provincial education acts, child and family services acts, hospitals acts, and mental health acts (Solomon and Visser, 2005).

For social workers working within organizations, specific policies regarding privacy and confidentiality of personal information have typically been developed by organizations in compliance with the requirements of applicable legislation. Social workers not working in organizations, however, are required to develop their own privacy policies, practices, and procedures in accordance with the law. The Ontario College of Social Workers and Social Service Workers' *Privacy Toolkit* (OCSWSSW, 2005) is recommended as an excellent resource for this purpose.

Client Access to Records

As stated earlier, a basic principle of privacy legislation is access and clients should have the opportunity to access personal information in the custody or control of the practitioner or organization, subject to limited exceptions. Privacy legislation codifies the common law, and in particular, an earlier judgment of the Supreme Court of Canada (*McInerney v. MacDonald*, 1992) that established the right of clients to have access to all mental health and medical records regarding their care. This includes not only records compiled in the treatment facility to which the request for access is directed, but also all records obtained from other facilities and which form part of the individual's health record. If a treating professional has reason to believe that access to the information contained in a clinical record may be harmful to the client or a third party (such as a family member who has provided information), she or he may, as defined by legislation, be able to deny the request for access or apply to the court to deny the request for access. For instance, under the Ontario Personal Health Information Protection Act, a health information custodian may refuse to provide access to all or part of the record if the custodian believes that the access may cause serious harm to the individual or another. Similarly, under the Ontario Mental Health Act, the attending physician may refuse to allow disclosure of a mental health record provided that he or she states in writing the opinion that disclosure will be harmful. However, if the potentially dangerous information is contained in records that have been forwarded to another facility subsequent to a signed release of information form, the worker who authored the records may not be informed that the information is to be released and therefore may not have the opportunity to make application to have the information kept private.

Although initially viewed with alarm by practitioners, client access to records is now seen by some as having benefits. For instance, clients are given the opportunity to request correction or amendment to erroneous records. Further, when aware that clients will access records, social workers tend to ensure that records are better organized, shorter, more factual, and more goal-oriented (Gelman, 1992). It has also been suggested that involving clients in the production of case records can be an effective tool in the treatment process (Badding, 1989).

Access to Records in Criminal and Civil Cases by Third Parties

Third-party access to the treatment records of victims has been the centre of considerable controversy over the past few years (Regehr, Bryant, and Glancy, 1997). In criminal court proceedings,

arguments have focused on balancing the legal rights of the defendant, particularly in sexual assault trials, with the privacy rights of the victim. As a result of the vocal concerns of therapists and other victim advocacy groups, changes to the Criminal Code have placed restrictions on access to victim's treatment records (Statutes of Canada, 1997). Although subsequent court decisions challenged the legislation on the basis that it violated the Canadian Charter of Rights and Freedoms (1982), these provisions were upheld by the Supreme Court of Canada (R. v. Mills, 1997). Nevertheless, if victim records are determined to be relevant to the case, they can become a part of the criminal trial.

A professional who is subject to a subpoena to attend court with client records may seek standing to object to an order to produce the confidential files. For example, in criminal cases involving sexual assault or similar charges, the accused may apply to a judge trying the case for the production of clinical records and set out the grounds on which the records are relevant to an issue at trial or to the competence of a witness to testify. Seven days' notice of the application must be served on the prosecutor, the complainant, or witness, and the record-holder. An in-camera hearing is held at which the record-keeper may appear and make submissions. Following this, a judge may order production of the record if he or she deems it necessary in the interest of justice. In doing so, the judge is mandated to take into consideration a number of defined factors including the salutary and deleterious effects on the accused's right to make full answer and defence, the right to privacy and personal dignity of the complainant or witness, society's interest in encouraging the reporting of sexual offences, society's interest in encouraging treatment for complainants of sexual offences, and the effect of the determination on the integrity of the trial process (Glancy, Regehr, and Bryant, 1998b). If the judge orders production of the record, he or she has the discretion to impose conditions in order to ensure, to the greatest extent possible, the privacy of the complainant or witness. These conditions can include that the record be edited as directed by the judge, that a copy of the record rather than the original be produced, that the record be viewed only at the offices of the court and the contents not be disclosed, and that names and addresses regarding any person be severed from the record.

Despite the fact that subpoenas represent both significant risk to the privacy of the client and inconvenience to the social worker who is receiving it, serious sanctions can be imposed by the courts if a subpoena is ignored. However, a subpoena is just an order to attend, it is not a licence to breach client confidentiality (College of Physicians and Surgeons of Nova Scotia, 2004) and it does not grant the social worker permission to speak to a lawyer, police officer, or anyone else about the content of the records or any aspect of the client's treatment. It simply directs the social worker to bring the record to the court or tribunal for a determination of whether or not it should be produced. The social worker cannot speak to anyone about the record or produce the record to a third party until and unless the court orders the social worker to do so.

In the case of civil litigation, individuals who initiate legal proceedings that put their treatment, medical condition, or health in issue are viewed as waiving the right to confidentiality and implicitly consenting to the disclosure of confidential information relevant to the action (P.(L.M.) v. F. (D.), 1994). Thus, the defendant in a civil action has access to records of the complainant's care. This has significant implications in cases where victims choose to sue their abusers. In addition, access to records may also be granted in family law disputes. For example, during a custody dispute, a husband requested the psychiatric records of his wife be disclosed to support his claim that she could not care for children (Gibbs v. Gibbs, 1985). The court concluded that the potential harm to the children was the greater risk and thus ordered disclosure of records despite her doctor's conclusion that it would likely be harmful to her. The demand for clinical records generally comes in the form of a subpoena. The development of law in this area arose in the context of high-profile

sexual assault cases (R. v. O'Connor, 1995; R. v. Mills, 1997) and subsequently resulted in changes to the Criminal Code.

What Are the Implications of the Confidentiality and Privacy Obligations on Record-keeping?

As stated earlier in this chapter, social workers have both legal obligations to protect the confidentiality of records defined by statute and by case law and ethical obligations to protect records as defined by the Code of Ethics. Because social workers in Canada are increasingly faced with limits to the privacy of client information, we must evaluate the impact of these changes on practice. Health records are often producible as evidence in legal proceedings and are subject to access and correction requests; both situations may effect recording practices and remind social workers that clinical records must be written in a factual manner that respects the best interests of clients and their families. Social work records should avoid speculation and record only details that are clearly pertinent to the assessment and treatment of clients. In particular, when providing treatment to victims or offenders, clinical records must exclude any speculation as to the legitimacy of a victim's story or the culpability of the alleged offender. As always, it is important to clarify what is opinion and what is 'fact' as presented by the client.

While information presented by the client is necessary for a comprehensive assessment, specific details of victimization or criminal activity should be avoided. As therapists attempt to reconstruct the client story from their notes and memory into an assessment, some facts can become distorted. These distortions may ultimately result in a miscarriage of justice, because it may appear that the client is providing inconsistent information. In addition, in sexual assault cases, extreme caution should be exercised in recording information about the client's previous sexual history since it is very likely that these notes will be required for court.

Earlier, Barsky (1997) recommended the separation of client records for the various services that a client receives, such as vocational counselling and sexual assault treatment. Sexual assault care centres in hospitals often elected to keep a set of records that is distinct from the main hospital record. Therefore, if the sexual assault chart is subpoenaed, the defendant does not necessarily receive all information about such things as psychiatric admissions or previous abortions. However, these records could equally be obtained by demonstrating relevance to the action before the court. It is recommended to seek legal advice prior to instituting a policy of separate records for any services rendered and certainly prior to making only a partial response to a subpoena. Further, the practice of keeping separate records clearly contravenes the CASW Code of Ethics that states: 'The social worker shall maintain only one master file on each client' (CASW, 2005a, section 5.9). The master file as defined by the code must include all information pertaining to the client. It is cautioned by the code that this document should be prepared with the anticipation that the file may be revealed to the client or disclosed in legal proceedings.

As a final point, notes once made should not be destroyed or altered in order to avoid the problem of court access. Such destruction has led to a dismissal of charges against an accused (Barsky, 1997). Destruction of records after the issuance of a subpoena could also lead to charges being laid against the record-keeper for obstruction of justice, or to disciplinary proceedings. In addition, corrections or additions to client records should be done in accordance with professional documentation practices, in such a way that the original documentation and amended version are legible and can be traced.

When discussing confidentiality in the context of treatment, social workers must be clear about the limits of confidentiality of social work records, particularly when the situation of the client may result in some type of legal action. Finally, social workers have an ethical duty to remain current about legal threats to confidentiality and to make all reasonable efforts to protect the privacy of clients within the confines of legal requirements.

What Should Be Contained in Documents Prepared for a Court?

Two types of court documents are prepared by social workers in the majority of situations: an affidavit and an expert report. Other documents may be prepared by clients, assisted by social workers, such as victim impact statements or refugee claims.

Affidavits

As noted in Chapter 4 on child-protection law, increasingly, family court proceedings regarding child welfare issues are being dealt with through the use of affidavit evidence. Affidavits are sworn, written statements that provide information that would otherwise have been presented in testimony. Depending on the legal process, the affidavit may have to be witnessed by a lawyer, notary public, or commissioner of oaths (Barsky, 1997). In general, affidavit evidence excludes hearsay and is limited to direct knowledge, although some court rules do allow for information conveyed by others and beliefs formed by the person providing the affidavit (Thompson, 2004). However, the source of any second-hand information contained in the affidavit should be clearly identified: for instance, 'Kelly Smith provided the following information . . .'. Because health care professionals often work as teams, it is not uncommon that one affidavit will contain information gathered by various team members. It is then at the discretion of the opposing party whether to accept the second-hand information as fact or demand testimony or an affidavit from the named person. As affidavits are quite specific in their language and style, frequently the lawyer will draft the affidavit based on discussions with the witness. This is especially true in situations where the social worker has limited or no experience in the preparation. However, affidavits are the statements of the witness, not the lawyer, and thus if one has been prepared for you, it is vital to ensure that the opinions, tone, and wording accurately reflect your voice and that you are comfortable with every word of the affidavit because you may be cross-examined on it.

There is no obligation on a witness, even under a subpoena, to discuss his or her testimony prior to appearing or to provide affidavit evidence (Thompson, 2004) and a social worker cannot do so when the client has not given consent for disclosure of confidential information (if it is not a mandated case, such as a child-protection hearing) unless the court orders the worker to do so. That being said, social workers may want to cooperate as much as possible without breaching confidentiality because this will facilitate the worker being accommodated later on in the proceedings (for example, for scheduling of testimony, etc.).

Court Reports

Unlike the term 'affidavit', the term 'report' does not have a legal definition; rather, it applies to an assessment prepared by a clinician for a legal purpose (Barsky, 1997). Reports, though not sworn as affidavits, can be heavily relied upon by the courts and can be highly persuasive. They are a way in which professionals can structure and support their expert opinion in a manner that is understandable and accessible to the various officers of the court. If requested to prepare a report the social worker should ensure it is pertaining to an area that is within the scope of expertise of the worker. Prior to writing the report, the social worker should obtain a letter from the requesting lawyer indicating that he or she is being officially retained and outlining the issues to be addressed. These issues can include social factors that may be useful considerations in sentencing of a person convicted of an offence; the ability of someone to parent their child; or the social and emotional consequences for the victim of an assault or accident. The social worker should ensure that she or he has been provided with complete information about the situation in question. Are there medical or social work records that will be entered into the court? Is there a police report or a probation report? As the assessment progresses, it is important to communicate with the retaining lawyer as frequently as necessary in order to ensure that the report is relevant and considers all available data. The social worker should keep in mind that he or she may be cross-examined on the content of the report.

A report prepared for the court should be the end result of a well-planned, objective, and systematic search for clinical facts in order to answer a legal question. It should be based on facts collected from a variety of sources, augmented with knowledge of the research literature in the field and offered in an impartial manner. 'It is not sufficient to offer a sincere belief; what is required is logical and compelling knowledge' (Rosner, 1984, p. 13). Because the report is a representation of the professional, it should be professionally presented, grammatically correct, and free of errors. It should be easy to follow, demonstrate clear thinking, and flow logically towards the conclusion (Arboleda-Florez and Deynaka, 1999). For clarity and flow, it is helpful to divide professional reports into sections using a standard format. Table 11.2 lists the format recommended by the American Board of Forensic Psychiatry.

What Are the Ethical Issues to Be Considered in Providing Court Assessments?

When providing assessments for the courts, social workers are faced with ethical dilemmas that they do not encounter in other areas of practice (Regehr and Antle, 1997). A central issue in these dilemmas is that of informed consent. As we have discussed in earlier chapters, the client's right to self-determination is a key tenet of social work practice, and informed consent is one of the ways

Table 11.2   Elements of a Forensic Report

Introduction

- name of the person being assessed
- agency requesting the assessment (the Crown, defence . . .)
- the purpose or legal question to be addressed

Opinion

- summary of the assessor's opinion based on the facts considered and the question posed

Sources of information

- all documents reviewed
- interviews conducted (with whom, how long, what dates)

Confidentiality

- the nature of confidentiality that was explained to the person being assessed and all others interviewed
- an estimation of those individuals' degree of comprehension

Data surrounding the question

- description of the event by all persons and documents (use quotes where possible)

Relevant past history

- family and developmental history
- prior medical, criminal, and psychiatric history

Summary of special studies

- any tests that have been administered either by the social worker or by other members of the team may be included

Formulation

- organizing of preceding data for conclusions
- clinical findings should be specifically related to the legal question and be relatively free of jargon.

in which we codify the principle of self-determination in our day-to-day practice. Clients have a right to information about the type of social work treatment they are about to receive and the efficacy of that treatment in addressing their particular problem. Social workers have both a legal and ethical responsibility to provide this information (NASW, 1999; CASW, 2005). However, when conducting court-ordered assessments—for clients facing charges in the criminal justice system, for divorcing parents seeking custody and visitation rights, or for parents requiring assessment in child welfare—social workers are often placed in the role of working for the greater good. That is, they must balance the safety of a child with the individual rights of one or both parents, or balance the risk to society with the rights of the accused. Practice norms would command that in these situations social workers give clear information about the nature of the assessment and the limits of confidentiality, for instance, stating: 'This assessment is being conducted for the courts on the request of your lawyer. As such, any information that you provide may be included in my report, which then may become a matter of public record. Thus, our interview is not confidential as your statements and my opinion will be shared with others outside this room.'

It is likely that social workers assume that by providing information about these limits to confidentiality, they will have met their ethical requirements of informed consent. However, several factors are neglected in this approach to informed consent. The first is that the risks and benefits of an assessment for the individual/family cannot always be anticipated in advance. We do not know how the judge may rule, we do not know what additional information will come forward, and we do not know whether our opinion evidence will be accepted. Further, the power imbalance between the worker and the client can result in client vulnerability and the undermining of freedom to consent. Can clients in court-mandated practice be understood to freely consent? What are the consequences of refusing to consent? If refusal to consent to the assessment means that they are more likely to lose custody of their child or are less likely to receive a reduced sentence for a criminal offence, consent is not truly free. While social workers may not be able to change this fact, they must be cognizant of the imbalance and cautious in their approach.

A second dilemma is the dual role that social workers carry with regard to court-mandated assessment (Regehr and Antle, 1997). In these situations, social workers must consider the interests of individuals weighed against the needs of the larger community. Social workers have a fiduciary duty to act in the best interest of the client (NASW, 1999; CASW, 2005a). In court-mandated practice, however, it is not always clear which party is the client. The social worker may regard the court or the prosecuting attorney who is requesting the assessment to be the client, or perhaps regard the vulnerable child of the person being assessed to be the client. The person being assessed, however, may regard themselves as the client and assume that the social worker is acting in their best interests, not the best interests of other vulnerable members of society. This problem is intensified by the therapeutic alliance that develops between the social worker and the client during the assessment process. Social workers are selected to perform the role of assessors in quasi-coercive situations because of their relationship skills.

Therefore, while it is this ability to form a therapeutic alliance and obtain relevant information that is valued by the court, the therapeutic alliance may not always serve the best interests of the individual being assessed. This person may not be aware of the complexity of the relationship and may assume that the social worker will provide an assessment that is in his or her best interest, in spite of the nature of the referral and the social worker's obligation to address the needs, interests, and safety of others. Social workers have a duty to clarify their role when providing services to two or more individuals who have a relationship with one another, such as for a family. In court-mandated practice, social workers must similarly identify to all parties at the onset of the contract both the limitations of their role and the extent of their obligation to the safety of others (Regehr and Antle, 1997).

As a final point, when requested to perform a court-ordered assessment, social workers should take due care to ensure that they have not previously provided treatment to the party to be assessed. A fiduciary duty is owed to all clients and this will restrict the ability of the practitioner to act as an independent assessor.

What Is an Expert?

There are two instances where a social worker may be called on in a legal situation involving clients (Diamond, 1983). In Case Example 1, the social worker is the counsellor working with a client who is involved in a criminal or civil proceeding. The social worker is then called on to testify regarding the treatment. This may involve only factual evidence or both factual and expert opinion evidence. In Case Example 2, the social worker is retained as an expert, solely for the purposes of providing a forensic report. The social worker in this case usually has forensic training and provides expert-opinion evidence. Unlike a witness who may only testify about what he or she saw or heard and is not expected to evaluate the facts and offer an opinion, an expert witness offers an opinion regarding matters beyond the experience of the average layperson. The primary role of the expert is to serve as a consultant and educator of the court about matters that the court knows little about.

Generally, expert opinion evidence is viewed as scientific evidence. Accordingly, to ensure scientific validity of the opinion, the expert must ensure that sound science and research has led to the theories and evidence that support his or her opinion (Arboleda-Florez and Deynaka, 1999). The quality of an expert opinion is dependent on the facts that form the foundation for the opinion. The more solid the facts, the greater confidence the court places on the opinion (*R. v. Olscamp*, 1994).

Expert evidence is admissible if it is: relevant to the issues in the case; necessary because the issue requires someone with special knowledge and this knowledge is beyond that of the judge or jury; is being put forward by a properly qualified expert and is reliable (*R. v. Monahan*, 1994). There are no specific professional qualifications regarding who qualifies as an expert in Canada and no single test of expertise; however, the court will generally consider the person's training, experience, and knowledge. Information considered may include professional position, degrees, licences, years of experience, awards, provisions of training to others, previous court appearances, research conducted, articles and books written, and whether or not these were in peer-reviewed academic journals or presses. These qualifications will be presented in court and often challenged by the opposing counsel.

Similar to court-ordered assessments, when requested to act as expert witnesses, social workers should verify if they have previously provided any professional services to the individual whose behaviour they have been asked to comment on. It would be a breach of the worker's fiduciary duty to act as an expert for a party adverse in interest to his or her current or previous clients (*Burgess v. Wu*, 2003).

What Happens If I Am Asked to Testify in Court?

The court process begins for a fact or expert witness with the oath to tell the truth. There will then be a review of the witness's qualifications, which may or may not be contested by opposing counsel, and a determination by the judge about whether the witness can be accepted as an expert. The testimony of the witness then follows three steps: the examination in chief (also known as the direct examination), the cross-examination, and the re-examination (or redirect).

Preparing to Testify

It is natural to feel anxious about testimony in court and the most effective way to reduce anxiety and increase confidence is to prepare in advance. Prepare your testimony in consultation with the lawyer who called you as an expert, or if you are the defendant, with your own lawyer. You should ask questions regarding: 1) why you have been asked to testify; 2) what types of questions the lawyer calling you might ask on examination in chief; 3) what you might expect on cross-examination; 4) what controversial issues may arise from your résumé and how these can be addressed; and 5) what you should review prior to testimony, for example, your records, other reports, relevant literature (Ross, 1999). For instance, a common question in reviewing your résumé is: 'What is the basis of your expertise?' You should prepare in advance an answer to a query about what makes you an expert. Be very familiar with the case in question and ensure that you have read over all the notes carefully. You do not want to be surprised by a question regarding records that you should have read.

If you have never been to court before you may find it helpful to visit a courtroom to learn about the layout of the room, where you are expected to sit when testifying and when not testifying, and the general process of the court proceeding (Hoffman, 1997; Ross, 1999). Do not expect that it will follow the examples you have seen in TV courtroom dramas. Plan the route to the court in advance and ensure you arrive in plenty of time. You don't want to begin your testimony still sweating and panicked because you couldn't find a parking spot and had to run the last 10 blocks. Dress in business attire that is comfortable, conservative, and not overly expensive or flashy. The judge and jury need to be impressed with both your evidence and your credibility as assessed by the first impression you create.

Examination in Chief

The examination in chief, or direct examination, allows the lawyer who has called the witness to review evidence presented in a report (if there is one) and to present information necessary to his or her case through the process of asking the witness open-ended questions and eliciting responses (for example, who, what, when, why). The lawyer aims to create a record of the evidence in a logical and persuasive manner. Ideally, the lawyer and the witness will have discussed the examination in advance and therefore the process is relatively smooth and stress-free. Pointers for witnesses are found in Table 11.3 (Barsky, 1997; Ross, 1999; Thompson, 2004). During the process of examination, the witness may consult notes, but only after having requested permission to do so of the judge. This can be helpful to ensure that details such as dates are accurate. However, it must be noted that once notes have been admitted, the entire record can be open to examination by opposing counsel and to cross-examination.

An expert witness does need to be cognizant of social pressures to overextend their testimony, that is, go beyond what is known into the realm of speculation and advocacy (Wasyliw, Cavanaugh, and Rogers, 1985). The first pressure is the existence of a social problem in need of resolution. Experts can feel compelled to assist the courts in addressing a serious social issue, such as wife battering, by taking an advocacy role with a particular case, selecting supportive data, and ignoring non-supportive data. As discussed earlier, the multiple duties of ensuring community safety, seeking justice for a group, and seeking justice for an individual before the courts can exacerbate the dilemma of balancing advocacy with impartiality often faced by social work experts. A second issue is that, increasingly, social sciences and behavioural sciences are being accepted as explanations for behaviour. Experts must be cautious about stating with certainty that a psychological or social theory definitively explains a particular offence or the motivations of a parent seeking custody. The court's willingness to accept expert testimony as a means of dealing with complex situations entices the expert to go beyond what is truly evidence-based. Further, the adversarial process can move the expert into a polarized position, where they no longer offer a balanced view but become wedded to one viewpoint. These combined forces can cloud the distinction between legal issues and scientific knowledge, and they can pressure the expert to testify beyond the limits of their expertise. Such testimony does little to assist the courts or to bolster the credibility of the witness and support the cause he or she believes in.

Table 11.3   Pointers for Expert Witnesses

1. Tell the truth and always avoid exaggeration.
2. Acknowledge uncertainty when there is not a clear answer or scientific fact.
3. Convey professionalism and address all answers to the judge.
4. Understand the question and seek clarification as required.
5. Take your time and provide a considered answer.
6. Answer questions slowly, clearly, and concisely—do not ramble.
7. Do not act as an advocate or appear partisan.
8. Do not argue with counsel.
9. Remain composed, polite, and unemotional.
10. If you are wrong, admit it.
11. If you are certain, don't back down.

Cross-examination

Cross-examination has three main purposes: to obtain evidence useful to the opposing side's case; to test and discredit the witness by exposing inconsistencies, errors, and gaps; and to undermine the credibility of the witness (Thompson, 2004). During cross-examination, a lawyer is given more latitude by the courts to ask leading questions and control the witness. The goal is to ensure that potential biases presented by one side do not result in a miscarriage of justice. Reder and colleagues (1994) identify four techniques used in cross-examination of an expert witness: discrediting the witness; controlling the range of information; changing the meaning; and overgeneralization. Discrediting the witness could be through the use of personal questions such as asking a child welfare social worker whether she has children, or by suggesting that the expert's training, experience, or knowledge are substandard. Controlling range of information may include entering new information, for instance, 'If you knew . . . would it change your opinion?' Alternatively, the lawyer may request that only information related to a particular time period be considered, which compromises the facts on which the opinion evidence is based. Changing the meaning occurs when a particular event is put in a different light, such as 'maybe the parent was not abusing their child when the child's arm was wrenched, but rather was protecting him from oncoming traffic'. Overgeneralizing, such as 'Is it not true that children are better off living with their parents?' can lead to false conclusions regarding the case at hand. Experts should monitor their own emotional reactions to these types of cross-examination strategies, carefully consider their responses, and continue to focus on the case at hand and the evidence in the particular situation in question. Excellent books that provide strategies for testifying and managing cross-examination have been written by Brodsky (1999) and Gutheil and Simon (2002).

Re-examination or Redirect

Redirect is an opportunity for the lawyer who has called the witness to clarify points raised on cross-examination or further develop answers that could not be fully discussed during cross-examination. In this way, the lawyer can correct any distortions that may have occurred as a result of the nature of questioning during the cross-examination. No new issues can be raised at this point in the examination.

CASE EXAMPLES 1 and 2 REVIEWED

In summary, there are two main ways in which social workers may become involved with the courts regarding their clients (excluding the possibility that they may be the target of the action due to alleged negligence or malpractice—see Chapter 12). In the first case example, the social worker was treating an individual who became involved with the courts. In this case, the social worker may discover that his or her records are called into evidence, and he or she may be called to testify as a fact or expert witness. Realistically, clinical records are no longer the private domain of the social worker; rather, they are increasingly open to a variety of reviews. As such, they should be written with the expectation that they may be read by others and may become central to a legal battle. It is the ethical and legal responsibility of all social workers to maintain records that accurately reflect a client's situation and all contacts between the social worker and the client. These records should be clear, concise, and should focus on facts obtained from the client and other collateral sources. The social worker's opinion must be clearly differentiated and based on information gleaned about the individual client's situation, not based on pre-existing biases or assumptions. Finally, in the event that access of others to the record is made possible by a court order, the social worker must make every effort to ensure that confidentiality is maintained within the bounds of the law.

CASE EXAMPLES 1 and 2 REVIEWED *(Continued)*

A second situation in which social workers may interface with the courts is when they are retained as experts to assist the courts by providing an opinion on a particular matter. In these situations, social workers must follow ethical and legal guidelines of ensuring that they have provided a full assessment and that their opinion is grounded in both the facts of the case and scientific evidence that supports their opinions. They must ensure that during the process of examination and cross-examination in the courts, that they maintain their credibility, maintain their objectivity, and do not become polarized into an advocacy position that is no longer supported by the evidence at their disposal.

Key Terms

Affidavit
A sworn, written statement that provides information derived from direct knowledge that would otherwise be presented in a testimony; in some instances, second-hand knowledge can be used provided that it is clearly identified as such in the document

Court Report
A clinician or professional's written assessment and expert opinion based on well-researched clinical facts for a legal purpose

Cross-examination
When a witness is questioned by the opposing side to obtain useful evidence, to discredit the witness by exposing inconsistencies, errors, and gaps, and to undermine the credibility of the witness

Examination in Chief/Direct Examination
When a witness is called in court to review evidence in a report or to present information necessary to the lawyer's case

Expert Opinion
When a social worker is retained due to his or her professional qualifications to provide forensic evidence and offer an opinion based on research-supported theories and evidence regarding matters beyond the experience of the average layperson; the primary role is to serve as a consultant and educator of the court about matters the court knows little about

Re-examination/Redirect
The opportunity for the side who called the witness to clarify points raised on cross-examination or further develop answers that could not be fully discussed during cross-examination to correct any distortions that may have occurred; no new points can be raised at this point

Discussion Questions

1. What is a social worker's obligation to ensure the confidentiality of the clinical record and under what circumstances will the social worker be required to reveal the record?
2. What precautions should a social worker take in preparing clinical records in order to ensure that clients' rights are protected?
3. How might a social worker best prepare for a court appearance?
4. What are the ethical obligations of social workers when preparing assessments for the courts?

Relevant Legislation

Federal
Personal Information Protection and Electronic Documents Act, S.C. 2005, c. 5
http://laws.justice.gc.ca/en/p-8.6/
Privacy Act, S.C. 1985, c. P-21
http://laws.justice.gc.ca/en/P-21/

Alberta
Health Information Act, R.S.A. 2000, c. H-5
http://www.canlii.org/ab/laws/sta/h-5/
Personal Information Privacy Act, R.S.A. 2003, C-P6.5
http://pipa.alberta.ca/index.cfm?page=legislation/act/index.html

British Columbia
Freedom of Information and Protection of Privacy Act, R.S.B.C. 1996, c. 165
http://www.qp.gov.bc.ca/statreg/stat/F/96165_01.htm
Personal Information Act, 2003, c. 63
http://www.qp.gov.bc.ca/statreg/stat/P/03063_01.htm

Manitoba
Freedom of Information and Protection of Privacy Act, 1997, C-F175
http://web2.gov.mb.ca/laws/statutes/ccsm/f175e.php
Personal Health Information Act, S.M. 1997, c. 51
http://web2.gov.mb.ca/laws/statutes/ccsm/p033-5e.php

New Brunswick
Protection of Personal Information Act, 1998, P19.1
http://www.gnb.ca/0062/acts/acts/p-19-1.htm

Newfoundland and Labrador
Access to Information and Personal Privacy Act S.N.L. 2002, c. A1.1
http://assembly.nl.ca/Legislation/sr/statutes/a01-1.htm

Nova Scotia
Freedom of Information and Protection of Privacy Act, 1993, c. 5
http://www.gov.ns.ca/legislature/legc/statutes/freedom.htm

Ontario
Freedom of Information and Protection of Privacy Act, R.S.O. 1990, C-F31
http://www.e-laws.gov.on.ca/html/statutes/english/elaws_statutes_90f31_e.htm
Municipal Freedom of Information and Protection of Privacy Act, R.S.O.1992, C-32
http://www.efc.ca/pages/law/ontario/M.56.head.html
Personal Health Information Protection Act, R.S.O. 2004, c. 3
http://www.e-laws.gov.on.ca/html/statutes/english/elaws_statutes_04p03_e.htm

Prince Edward Island

Freedom of Information and Protection of Privacy Act, R.S.P.E.I. 1988, c. F-15.01

http://www.canlii.org/pe/laws/sta/f-15.01/

Quebec

An Act Respecting Access to Documents Held by Public Bodies and the Protection of Personal Information, R.S.Q. 1982, c. A-2.1

http://www2.publicationsduquebec.gouv.qc.ca/dynamicSearch/telecharge.php?type=2&file=/A_2_1/A2_1_A.html

Saskatchewan

Health Information Protection Act, S.S. 1999, c. H-0.021

http://www.canlii.org/sk/laws/sta/h-0.021/

Northwest Territories

Access to Information and Protection of Privacy Act, S.N.W.T. 1994, c. 20

http://www.canlii.org/nt/laws/sta/1994c.20/

Nunavut

Access to Information and Protection of Privacy Act, 1994, C-20

http://www.canlii.org/nt/laws/sta/1994c.20/

Yukon Territory

Access to Information and Protection of Privacy Act, R.S.Y. 2002, c. 1

http://www.canlii.org/yk/laws/sta/1/

References

Alexander, R. (1995), 'Social Workers and Immunity from Civil Lawsuits', *Social Work*, 40(5): 648–54.

Ames, N. (1999), 'Social Work Recording: A New Look at an Old Issue', *Journal of Social Work Education*, 35(2): 227–37.

Arboleda-Florez, J. and Deynaka, C. (1999), *Forensic Psychiatric Evidence* (Toronto: Butterworths).

Badding, N. (1989), 'Client Involvement in Case Recording', *Social Casework*, 70(9): 539–48.

Barsky, A. (1997), *Counsellors as Witnesses* (Aurora, ON: Aurora Professional Press).

Brodsky, S. (1999), *The Expert Witness* (Washington, DC: American Psychological Association).

Burgess v. Wu (2003), 68 O.R. (3d) 710.

Canadian Association of Social Workers (CASW) (1994), *Social Work Code of Ethics* (Ottawa: Canadian Association of Social Workers).

——— (2005a), *Social Work Code of Ethics* (Ottawa: Canadian Association of Social Workers).

——— (2005b), *Code of Ethics, Guidelines for Professional Practice* (Ottawa: Canadian Association of Social Workers).

Canadian Charter of Rights and Freedoms (1982), Part 1 of the Constitution Act, 1982, being Schedule B to the Canada Act 1982 (UK), 1982, c. 11.

Coady, N. (1993), 'The Worker-Client Relationship Revisited', *Families in Society*, 74: 291–8.

College of Physicians and Surgeons of Nova Scotia (2004), *A Physician's Guide to Medical Records* (accessed 21 November 2004 at http://www.cpsns.ns.ca/guidetomedrec.html#31).

College of Social Workers and Social Service Workers (2005), *Privacy Toolkit: Guide to the Personal Health Information Protection Act, 2004* (Toronto: College of Social Workers and Social Service Workers) (accessed at http://www.ocswssw.org/sections/membership_info/documents/PHIPA%20Toolkit.pdf).

Diamond, B. (1983), 'The Psychiatrist as Expert Witness', in J. Quen (ed.), *The Psychiatrist in the Courtroom: Selected Papers of Bernard L. Diamond* (Hillsdale, NJ: Analytic Press).

Edwards, R. and Reid, W. (1989), 'Structured Case Recording in Child Welfare: An Assessment of Social Workers' Reactions', *Social Work*, 34(1): 49–52.

Gelman, S. (1992), 'Risk Management through Client Access to Case Records', *Social Work*, 37(1): 73–9.

Gibbs v. Gibbs (1985), 1 W.D.C.P. 6 (Ont. S.C.).

Glancy, G., Regehr, C., and Bryant, A. (1998a), 'Confidentiality in Crisis: Part I–The Duty to Inform', *Canadian Journal of Psychiatry*, 43(12): 1001–5.

——— (1998b), 'Confidentiality in Crisis: Part II–Confidentiality of Treatment Records', *Canadian Journal of Psychiatry*, 43(12): 1006–11.

Gutheil, T. and Simon, R. (2002), *Mastering Forensic Psychiatric Practice: Advanced Strategies for the Expert Witness* (Washington, DC: American Psychiatric Association).

Hoffman, B. (1997), 'Courts and Torts: The Psychiatrist Preparing for Trial', *Canadian Journal of Psychiatry*, 42(6): 497–501.

Kagle, J. (1983), 'The Contemporary Social Work Record', *Social Work*, 28(2): 149–53.

—— (1984), 'Restoring the Clinical Record', *Social Work*, 29(1): 46–50.

—— (1993), 'Record Keeping: Directions for the 1990s', *Social Work*, 38(2): 197–203.

McInerney v. MacDonald (1992), 2 S.C.R. 138.

Mental Health Act, R.S.O. 1990, c. M7, ss. 29 (2) and (3).

National Association of Social Workers (NASW) (1999), *Code of Ethics* (Washington, DC: National Association of Social Workers).

Ontario College of Social Workers and Social Service Workers (OCSWSSW) (2000), *Code of Ethics and Standards of Practice* (Toronto: Ontario College of Social Workers and Social Service Workers).

P.(L.M.) v. F. (D.) (1994), 22 C.C.L.T. (2d) 312 (Ont. Gen. Div.).

R. v. Mills (1997), A.J. 891 (Alta. Ct. Q.B.).

R. v. Monahan (1994), 89 C.C.C. (3d) 402 (S.C.C.).

R. v. O'Connor (1995), 4 S.C.R. 411.

R. v. Olscamp (1994), 91 CCC (3d) 180 (Ont. Gen. Div.).

Reamer, R. (2005) 'Documentation in Social Work: Evolving ethical and risk-management standards', *Social Work*, 50(4): 325–34.

Reder, P., Lucey, C., and Fellow-Smith, E. (1994), 'Surviving Cross-examination in Court', *Journal of Forensic Psychiatry*, 4(3): 489–95.

Regehr, C. (2002), 'Record Keeping in Clinical Social Work Practice', in F. Turner (ed.), *Social Work Practice: A Canadian Perspective*, 2nd ed. (Toronto: Prentice-Hall).

—— and Antle, B. (1997), 'Coercive Influences: Informed Consent in Court Mandated Social Work Practice', Social Work, 42(3): 300–6.

——, Bryant, A., and Glancy, G. (1997), 'Confidentiality of Treatment for Victims of Sexual Violence', *The Social Worker*, 65(3): 137–45.

Rosner, R. (1984), *Principles and Practice of Forensic Psychiatry* (Boston: Chapman and Hall).

Ross, M. (1999), 'Effective Testifying, Fact Sheet' (Ottawa: Canadian Medical Protection Association).

Solomon, R. and Visser, L. (2005), *A Legal Guide for Social Workers* (Toronto: Ontario Association of Social Workers).

Statutes of Canada (1997), c. 30 (Bill C-46, 1996) An Act to Amend the Criminal Code.

Streat, Y. (1987), 'Case Recording in Children's Protective Services', *Social Casework*, 68(9): 553–60.

Tebb, S. (1991), 'Client-focused Recording: Linking Theory and Practice', *Families in Society*, 72(7): 425–32.

Thompson, R. (2004), 'Rules of Evidence and Preparing for Court', in N. Bala, J. Hornick, R. Vogl, R.J. Williams, and M. Zapf (eds), *Canadian Child Welfare Law: Children, Families and the State* (Toronto: Thompson Educational).

Wasyliw, O., Cavanaugh, J., and Rogers, R. (1985), 'Beyond the Scientific Limits of Expert Testimony', *Bulletin of the American Academy of Psychiatry and the Law*, 13(2): 147–57.

CHAPTER TWELVE

Liability for Social Workers

OBJECTIVES

- To identify legal forums in which social workers may be held accountable for their actions and inactions
- To review various duties of social workers and highlight potential grounds of liability
- To discuss ways that social workers may protect themselves from liability

CASE EXAMPLE

Shock waves rippled through the social work community in Canada when child welfare worker Angie Martin was charged with criminal negligence causing death in connection to the death of Jordan Heikamp. Jordan was born in Toronto on 18 May 1997 and he died five weeks later of chronic starvation, weighing just 4 pounds, 2 ounces. His mother, then 19, was estranged from her family, lived in shelters, and had no source of income. With the approval of their child welfare worker, Ms Martin, Jordan and his mother moved to a shelter for homeless women, where he slowly starved to death. After a seven-month preliminary hearing, Ms Martin's charges were discharged in 1997. Madam Justice Mary Hogan of the Ontario Court of Justice found that Ms Martin had a reasonable belief that Jordan was being monitored by medical personnel and shelter staff and that the shelter itself was an appropriate residence. She further indicated that while Ms Martin should have verified Ms Heikamp's claims about the care of her child, there was no evidence that 'Ms Martin's acts or omissions were a contributing cause of Jordan's death by chronic starvation' (*R. v. Heikamp and Martin*, 1999, p. 20). Two years later a coroner's inquest into Jordan's death highlighted problems in the system and yet ruled the death a homicide. Much of the press remained negative towards Ms Martin, the child welfare agency that employed her, and social workers as a group. One reporter concluded, 'They proved if nothing else, that while you can fool all of the social workers some of the time and some of the social workers all of the time, you can't snow the ordinary Joe [on the jury]' (Blatchford, 2001).

- What are the forums in which social workers accused of misconduct or professional negligence may be held liable?
- What are the grounds of liability for social workers in Canada?
- What protections exist for social workers?
- How might social workers protect themselves from liability?

What Are the Forums for Accountability?

Professional Discipline

Social work as a profession is regulated throughout Canada by provincial acts that: identify which professionals can use the designation of social worker or social service worker; define the responsibilities and scope of practice; specify which governing body regulates the profession; and ensure the competence of individual professionals. In each province (with the exception of Alberta, where social workers are covered under the Health Professions Act), the Act is specific to social workers (and in Ontario social workers and social services workers). In the Yukon, Northwest Territories, and Nunavut, one professional association, the Association of Social Workers in Northern Canada, binds the profession; however, there is no governing legislation to date nor any regulating body overseeing social work practice (Doucette, 2004). The specific nature of the governing acts for each province can be found in Table 12.1. In addition, in March 2007, Alberta, British Columbia, Manitoba, New Brunswick, Newfoundland, Nova Scotia, Ontario, Prince Edward Island, Quebec, and Saskatchewan entered into a Mutual Recognition Agreement on Labour Mobility for Social Workers in Canada which establishes the conditions under which a social worker registered in one Canadian jurisdiction can have his/her qualifications recognized in another Canadian jurisdiction that is a party to the agreement.

Each province has a mechanism by which members of the public can raise a concern or lodge a complaint against a registered social worker who has behaved unethically or provided incompetent service. These complaints may be reviewed by a disciplinary body and via a process specified by the legislation. For instance, in Alberta anyone who believes that they or someone they know has been harmed by a social worker may file a complaint with the Alberta College of Social Workers. The complaint must be submitted in writing and in most cases the registered social worker named in the complaint is notified and may be asked to respond in writing. The complaints director has 30 days to determine what action to take (ACSW, 2006). Complaint committees across the country generally have the option to: dismiss the complaint; attempt to resolve the matter informally; refer the matter for mediation; counsel the social worker; reprimand the social worker; require the person to undergo treatment or re-education; or refer the matter to a discipline committee (NSASW, 2007). Discipline committees generally include members of the public as well as registered social workers (see, for example, MIRSW, 2005). Sanctions that can be imposed by discipline committees include: revoking the right to practise; suspending the right to practise; imposing limitations on practice; reprimands; imposing a fine; publishing the findings; and charging the costs of the proceedings to the member (SASW, 2005).

Disciplinary hearings do not occur with great frequency. The New Brunswick Association reported three disciplinary hearings in 2006–7 involving a social worker having a sexual relationship with a client, a social worker asking a client to obtain drugs and then using the drugs with the client, and a social worker not keeping clear professional boundaries between professional and personal life (NBASW, 2007). In British Columbia since 2002 there have been only two citations issued for formal disciplinary hearings to be held and in each case the social worker resigned before the hearing was held. *The Saskatchewan Social Worker* reports only one discipline case between 2003 and 2009. The findings of disciplinary hearings may be reported to the public through publication (for example, the Saskatchewan Association has published findings with and without the members' names in the *Regina Leader Post*, the *Star Phoenix*, the *Moose Jaw Herald*, and the *Prince Albert Times*) or on provincial association websites (for example, Discipline Committee decision summaries on the Ontario College of Social Workers and Social Service Workers website), although, again, there are not large numbers of reported discipline cases in any jurisdiction.

Thus, as with other professions across the country, social workers may be subject to scrutiny on the basis of complaints made against them at the level of the professional college and these complaints may result in a variety of sanctions from revocation of the right to practise to reprimand or suggestions for improved practice.

Civil Liability

A second option available to those with complaints against a particular social worker or social work agency is seeking compensation for damages through the civil courts. Suits against social workers generally involve boundary violations, incompetence, failure to protect, or malicious prosecution actions by parents where child abuse has been alleged (these are discussed in greater detail later in the chapter). The grounds for initiating a civil action and the process of civil litigation are discussed extensively in Chapter 9. If a finding is made in favour of the plaintiff and against the defendant, in this case a social worker, the courts can order that damages be paid to the plaintiff. Damages are restitutionary in nature, designed to place the victim in the position he or she would have been in if the tort had not occurred. It is common for social workers and the agencies which they represent to both be sued in civil actions. However, although in such cases the worker and agency are often both found liable, in practice the agency (or its insurance company) will likely pay the damage award. Agencies are aware that it would be unfair and demoralizing to its staff if social workers were forced to personally pay the damage awards. In spite of the fact that workers employed by an agency or other organization will generally not have to personally satisfy damages awards, social workers who are sued will inevitably experience stress from the civil litigation process (Bernstein, Regehr, and Kanani, 2004).

Criminal Liability

In rare circumstances, criminal charges can be laid against social workers related to the duties that they perform. For example, criminal charges have been laid against child welfare social workers. The case of Angie Martin, previously described, resulted in the social worker being discharged from further criminal prosecution. Similarly, in 1982 the executive director, the social work supervisor, and a child protection social worker with Brockville Children's Aid Society were acquitted at trial of charges of child abandonment and exposure regarding a boy who was brutally beaten by his mother while under CAS supervision. In rendering his decision, His Honour Judge Newton considered the background of the case prior to CAS involvement, the services offered, the necessity of weighing competing factors of child protection and family preservation, and the worker's competence and dedication. He concluded that the Crown had failed to prove beyond a reasonable doubt that the conduct of the worker was so negligent as to constitute a reckless or callous disregard for the safety of the child (Bernstein, 1983). This case raised the threshold required for criminal prosecution of child welfare workers. Alexander and Alexander (1995), in their review of the US criminal prosecutions of caseworkers, found that of the less than a dozen reported cases across the United States, in only two were the workers actually convicted. Thus, it is rare for social workers to be criminally prosecuted and even less likely that they will be convicted.

Coroner's Inquests, Fatality Inquiries, and Public Inquiries

Coroners in Canada are mandated by provincial legislation (differentially called the Coroners Act, Fatalities Investigation Act, or the Fatalities Inquiries Act) to perform an investigation when a death occurs that meets specified criteria. For instance, under the Coroners Act in PEI the coroner must investigate when a death is the result of violence, misadventure, malpractice, or negligence, if it occurs in a jail or if it occurs in a hospital during an operation or within 24 hours of admission. The coroner can then call an inquest into the circumstances of the death at his or her discretion.

Table 12.1   Legislation Governing Social Work Practice

Province/Territory	Governing Legislation	Type of Regulation	Penalty	Governing Body	Discipline	Minister Responsible
British Columbia	Social Workers Act, S.B.C. 2008, C-31	Control over use of title 'registered social worker' and limited control over 'social worker' and voluntary private practice roster	Not more than $1,000 fine for inappropriate use of the title	British Columbia College of Social Workers	Inquiry Committee & Discipline Committee	Minister for Children and Family Development
Alberta	Health Professions Act, R.S.A. 2000, c. H-7	Control over use of title 'registered social worker' and 'clinical social worker'; mandatory registration for all social workers	Unspecified	Alberta College of Social Workers	Competence Committee, Complaints Director	Minister of Health and Wellness
Saskatchewan	The Social Workers Act, S.S. 1993, c. S-52.1	Control over title 'social worker'	1st offence—up to $2,000 2nd—up to $4,000 Each subsequent— up to $6,000 and/or imprisonment of up to 6 months	Saskatchewan Association of Social Workers	Discipline Committee	Minister of Social Services
Manitoba	The Manitoba Institute of Registered Social Workers Incorporation Act, R.S.M. 1990, c. 96	Voluntary registration and control of title 'registered social worker'	Fine of not less than $100 and not more than $200 and costs	Manitoba Institute of Registered Social Workers	Complaints Committee, Discipline Committee	None
Ontario	Social Work and Social Service Work Act, S.O. 1998, c. 31	Control over titles 'social worker', 'registered social worker', 'social service worker', and 'registered social service worker'	Fine of not more than $5,000 for first offence and not more than $10,000 for subsequent	Ontario College of Social Workers and Social Service Workers	Complaints Committee, Discipline Committee, Fitness to Practice Committee	Minister of Community and Social Services
Quebec	Représentation au Bureau de l'Ordre professionnel des travailleurs sociaux du Québec et sur la délimitation des régions électorales, Règlement sur la, R.Q. C-26, r. 188.2	'travailleur social/travailleuse sociale'	Fine of no more than $6,000 and no less than $600	Ordre professionnel des travailleurs sociaux du Québec	Professional Inspection Committee, Discipline Committee	Minister of Justice (one professional code for all professions in Quebec and the 'Office des professions' is responsible for overseeing its application under the Ministry of Justice)

Table 12.1   Legislation Governing Social Work Practice *(Continued)*

Province/ Territory	Governing Legislation	Type of Regulation	Penalty	Governing Body	Discipline	Minister Responsible
New Brunswick	New Brunswick Association of Social Workers Act, 1988	Regulation of practice and control over titles 'social worker' and 'registered sw'	1st offence, $500–$2,000 and costs, subsequent offences $1,000–$5,000 and costs and/or up to 6 months in prison	New Brunswick Association of Social Workers	Complaints Committee, Discipline Committee	Minister of Health and Community Services
Nova Scotia	Social Workers Act, S.N.S. 1993, c. 12	Regulation of practice and control over titles 'social worker' and 'registered sw'	1st fine of not less than $500 and costs, subsequent fine of not less than $1,000 and costs and/or up to 6 months in jail	Nova Scotia Association of Social Workers	Complaints Committee, Discipline Committee	None
Prince Edward Island	Social Work Act, R.S.P.E.I. 1988, Cap S-5	Regulation of practice and control over titles 'social worker' and 'registered sw'	A fine not to exceed $500	PEI Social Work Registration Board	Complaints Committee, Discipline Committee	Minister of Social Services and Seniors
Newfoundland and Labrador	Social Workers Association Act, S.N.L. 1992, c. S-18.1	Regulation of practice and control over titles 'social worker' and 'registered sw'	1st offence $500–$2,000 and costs, subsequent fine of not less than $1,000 and/ or 6 months in jail	Newfoundland and Labrador Association of Social Workers	Complaints Committee, Discipline Committee	Minister of Health and Community Services
Northwest Territories and Nunavut, Yukon	No governing legislation					

An inquest is a formal hearing into the events surrounding a death with the coroner acting in the position of chair of the proceedings and jury members hearing the evidence and making recommendations designed to prevent similar deaths in the future. Though not legally binding, these recommendations may have local or province-wide impact (Regional Forensic Unit, 2005).

Public inquiries (sometimes called royal commissions, as a remnant of Canada's British heritage, or provincial task forces) began with the federal Inquiries Act passed by Parliament in 1868 (CBC, 2004). Inquiries are called by a governmental body to address an issue of concern to the public. In these situations, a chair and several committee members are appointed, various people are called to make submissions on the issue, and recommendations are made back to the body convening the inquiry. Again, these are not legally binding.

Recently there has been a great deal of attention paid to inquests and public inquiries related to deaths associated with health and social services and they have emerged as powerful political forces. Examples are plentiful in child welfare services. In April 1996 the Ontario Child Mortality Task Force was established in response to five coroner's inquests that were conducted to examine the deaths of children who were known to children's aid societies (Buck, 1998). The more than 400 recommendations emanating from the inquests and 16 resulting from the Ontario Child Mortality Task Force resulted in the provincial government initiating a Child Welfare Reform Agenda. In New Brunswick, stung by suggestions that child-protection officials failed to save a little girl from neglectful parents, the New Brunswick government, in 1997, created an independent committee to review deaths in the child-protection system (Morris, 1997). Specific expressed concerns were that social workers had become too family-oriented and tried at all costs to keep the family together rather than put the needs of children first. These inquiries resulted in the production of the Gove Report on child welfare reform (Brunet, 1998).

Inquests and public inquiries do not only target systemic changes, they also look at the actions and responsibilities of individual workers, at times with devastating consequences. The emotional costs of these inquiries on firefighters and paramedics (Regehr et al., 2003a), police officers (Regehr et al., 2003b) and child welfare social workers (Regehr et al., 2002) have been previously documented. In addition to emotional consequences, however, there can also be legal consequences. For example, although Quebec is the only jurisdiction where a coroner can recommend that criminal charges be laid, following a coroner's inquest into the death of a child in a hospital, two nurses in Ontario were criminally charged, based on the evidence presented at the inquest (*Maclean's*, 2001).

It is important to know that inquests and inquiries are not courts and therefore the processes and safeguards in place in a court process do not apply. A coroner has wide powers regarding inspecting records or writings related to the deceased person and can seize anything that he or she has reasonable grounds to believe is relevant to the investigation. The rules of evidence are less structured than that in a civil or criminal court and information that would not be admissible in court can be considered in the inquest. Jury members are permitted to ask questions. Others outside the process (such as family members of the deceased) can be given standing and are entitled to legal representation. These individuals or their lawyers can then question witnesses, cross-examine witnesses, or make submissions.

Workers whose cases are being reviewed in an inquest or inquiry should be aware that while they do not require legal representation, it is often advisable considering that criminal charges or civil action may follow. Depending on the degree of involvement, a worker may want to ensure that the agency seeks standing or considers seeking standing themselves. Further, workers should not rely solely on the assistance of the lawyer hired by the agency or organization for which they work because that lawyer is required to protect the organization's interests, which may or may not be in keeping with the interests of the social worker on the case.

Duties of Social Workers and Potential Grounds of Liability

The Duty to Protect Children

In Chapter 4 on child-protection law we discussed at length the duty to report child abuse. To summarize, in all jurisdictions throughout Canada there is a positive duty to report suspected child abuse or neglect. Nevertheless, there are many children who continue to suffer maltreatment after their plight becomes known to a child-protection agency. In such cases the child welfare social worker can be held civilly or criminally liable for inadequately protecting the child by failing to accept a report for investigation, failing to conduct an adequate investigation, or failing to place a child in protective custody (Besharov, 1983).

Civil lawsuits of this kind are most often based on the tort of negligence. Essentially, the complainant would state that the worker owed a duty to the child to protect him or her from further harm, that the worker responded in a substandard fashion, and as a result the child was injured. Two cases in the Canadian courts addressing this issue have reached different conclusions. In one, the social worker was not seen as liable, and in the other, it was held that the social worker did breach the duty of care. In the Alberta case of *D. (S.) v. S. (D.W.)* (1994), the plaintiff sued her social worker, alleging that she had been regularly sexually assaulted in her parents' home. Although she did not tell the defendant social worker of the assaults until after they had stopped and she had left the home, she contended that the social worker should have investigated her case more fully and instituted protective measures to remove her from the home or to ensure that she be safe from abuse. The court held that there was no cause of action against the social worker. However, in the Manitoba case, *A.J. v. Cairnie* (1999),

the plaintiff alleged that she had been sexually abused by her stepfather when she was a child and that Cairnie, the defendant social worker, had failed to take steps to remove her from the abusive situation. A.J. had spoken to Cairnie about the abuse and was subsequently beaten by her stepfather and threatened that she would be killed if she spoke to the worker again. Cairnie called on a couple of occasions and A.J. lied out of fear, stating that everything was fine. The abuse continued to escalate to the point of regular rapes. Another social worker then phoned A.J. and she admitted she was still being abused. A.J. was then immediately taken into care. The court found that Cairnie owed A.J. a duty of care and that she breached that duty by failing to apprehend as a reasonable social worker would have done. Damages were assessed in the amount of $116,800. Cairnie's liability was apportioned at 25 per cent. However, it appears that the more costly lawsuits in both Canada and the United States have not occurred as a result of failure to remove a child from an abusive home but rather when there has been a failure to assure the safety of children once in placement. In these cases however, the focus has been on offending organizations and not individual social workers.

Even more chilling than the civil suits with large monetary damages is the possibility of criminal charges that, upon conviction, can in some cases, such as criminal negligence causing death, carry the possibility of life imprisonment. As stated earlier, cases involving such issues to date have not resulted in the conviction of social workers.

The duty to protect children from harm is often challenging for social workers to balance with respect for parental rights. Indeed, while the provincial laws give child-protection caseworkers the authority to intervene into the privacy of the family, the need to protect children from abuse or neglect is not a justification for unnecessarily violating or ignoring parental rights. The inherent conflict in fulfilling the duty to protect children from harm was highlighted in Canada by Lord Nicholls when he stated:

Cruelty and physical abuse are notoriously difficult to prove. The task of social workers is usually anxious and often thankless. They are criticized for not having taken action in response to warning signs which are obvious enough when seen in the clear light of hindsight. Or they are criticized for making applications based on serious allegations which, in the event, are not established in court. Sometimes, whatever they do, they can not do right (*Re H. (Minors)*, 1996, p. 592).

We have discussed circumstances where social workers could be held liable for failing to fulfill their duty to protect children from harm. On the flipside of that coin, social workers who intervened to protect children from harm have also been held liable for violations of parental rights including slanderous investigations, wrongful removal of children, and malicious prosecution (Besharov, 1983). Of the five Canadian cases in which child-protection workers have faced civil suits for violating parental rights, in three cases the social workers (in British Columbia and Nova Scotia) were found not liable, and in two, social workers (in Ontario) were found liable.

In *Farchels v. British Columbia (Minister of Social Services and Housing)* (1988), the defendant social worker was accused of wrongful apprehension, detention, and slander based on her decision to bring a child into care. On the day in question, the mother presented at an emergency room in an agitated state. She refused to talk to the emergency room social worker, began yelling, fled from the hospital with her son, and was eventually cornered by police. The child welfare worker, who had previous contacts with the family and information from the family physician that the mother was delusional and mentally disturbed, concluded that the child was in need of protection. Three months later the child was returned to the mother. The court dismissed the cause of action, holding that the social worker had an honest belief that the child was in need of protection, acted in good faith, and was perfectly justified.

In his decision, His Honour Judge Shaw quoted section 23 of the British Columbia Child and Family Services Act (1990) that states: 'No person is personally liable for anything done or omitted in good faith in the exercise or purported exercise of powers conferred by this Act.' The judgment that the social workers should not be held liable when acting in good faith was similarly upheld in *G. (A.) v. British Columbia (Superintendent of Family and Child Services)* (1989), where a mother, father, and seven children brought an action against the defendant social workers in a child welfare agency for negligence for apprehending the children based on what were later determined to be unfounded allegations of child abuse. The court held that there was no basis for liability because even though the social workers made significant errors of judgment, they did not fail to carry out their duty to consider the matter nor did they reach a decision so unreasonable as to show failure to do their duty. In *Ashford v. Children's Aid Society of Cape Breton-Victoria* (2008), the plaintiff was a mother of several children and had a lengthy history of protection proceedings with the defendant children's aid society. She brought an action for six million dollars in damages for negligence, abuse of position, abuse of process, malicious prosecution, failing fiduciary duty, defamation of character, and child endangerment. The claims were dismissed for disclosing no reasonable cause of action.

In contrast, in the two Ontario cases the social workers were found liable. In *B. (D.) v. Children's Aid Society of Durham* (1996), an Anglican minister was accused by his ex-wife of sexually abusing their two daughters. The child welfare social worker conducted an assessment following which she sought court intervention to restrict D.B.'s access to his children. D.B. was later cleared of the allegations and awarded full custody. The court held the social worker liable for negligence in conducting a biased, unfair, and unbalanced investigation that fell below the standard of care expected of a professional social worker. D.B. was awarded $60,000. In the case of *W. (D.)*

v. W. (D.) (1998), the child-protection worker received a report of sexual abuse from a mother. The worker spoke to the daughter who had been allegedly abused and then reported the incident to the police. Charges were laid against the father and then later withdrawn. He brought an action against the social worker for negligence, malicious prosecution, wrongful arrest, false imprisonment, abuse of process, defamation, and infringement of constitutional rights. The judge held that there was evidence to support the allegations that the caseworker had formed a biased opinion, was not acting in good faith, and was thus negligent. However, no damages were awarded.

In 2007 the Supreme Court of Canada also considered the issue of whether once a child has been apprehended the organization and employees into whose care the child has been placed owes an unrecognized legal duty of care to the family of the child that they have been ordered to protect (*D. (B.) v. Children's Aid Society of Halton (Region)*, 2007). In this case the child was apprehended and placed in a foster home. The child subsequently attempted suicide on three occasions, was placed in a secure treatment facility and made a permanent ward of the Crown. The family filed a claim seeking damages for negligence, arguing that negligence in the child's treatment caused the child not to be reintegrated into the family. The court held that the child's best interest takes primacy over parental rights and to impose a duty of care on the relationship between a family and court-ordered service provider creates the potential for 'serious and significant' conflict with the service provider's duty to promote the best interest, protection, and well-being of children in their care. Madam Justice Abella stated (at paras. 50, 51, and 64):

> If a corresponding duty is also imposed with respect to parents, service providers will be torn between the child's interests on the one hand, and parental expectations which may be unrealistic, unreasonable, unrealizable on the other. This tension creates the potential for a chilling effect on social workers, who may hesitate to act in pursuit of the child's

best interests for fear that their approach could attract criticism—and litigation—from the family. They should not have to weigh what is best for the child on the scale with what would make the family happiest, finding themselves choosing between aggressive protection of the child and a lawsuit from the family. I appreciate that the family of a child in care would, understandably, generally wish for the return of the child. But that cannot always be accommodated.

. . .

Child protection work is difficult, painful and complex. Catering to a child's best interest in this context means catering to a vulnerable group at its most vulnerable. Those who do it, do so knowing that protecting the child's interests often means doing so at the expense of the rest of the family. Yet their statutory mandate is to treat the child's interests as paramount. They must be free to execute this mandate to the fullest extent possible.

The Duty to Protect Adults from Harm

The duty to protect adults from harm encompasses two key areas: warning third parties of harm and protection from adult abuse.

Warning Third Parties of Harm

Chapter 7 on serious mental illness and the law discussed the duty to protect family members from harm when a professional has reason to believe that their client may harm another person. The positive duty to warn was established in Canada in the Supreme Court of Canada case of *Smith v. Jones* (1999), where a patient of a psychiatrist disclosed that he intended to rape and murder prostitutes in Vancouver. In that case, the Supreme Court ruled that danger to the public overrules confidentiality, enshrining the duty to protect when the following three elements are in place: 1) risk to a clearly identified person or group of persons is determined; 2) the risk of harm includes bodily injury, death, or serious psychological harm; 3) there is an element of imminence, creating a sense of urgency (Chaimowitz and Glancy, 2002). This directive to protect others from harm is also clearly identified in the ethical guidelines of the Canadian Association of Social Workers (CASW, 2005b) that state: 'Social workers who have reason to believe that a client intends to harm another person are obligated to inform both the person who may be at risk (if possible) and the police' (section 1.6.1). Therefore, social workers have a duty to warn and protect the intended victim(s) of a client or patient who discloses the intent to harm others. Failure to do so could result in sanctions at the professional disciplinary level or in civil or criminal courts.

Adult Abuse

Knowledge of the abuse of adults is another area involving the duty to protect. Much of the legislative effort in Canada for protecting adults has focused on those who are incompetent to make decisions regarding health care or those who are vulnerable to financial abuse (see Chapter 6 for a discussion of substitute decision-making). A different issue arises in situations where adults are physically abused or neglected by others, particularly family members. The Social Work Code of Ethics (CASW, 2005a) advises social workers with knowledge of an adult who is being abused to take action consistent with their provincial/territorial legislation, recognizing that not all provinces have mandatory reporting of adult abuse. The Atlantic Provinces in Canada have led the way in enacting adult protection legislation that is heavily influenced by child welfare models and includes such elements as legal powers of investigation and mandatory reporting (Gordon, 2001; McDonald, Collins, and Dergal, 2005). Nova Scotia and Newfoundland have a general mandatory reporting requirement. The Adult Protection Act of Nova Scotia (1989), for instance, states: 'Every person who has information, whether or not it is confidential or privileged, indicating that an adult is in need of protection and who fails to report that information to the Minister is guilty

of an offence under this Act.' Manitoba requires mandatory reporting by service providers under the Vulnerable Persons Living with a Disability Act (1993). Alberta requires mandatory reporting of abuse against a client under the Protection for Persons in Care Act (2000). British Columbia, Prince Edward Island, New Brunswick and the Yukon have voluntary reporting. The PEI Adult Protection Act (1988) states: 'Any person who has reasonable grounds for believing that a person is, or is at serious risk of being, in need of assistance or protection *may* [emphasis added] report the circumstances in such a manner and to such authority or person as may be designated by the Minister.' Thus, the requirement and the right to report the abuse of adults varies across the country. Further, while Nova Scotia and Prince Edward Island have legislation pertaining to all adults, Newfoundland specifies only neglected adults, Manitoba specifies vulnerable adults living with a disability, and New Brunswick limits intervention to those who are elderly or disabled.

The Duty to Maintain Professional Boundaries

The responsibility of social workers and other professionals to maintain clear boundaries in the professional relationship is based on the imbalance in power between clients and professionals and the manner in which the therapeutic relationship may undermine the ability of clients to make decisions in their own best interests when such interests are in contradiction to what is being suggested by the therapist (Regehr and Antle, 1997). The power held by professionals is acknowledged in the legal concept of fiduciary relationships. 'Fiduciary relationships emanate from the trust that clients must place in professionals. Because professionals have knowledge and use techniques that require special expertise, clients must trust workers to act in their best interest' (Kutchins, 1991, p. 106). As a consequence, those with a fiduciary duty are held to a higher standard in interpersonal relationships with clients and are solely responsible for maintaining the professional boundary. This concept is exemplified in the Social Worker Code of Ethics (CASW, 2005a), which includes the following statements:

> 2.2.1 Social workers do not exploit the relationship with a client for personal benefit, gain, or gratification.
>
> 2.4.1 Social workers take care to evaluate the nature of dual and multiple relationships to ensure that the needs and welfare of clients are protected.
>
> 2.5.1 Social workers avoid engaging in physical contact with clients when there is a possibility of harm to the client as a result of the contact.
>
> 2.6.1 Social workers do not engage in romantic relationships, sexual activities, or sexual contact with clients, even if such contact is sought by clients.
>
> 2.6.2 Social workers who have provided psychotherapy or in-depth counselling do not engage in romantic relationships, sexual activities, or sexual contact with former clients.
>
> 2.6.3 Social workers do not engage in romantic relationships, sexual activities, or sexual contact with students whom they are supervising or teaching.
>
> 2.7.1 Social workers do not sexually harass any person.

Over the past two decades, the professional literature has devoted considerable attention to the issue of sexual exploitation of patients by health care practitioners. Considering the rates of reported incidents of sexual exploitation of patients, this attention certainly appears justified. Various studies conducted in the 1970s and 1980s utilizing self-report surveys of professionals found that 10 per cent of psychiatrists (Kardener, Fuller, and Mensh, 1973), 11 per cent of male psychologists, 2 per cent of female psychologists (Holroyd and Brodsky, 1977), and 3.8 per cent of male social workers (Gechtman, 1989) admitted to sexual contact with a patient. Obtaining accurate estimates of the number

of social workers who have engaged in sexual behaviour with clients is difficult with most self-report studies yielding consistently low rates of social worker sexual involvement with clients. In a recent study, Hutchinson Mittendorf and Schroeder (2004) asked 144 social workers in private-care settings if they ever had a client who reported having sexual contact with a previous therapist. Approximately half answered in the affirmative and identified the professions of the exploitive therapists as social workers (21 per cent), psychiatrists (21 per cent), psychologists (21 per cent), clergy (21 per cent), licensed professional counsellors (10 per cent), and unspecified other professionals (6 per cent). Fewer than one-third of the respondents reported the exploitive therapist to a licensing body or other authority. Further, over one-third of the respondents reported knowing other social workers who had sexual contact with a client. Several findings of professional misconduct have been made against social workers regarding sexual relationships with clients. It is common for other complaints to accompany the complaint about sexual boundary violations. For instance, the *Alberta Advocate* (ACSW, 2002) reports the case of a social worker, Mr Smith, who was treating a client for childhood sexual abuse. One month after the end of therapy, Mr Smith developed a personal relationship with the client; one year later this relationship became sexual, and six months after that the former client and Mr Smith began to live common-law. Other complaints included that Mr Smith had improperly documented case notes, took client calls concerning professional relationships in his home, that his files were not safe from others, and that others therefore had access to client information. A finding of misconduct was made against Mr Smith and as a result he was suspended from practice for six months, ordered to attend counselling, reprimanded, required to have supervision for 18 months following his suspension, ordered to pay costs, and have the decision published. Mr Smith did not comply with some of the sanctions and consequently also had his licence suspended for five years (ACSW, 2003a).

Similarly, in a Nova Scotia case, a registered social worker, Mr Campkin, was found in violation of professional ethics for engaging in a sexual relationship with a client, giving her advice with regard to the disposition of her matrimonial assets, obtaining money from the client, and upon her moving to another province, providing her with his résumé in the hope that she would help him find a job in that province (NSASW, 2004). In yet another case, a social worker, Mr Cunningham, provided his home phone number to clients, made personal comments about a client's body, sent an intimate letter to a client, arranged for a client to be sheltered in the home of his friend and in his own home, and continued a personal relationship with the client after termination of his employment (ACSW, 2003b). He was found guilty of boundary violations, harassment, using EMDR treatment without proper competence, failing to maintain proper records, and failing to maintain confidentiality.

Boundary-violation cases are not dealt with solely by professional discipline committees; they also frequently find their way into the court system. Examples of these cases involve doctors (*Mussani v. The College of Physicians and Surgeons of Ontario*, 2003; *R. v. Orpin*, 2002; *A.B. v. College of Physicians and Surgeons of Prince Edward Island*, 2001; *T.C. v. Scott*, 1997), psychologists (*N.C. v. Blank*, 1998), nurses (*Bennet v. Registered Nurses' Assn. of Manitoba*, 2003; *Carruthers v. College of Nurses of Ontario*, 1996), and social workers (*J. Doe v. New Brunswick Minister of Family and Community Services*, 2004). For instance, the Elizabeth Fry Society terminated a social worker's employment because she refused to end her relationship with her boyfriend who was a client of the agency. The social worker appealed to the courts, claiming wrongful dismissal by her employer (*Smith v. Kamloops and District Elizabeth Fry Society*, 1996). The trial judge held that the dismissal was justified.

The Duty to Maintain Confidentiality

The legal obligations on social workers to maintain confidentiality and privacy of patient information have been discussed in Chapters 6 and 11.

In addition to the statutory obligations, both the Canadian Association of Social Workers' (2005a) and North American Association of Social Workers' (1999) codes of ethics also well establish the duty to maintain confidentiality and privacy. The duty to hold information received from or about a patient in confidence arises as part of a fiduciary relationship between a practitioner and a patient. As discussed, the social worker may be authorized or obligated by law to disclose confidential information in the context of criminal proceedings, to warn third parties of harm, or to protect the public interest (Regehr, Glancy, and Bryant, 1998). However, disclosure of confidential client information outside the grounds mandated by law are actionable under statute as professional misconduct. In Canada, there has traditionally been no tort of breach of privacy, and breach of confidentiality was actionable under common law through related actions such as nuisance, trespass, libel, slander, defamation, assault, battery, and breach of contract (Marshall and Von Tigerstorm, 1999). With the advent of privacy legislation, breach of confidentiality may now be actionable as a cause of action in and of itself.

In recent years new challenges to confidentiality have arisen with the advent of online communications, electronic health records, and increasing use of e-health. Data from Statistics Canada indicates that almost three-quarters (73 per cent), or 19.2 million Canadians aged 16 and older, used the Internet for personal reasons in 2007. Almost all (96 per cent) of persons aged 16 to 24 in Canada went online, yet even 29 per cent of those over the age of 65 used the Internet in 2007 (Statistics Canada, 2008). Therefore, the Internet offers opportunities for improving access to counselling interventions to a larger and more diverse segment of the population (Recupero and Rainey, 2006; Bell, 2007; Postel, de Haan, and De Jong, 2007). Kanani and Regehr (2003) provide a more complete discussion of issues relating to e-therapy that are beyond the scope of this chapter. Briefly, however, there are several limits to confidentiality in the online world and these can be distilled into two primary areas of risk: access during transmission and access at the therapist and client end. The Internet relies on the electronic copying of information for transmission and this creates the possibility of interception at many points (Elleven and Allen, 2004). Regular email correspondence can be easily snooped and intercepted by hackers satisfying their voyeuristic curiousity, by Internet service providers, or even by an employer if the email is being received at work. In addition, with a slip of the finger a client or a therapist may accidentally send a confidential email to an unintended recipient. Further, because people regularly share computing resources, email communications can be easily accessed by a member of the therapist's staff or the client's family at home. Even if people attempt to destroy messages, they may not be aware that deleting files from a computer's hard drive means that the space previously occupied by the file is made available to be written over, but until the disk space is used the file may still be recovered.

Encryption software deals with many of the issues related to interception of messages. However, in contrast to traditional therapy where confidentiality is the duty and responsibility of the social worker, in e-therapy the client must assume some responsibility for confidentiality maintenance by taking proactive measures to protect information held within his or her computer. Therefore, the social worker will have a duty to maintain confidentiality of the information received from the client, but the confidentiality responsibility will have to be shared between social worker and client. Accordingly, liability for social workers engaging in e-therapy may arise by a direct breach of the confidentiality duty or through breach of informed consent for failing to inform the client of his or her confidentiality burden.

In addition, social workers have the same obligations with respect to confidentiality of electronic health records and through the provision of e-health as they do when using paper records or providing more traditional types of therapies. They have an obligation to protect the privacy, security, and confidentiality of information that is entrusted to them. For example, social workers must take reasonable measures to safeguard health information through administrative means (such as policy development, ensuring access on a need to know basis only), technical means (such as passwords and use of encryption as discussed above), and physical measures (such as locked areas).

The Duty to Maintain Competence

The Canadian Code of Ethics requires that social workers practice within their areas of competence. Social workers must 'demonstrate due care for client's interests and safety by limiting professional practice to areas of demonstrated competence' (CASW, 2005a, p. 8). In addition to acquiring a level of competence in the practice modality chosen, the social worker must also carry out his or her professional duties and obligations with integrity and objectivity. An aspect of such integrity is a social worker's appropriate declaration of his or her expertise: 'Social workers do not claim formal social work education in an area of expertise or training solely by attending a lecture, demonstration, conference, workshop or similar teaching presentation' (CASW, 2005b, section 7.1.4). Thus, in order to provide a particular client service free of professional misconduct, social workers must be competent in their chosen practice modality and have sufficient education to declare their expertise. The New Brunswick Association of Social Workers issued a decision on 21 June 2004 against a social worker in a health facility for failing to maintain an acceptable level of knowledge and skill to meet the standards of practice of the profession (NBASW, 2004). Further, as noted earlier, in an Alberta case, a social worker was found to be incompetent for using EMDR treatment without proper training (ACSW, 2003b).

In addition, under the common law, competence requires the social worker to render services to the standard of care generally accepted in the profession. For example, S.T. v. Gaskell (1997) was a civil case where a woman who had been receiving counselling from a social worker for sexual abuse issues brought a malpractice action against the social worker. The woman stated that the counselling services were negligently provided, causing her to go out of control and enter into a period of self-destructive behaviour, which included criminal acts, alcoholism, drug abuse, and suicidal depression. In the end she was involved in a motor vehicle accident while intoxicated which resulted in her losing the potential for employment as a constable. The judge dismissed the action because the social worker's conduct did not fall below standards as articulated by other practitioners in the community.

The Duty to Act in a Manner Becoming of a Social Worker

The duty to act in a manner becoming of a social worker generally requires that social workers follow the ethical standards of their profession and of the organizations for whom they work. This is being used as a catch-all category to include a variety of infractions that have resulted in disciplinary decisions being brought against social workers by their professional licensing bodies, such as failure to keep records (ACSW, 2004), dishonesty in filing expense claim forms (ACSW, 2004), and misrepresenting oneself as a registered social worker (SASW, 2004).

What Are the Legal and Statutory Protections for Social Workers?

Child protection has been one of the primary areas for civil and criminal actions against social workers and is thus a logical area to discuss and describe the legal and statutory protections for social workers.

There has been wide criticism that child-protection caseworkers are being unfairly blamed for a societal problem with no immediate solutions (Alexander and Alexander, 1995; Davies et al., 1999). Child-protection work is difficult and workers are well aware of the consequence of making a wrong decision. However, the system

is based on the ability of the workers to exercise discretion and make decisions based on available information in high-stress situations. Therefore, it is argued that the law holding workers responsible for what they cannot prevent raises an inherently stressful responsibility to an unattainable and morale destroying level of accountability.

Most provincial legislatures in Canada acknowledge this and have therefore instituted statutory protections against the civil liability of child-protection workers. For example, section 15(6) of Ontario's Child and Family Services Act (1990) reads as follows: 'No action shall be instituted against an officer or employee of a society for an act done in good faith in the execution or intended execution of the person's duty or for an alleged neglect or default in the execution in good faith of the person's duty.' This is referred to as an immunity provision. Immunity shields a person from liability and may be either absolute or qualified. The immunity from civil liability provided above for child-protection caseworkers is a form of qualified immunity called 'good faith' (AFSCME, 1999). Good faith suggests that a worker acted on his or her best judgment and knowledge by seeking out the most positive outcome for all parties based on an honest belief that the action taken was necessary. Good faith may accommodate errors of judgment but it will not protect practice that was biased, vengeful, or indifferent (Holder, 1984). Thus, the legislature has provided outright protection to social workers while still holding them accountable for egregious malpractice.

The effect of this protection of good-faith decisions for or against apprehension is that workers should be able to focus on making professional decisions in good conscience instead of making decisions based on the risk of liability. This was recently underlined by the court in a case against a child welfare worker (G. (A.) v. British Columbia (Superintendent of Family and Child Services), 1989) where the judge quoted an earlier decision as follows: 'Where Parliament confers a discretion . . . [t]hen there may, and almost certainly will, be errors of judgment in exercising such discretion and Parliament cannot have intended that members of the public should be entitled to sue in respect of such errors.' Further, in *D. (B.) v. British Columbia (Superintendent of Family and Child Services)* (1997), the British Columbia Court of Appeal held:

> The theme running through the important cases in this area is the difficulty facing those who work with disturbed children. Decisions have to be made about care when outcome is unpredictable. It is too easy to say when things turn out badly that it was the fault of the person who made the judgment. Social workers should not be so afraid of making a mistake that they can not do their job properly. The statutory immunity is intended to protect workers in the field so their judgments will be focused on child welfare and not their exposure to liability.

Thus, the Canadian legislature and the courts have taken a social work–friendly approach to accountability by not only respecting the expertise that underlies discretionary decision-making in general but also by undertaking a contextual analysis that appreciates the dynamics of child-protection practice. It is important to note, however, that 'immunity does not prevent a lawsuit being filed against a professional' (Myers, 2001, p. 46). Rather, it merely provides a means by which the defendant social worker can request to have the case dismissed.

In areas where statutory immunity is not provided, social workers are nevertheless protected under the common law so long as they deliver services to the standard of care expected in the profession (that is, what a reasonable social worker would do). Further, in circumstances of child protection, the Supreme Court of Canada case *D. (B.) v. Children's Aid Society of Halton (Region)* (2007) discussed earlier has established that no duty of care is owed to a family of a child in care and thus there is no basis for claims of negligence. This case has been interpreted to indicate a 'blanket immunity for care providers performing their statutorily defined responsibilities' (*Ashford v. Children's Aid Society of Cape Breton-Victoria*, 2008, para. 20).

The constructs of good faith and the provision of services that are consistent with acceptable standards of practice within the profession are common principles of law. Insofar as social workers provide services and make decisions within this basis, they are unlikely to be found liable. However, when social workers fail to follow these principles, the client has a right to hold the worker accountable for the failure.

How Can Social Workers Protect Themselves from Liability?

Social workers' increased exposure to liability is an indicator of their increased professional status, visibility, and sphere of responsibility. Signs of a recognized profession include consumers with expectations of providers and providers' accountability for their professional behaviour (Houston-Vega, Nuehring, and Daguio, 1996). The profession has arrived. While no professional can ever be completely immune to liability, social workers can practice in a manner that reduces the risk of liability and prosecution. What follows are some general guidelines for social work practice.

Complying with Ethical Standards and Applicable Laws

The first way in which social workers can protect themselves is also the most obvious: that is, providing services in a manner that complies with all legal obligations and the ethical guidelines of the profession. Acting in an ethical manner, exercising good faith, complying with legal requirements, and delivering service in accordance with the standards of the profession are key factors. When grey areas emerge or concerns arise about one's own practice, it is necessary to seek consultation with colleagues, the governing college, or legal counsel. Such issues can arise regarding confidentiality, the capacity of clients to consent, and the duty to warn and protect.

Maintaining Competence

Social workers must demonstrate sound practice skills based on accepted theories and standards of practice. This requires not only that they successfully complete required degrees and diplomas, but also that they continuously upgrade skills and knowledge. Increasingly, it is required that practice follow evidence-based guidelines. Evidence-based practice is the conscientious, explicit, and judicious use of current best evidence in making decisions about the care of individual clients. It involves integrating individual practice expertise with the best available external evidence based on systematic research (Sackett et al., 1997). It is not expected that individual practitioners will be able to conduct reviews in all the areas that they practice and thus evidence-based practice reviews are increasingly available through journals and online sources such as the Cochrane Collaboration (which focuses more on medical treatments) and the Campbell Collaboration (for social science reviews). Universities and colleges also offer evidence-based practice updates in continuing education offerings.

In addition, as social workers enter new areas of practice, it is incumbent upon them to obtain training and education. An example of this, discussed earlier in this chapter, is e-therapy where, as in many new areas of practice, few educational opportunities exist. Social workers who learn new therapies solely through seminars and conferences may not have sufficient training to declare an expertise in this modality and thus may be held liable. Social workers practising in new areas such as e-therapy should lobby for the development of courses and certificates through established social work programs.

Careful Documentation

Thorough documentation allows social workers to maintain a record of their clinical assessment and clinical interventions in order to assist with ongoing work in the case and in order to clearly communicate their opinions, findings, and interventions to other members of the team. In addition, careful records can be the key to ensuring that practice decisions were well considered and adequate measures were taken to ensure the safety and well-being of clients and others in the face of possible legal action. Elements of clinical records are discussed at length in Chapter 11.

Obtaining Collateral Information

Social workers will be better protected from potential criminal or civil responsibility where they engage in effective communication with their clients, other team members, their supervisors, and not the least of which, other collaterals involved in the case. Social workers are frequently asked to make judgments about such issues as the future risk that a youth offender presents to society, the risk that someone will injure themselves, or the risk that a client will injure a third party. In these situations, there is a need to verify important information, which, in turn, should be carefully documented. This has been clearly stated by the courts in child welfare cases. Madam Justice Hogan in the *Heikamp and Martin* case (1999) emphasized the importance of the verification and clarification of roles and responsibilities with collaterals, either by confirming letter or agreement, particularly where there is room for misunderstanding or some perceived antipathy exists between the professionals providing services to the child and family. She also underscored the need to verify important information, such as follow-up medical appointments and weight gains for a premature infant, especially where high risk and/or unreliable and manipulative caretakers are providing the information.

Obtaining Insurance

Although insurance cannot compensate for the emotional costs of being sued, criminally charged, or brought before a disciplinary board or coroner's inquest, it can provide vitally needed financial protection. Workers must find out if their agencies carry insurance or have indemnification programs and the coverage areas and rates. Coverage for civil matters is common, but not necessarily comprehensive. Most agencies will have limited or no criminal defence costs coverage. Where such coverage exists, it is usually predicated upon an ultimate acquittal or withdrawal/dismissal of the charges against the worker. At inquests, agencies will employ lawyers to represent the organization but may not cover the costs of an independent lawyer for the worker (whose interests may not be the same as those of the agency). It is useful to ask how the agency has handled these matters in the past and whether the agency will assume financial responsibility for all interim billings by lawyers until such time as a final acquittal verdict has been delivered. Depending on the agency coverage, the social worker may wish to consider obtaining liability insurance privately. When selecting a plan, ensure that it covers professional liability and disciplinary defence and inquire about coverage for criminal matters and representation at inquests.

Collectively Working to Improve the Image of Social Workers

The root of negative defensive strategies in social work lies in the power of the sociopolitical environment to ostracize social workers following major events, such as the injury or death of a child under their supervision. All social workers must embrace their identity and expertise as professionals and maintain responsible decision-making even in the face of negative publicity, thereby reflecting to the public their confidence in their practice and their profession. Social workers must advocate for public policies that protect the rights of vulnerable clients and promote safe environments. Finally, they must advocate for economic resources necessary to enable the provision of quality service to their clients through worker training, manageable case loads, and accessible community services for their clients.

CASE EXAMPLE REVIEWED

What are the forums in which social workers may be held liable for their actions and inactions?

Social workers can be held accountable for their actions or inactions through complaints made to licensing bodies, civil actions initiated through the courts, or more infrequently, criminal charges.

What are the grounds of liability for social workers in Canada?

In general, social workers can be held liable for: misconduct and incompetence. Misconduct refers to the breach of professional or legal duties such as boundary violations, not keeping records, or falsifying expense claims. Incompetence refers to the provision of service below the accepted standard for the profession.

What protections exist for social workers?

Good-faith provisions in legislation protect social workers in the area of child welfare. Further, where statutory immunity is not available, the courts will consider the actions of social workers according to acceptable standards of practice in the profession. Consequently, social workers who exercise reasonable caution and engage in good clinical social work practice, good record-keeping, and effective communication and verification of information can continue to strive to offer the high-quality services without any serious fear of recrimination. This point is reflected in Justice Hogan's judgment discharging the social worker Angie Martin at the *Heikamp and Martin* preliminary inquiry, where she stated:

CASE EXAMPLE REVIEWED *(Continued)*

I should emphasize here that having found that mistakes or errors in judgment were made does not, therefore, mean that there is evidence on any of the essential elements of criminal negligence. People make mistakes all the time, professionals make errors in judgment but this doesn't mean that these mistakes or errors constitute criminal negligence unless it can be proved that they were of such a nature as to satisfy the essential elements of the charge. In this case, I have found that they did not (*R. v. Heikamp and Martin*, 1999, p. 20).

How might social workers protect themselves from liability?

Social workers can protect themselves through ethical and competent practice as noted above. Insurance is also key to financial protection when claims are made against the worker.

Key Terms

Civil Liability

An action is brought against a social worker in civil court—if a finding is made against the social worker, the court can order that damages be paid to place the victim in the position he or she would have been in had the wrong not occurred; civil suits against social workers may involve boundary violations, incompetence, failure to protect, or malicious prosecution actions by parents where child abuse has been alleged

Coroner's Inquest

A formal hearing into the events surrounding a death where the coroner is the chair of the proceedings and jury members hear the evidence and make recommendations to prevent similar deaths in the future; an inquest may be called at the coroner's discretion after completing an investigation—coroners are mandated by legislation to investigate all deaths that meet specific criteria

Criminal Liability

Criminal charges laid against a social worker related to the duties he or she performed; it is rare for social workers to be criminally charged and even less likely that they will be convicted

Good Faith

Where a worker acts on his or her best judgment and knowledge by seeking out the most positive outcome for all parties, based on an honest belief that the action taken was necessary; this form of qualified immunity from liability allows for errors of judgment but will not protect biased, vengeful, or indifferent practice

Immunity

Legislative provisions or common law that provides explicit protection for workers from liability; immunity may be absolute or qualified, such as acts done in good faith

Professional Discipline

Social work practice is regulated, including who may practice and standards of practice; each province has a mechanism for the public to lodge a complaint against a social worker and the complaints may be reviewed by a disciplinary body through a process specified under provincial legislation

Public Inquiry
Also sometimes called a royal commission or provincial task force, it is called by a governmental body to address an issue of concern to the public; a chair and several committee members are appointed and various people are called to make submissions on the issue; recommendations are made to the body that called for the inquiry

Discussion Questions

1. What is a discipline committee? What sanctions may be imposed upon a social worker by a discipline committee?
2. When are coroner's inquests called?

3. Identify two duties to be observed by social workers and give an example of breach of each that could give rise to liability.
4. List three strategies that social workers can employ to protect themselves from liability.

Relevant Legislation

Federal Agreement
Mutual Recognition Agreement on Labour Mobility for Social Workers in Canada
http://www.cicic.ca/docs/mra/social-workers.en.pdf.

Alberta
Fatal Inquires Act, R.S.A. 2000, c. F-9
http://www.canlii.org/ab/laws/sta/f-9/2005 0801/whole.html
Health Professions Act, R.S.A. 2000, c. H-7
http://www.canlii.org/ab/laws/sta/h-7/
Protection for Persons in Care Act, R.S.A. 2000, c. P-29
http://www.canlii.org/ab/laws/sta/p-29/2008 0818/whole.html

British Columbia
Coroners Act, R.S.B.C. 2007, c. 15
http://www.qp.gov.bc.ca/statreg/stat/C/07015_ 01.htm
Health Care (Consent) and Care Facility (Admission) Act, R.S.B.C. 1996, c. 181 (enacted in part only)
http://www.qp.gov.bc.ca/statreg/stat/H/96181_ 01.htm
Social Workers Act, R.S.B.C. 1996, c. 432
http://www.qp.gov.bc.ca/statreg/stat/S/96432_ 01.htm

Manitoba
Fatal Inquiries Act, C.C.S.M., c. F52
http://www.canlii.org/mb/laws/sta/f-52/ index.html
Manitoba Institute of Registered Social Workers Incorporation Act, R.S.M. 1990, c. 96
http://web2.gov.mb.ca/laws/statutes/private/ c09690e.php
Vulnerable Persons Living with a Mental Disability Act, 1993, C.C.S.M., c. V90
http://www.canlii.org///mb/laws/sta/v-90/2008 0715/whole.html

New Brunswick
Coroners Act, S.N.B., c. C-23
http://www.canlii.org/nb/laws/sta/c-23/
Family Services Act, S.N.B. 1980, c. F-2.2
http://www.canlii.org/nb/laws/sta/f-2.2/2005 0801/whole.html
New Brunswick Association of Social Workers Act, 1988

Newfoundland and Labrador
Fatalities Investigation Act, S.N.L. 1995, c. F-6.1
http://www.canlii.org/nl/laws/sta/f-6.1/
Neglected Adults Welfare Act, R.S.N.L. 1990, c. N-3
http://www.assembly.nl.ca/Legislation/sr/ statutes/n03.htm

Social Workers Association Act, S.N.L. 1992, c. S-18.1
http://www.assembly.nl.ca/Legislation/sr/statutes/s18-1.htm

Nova Scotia

Adult Protection Act, R.S., c. 2, s. 1
http://www.gov.ns.ca/legislature/legc/statutes/adultpro.htm

Fatality Investigations Act, S.N.S. 2001, c. 31
http://www.gov.ns.ca/legislature/legc/statutes/socialwk.htm

Social Workers Act, S.N.S. 1993, c. 12
http://www.gov.ns.ca/legislature/legc/statutes/socialwk.htm

Ontario

Coroners Act, R.S.O. 1990, c. C.37
http://www.canlii.org/on/laws/sta/c-37/20050801/whole.html

Health Professions Procedural Code (1991), Schedule 2 of the Regulated Health Professions Act, S.O. 1991, c. 18
http://www.cpso.on.ca/policies/profmisc.htm

Social Work and Social Service Work Act, S.O. 1998, c. 31
http://www.canlii.org/on/laws/sta/1998c.31/

Prince Edward Island

Adult Protection Act, R.S.P.E.I. 1988, c. A-5
http://www.canlii.org/pe/laws/sta/a-5/20080715/whole.html

Coroners Act, R.S.P.E.I. 1988, c. C-25.1
http://www.canlii.org/pe/laws/sta/c-25.1/index.html

Social Work Act, R.S.P.E.I. 1988, Cap S-5
http://www.gov.pe.ca/law/statutes/pdf/s-05.pdf/

Quebec

Determination of the causes and circumstances of death, An Act respecting the, R.S.Q., c. R-0.2/index

Représentation au Bureau de l'Ordre professionnel des travailleurs sociaux du Québec et sur la délimitation des régions électorales, Règlement sur la, R.Q. C-26, r.188.2
http://www.canlii.org/qc/legis/regl/c-26r.188.2/20040901/tout.html

Saskatchewan

Coroners Act, 1999, S.S. 1999, c. C-38.01
http://www.canlii.org/sk/laws/sta/c-38.01/index.html

Social Workers Act, S.S. 1993, c. S-52.1
http://www.qp.gov.sk.ca/documents/English/Statutes/Statutes/S52-1.pdf

Northwest Territories

Coroners Act, R.S.N.W.T. 1988, c. C-20
http://www.canlii.org/nt/laws/sta/c-20/

Yukon

Decision-Making Support and Protection to Adults Act, S.Y. 2003, c. 21
http://www.gov.yk.ca/legislation/acts/dmspa.pdf

References

A.B. v. College of Physicians and Surgeons of Prince Edward Island (2001), P.E.I.J. No. 89

A.J. v. Cairnie (1999), M.J. No. 176.

Alberta College of Social Workers (ACSW) (2002), 'Findings in Case 00.8', *The Advocate*, 27(1): 4–5.

———— (2003a), 'Findings in Case 00.8', *The Advocate*, 28(2): 12–13.

———— (2003b), 'Findings in Case 01.6', *The Advocate*, 28(2): 14–15.

———— (2004), 'Findings in Case 01.4', *The Advocate*, 29(1): 28–29.

———— (2006), 'Complaint Procedures: Information for the Public' (accessed at http://www.acsw.ab.ca/complaints/make_a_complaint).

Alexander, R. and Alexander, C. (1995), 'Criminal Prosecution of Child Protection Workers', *Social Work*, 49(6): 809–14.

American Federation of State, County and Municipal Employees (AFSCME) (1999), 'Liability and Child Welfare Workers', *Child Welfare Watch*, 2 (accessed at http://www.afscme.org/publications/child/cww99205.htm).

Ashford v. Children's Aid Society of Cape Breton-Victoria (2008), NSSC 73.

B. (D.). v. Children's Aid Society of Durham (1996), 136 D.L.R. (4th) 297 (Ont. C.A.).

Bell, V. (2007), 'Online Information, Extreme Communities and Internet Therapy: Is the Internet Good for Our Mental Health?', *Journal of Mental Health*, 16(4): 445–57.

Bennet v. Registered Psychiatric Nurses' Assn. of Manitoba (2003), M.J. No. 163.

Bernstein, M. (1983), 'The Brockville Case: Legal Analysis', *Family Law Review*, 6: 92–113.

———, Regehr, C., and Kanani, K. (2004), 'Liability for Child Welfare Workers: Weighing the Risks', in N. Bala, M. Zapf, J. Williams, R. Vogl, and J. Hornick (eds), *Child Welfare in Canada* (Toronto: Thompson Educational).

Besharov, D. (1983), *Criminal and Civil Liability in Child Welfare Work: The Growing Trend* (National Legal Resource Center for Child Advocacy and Protection, American Bar Association, Young Lawyers Division).

Blatchford, C. (2001, 12 April), 'She Should Be Sterilized: My Four Extra Recommendations to Add to the Jurors', *National Post*, pp. A1, A10.

Brunet, R. (1998), 'BC's Only Growth Industry: Complaints Quadruple Against Aggressive Children and Families Ministry', *British Columbia Report*, 9(33): 14–17.

Buck, C. (1998), 'Managing an Inquest: The Ontario Experience', *Canada's Children* (Fall/Winter): 15–18.

Canadian Association of Social Workers (CASW) (2005a), *Code of Ethics* (Ottawa: Canadian Association of Social Workers).

——— (2005b), *Guidelines for Ethical Practice* (Ottawa: Canadian Association of Social Workers).

Carruthers v. College of Nurses of Ontario (1996), 31 O.R. (3d) 377 O.J. No. 4275.

CBC (2004, 11 February), 'Canada and Public Inquiries', *CBC News Online* (accessed 24 August 2005 at http://www.cbc.ca/news/background/ cdngovernment/inquiries.html).

Chaimowitz, G. and Glancy, G. (2002), 'The Duty to Protect', *Canadian Journal of Psychiatry*, 47: 1–4.

Child and Family Services Act, R.S.O. 1990, c. C.11, s. 15(6).

D. (B.) v. British Columbia (Superintendent of Family and Child Services) (1997), 26 R.F.L. (4th) 273, No. 674 at para. 40 (B.C.C.A.).

D. (B.) v. Children's Aid Society of Halton (Region) (2007), 3 S.C.R. 83.

D. (S.) v. S. (D.W.) (1994), 160 A.R. 61 (Master).

Davies, L., McKinnon, M., Rains, P., and Mastronardi, L. (1999), 'Rethinking Child Protection Practice', *Canadian Social Work Review*, 16(1): 103–15.

Doucette, E. (2004), president of the Association of Social Workers in Northern Canada, personal communication.

Elleven, R. and Allen, J. (2004), 'Applying Technology to Online Counseling: Suggestions for the Beginning E-therapist', *Journal of Instructional Psychology*, 31(3): 223-7.

Farchels v. British Columbia (Minister of Social Services and Housing) (1988), B.C.J. No. 493.

G. (A.) v. British Columbia (Superintendent of Family and Child Services) (1989), 61 D.L.R. (4th) 136.

Gechtman, L. (1989), 'Sexual Contact Between Social Workers and Their Clients', in G. Gabbard (ed.), *Sexual Exploitation in Professional Relationships* (Washington, DC: American Psychiatric Association).

Gordon, R. (2001), 'Adult Protection Legislation in Canada: Models, Issues and Problems', *International Journal of Law and Mental Health*, 24: 117–34.

Holder, W. (1984), 'Malpractice in Child Protective Services: An Overview of the Problem', in W. Holder and K. Hayes (eds), *Malpractice and Liability in Child Protective Services* (Longmont, CO: Bookmakers Guild).

Holroyd, J. and Brodsky, A. (1977), 'Psychologists' Attitudes Toward and Practices Regarding Erotic and Non-erotic Physical Contact with Patients', *American Psychologist*, 32: 843–9.

Houston-Vega, M., Nuehring, E., and Daguio, R. (1996), *Prudent Practice: A Guide for Managing Malpractice Risk* (accessed at http://www.naswpress.org/publications/books/clinical/ prudent/prudent-chap.html).

Hutchinson Mittendorf, S. and Schroeder, J. (2004), 'Boundaries in Social Work: The Ethical Dilemma of Social Worker-Client Sexual Relationships', *Journal of Social Work Values and Ethics*, 1(1) (accessed at http://www.socialworker.com/jswve/content/view/11/30/).

J. Doe v. New Brunswick (Minister of Family and Community Services) (2004), N.B.J. No. 276.

Kanani, K. and Regehr, C. (2003), 'Clinical, Ethical and Legal Issues in E-therapy', *Families in Society*, 84(2): 155–62.

Kardener, S., Fuller, M., and Mensh, I. (1973), 'A Survey of Physician's Attitudes and Practices Regarding Erotic and Non-erotic Physical Contact with Patients', *American Journal of Psychiatry*, 130: 1077–81.

Kutchins, H. (1991), 'The Fiduciary Relationship: The Legal Basis of Social Workers' Responsibilities to Clients', *Social Work*, 36: 106–13.

McDonald, L., Collins, A., and Dergal, J. (2005), 'The Abuse of Older Adults in Canada', in R. Alaggia and C. Vine (eds), *Cruel but Not Unusual: Violence in Canadian Families* (Waterloo, ON: Wilfrid Laurier University Press).

Maclean's (2001, 5 November), 'Nurses Charged', p. 16.

Manitoba Institute of Registered Social Workers (MIRSW) (2005), 'Complaints' (accessed at http://www. geocities. com/masw_mirsw/masw_enter.htm).

Marshall, M. and Von Tigerstorm, B. (1999), 'Confidentiality and Disclosure of Health Information', in J. Downie and T. Caulfield (eds), *Canadian Health Law and Policy* (Toronto: Butterworths).

Morris, C. (1997, 26 November), 'NB to Review Suspicious Child Deaths', Canadian Press Newswire.

Mussani v. The College of Physicians and Surgeons of Ontario; The Ontario Medical Association et al., Intervenors (2003) O.J. No. 1956.

Myers, J. (2001), 'Risk Management for Professionals Working with Maltreated Children and Adult Survivors', in J. Myers, L. Berliner, J. Briere, C. Jenny, T. Hendrix, and T. Reid (eds), *The APSAC Handbook on Child Maltreatment* (Thousand Oaks, CA: Sage).

National Association of Social Workers (NASW) (1999), *Code of Ethics* (Washington, DC: National Association of Social Workers).

N.C. v. Blank (1998) O.J. No. 2544.

New Brunswick Association of Social Workers (NBASW) (2004, November), *Dossier*, 15(1).

———— (2007) Annual Report.

Nova Scotia Association of Social Workers (NSASW) (2004), 'Recent Discipline Decision', *Connection*, 11(1): 12–15.

———— (2007), 'Complaints and Discipline' (accessed at http// www: nsasw.org/complaints.html).

Postel, M., de Haan, H., and De Jong, C. (2007), 'E-therapy for Mental Health Problems: A Systematic Review', *Telemedicine and e-Health*, 14(7): 707–14.

Re H. (Minors) (Sexual Abuse: Standard of Proof) (1996), A.C. 563 (H.L.).

R. v. Heikamp and Martin (3 December 1999), Toronto (O.C.J.) (Judgment at preliminary inquiry).

R. v. Orpin (2002), O.J. No. 1541.

Recupero, P. and Rainey, S. (2006), 'Characteristics of E-Therapy Web Sites', *Journal of Clinical Psychiatry*, 67(9): 1435–40.

Regehr, C. and Antle, B. (1997), 'Coercive Influences: Informed Consent in Court Mandated Social Work Practice', *Social Work*, 42(3): 300–6.

———— , Chau, S., Leslie, B., and Howe, P. (2002), 'Inquiries into the Deaths of Children: Impacts on Child Welfare Workers and Their Organizations', *Child and Youth Services Review*, 21(12): 885–902.

———— , Glancy, G., and Bryant, A. (1998), 'Breaking Confidentiality: Legal Requirements for Canadian Social Workers', *Journal of Law and Social Work*, 8(1): 115–29.

———— , Hill, J., Goldberg, G., and Hughes, J. (2003a), 'Postmortem Inquiries and Trauma Responses in Paramedics and Firefighters', *Journal of Interpersonal Violence*, 18(6): 607–22.

———— , Johanis, D., Dimitropoulos, G., Bartram, C., and Hope, G. (2003b), 'The Police Officer and the Public Inquiry', *Brief Treatments and Crisis Intervention* 3(4): 383–96.

Regional Forensic Unit, Kingston General Hospital (2005), *What Is an Inquest?* (accessed 24 August 2005 at http:// www.path.queensu.ca/kgh/ pathology/forensic.htm).

Sackett, D., Richardson, W., Rosenberg, W., and Haynes, R. (1997), *Evidence-based Medicine* (New York: Churchill Livingston).

Saskatchewan Association of Social Workers (SASW) (2004), 'Discipline Decision', *Saskatchewan Social Worker*, 15(3): 6.

———— (2005), 'Discipline' (accessed at http://www. sasw.ca/ discipline.html).

Smith v. Jones (1999), 1 S.C.R. 455, 1999 CanLII 674 (S.C.C.).

Smith v. Kamloops and District Elizabeth Fry Society (1996), B.C.J. No. 1214.

Spillane, S. (1990), 'AIDS: Establishing a Physician's Duty to Earn', *Rutgers Law Journal*, 21: 645.

S.T. v. Gaskell (1997), O.J. No.2029.

Statistics Canada (2008), 'Canadian Internet Use Survey', *The Daily* (accessed 12 June at http://www.statcan.gc.ca/daily-quotidien/080612/dq080612b-eng.htm).

T.C. v. Scott (1997), O.J. No. 2389.

W. (D.) v. W. (D.) (1998), O.J. No. 2927 (O.C.J.).

Index

Social Work Texts from Oxford University Press

Oxford University Press Canada publishes a wide range of texts for both undergraduate and graduate social work programs. Some of our bestselling titles are described below.

Mental Health Social Work Practice in Canada

CHERYL REGEHR • GRAHAM GLANCY

Written by two of the discipline's foremost researchers and practitioners, this is the only Canadian textbook to offer a comprehensive overview of the legal and policy framework for mental health practice in social work. Combining analysis of case studies with careful examination of evidence-based practices, the authors outline the social work practices that will best assist individuals and families struggling with mental health challenges. Accessible, rigorous, and grounded in research, *Mental Health Social Work Practice in Canada* is a useful reference for social work practitioners and an ideal text for courses in social work and mental health.

CONTENTS: Preface. 1. The Context of Mental Health Social Work Practice in Canada. 2. A Policy Framework for Mental Health in Canada. 3. Mental Health Law in Canada. 4. Social Work Assessment in Mental Health. 5. Suicide and Self-Harm. 6. Trauma and Traumatic Grief. 7. Schizophrenia and Related Psychotic Illnesses. 8. Depression and Mania. 9. Anxiety. 10. Delirium and Dementia. 11. Substance Abuse. 12. Personality Disturbance. Glossary. References. Index.

Paper, 2009, 232 pp., ISBN 9780195429718

Challenging Oppression and Confronting Privilege: A Critical Social Work Approach, Second Edition

BOB MULLALY

The definitive guide to anti-oppressive social work, which is a prominent part of social work theory and practice in Canada. Bob Mullaly examines the many forms that oppression can take, at the personal, cultural, and structural (or institutional) levels. The text outlines the necessary practices and approaches that social work must adopt in order to fight against oppression and assist those who have been oppressed. In this second edition, every chapter has been thoroughly revised to include new research and updated resources. As well, a chapter has been added explaining the dynamics of privilege and how an understanding of privilege can improve social work practice.

CONTENTS: 1. Theoretical and Conceptual Considerations. 2. Oppression: An Overview. 3. Oppression at the Personal Level. 4. Oppression at the Cultural Level. 5. Oppression at the Structural Level. 6. Internalized Oppression and Domination. 7. The 'Web': The Multiplicity, Intersectionality, and Heterogeneity of Oppression. 8. Anti-Oppressive Social Work Practice at the Personal and Cultural Levels. 9. Anti-Oppressive Social Work at the Structural Level and Selected Principles of Anti-Oppressive Social Work. 10. Unpacking Our Knapsacks of Invisible Privilege.

Paper, 2009, 376 pp., ISBN 9780195429701

Social Work Texts from Oxford University Press

Oxford University Press Canada publishes a wide range of texts for both undergraduate and graduate social work programs. Some of our bestselling titles are described below.

Working with People: Communication Skills for Reflective Practice, Canadian Edition

LOUISE HARMS • JOANNA PIERCE

Seamlessly integrating Canadian research and examples, this multidimensional guide to interpersonal communication in the human services offers practical instruction on the basics of relationship-building, interviewing, assessment, and in-the-field communication, with case studies from experienced practitioners included throughout. Topics covered include the worker–client relationship, the steps involved in developing discipline-specific communication skills, and the importance of cross-cultural knowledge and self-awareness on the part of the case worker. The strengths and shortcomings of various theoretical approaches are discussed, and the authors note the need for continuing self-assessment and self-care in a profession that can often be physically and emotionally stressful. A perforated appendix ('Practice Pack') includes Canadian social work references; tips on making ethical decisions; a summary of the Harms model of decision-making; the Holmes and Rahe social readjustment scale; drug and alcohol addiction abuse assessment; First Nations code of ethics; core social work values and principles as outlined in the Canadian Association of Social Workers, *Code of Ethics* (2005); and additional resources, making it an invaluable tool for fieldwork.

CONTENTS: Part I. Framing the Relationship. 1. Working Towards Change. 2. Understanding Communication and Change. 3. Communication and Change. Part II. Basic Skills: Forming the Relationship. 4. Preparing for Practice. 5. Sustaining Your Self in Practice. 6. Establishing a Good Working Relationship. Part III. Basic Skills: Focusing the Communication. 7. Establishing the Story. 8. Paraphrasing and Summarizing. 9. Forming an Assessment—Setting the Agenda. 10. Assessing Risk Situations. Part IV. Applying the Skills: Focusing the Intervention. 11. Task-Centred and Crisis-Intervention Skills. 12. Psychodynamic and Cognitive Behavioural Skills. 13. Narrative and Solution-Focused Skills. 14. Feminist and Critical Theory Skills. Part V. Finishing the Work. 15. Finishing the Work. Appendix: Practice Pack. Glossary.

Paper, 2011, 336 pp., ISBN 9780195433548

Interventions with Children and Youth in Canada

MAUREEN CECH

Written specifically for Canadians, *Interventions with Children and Youth in Canada* provides an introduction to the structural and strengths-based approach to working with at-risk children and youth. Weaving discussions of class, cultural analysis, and Aboriginal issues throughout, the text helps students develop the skills required to practice effective helping relationships. Interdisciplinary in scope, the text integrates information from Canadian medical, psychological, sociological, and educational sources, reflecting the way social workers and child and youth care workers practice their craft. The comprehensive exploration of both the theory and practical application of working with children and youth makes this text a valuable tool for both practicing and aspiring social workers.

CONTENTS: 1. The Structural and Strengths-Based Approach. 2. The Social Construction of the Child. 3. Developmentally Appropriate Practice. 4. Attachment. 5. Relationships. 6. The First Meeting. 7. The Child's Story. 8. Listening to Play. 9. Understanding Behaviours. 10. High-Risk Interventions. 11. Groups and Gangs. Afterword: Setting Structural and Strengths-Based Targets. Glossary. References. Index.

Paper, 2010, 336 pp., ISBN 9780195430240

Social Work Texts from Oxford University Press

Oxford University Press Canada publishes a wide range of texts for both undergraduate and graduate social work programs. Some of our bestselling titles are described below.

Connecting Policy to Practice in the Human Services, Third Edition

BRAD McKENZIE • BRIAN WHARF

Traditionally, human services policy has been made by people whose own lives are unaffected by their decisions. As a consequence, that policy often fails to meet the needs of service users. In this third edition of *Connecting Policy to Practice in the Human Services*, Brad McKenzie and Brian Wharf suggest that a more inclusive process will produce better results. Following a careful examination of current practices, they look at a number of alternative strategies, including shared decision-making, policy communities, community governance, and family group conferences. This edition has been updated throughout and features a new chapter on policy resistance, new chapter summaries, end-of-chapter activities, and a glossary, making it the most current and engaging text available. Linking Canadian social welfare policy with social welfare practice, this indispensable resource encourages and facilitates participation in a process that has significant consequences for many lives.

CONTENTS: Introduction. 1. Policy-Making and Policy-Makers. 2. The Social Policy Environment. 3. Making Social Policy in Canada: Structures and Processes. 4. Stages of the Policy-Making Process. 5. The Implementation Stage. 6. Inclusive Approaches to Policy-Making. 7. Influencing Policy from Outside the System. 8. Chalk and Cheese: Feminist Thinking and Policy-Making (Marilyn Callahan). 9. Policy Resistance: The Rise and Fall of Welfare Time Limits in BC (Bruce Wallace and Tim Richards). 10. Policy-Making in Aboriginal Child and Family Services. Conclusion. Appendix: Annotated Websites and Selected Canadian Journals. References. Index.

Paper, 2009, 272 pp., ISBN 9780195430097

Skills for Human Service Practice: Working with Individuals, Groups, and Communities, Canadian Edition

AGI O'HARA • ZITA WEBER • KATHY LEVINE

This practice-based text is a comprehensive guide to the skills used in social work and other human services professions across a variety of contexts. Taking a unique approach to the study of social work, it integrates theory and practice throughout to help students build real-world skills for their future careers. Pedagogical features include 'Practice Example' boxes—short case studies on such topics as handling anxiety in a group, training opportunities, and community development; 'Practice Points' boxes, which summarize key issues and facts from the case studies; and 'Activity' boxes, where students will learn how to build their skills and confidence through social work activities such as self-disclosure, negotiating, group experiences, and interpreting silence.

CONTENTS: Introduction. 1. Practising Critical Reflection. 2. Professional Values and Ethical Practice. 3. Making the Most of Supervision. 4. The Practitioner's Use of Self in the Professional Relationship. 5. Cultural Diversity in Practice: Working with Immigrants and Refugees. 6. Cultural Diversity in Practice: Working with Indigenous People—A Meeting of Minds and Hearts. 7. Risk Assessment: Working within a Legal Framework. 8. Effective Communication. 9. The Microskills of Interviewing. 10. Conducting Assessment: Some General Guidelines. 11. Advocacy in Practice. 12. Understanding and Managing Conflict. 13. Introduction to Working with Groups. 14. Intervention Strategies for Working with Groups. 15. Working Effectively in Teams. 16. Asset-based Community Development: Recognizing and Building on Community Strengths. 17. Community Education.

Paper, 2010, 336 pp., ISBN 9780195430103

Social Work Texts from Oxford University Press

Oxford University Press Canada publishes a wide range of texts for both undergraduate and graduate social work programs. Some of our bestselling titles are described below.

The New Structural Social Work, Third Edition

BOB MULLALY

The New Structural Social Work uncovers the shortcomings of the current social system and voices the need for an alternative to conventional methods of social work. The text presents a coherent and consistent theory of progressive social work, focussing on oppression and examining current political practice, while promising both to engage students in debates about how to address social issues and to challenge them to re-evaluate existing modes of social work and their implications.

CONTENTS: Part I. In Search of a Paradigm. 1. Capitalism, Crises, and Paradigms. 2. The Social Work Vision: A Progressive View. 3. The Neo-Conservative Paradigm. 4. The Liberal and Neo-Liberal Paradigms. 5. The Social Democratic Paradigm. 6. The Marxist Paradigm. 7. Feminist, Anti-Racist, and Postmodern Critiques. 8. The Third Way. Part II. Structural Social Work Theory and Oppression. 9. A Reconstituted Theory of Structural Social Work. 10. Oppression: The Focus of Structural Social Work. Part III. Structural Social Work: Practice Elements. 11. Working within (and against) the System: Radical Humanism. 12. Working outside (and against) the System: Radical Structuralism and Working within Ourselves. Appendix: Structural Analysis of Agency/Field Placement.

Paper, 2007, 408 pp., ISBN 9780195439137

Multicultural Social Work in Canada: Working with Diverse Ethno-Racial Communities

ALEAN AL-KRENAWI • JOHN R. GRAHAM, editors

Multicultural Social Work in Canada is divided into two sections. Section One outlines the knowledge and skills required for effective multicultural practice. Chapters in this introductory section discuss such topics as culturally competent social work with individuals, families, and communities; social policy; working with people who immigrated to Canada; and working in the context of racial plurality in diverse communities of Canadian society. Section Two contains personal narratives of social work with Canadians of different ethno-racial backgrounds, such as Italian, Arab, Jewish, Ukrainian, Aboriginal, African, Caribbean, South Asian, and Franco-Ontarian. Each chapter in this section focusses on the author's experiences working with the community under study at varying levels of practice—family, group, and community. This analysis offers a starting point for readers to reflect on their own experiences and assumptions of multicultural practice with diverse ethno-racial communities. Major themes include differential processes in seeking help and the importance of taking into account a community's history or an individual's age, gender, acculturation, or socio-economic status when developing strategies for social work in multicultural settings.

CONTENTS: 1. Introduction. 2. Culturally Appropriate Knowledge and Skills Required for Effective Multicultural Practice with Individuals, Families, and Small Groups. 3. Culturally Appropriate Social Work for Successful Community Development in Diverse Communities. 4. Canadian Society: Social Policy and Ethno-Racial Diversity. 5. Whiteout: Looking for Race in Canadian Social Work Practice. 6. Practice with Immigrants in Quebec. 7. Social Work with Canadians of Italian Background: Applying Cultural Concepts to Bicultural and Intergenerational Issues in Clinical Practice. 8. Social Work with Canadians of Arab Background: Insight into Direct Practice. 9. Social Work with Canadians of Jewish Background: Guidelines for Direct Practice. 10. Social Work with Canadians of Ukrainian Background: History, Direct Practice, Current Realities. 11. Social Work Practice with Canadians of Aboriginal Background: Guidelines for Respectful Social Work. 12. The Franco-Ontarian Community: From a Period of Resistance to New Social Solidarities and Practices. 13. Social Work Practice with African Canadians: An Examination of the African–Nova Scotian Community. 14. Canadians of Caribbean Background: Postcolonial and Critical Race Perspectives for Practice. 15. The Context of Culture: Social Work Practice with Canadians of South Asian Background.

Paper, 2003, 352 pp., ISBN 9780195415308

Social Work Texts from Oxford University Press

Oxford University Press Canada publishes a wide range of texts for both undergraduate and graduate social work programs. Some of our bestselling titles are described below.

Child Poverty in Canada

PATRIZIA ALBANESE

This short, engaging book provides the latest research on child poverty by Canadian sociologist Patrizia Albanese, who explores trends over time, across provinces, and among various groups. Her research reveals which children are most vulnerable and why, and describes the physical, behavioural, and educational impact of poverty.

CONTENTS: 1. Defining and Measuring Child Poverty. 2. Child Poverty Rates and Trends. 3. Incomes and Outcomes: Impact of Poverty on Children. 4. Exploring Causes I: Family and Neighbourhood Factors. 5. Exploring Causes II: Canada's Changing Economy. 6. Exploring Causes III: Canada's Changing and Unchanging Policies. 7. International Comparisons and Accounting for the Differences. 8. Solutions Proposed and Tested and Recommendations for Change.

Paper, 2010, 184 pp., ISBN 9780195432053

Social Welfare in Canada, Fourth Edition

ANDREW ARMITAGE

This comprehensive text examines the development of Canada's welfare state, various views of social policy, and the contributions of liberal thought to social welfare in Canada. Armitage evaluates what has been gained, and what has been lost, in regard to seven fundamental liberal values: concern for the individual, faith in humanity, equity, equality, community, diversity, and faith in democracy.

CONTENTS: Part I. Overview. 1. Social Welfare: Ideals and Context. Part II. Income Distribution: Seeking Fairness. 2. The Redistribution of Income: Theory, Principles, and Resources. 3. Canada's Record: Redistribution, Poverty, and Programs. Part III. Building Communities. 4. Community and Social Welfare: Theory, Principles, and Resources. 5. Canada's Record: Community Welfare and the Social Services. Part IV. The Political and Ideological Context. 6. Social Welfare: Power, Politics, and Organizations. 7. Social Welfare: Ideologies and Research. Part V. Conclusion. 8. The Uncertain Future of Social Welfare.

Paper, 2003, 248 pp., ISBN 9780195417838

Social Policy in Canada

ERNIE LIGHTMAN

Social Policy in Canada provides and important and timely examination of the past, present, and future of Canadian social policy. In particular, Lightman looks closely at how social benefits are allocated and explains in detail the mechanisms and tools of income transfer and redistribution that are central to all aspects of social policy. What makes the book unique is its central organizing premise: not merely that social policy should be understood in juxtaposition to economic policy, but that economic policy is in fact a subset of social policy. The result is a comprehensive overview of key issues in the realm of social policy that highlights commonalities and differences in such pivotal areas as privatization, user fees, and universality.

CONTENTS: Part I. Introduction. 1. Setting the Context. Part II. Approaches to Social Policy. 2. Defining Social Policy. 3. Social Policy and Economic Markets. Part III. Allocating Benefits. 4. Allocating Benefits: Privatization, Commercialization, and Welfare Pluralism. 5. Allocating Benefits: What? 6. Allocating Benefits: To Whom? Part IV. Generating Resources. 7. Paying Through Taxes. 8. Fees, Charges, and Premiums. 9. Volunteers, Charities, and Gamblers. Part V. Conclusion. 10. Looking Ahead. Glossary.

Paper, 2002, 288 pp., ISBN 9780195416480

About Oxford University Press

Oxford University Press (often referred to as 'OUP') is one of the oldest publishing companies in the world, as well as one of the largest. Its imprint carries authority, its editorial and production standards are high, and its range of interests is wide. It is a department of the University of Oxford, and like the University as a whole, it is devoted to the spread of knowledge: any surplus generated by the Press through its activities is directed toward the publication of works which further scholarship and education, or to encouraging and sustaining research on which these books may be based.

The Press dates its origins back to the fifteenth century. The first book to be printed in Oxford—the *Commentary on the Apostles' Creed*, attributed to St Jerome, by Theodoric Rood—was issued in 1478, only two years after Caxton set up the first printing press in England, and barely a quarter-century following the invention of the printing press by Johann Gutenberg in 1450.

Matters developed in a somewhat haphazard fashion over the following century, with a number of short-lived private businesses, some patronized by Oxford University, taking the field. But in 1586, the University itself obtained a decree from the Star Chamber confirming its privilege to print books. In the same year, Oxford University lent £100—a small fortune at that time—to a local bookseller, Joseph Barnes, to set up a press. Barnes produced many books now prized by collectors, including the first books printed at Oxford in Greek (1586) and Hebrew (1596), and Captain John Smith's *Map of Virginia* (1612). The Great Charter, secured by Archbishop Laud from King Charles I in 1632, increased the independence and latitude of the press, entitling the University to print 'all manner of books', and approximately 300 books were printed before Barnes retired in 1617.

In 1633, the University first appointed delegates to oversee printing and publishing activities. Minute books recording their deliberations date back to 1668, and the Press as it exists today began to develop in a recognizable form from that time. To this day, the worldwide Press' activities are overseen by delegates, who are appointed from the academic staff of Oxford University to 'have charge of the affairs of the Press' and to govern it under the University statutes. The delegates are actively involved in the publishing program and maintain an active dialogue with editors in their specialist subject areas. The operations of the Press as a whole are overseen by a board that includes the vice chancellor of the University and other University administrators, as well as a number of delegates and officers of the Press.

The University established its right to print the King James Authorized Version of the Bible in the seventeenth century. This 'Bible Privilege' formed the basis of a successful publishing business throughout the next two centuries and was the spur for OUP's expansion. In London, the Press established a Bible warehouse, which later grew into a major publisher of books with educational and cultural content aimed at the general reader. Then, OUP began to expand internationally, starting with the opening of an American office in New York in 1896 and the Canadian branch in 1904.

Today, the OUP group of publishing companies constitutes the world's largest university press—larger than all of North America's university presses and Cambridge University Press combined. Worldwide, OUP publishes more than 6,000 new titles a year and employs approximately 5,000 people in 50 countries. As a result of its diverse, international publishing program, the 'Oxford University Press' imprimatur has become familiar worldwide, standing for scholarly, educational, and research excellence and authority.

Few if any organizations publish a more diverse range of titles than Oxford, including scholarly works in all academic disciplines; bibles; music reference works as well as sheet music; textbooks; children's books; materials for teaching English as a foreign language; dictionaries and reference books; professional books in fields such as law, brain science, and medicine; academic journals; and a burgeoning online publishing program of electronic resources and publications. Oxford and New York are the two largest publishing centres within the Press, but other publishing programs of significant size and scope exist the world over, in such countries as Canada, Australia, China, India, Kenya, Malaysia, Mexico, Pakistan, South Africa, and Spain.

Additional information about Oxford University Press is available at our global website: www.oup.com.

About Oxford University Press Canada

OUP Canada: A Brief History

The Canadian branch of Oxford University Press was established in 1904. It was the first overseas branch to be set up after an office was established in New York in 1896. Although the branch did not open until 1904, the first book published for the Canadian market actually appeared eight years earlier—a hymnal for the Presbyterian Church of Canada.

Before the twentieth century, the main suppliers of books to the trade in Canada were the Copp Clark Company, the W.J. Gage Company, and the Methodist Bookroom (in 1919 renamed The Ryerson Press after its founder, Egerton Ryerson). These three firms acted as

'jobbers' for other lines that were later to be represented either directly by branches of their parent houses or by exclusive Canadian agents. Prior to 1904, Oxford books had been sold in Canada by S.G. Wilkinson, who, based in London, England, travelled across Canada as far west as Winnipeg. Wilkinson did a large trade with S.B. (Sam) Gundy, the wholesale and trade manager of the Methodist Bookroom. When Oxford University Press opened its own branch in Canada, Gundy, already familiar with Oxford books, was invited to become its first manager. The premises were at 25 Richmond Street West and, lacking an elevator of any kind, were hardly ideal for a publishing house.

In 1929, the branch moved to Amen House, located at 480 University Avenue, and in 1936, after Gundy's death, the branch became closely allied with Clarke, Irwin and Company under W.C. Clarke. This association continued until 1949 when Clarke, Irwin moved to a separate location on St Clair Avenue West. In 1963, the Press moved to a new building at 70 Wynford Drive

OUP Canada's first home, at 25 Richmond Street West in Toronto.

The original reception area and library at 70 Wynford Drive. The library was later removed to make room for offices.

An etching of Amen House on University Avenue, created by Stanley Turner.

in Don Mills, which served it well for the next 46 years. By 2009, however, the branch had outgrown the 70 Wynford site. An extensive search process culminated in the move that November to a split-site configuration. The offices relocated to new premises at the Shops at Don Mills, an innovative retail/office/residential development, while the warehouse moved to a site in Brampton that not only offered more affordable rent and carrying charges but also provided a modern high-bay space much closer to major customers and Pearson International Airport.

Today OUP Canada is a major publisher of higher education, school, and English-as-a-second-language textbooks, as well as a significant trade and reference publisher. The Higher Education Division publishes both introductory and upper-level texts in such disciplines as sociology, anthropology, social work, English literature and composition, geography, history, political science, religious studies, and engineering. The division publishes more than 60 new Canadian texts and 150 student and instructor supplements each year, and derives about 60 per cent of its total sales from books and other learning materials written, edited, and published in Canada.

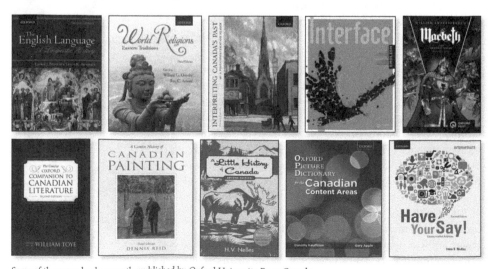

Some of the many books recently published by Oxford University Press Canada.